Anti-Submarine Warfare

Anti-Submarine Warfare

Warfare

An Illustrated History

David Owen

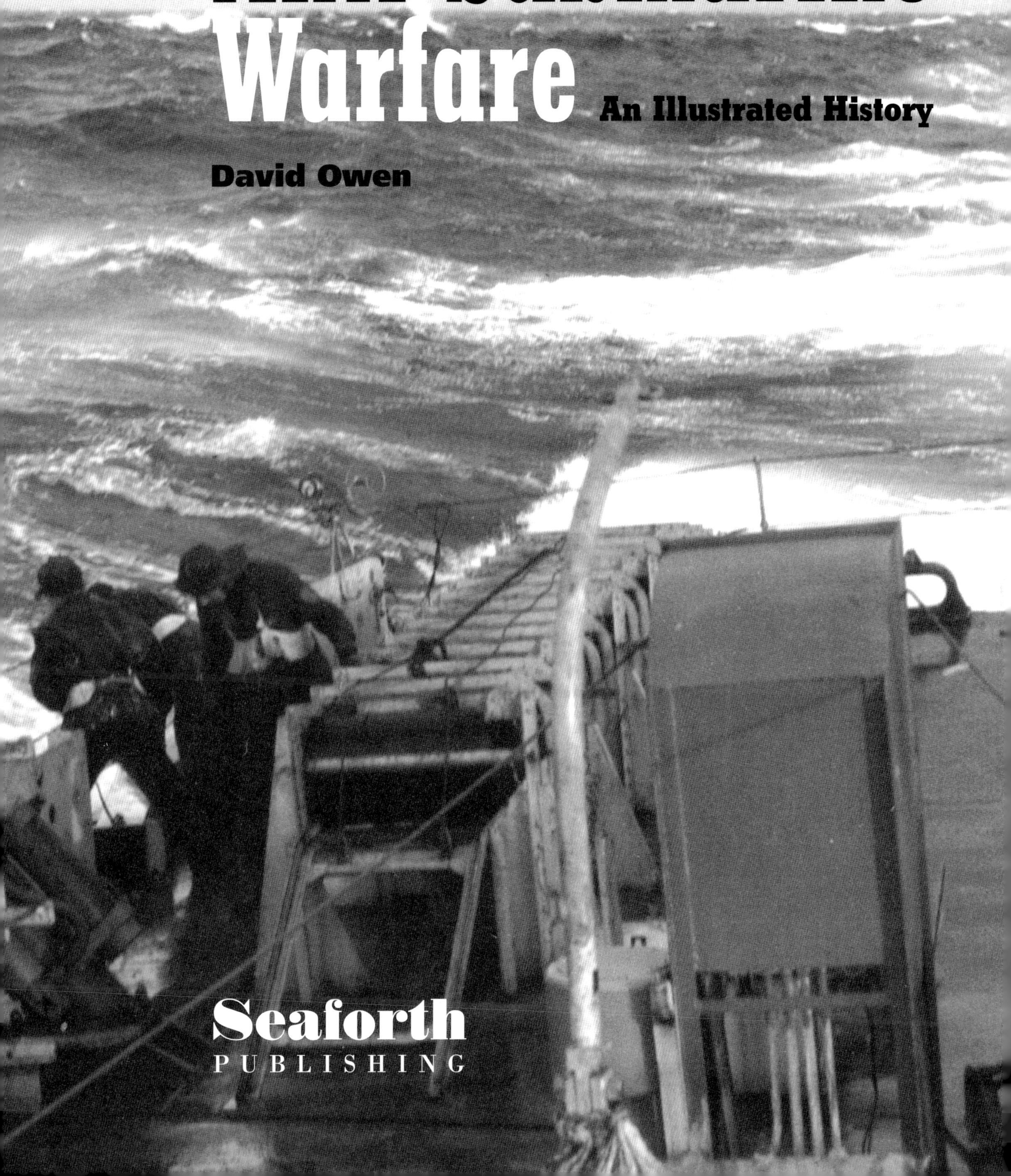

Seaforth
PUBLISHING

Copyright © David Owen 2007

First published in Great Britain in 2007 by
Seaforth Publishing,
Pen & Sword Books Ltd,
47 Church Street, Barnsley, S70 2AS

British Library Cataloguing in Publication Data

Owen, David, 1939-
Anti-Submarine Warfare: An Illustrated History
1. Anti-submarine warfare - History
    I. Title
    359.9'3'09

ISBN 978-1-84415-703-7

Designed and Typeset by Roger Daniels
Printed and bound in China through Printworks Int. Ltd.

Half-title: Launching depth charges. See page 68
Title page: HMCS *Swansea*. See page 54

CONTENTS

ACKNOWLEDGEMENTS

One of the most pleasant duties in producing a book like this is to thank everyone who helped along the way between idea and publication. In this case, the first person on the list should surely be Paul Wilderson, formerly of the US Naval Institute Press, with whom I first discussed the subject more than ten years ago now. Since then, many different people have provided essential and much appreciated input. Some remain anonymous, like the ever-helpful staff of the Liverpool and Manchester Reference Libraries, but others I can at least thank by name. These include Tim Padfield of the UK National Archives for permission to quote from Gunther Hessler's massive three-volume work on the U-boat war, published originally by HM Stationery Office, Mary Bergin-Cartwright of the Oxford University Press for permission to quote from *From Dreadnought to Scapa Flow* by Professor A J Marder (1960), David Page and Peter Swarbrick of Navy Photos for supplying such a varied selection of pictures, Susan Brook of the US Naval Institute Press for a splendid selection of photos from their large library, and Susan and Cyndy of Do You Graphics for processing a stack of US National Archives pictures at a very difficult time. Lastly, but most definitely not least, I should like to thank my family for putting up with the pressures and deadlines of producing a work like this, and particularly my daughter Felicity who spent many an hour in libraries checking names, facts and sources, and returning with masses of much appreciated and useful material. To all of them, and anyone not specifically mentioned here, my sincere and grateful thanks for all your help.

INTRODUCTION

From the very beginning of naval warfare, one of the factors that set it apart from fighting on land was the virtual impossibility of camouflage or concealment. With any reasonably efficient ship of war, well designed and beyond the range at which the intruder could present a serious threat, the size and armament of the approaching enemy could easily be estimated, and the way in which it was handled was a clue to the chances of defeating her in combat. Given the difficulty for one sailing ship to overhaul another of similar performance and bring her to battle, escape was invariably an option.

Yet the idea of a warship so designed and equipped that she could use the water in which she floated to provide a cloak of invisibility was a seductive prospect. It was one that attracted inventors in every country, but it gave them an almost insurmountable challenge. In theory, all was straightforward enough. If a means could be found to reduce the buoyancy of a surface warship, she could disappear beneath the waves under full control. Once hidden below the surface, she could navigate close enough to an adversary to damage or sink it, and then escape the enemy's response to return safely to base.

The reality was all too different. Simply building a hull that could withstand the increased pressure even at shallow depths, and then providing it with control and propulsion would be difficult enough. Supplying its crew with air to keep them alive, and the means of persuading their craft to submerge, find its way to its target and back and then surface on demand proved far more daunting. The death toll of those who experimented with the early experimental underwater craft deterred all but the most determined from trying to solve these problems, and it was not until the opening years of the twentieth century that their quest finally proved successful.

The result was a radical leap in weaponry that promised to overturn the established order of precedence of the world's navies. Submarines were small and relatively cheap, yet packed a potential punch out of all proportion to their limited size and displacement. Weaker navies could spend a fraction of the money needed to build one new battleship on flotillas of submarines that could easily sink a whole squadron of an opponent's dreadnoughts. To the appalled commanders of the world's greatest fleets, the threat of the submarine promised chaos and ruin, and attempts were made to outlaw it from the start.

Once this proved impossible, and once the submarine had shown its capabilities all too clearly within weeks of the opening of the First World War, huge efforts were made to develop defences against it and the weapons it wielded with such effect. In essence, this meant finding a quick solution to two extremely difficult problems. First, it was essential to locate the position of a submerged submarine as accurately as possible. Secondly, it was necessary to develop a means of destroying it, before it could attack vulnerable surface ships. In the event, the second problem proved to be the easier, with the development of the mine and the depth charge, but finding a way of stripping away the submarine's cloak of invisibility proved much more troublesome and time consuming.

From the opening of the First World War until the present day, the vital need to develop the technology and the tactics to defend against submarines, to defeat them in combat, and finally to destroy them as a threat has been a major priority for the Royal Navy and the United States Navy in particular. As the fleets that had most to lose from the submarine threat, they had the most powerful incentive to make anti-submarine warfare both viable and effective. Faced with the formidable German U-boat force in both world wars, and with the Japanese submarine force in the second, they were spurred on to produce every kind of ingenious device, from the homing torpedo to the Hedgehog cluster bomb, the Mousetrap rocket and the Squid and Limbo mortars, to sink and destroy their enemies. Centimetric radar, magnetic anomaly detection, active and passive sonar and high-frequency direction finding all helped to locate their targets and ensure their destruction.

Yet the submarines that triggered this technological arms race were not true submarines at all; they were only able to submerge to hide from potential targets or to evade potential attacks. When they did so, their speed and range were dramatically cut, and their endurance hampered by limited reserves of air and battery power. New tactics to exploit these weaknesses proved more and more effective, at the very time when the first true submarines were about to make their appearance in the world's oceans.

With the advent of hydrogen-peroxide power and eventually nuclear submarines, the tables were turned once again. Escort vessels that could catch and destroy the old submersibles were suddenly left behind by submarines that could outrun them and evade them with ease. Weapons that were adequate to shatter the pressure hulls of wartime submarines were incapable of delivering a powerful enough blow against the much larger and stronger nuclear boats, and a whole new armoury of weapons and tactics had to be developed to contain the more urgent threat they presented.

Though surface escorts continued to play a powerful role in post-war anti-submarine warfare (ASW), the chief burden of anti-submarine operations soon passed to the submarines themselves. Nuclear-powered hunter-killer craft seemed to offer the only viable way of pursuing enemy nuclear boats at the speeds and depths of which they were capable, and delivering a knock-out punch without being handicapped by their own vulnerability.

Finally, in the closing years of the century of the submarine, the wheel has almost turned full circle, from the size, power and complexity of the nuclear submarines, which could only be built and operated by the wealthiest naval powers, to the idea of a submarine as a weapon that could be used by smaller countries to exert military power against larger and better equipped opponents. These latest-generation submarines use different methods of propulsion, including fuel cells and other power units that can run without an external air supply, to operate as true submarines. Because they are smaller and quieter than nuclear submarines they are once again more difficult to locate, though they are easier to sink once found, and this change in the nature of the submarine threat has forced yet another major change in ASW tactics. Almost universal reliance on passive sonar to find submarines, in case the loud pulses of active sonar reveal the position of the transmitter, has given way to multi-platform searches using towed array active sonars, aircraft carrying dipping sonars and arrays of seabed sensors and sonobuoys to pinpoint the quietest submarine targets. Meanwhile, the spread of these non-nuclear submarines through navies that could never have afforded to have joined the nuclear club make it almost inevitable that the counter-measure, counter-counter-measure progression of ASW development will long outlast the ending of the Cold War and be maintained far into the twenty-first century.

This is the story that *Anti-Submarine Warfare* sets out to tell – the mixture of ingenious technology and clever tactics that has prevented the submarine from achieving complete dominance over naval warfare during the hundred and more years since its first hesitant appearance.

However, in covering this vast and varied canvas, inevitable compromises have to be made. This does not set out to be a history of naval operations, nor even of submarine operations *per se*, since these subjects have been covered very well elsewhere. For example, it devotes much of its coverage to the Anglo-American campaigns against the U-boats, because the especially urgent problems posed by German attacks on merchant shipping forced the British and Americans to carry out most of the work to develop the tactics and technology needed to defeat them.

Consequently, when the Axis forces hunted Allied submarines, many were lost to determined and skilful attacks by German, Italian and Japanese aircraft and escort vessels. But the techniques and weapons they used were based on those already in use by the Allies, and reviewing them in detail would merely be repetitive. However, as the main target of Allied ASW forces, the German U-boat arm was forced to develop tactics and technology of its own to counter the attacks, and these *are* reviewed in detail.

This same focus is maintained when looking at the

fighting between submarines, aircraft and escort vessels around particular convoys. No attempt has been made to review every convoy battle, nor even all those conflicts where losses were particularly heavy. Instead, more attention has been given to operations where a new tactic or a new weapon was first used, or used to maximum effect – for example, the invention of the 'plaster' and 'creeper' tactics for massed depth-charge attacks, or the first German use of the *Zaunkönig* homing torpedoes.

Overall, the reason for the emphasis on the anti-U-boat campaign of the Second World War is that this remains the only period where large-scale developments in ASW tactics and technology were actually put to the test, and many of the devices and weapons that form part of today's ASW armoury were originally perfected in principle. The First World War has been covered in less detail, as the U-boats' astonishing successes in that campaign were achieved against a frantic but ultimately almost fruitless struggle to find a way of hitting back at them. Trawler nets, high-speed paravanes, mine barrages and other expedients of the time were to prove dead-ends in terms of effective ASW for the future. The one measure that proved decisive, was the extremely simple one – in its basic principle – of returning to the eighteenth-century defence against raids by privateers. Grouping merchant ships into convoys did more to reduce losses than any technical ASW development of the time.

It is a similar case for other campaigns like the ASW war (conducted by both sides against one another's submarines) in the relatively confined waters of the Mediterranean. German and Italian submarines operating against Allied targets achieved some dramatic successes. However, Doenitz regarded U-boats sent into the Mediterranean on Hitler's express orders as permanently lost to what he considered the decisive theatre of operations – the North Atlantic convoys. When the Allies developed special techniques like 'swamping' to hunt individual submarines to destruction using their increasing ASW resources, those losses became all too real. And, in spite of Axis ASW vessels sinking British submarines in their efforts to protect Rommel's supply convoys, their tactics were conventional and the capture of North Africa brought this campaign to a close.

In the Pacific, the submarine ASW war was effectively turned around to face the opposite way. Though the big Japanese submarines achieved some remarkable successes against American warships early in the war, the idea of using them in a determined campaign against seaborne supplies never appeared attractive enough to the Imperial Navy. Initially a prisoner of its own doctrine that submarines were to be reserved for a series of blows against the oncoming US battle fleet before it could meet the Japanese capital ships in a massive and decisive encounter to settle

the Pacific naval war at a stroke, the Imperial Navy was forced to use its underwater craft to solve other problems in the face of growing American ascendancy, like the urgent need to deliver supplies and reinforcements to beleaguered Japanese garrisons on isolated islands.

At first, the US Navy also remained unaware of the vast opportunity opening up before its own submarine forces. In thrall to the almost universal pre-war doctrine which saw the greatest value of submarines in their ability to sink enemy warships, it later realised that their opponents' conquests of island bases across the Pacific left them totally dependent on supplies, munitions and reinforcements carried aboard largely unprotected merchant ships. Once the American submarines were unleashed against these targets, they went on to achieve the almost complete destruction of Japanese merchant shipping.

Though this was no walkover, and the US Navy suffered relatively heavy submarine losses due to Japanese warships and aircraft, resulting from their determination to head into harm's way and press home their attacks with the utmost resolution, the results were spectacular. The Japanese offered little in the way of new ASW tactics or technology, but they provided an instructive example of the terrible results of neglecting ASW against a clever and determined enemy. The fate they suffered in the closing years of the Second World War could instead have been suffered by the Allies, and Britain in particular, had the Allies not developed effective anti-submarine defences.

Following the end of the Second World War, the submarine reverted to being a potential threat rather than an actual weapon. But the termination of the ASW campaign against the U-boats had shown some ominous signs of future developments in the direction of the true submarine, which would be much more difficult to find and destroy than its wartime predecessors. As in so many other technological advances, like the swept-wing jet fighter and the ballistic missile, German ingenuity came within a worryingly short distance of success. Their new U-boats possessed speed, range and endurance so far improved over the wartime type VIIs and IXs that existing escort forces would have found them a daunting prospect to defeat. Production delays, design faults, materials shortages and the crippling effects of Allied bombing stopped the threat from being turned into reality, but the prospect of similar craft being built in large numbers by the Soviet Union meant a huge effort to produce faster escorts fitted with sensors and weapons that were longer in range and heavier in their impact. This kept ASW at the forefront of naval development through the 1950s and 1960s.

Undoubtedly the greatest change in ASW methods was made necessary by the development of the first true submarines, able to operate independently of the surface for an entire patrol if need be, with undreamt-of range and speed and endurance. The nuclear submarine changed the entire face of ASW and seemed at first to be entirely immune to ASW forces. In time, its Achilles heel became more apparent, in terms of the noises it emitted, which could be picked up by passive sonar to give its adversaries its position and allow them to target it with high-speed homing torpedoes, anti-submarine missiles and nuclear depth charges.

Fortunately for the balance of naval power, just as the submarine appeared to be achieving an even greater immunity from the forces ranged against it than was the case in 1914, an idea from that far-off conflict provided the necessary means of defence. In 1917, Admiral Sims of the US Navy suggested that a promising way of striking back at the U-boats was to use Allied submarines to hunt them down and sink them. At the time the idea had already proved moderately successful – by the Armistice a total of 18 U-boats had been sunk in this way, compared with a single one that fell victim to bombs dropped from an aircraft. In the Second World War, another 25 would fall victim to Allied submarines, but no fewer than 382 would be sunk by aircraft and another 51 to aircraft operating in co-operation with surface warships.

In the world of the nuclear submarine, though, no other warship had the right qualities of stealth, weaponry and performance in such abundance as another nuclear submarine, and the ASW emphasis tended to pass from the surface ship and the maritime patrol aircraft to the submarine service itself. Skippers of nuclear boats became adept at tailing their potential adversaries through the ocean depths, and at learning the exact mix of noises that would identify the class or even the individual identity of the boat they were tailing, while doing everything they could to conceal their own presence and position from their opponent.

Finally, as the twentieth century gave way to the twenty-first, ASW faced yet another turning point. Just as the balance of power between the major navies had become stabilised, so that each knew the other's numbers, capabilities, resources, routines, weapons, advantages, drawbacks, strengths and weaknesses to as great an extent as was possible without actually going to war against one another, conditions changed yet again. Just as the German Professor Walther's experiments with hydrogen peroxide had seemed to make the true submarine possible during the 1930s and 1940s, so his successors in naval research bureaux around the world began to develop different means of attaining the same ideal.

The result has been a different type of genuine submarine, using air-independent propulsion provided by power units ranging from Stirling engines to fuel cells to power a smaller, quieter and much more manoeuvrable submarine than the nuclear giants, some of whom displace as much weight as a heavy cruiser or a battleship of wartime days. Because they are quieter, they are much more difficult to track and identify using existing ASW techniques, and because they are much cheaper, they are being built for more and more navies around the world.

Inevitably, some of these will be operated by countries that may become opponents in a future conflict, and ASW tactics and technology will have to be developed to cope with their advantages and make good use of their weaknesses. As this book goes to press, the reliance on passive sonar used by the nuclear hunter-killer boats has already given way to using active sonar as the wartime escorts did, albeit with far greater range, sensitivity, accuracy and discrimination. The overriding drawback of this technique – that it gives away the user's position even more clearly and obviously than that of its target – is being diluted by combinations of surface ASW vessels using towed array sonar with aircraft dropping sonobuoys and helicopters using dipping sonars to build up additional information on the target.

Perhaps the greatest threat to future ASW forces is from new generation submarines designed to achieve greater speeds to make it more difficult for potential targets to evade their attacks. Add to that the introduction of submarine-launched anti-shipping cruise missiles and super-high-speed torpedoes that use bubble generators in the nose of the weapon to create a cavitation bubble around the torpedo to enable it to reach very high speeds indeed, and the ability of the submarine to hit back at attackers has been made much more formidable. Here too technology may have the answer, with cluster bombs dropped from aircraft in a re-run of the wartime Hedgehog to decoy torpedoes and missiles designed to confuse and divert incoming enemy weapons.

It all adds up to a story that clearly has a long way to run. The book can only attempt to tell the tale of this complex and challenging subject up to the present day, and try to offer some ideas for the short- to medium-term future. Any attempt to reach further than that risks entering the realms of astrology or science fiction. If the history of ASW thus far has anything to teach us, it is that all too often it is the more difficult and less promising of tactical ideas or technological projects that ultimately have the greatest effect. In fact, the only predictable quality of future anti-submarine warfare is its very unpredictability.

CHAPTER 1

DEVELOPING THE THREAT

1578–1913

This plaque at the Submarine Library in Groton, Connecticut, commemorates the creator of the first submarine to sink an enemy warship, even though Hunley himself died with all his crew on a test dive before the actual operation.

(US Naval Historical Center)

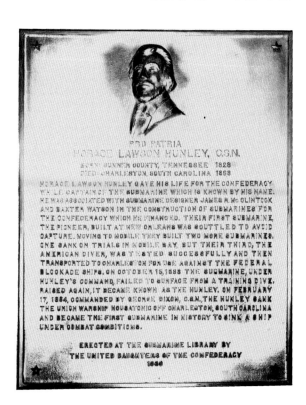

T HE night of 17 February 1864 was cold and clear, with a bright moon lighting up the sea off the coast of South Carolina. Watchers on the shore could clearly see the towering masts of the 1,200-ton steam-powered sloop USS *Housatonic*, anchored three miles off the Confederate port of Charleston, and part of the tight Federal blockade that was crippling Southern trade in the US Civil War. On board, all seemed well, as the lookouts scanned the waters around the ship, until, at approximately 8.40pm, their attention was aroused by something strange and threatening. At first it seemed like a large and rather slow dolphin, common in those waters, though with none of their grace and exuberance. Instead, it moved deliberately through the water, just below the surface, and it seemed to show two faint lights on its upper side. And it was heading straight for the ship.

The startled sentries soon realised that the mysterious object must be some kind of weapon, and that their ship was unmistakably its target. They sounded the alarm and opened fire on the object with rifles, muskets and a shotgun, but the rounds that hit it simply ricocheted off its iron structure. Down below, in the *Housatonic*'s engine room, men were striving to move the ship astern to evade the attack, and on the forecastle hands were struggling to slip the anchor. It was all in vain, and far too late. Ahead of the submerged vessel was a 90-pound explosive charge carried on a long spar, and when this made contact with the hull of the *Housatonic,* just ahead of the mizzen mast, it exploded with a massive concussion. The shock of the detonation blew the sloop in half, and water rushed in through the gap, sending her to the bottom in just three minutes, so quickly that she dragged five of her crew down with her.

The anxious watchers on the shore heard the explosion and saw the Union ship sinking. Some said they saw a signal from out at sea, confirming the attack had been successful, but there remained no sign of the mysterious vessel that had caused the destruction, and she and her crew would not be found again for more than 130 years. Yet all those present on that cold February night had seen history being made. In addition to a Southern victory at a time when these were few and far between, the *Housatonic* was the first enemy warship to be sunk by a submarine, and her five casualties were the first victims of a submarine attack.

The submarine in this case was the Confederate naval vessel *H L Hunley*. Before reaching this point, her history had been less than promising. She had been designed by two New Orleans inventors, James McClintock and Baxter Watson, who already had two unsuccessful submarine designs to their credit. The first had been produced in the opening winter of the war as an ambitious design called the *Pioneer*, which was actually granted letters of marque as a privateer (a licence for a civilian ship to prey on enemy merchant ships). After a promising demonstration when the 4-ton, iron-hulled craft, hand propelled with a crew of three, sank three targets using towed torpedoes with contact fuses, she had to be abandoned when the Northern army captured New Orleans.

The same inventors produced a larger design, the *American Diver*, which sank at sea when under tow. By then, they were short of funds, and they simply adapted their third design from an old ship's boiler, which they lengthened to forty feet overall and fitted with a keel, diving planes, hand cranks for propulsion and two deck hatches with observation portholes. The finished craft was taken by rail to Charleston, where a series of tests merely confirmed how dangerous submarines could be to their own crews. On one test, she submerged without the hatches being properly closed, drowning five of her crew of nine naval volunteers.

A second crew was been assembled, this time of civilians, headed by Horace Hunley, a New Orleans customs officer who had helped with the original design. Unfortunately, his experience with the development of the submarine did not prevent him from making mistakes and under his command she foundered a second time, plunging to the bottom of the harbour and drowning the entire crew. She was raised, named the *Hunley* after her late commander, and made ready with a third crew of eager volunteers, from both navy and army personnel, this time skippered by Lieutenant George Dixon of the 21st

Alabama Regiment. On that chilly moonlit evening in February 1864 she set off on her hazardous mission to sink the Union warship, with eight of her nine-man crew laboriously turning the hand crank connected to the propeller that moved the vessel through the water just beneath the surface

The *Hunley* never returned, and nothing more was known about her fate or that of her crew, until her hull was found on the seabed off Charleston in May 1995. When the boat was raised and examined, the bodies of her crew were found at their stations, but the hull had a hole in the side plating measuring a yard across. Different theories have attempted to explain her loss: she might have been overwhelmed by a sudden deterioration in the weather, or she might have been crippled by the shock of an explosion heavy enough to sink a relatively large warship in minutes, set off only twenty feet or so from her own hull.

Whatever the cause of her loss, she established several truths about submarines. The cloak of secrecy provided by sailing beneath the surface made them deadly weapons, as they could approach to much closer quarters with their targets than any surface warship could hope to do. However, the objective of designing and building a boat capable of doing this called for a number of complex technological advances to be made, and until these were proved to be efficient and reliable, early submarines would prove even more dangerous to their own crews than they were to those of the enemy ships they attacked. The *Hunley* was the most successful submarine of her time, but she had

The *Hunley* depended on its crew for propulsion, using a hand-turned crank running most of the length of the hull.

(US Naval Historical Center)

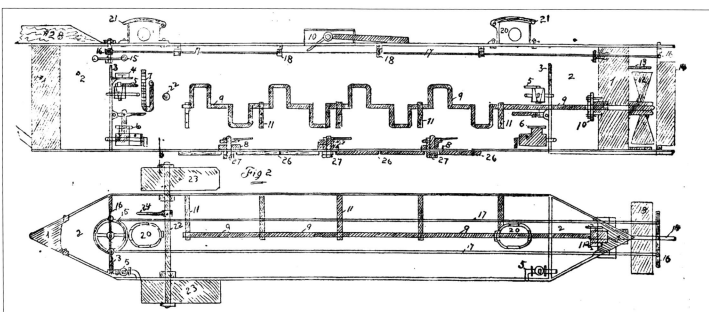

LONGITUDINAL ELEVATION IN SECTION AND PLAN VIEW OF THE CONFEDERATE SUBMARINE BOAT HUNLEY.
From Sketches by W. A. Alexander.

No. 1. The Bow and Stern Castings. No. 2. Water ballast tanks. No. 3. Tank bulkheads. No. 4. Compass. No. 5. Sea cocks. No. 6. Pumps. No. 7. Mercury gauge. No. 8. Keel ballast stuffing boxes. No. 9. Propeller shaft and cranks. No. 10. Stern bearing and gland. No. 11. Shaft braces. No. 12. Propeller. No. 13. Wrought ring around propeller. No. 14. Rudder. No. 15. Steering wheel. No. 16. Steering lever. No. 17. Steering rods. No. 18. Rod braces. No. 19. Air box. No. 20. Hatchways. No. 21. Hatch covers. No. 22. Shaft of side fins. No. 26. Cast-iron keel ballast. No. 27. Bolts. No. 28. Butt end of torpedo boom. No. 23. Side fins. No. 24. Shaft lever. No. 25. One of the crew turning propeller shaft. No. 31. Keel ballast.

The *Intelligent Whale* was the second submarine developed for the Union forces (the first was the *Alligator* which sank under tow in 1863). Known to her critics as the Disastrous Jonah, she flooded and sank on a test dive, though the crew escaped and she was later raised, to be kept at a National Guard Museum in New Jersey.
(*US Naval Institute Press*)

practical submersible, as a new design contributed often another 'first' needed to solve yet another problem. The need for ballast tanks, surface and underwater propulsion, stability while submerged, fresh air for the crew, a clear view of the enemy target and a weapon to sink it when spotted, were requirements that would be met one by one. The most glaring omission in the long and painful process of the birth of the submarine, though, was a true vision of what it could be used for once it was perfected: as a potential war-winning weapon against trade rather than warships. The development of ASW, the tactics and weapons that would eventually be used to defeat the menace that the submarine represented to established navies would take even longer to perfect. Only when the weapon existed could measures be developed to produce a defence against it.

Another common factor of many of the early submarines was that they tended to be developed by or for the world's weaker navies, facing a mightier opponent and looking for a means to redress that imbalance. Many of the projects were intended to be used against British naval supremacy, like the work of a pair of French clerics, Marin Mersenne and Georges Fournier, a decade after Drebbel's experiments, though their abortive design was designed to run on wheels when it sank to the seabed.

This ingenious attempt at an underwater road vehicle was followed by a British attempt to take the buoyancy principles of the gas balloon down below the surface. In 1774, a Devonshire carpenter and betting man, John Day, modified the *Maria*, a 50-foot sloop, by constructing a watertight cabin in her hold, and adding positive buoyancy by lashing seventy-five sealed and empty casks at intervals around the hull. To make the craft submerge, two 10-ton iron weights were slung beneath it. Just as the occupants of a balloon could throw ballast overboard to make their craft rise, Day fixed the weights through ringbolts to allow them to be released when the time came to surface again.

Under the terms of the bet behind the project, Day took his craft into Plymouth Sound where she submerged decisively enough but failed to reappear. No buoys were released and nothing more was ever heard from the *Maria*. The water was 170 feet deep at the point where she disappeared and the most likely explanation was that the large increase in pressure caused the hull to leak catastrophically, or even collapse, before Day had time to release the ballast.

Nevertheless, just over a year later, on the other side of the Atlantic, another primitive submarine not only survived its first outing without killing its operator, but carried out the first attack on an enemy vessel. David Bushnell was a graduate of Yale University and his country had just begun a revolutionary war to win independence from British rule. The principal American harbours were closely blockaded

killed more than four times as many of her own side as she had of the enemy.

Yet, primitive and vulnerable as she was, she represented the fruit of more than two centuries' development. The first practical proposal for a submersible craft was made in 1578 by William Bourne, a Gravesend-born former naval gunner and self-taught navigator and mathematician. Ever since then, a succession of hopeful inventors had tried to solve the enormous technical problems of making a boat submerge beneath the surface of the water in which it floated, and then – infinitely more difficult – to make it regain the surface again afterwards.

Bourne's idea was to build a closed wooden hull waterproofed with leather, propelled by oars and made to dive or surface by applying or releasing screws compressing leather-bag ballast tanks. Though his boat was never built, Cornelius Jacobszoon Drebbel, son of a wealthy farmer from Alkmaar in Holland, a part-time inventor who had also produced microscopes and a perpetual motion clock, used Bourne's basic design in his submersible of 1620. This also had tubes supported by floats on the surface to provide the crew with a supply of fresh air, and was demonstrated on the Thames in London, though it leaked badly. But both the King and the Royal Navy were interested enough to fund Drebbel and his colleagues to develop weapons for his craft, including 'underwater explosive machines'. He also worked on explosives for fireships, but the insurmountable engineering obstacles to convert his experimental boat into a practical weapon of war led to the whole project sinking into abeyance.

This progression from a hopeful design to a promising debut succeeded by failure and final abandonment was echoed by most early submarines. Yet each represented another step on the road to a

Plunger was the first product of the newly-formed Holland Torpedo Boat Company in 1897, but the design was unsuccessful and the boat was never completed.

(*US Naval Historical Center*)

by British warships, and his submarine craft was designed to sink them with explosive charges.

Rather than using a conventional boat, Bushnell based the hull of his *Turtle* on the more practical example of a barrel. It was some seven feet tall from top to bottom and six feet in diameter, with room for a single crew member, and it was built from curved oak staves caulked with tar and held together by iron bands. An iron cylinder at the top of the barrel was fitted with portholes and the craft was propelled by hand-turned screws, one vertical and the other horizontal. It was armed with a single explosive charge carrying 150 pounds of gunpowder, to be attached to the hull of its target below the water line, using a drill attached to the *Turtle*'s vertical propeller.[1]

The submersible was demonstrated to American officers, who realised its potential, and on 6 September 1776, Sergeant Ezra Lee of the Continental Army set off to attack the 64-gun ship HMS *Eagle*, flagship of Admiral Howe, commanding the Royal Navy squadron blockading New York. Surprisingly, the *Turtle* reached its target without being spotted, but all attempts to attach the charge to the *Eagle's* hull failed, probably because iron-hard ship's timbers were impenetrable to Lee's struggles to drill into them. Meanwhile, a shore party of redcoats spotted the top of the *Turtle*, and a boat was launched to investigate. Lee primed the time fuse on the charge and dropped it while making his escape. The charge went off and the British gave up the pursuit, leaving Lee to return to safety. He had survived the first submarine attack, but so had his target.

With America independent of Britain and the Revolutionary War over, another, and much better

known, American inventor tried his luck in Europe with a submarine project. This was Robert Fulton, later famous for the first steamship, who in 1799 produced a sailing submarine, the *Nautilus*. This he showed to the warring British and French governments. His submersible was twenty-one feet long and the hull was sheathed in copper plates, with a folding mast that could be taken down before diving. Air was supplied to the crew in flasks, and in July 1801 the *Nautilus* completed a submerged test by staying on the bottom of the harbour of Brest for more than an hour at a depth of some thirty feet.

More encouraging tests followed. Napoleon himself supplied a 40-foot sloop which was sunk by an explosive charge carried ahead of the submarine on a long spar. This was the first ship to be sunk by submarine, but the French lost interest and Fulton turned to the British. His submarine sank another captive vessel, the brig *Dorothy*, with a 70-pound charge, in October 1805, but after the crushing victory of Trafalgar that very month the British too were lukewarm to the submarine's possibilities. Fulton's attempts to interest the Admiralty in the possibilities of the submarine and the torpedo through the offices of Prime Minister, William Pitt, drew the stinging rebuke from Lord St Vincent that 'Pitt was the greatest fool that ever lived to encourage a system of warfare that those who command the seas don't want and if successful would deprive them of it'. He returned to America to develop surface steamers, though at the time of his death in 1815 he was working on a project for a much larger steam-powered submarine, which died with him.

Possibly even more significant in the overall history of the submarine was a craft called the *Brandtaucher,* or 'Fire Diver', which made its appearance in 1850. This was the first German submarine, built by a 28-year-old former artillery sergeant named Wilhelm Bauer. Powered by its crew turning a treadmill linked to an external propeller, this was another unsuccessful design, marked only by its crew making the first successful escape from a submerged submarine, when it plunged to the seabed on its first test dive.

All these false starts provided a discouraging background for any prospective inventor, but the success of the *Hunley,* even at the price of the lives of her own crew, triggered a series of new designs. The steam-powered Confederate submarine *Saint Patrick,* of 1865, tried to attack the 10-gun Union paddle steamer USS *Octorara,* this time on the surface, but her spar-carried charge failed to detonate. *Saint Patrick* escaped, and was later used to sneak supplies to Confederate garrisons cut off by Union forces. There was even some evidence that James McLintock himself travelled to Halifax in Nova Scotia in October 1872 following discussions with the British Consul in Mobile, Alabama, during McLintock's supervision of dredging operations in Mobile Bay. His offer was to produce for the Royal Navy an improved model of the *Hunley,* more compact but faster, thanks to an improved propulsion system. Before he could carry out his intention of travelling to London for more discussions, he fell ill with 'typhoid pneumonia' on his way back to Alabama, and as a result of a delayed recovery and lack of funds, the planned meetings never took place. However, there is reason to believe that the interest caused by his approach finally helped tip the balance towards the Royal Navy buying their first, more viable submarines some two decades later.[2]

By comparison, the much stronger Union Navy barely dabbled in submarines: their first, the *Alligator* minelayer sank while being towed in April 1862, and the *Intelligent Whale* sank on her first official test, though the crew escaped with their lives. These disappointments resulted in the US Navy ignoring submarines for more than twenty years.

One of the biggest remaining limitations was the lack of proper underwater propulsion, and two French inventors used a compressed air engine on their *Le Plongeur* design, though this could not provide enough range for the boat to be a practical proposition. She also proved almost terminally unstable in the diving plane and was never used on an actual operation.

Another attempt to solve the propulsion problem was made by a minister, the Reverend George William Garrett, curate of Christ Church, Moss Side, in Manchester. In spite of a lack of engineering experience he was backed by his father and several city businessmen to build a submarine. His first egg-shaped experimental design was driven by hand cranking through a flywheel, but its successor, a tubular hull with conical bow and stern extensions, used the recently patented Lamy closed-cycle steam engine, which needed no external air supply except for the fire that heated the boiler.

Named *Resurgam,* (Latin: 'I shall rise again') the 45-foot boat displaced thirty tons. It was built at the port of Birkenhead in 1879 for a total cost of £1,538, and was launched on 26 November 1879 at the nearby Wallasey Docks. Its predicted performance was three knots on the surface and two knots underwater, after the furnace was put out and the engine ran on the remaining heat in the boiler, giving a predicted endurance of some four hours. It also had revolutionary weaponry, with two external torpedo tubes loaded with the new Whitehead torpedoes.

The Royal Navy asked Garrett to demonstrate his new submarine at Portsmouth Dockyard,[3] and, on 10 December 1879, he and two crewmen set off on the surface to sail around the coasts of Wales and Cornwall under the submarine's own power, heading for the Channel and Portsmouth. The heat of the boiler and furnace in the tiny iron hull soon raised internal temperatures to more than 100° Fahrenheit, and the boat had to put in to the small harbour at Rhyl, some twenty-five miles from its starting point for modifications to be made. The voyage was resumed on 24 February 1880, with the *Resurgam* towed by the steam yacht *Elfin,* but the yacht developed engine trouble, and two days later the tow parted in worsening weather. This left the submarine to broach-to in the steep seas and it flooded through the open conning-tower hatch. The crew abandoned their charge and boarded the yacht as the submarine vanished into the depths.

Garrett himself went into partnership with Thorsten Nordenfeld, a Swedish gunmaker, to make more steam submarines for the Greek, Turkish and, finally, Russian navies. They all suffered from pitching instability and performed poorly on tests, and the last straw was when their fourth boat ran aground in Denmark while being delivered to Russia. The Russians refused to pay, and Garrett was forced to leave England, the church and submarine-building, to find a new career teaching in the USA.

In spite of these setbacks, the submarine continued to edge slowly towards efficiency, reliability and viability as an operational weapon. In 1885, two more British inventors produced the 60-ton iron submarine *Nautilus* which relied on battery-driven electric motors for underwater propulsion. French inventors then produced a series of innovative designs ending in the *Gymnote* of 1890 and the *Narval* of 1899, which between them established the vital principles of dual propulsion. They used a steam engine on the surface and electric motors while submerged, with compressed air to empty the ballast tanks to make the submarine surface, and hydroplanes to control its depth.

But the big final step towards a viable submarine was taken by another unlikely inventor. John Holland was one of two Irish brothers who had emigrated to the USA in 1873. While working as a teacher in New Jersey, he read about the *Intelligent Whale* and became interested in the possibility of building a submarine. Like most others in this extraordinary story, he felt that lack of experience of marine engineering was no bar to success, and when his brother Michael provided a link to the Fenian Brotherhood, an organisation dedicated to overturning British rule in Ireland, he found backers for his efforts. The Fenians thought the submarine would be a wonderful weapon to use against British power, so provided funding, and John Holland set to work. However, his first three boats proved to be failures.

Holland I was a small iron boat weighing just two tons and powered by a small petrol engine. It was demonstrated to the Fenians in May 1877, who agreed a much larger boat was needed, and it was simply allowed to sink, literally and metaphorically, into oblivion. His second boat, originally the *Holland II* and later renamed the *Fenian Ram*, was a 19-ton iron boat fitted with a pneumatic gun that could fire a projectile underwater for up to sixty yards. His third boat was another small prototype, the *Fenian Model*, weighing just one ton, but in 1883 the Fenians reneged on the contract, seized both boats and towed them away up the East River. Their coup misfired: the *Fenian Model*

sank en route and the *Fenian Ram* stayed afloat as far as the port of New Haven in Connecticut, where she was beached and abandoned.

Holland's fourth and fifth designs were no more successful. His fourth prototype was a wooden boat that was remarkable for providing a platform for a fearsome new submarine weapon, designed by an army lieutenant named Edmund Zalinski. This was an experimental gun, or mortar, which fired cartridges filled with notoriously temperamental nitroglycerine, which would have almost certainly been more lethal to the craft carrying the weapon than to any of its targets.

Holland's hopes were transformed at last by a 1888 US Navy competition to design a submarine capable of maintaining eight knots submerged for two hours at depths down to 150 feet. This was a very demanding specification, but Holland won the competition, yet no contract was awarded. Instead, another competition followed in 1893, and this time Holland's design did not win. Instead, he built the *Holland VI*, fifty-three feet long and weighing seventy-four tons, driven by a 50-horsepower petrol engine promising a surfaced range of 1,000 miles. This was offered to the US Navy and, when they were shown it, could fire 17-inch Whitehead torpedoes; they finally bought it for the high price of $165,000 as USS *Holland*, or *SS*1.

She was a crude and uncomfortable boat on which to serve, with an open bucket for toilet facilities and sacks and newspapers on the steel deck instead of bunks. But she proved her capability as a weapon in

The USS *Holland*, seen here at Greenport, Long Island in the summer of 1899, was in fact the sixth boat produced by John Holland and the first to be accepted by the US Navy, to be commissioned on 12 October 1900.
(US Naval Historical Center)

the 1900 US Navy manoeuvres off Newport, Rhode Island, when she approached within 100 yards of a battleship before signalling that she could have launched a torpedo and scored a certain hit.

After this, most of the world's navies opted for Holland boats to threaten their enemies' fleets. The US Navy ordered seven boats of Holland's improved

John Holland, seen here in the conning tower of one of his designs, produced the first practical submersibles and went on to supply the world's navies.

(*US Naval Historical Center*)

no. 7 design. Now free of the Fenian Brotherhood, Holland himself was happy to allow the British shipbuilders Vickers-Armstrong to produce five boats under licence for the Royal Navy. The Japanese ordered five more which were then taken apart and shipped to Japan for reassembly, and the Dutch built another under licence in 1905.

Just about the only major navy that did not buy or build Holland boats was that of Imperial Germany. In fact, Holland's rival in the 1893 US Navy competition, one Simon Lake of New Jersey, had built a submarine called the *Protector*, which was then sold to the Russians. He had built more boats for the Russian and Austrian navies before supplying the Germans with their first submarine and then building the first non-Holland submarines for the US Navy. Finally, having set the world on the road to submarine warfare, John Holland himself died on 12 August 1914, eight days after the outbreak of a world war where his invention would play a vital and highly destructive part.

Though the Holland boats, and the other designs that followed them, were more successful at the basic requirement of being able to dive and surface under full control, and allowing their crews to survive the experience, much still had to be settled before the

submarine could finally develop into the formidable weapon it became. Propulsion was a continuing problem, the first submarines used petrol engines, which were highly dangerous. The Royal Navy's first post-Holland boats, the A class coastal submarines numbering thirteen boats in all, were completed between 1904 and 1908. Like the Holland boats, they were low on reserve buoyancy, and no less than eight were lost in different types of accident. The most significant loss, for future submarine development, was the loss of *A*5, which was refuelling at Queenstown on 16 February 1905 when petrol fumes caused an explosion that killed five of her crew. A direct consequence of this disaster was the switch to diesel engines in *A*13, the final boat of the class, in 1908, the first British submarine with diesel propulsion and part of a trend soon followed by the other major submarine powers.[4]

Nevertheless, the C class coastal submarines built soon afterwards also used petrol engines with more success, though these were the last to do so in Royal Navy service. In the meantime, the German Navy began using motors burning heavy fuel oil for propulsion on the surface in their first coastal submarines. Though they proved safer for the crews in one sense, they had another serious drawback: they produced clouds of exhaust smoke and sparks when running on the surface, which gave ASW forces a splendidly clear target.

These boats also set new standards in armament. Because the first torpedoes were temperamental, relatively unreliable and expensive, the boats were fitted with a 37-mm gun apiece, to be used to sink ships in surface attacks. By 1909, the Royal Navy's D class of diesel-engined overseas service submarines were being fitted with 12-pound deck guns, and by 1913 the process was virtually complete. Germany's four first ocean-going U-boats (*U*19 to *U*22) were fitted with diesel engines and an 88-mm deck gun, a specification that would be echoed in the type VII of three decades later.

Almost as soon as the first submarines entered service, controversy arose over how to use these powerful but dangerous new weapons. Some navies, like the US Navy and the Royal Navy, with large and well-established fleets, tended to see their usefulness as limited to defending harbours and vulnerable stretches of coastline from enemy raiders. Others, with more aggressive agendas in mind, like Germany and Japan, saw them as a means of attacking warships, to erode the advantages possessed by more powerful opponents in a major fleet action. But no one at that early stage realised the possibilities of turning the new submarines against their most vulnerable and most damaging targets: the merchant ships carrying the enemy's food and war materials.

IT was 5.45am on the morning of 22 September 1914. After two days' fierce equinoctial gales, which had brought to an end one of the loveliest summers in living memory, the weather was moderating again at last. Off the neutral Dutch coast, three ships of the Royal Navy's Seventh Cruiser Squadron sailed in line abreast formation through a shallow area of the North Sea called the Broad Fourteens. HMS *Aboukir*, HMS *Cressy* and HMS *Hogue* were all named after renowned British victories, but the ships themselves were less impressive, being obsolete four-funnelled cruisers, slow and desperately vulnerable. In the service they were known with grim humour as 'The Live Bait Squadron'. Their crews included reservists and Dartmouth cadets, and they were ill-equipped for the front line of this new naval war.

They were dangerously exposed. The Admiralty ordered a watch to be kept on this strategic area of the Narrow Seas, just 150 miles from the main German naval base at Wilhelmshaven, as there was a danger that German raiders might pass this way to lay mines off the British coast or, worse, head into the Channel to attack the convoys ferrying troops and equipment between England and France. Normally, most of the squadron patrolled further north in the less dangerous waters of the Dogger Bank. Even here, they were normally protected by an attendant destroyer screen, but the gales had forced the smaller vessels to shelter in Harwich.

A single successful U-boat had put a torpedo into the 'scout' (light cruiser) HMS *Pathfinder* on 5 September off the entrance to the Firth of Forth, setting off her magazine and sinking her with heavy casualties. Nevertheless, the main threat was still thought to be a raid by surface warships. In any case, if destroyers could not stay at sea in such rough weather, what danger could the smaller and much more fragile submarines pose?

Already the squadron was badly depleted. The leader, HMS *Euryalus*, had left for Sheerness two days before for repairs to her radio aerials and to refill her coal bunkers, and HMS *Bacchante* had had to return to port with engine trouble. A suggestion that, as the remaining three cruisers were also due for engine repairs, they should retreat to the safer, but rougher, waters south of the Dogger Bank had been vetoed by the Admiralty, though the decision had already been taken to pull them out altogether as soon as possible. In the meantime, with the weather improving, their escorting destroyers had sailed from Harwich almost an hour before to rejoin them.

For the moment, all seemed well. Yet, a few miles to the north, a German submarine, the already obsolescent *U9* was surfacing just before dawn after an anxious and bumpy night. The weather had been

CHAPTER 2

STRANGLEHOLD: WORLD WAR 1
1914–17

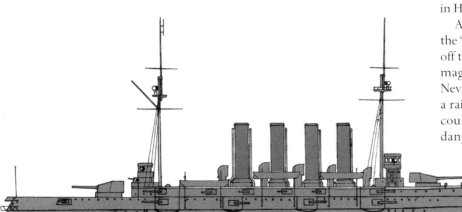

The *Cressy* class of armoured cruisers displaced 12,000 tons and were armed with 9.2in guns and protected by a belt of 6in armour. They were known in the Royal Navy as the 'Live Bait Squadron', and were fatally vulnerable to submarine torpedoes.

(Author's drawing)

too rough to rest on the bottom and shipping traffic had been too busy for her to remain on the surface. Now her skipper, thirty-two-year-old Kapitän-leutnant Otto Weddigen, was anxious to recharge batteries and search for enemy warships. He had scarcely begun his breakfast when his first officer reported smoke on the horizon. He dived immediately, with batteries still severely depleted and recharging barely begun.

The three cruisers headed steadily northeast, a course that took them away from the destroyers rushing to catch up, and towards *U9*. With no perceptible threat, and only a gentle swell as a reminder of the gales, conditions were relaxed. Guns were trained fore and aft and most were not loaded. The ships were roughly two miles apart, with *Aboukir* in the centre position and very slightly in the lead.

Weddigen's options were limited. His tiny craft had two torpedo tubes in the bow, with another pair of torpedoes as reloads, and two more loaded tubes at the stern; six shots in all, provided he had enough time to reload his bow tubes. But his underwater speed was slow, and trying to outmanoeuvre his adversaries would soon exhaust his limited battery power. In addition, he could not afford to try to evade attacks by retreating to the seabed as the air in *U9* was still foul from the night before.

HMS *Aboukir* was heading for a group of fishing boats on the horizon, when, at 6.25am, Weddigen fired his first bow torpedo. It hit the cruiser on her port side, abreast of the first and second boiler rooms. Water poured in through the huge hole, leaving her down by the stern, and with a steep list to port. So unexpected was the explosion that the crew believed that she had hit a mine, or that a boiler had exploded. For a time, it seemed possible to put her back on to an even keel by counter-flooding – admitting the sea to compartments on the starboard side – but this proved impossible as water continued to flood into the hull. Worse, the steep tilt to port meant that most of the ship's boats could not be lowered. *Aboukir*'s captain, still unaware of what had caused the explosion, signalled for help from his consorts. Once he realised the truth, he ordered the other ships to keep clear.[1]

Captain Nicholson of *Hogue* suspected what had

happened, but as he was on the opposite side of *Aboukir* from both *Cressy* and the site of the explosion, he assumed he was screened from any submarine by the hulk of the other ship. He moved closer, ordering *Cressy* to keep clear, and watch for any sign of a submarine periscope. He failed to see any sign of the tiny *U9* reversing her course, appearing from behind the *Aboukir* and closing on his ship.

Weddigen was probably the best shot with torpedoes in the entire Imperial Navy. In the 1913 war games, he was judged to have sunk three battleships with successive shots,[2] and the manoeuvres of the 'Live Bait Squadron' posed no particular problem. His crew had reloaded the number one tube and, exactly thirty minutes after firing his first torpedo at *Aboukir* to such deadly effect and, just as she vanished below the surface, he fired both bow tubes at *Hogue*. Both hit their target, and the ship's engine room flooded, sinking her in ten minutes.[3]

Cressy was now the sole survivor, and she kept a careful watch for periscope sightings while her boats continued to pick up survivors from the other two ships. Weddigen found his third attack a comparatively simple matter. At 7.20am he approached to within 1,100 yards of his final target and fired both stern tubes. One of these hit the cruiser on the starboard side but for once the damage was less than mortal, and the second one passed astern of the target.[4] Weddigen closed to within 500 yards to ensure a hit with his remaining bow torpedo. At 7.35 it hit *Cressy* and she finally sank twenty minutes later, taking with her the final hopes of an easy defeat of the submarine menace.

The loss of three cruisers in little more than an hour to one lone submarine proved a profound shock to both the Royal Navy and to their Imperial German adversaries. At the start of the war, both services had been in some doubt as to what these stealthy and still-misunderstood weapons might achieve. Because the early submarines were small, vulnerable and unreliable, it was difficult to take them seriously as a threat to much bigger and more heavily protected surface warships, and a number of theories were developed as to how they might be used in wartime fleet operations.

After Weddigen's victory, and the success of

The light cruiser HMS *Pathfinder* was the first warship sunk by a U-boat when a torpedo set off her magazine and sank her within minutes on 5 September 1914.

(Author's drawing)

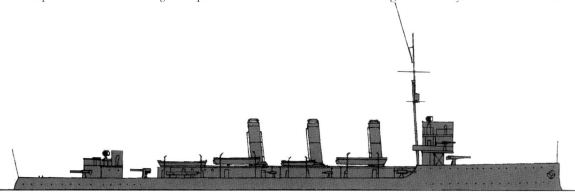

Lieutenant Max Horton RN (future Commander-in-Chief Western Approaches in the Second World War battle against the U-boats), when as skipper of the British submarine *E9* he had not only sunk the old German cruiser *Hela* on 6 September, but had partially redressed the balance by sinking the German destroyer *S119* with a single torpedo on 6 October,[5] the value of the submarine was no longer in doubt. What still needed to be decided was the best way to use this weapon, and ultimately how to defeat it when used by the enemy.

Ironically, German acceptance of the submarine had been surprisingly slow. Initially, they had seen submarines as playing a part in a major battle between the opposing fleets. As their chief fear was that the Royal Navy would take the strategic initiative and attack the German High Seas Fleet in their bases, much as Van Tromp had done to the English in the Dutch Wars of the seventeenth century, they decided their U-boats should be based on the island of Heligoland, to hack away at the flanks of the opposing British force and weaken it before the inevitable clash of the main battle fleets. If submarine-launched torpedoes could reduce the British advantage in heavy ships, Germany might yet win victory at sea against her strongest opponent.

As the months went by, however, they realised that the Royal Navy had no such end in view, however much individual officers might yearn for a decisive battle to do what Trafalgar and the Nile had done more than a century before, and eliminate the threat of the enemy fleet entirely. What was now in mind was a much more subtle legacy from the past, the weapon that had ultimately defeated a Napoleon who was hurt, but not crushed, by the loss of his fleet: blockade. With the British Isles lying athwart Germany's access to world trade as a simple fact of geography, it was all too easy for British warships to strangle Germany's imports of food and war materials as they had done those of Imperial France. And they could do it without sailing anywhere near German bases, or inviting a clash with adversaries increasingly reluctant to risk an open battle.

Against this strategic defence, there seemed to be only one viable tactic. German surface ships could not themselves take up the strategic offensive without risking destruction in the face of superior numbers, a defeat that might end the war with her armies still unbeaten. But the stealth and relative immunity of the submarine could be used to even the balance, and finally to tilt it in Germany's favour. Certainly British warships were becoming less available as targets. The shock of losing three elderly cruisers had galvanised the Royal Navy into taking precautions such as sailing at top speed, and on irregular zigzag courses that made it almost impossible for a slow submerged U-boat to manoeuvre into a position for launching torpedoes successfully.

On the other hand, merchant ships were much easier to find, and to hit. So if the British blockade could not be defeated directly, it might be possible to defeat it indirectly. If an even tighter counter-blockade could be imposed by submarines, then the British might be forced to negotiate terms for ending the

HMS *Aboukir*, first of *U9's* three victims on 22 September 1914.
(www.navyphotos.co.uk)

HMS *Hogue*, second of three cruisers to be torpedoed in quick succession.
(www.navyphotos.co.uk)

the surface, she could move faster and sail much further, but was frighteningly vulnerable to a single shot from a projectile heavy enough to pierce the pressure hull. Even if she then remained afloat, she would be unable to dive and would find herself easy prey.

The second problem was how exactly should British merchant ships be sunk? The routine was little changed from Nelson's time. In 1914, the internationally acceptable way to attack a merchant vessel was to stop it, confirm its nationality, route and cargo and then, if it was found to be an enemy ship carrying war material in its broadest sense, the crew had to be given time to take to the boats before the ship was sunk, by torpedo, by deck gun for the smaller merchant vessels, or by placing scuttling charges. Many U-boat commanders went even further, towing the lifeboats containing merchant survivors to the nearest land or a neutral ship that could take them on board.

However, this whole technique of intercepting and checking merchant ships was laborious and time consuming, and increasingly dangerous for the submarine and her crew. Consequently, there were more and more voices within the German Navy calling for a more ruthless approach, using torpedoes to sink enemy merchant ships on sight, as a way of bringing British trade to a halt as quickly as possible. As the first of these campaigns began to prove surprisingly effective, another objective slipped into the minds of Germany's naval commanders – the idea of sinking more merchant ships than Britain could build to replace them, especially at a time when more and more British shipyards had been given over to warship construction.

Neutral shipping, however, presented a problem. Many cargoes heading for British ports were carried in ships belonging to nations that had not entered the war on either side. If their ships were not targeted, the German blockade would not be complete. If they were, then their citizens would be killed, and public opinion at home might result in them joining the war against Germany. Bearing in mind that the largest and most powerful neutral nation was the USA, this represented a potentially unacceptable price for launching an unrestricted submarine campaign against British trade. American disapproval exerted a powerful influence on the course of Germany's submarine war.

In the meantime, the most important question for the Royal Navy arising from the demonstration of what submarines could do, was what kind of tactics and equipment could be brought to bear against these deadly and elusive opponents. The awful truth was that at the time there was almost nothing in the way of ASW technology or tactics that could be used to attack and sink a U-boat. Just about the only effective way of keeping them at bay was to restrict their range and speed by forcing them to dive, either by surface

embargo on German trade. Even if naval war went on otherwise unabated, the stranglehold on Germany's war economy and the food to feed her population could be relaxed.

This was perfectly possible in theory, but represented a huge change in priorities. Every nation that eventually made use of submarines thought first and foremost of using them against enemy warships, and preferably a battle fleet at that. Even having made the shift in doctrine, there were also practical difficulties. During both World Wars, there was no such thing as a true submarine, able to match its surface speed and endurance with similar performance underwater. So there was always a balance of advantages and drawbacks. Underwater, a submarine was difficult to find, but painfully slow and restricted in range: on patrols or by simply flying over them in airships or patrol planes. Even though U-boat crews knew perfectly well that air patrols as yet carried no weapons that could present a genuine direct threat, they could communicate with surface warships that could inflict lethal blows from gunfire so long as the submarine did not dive. If it did dive, its range and speed were cut and its usefulness temporarily eliminated.

In the longer term, and in the face of an intensifying German campaign against merchant shipping, this would never be enough. Something much more effective was needed. One of the first attempts to provide a solution was to organise Western Approaches Command, with headquarters at Queenstown on the southern coast of Ireland, controlling more than 400 miscellaneous vessels, from destroyers down to drifters, trawlers, sloops and armed motor yachts. The captains of this motley collection of ships were ordered to patrol all the waters between Ireland and the British mainland, together with the Bristol Channel and the western end of the English Channel.

This turned out to be hopelessly misconceived, and for once geography worked against the British. Offensive patrolling, as the doctrine was called, proved almost totally ineffective. The area involved was simply too vast. Even when the ships available to the Command increased almost eightfold by the final year of the war, there was still virtually no chance of simply running into a potential target. Even had they done so as a matter of luck, at this early stage of the war, they had nothing to attack it with.

At best, it was a colossal waste of resources, especially when a more practical alternative existed. There were still areas of sea confined enough to guarantee relatively dense U-boat traffic, around what would later become known as 'choke points'. Even here, for the time being, there were still no weapons that could be used against submerged submarines, so a great deal of effort was expended instead in preventing them from passing through these areas, mainly by laying huge minefields. In the first six months of the war, more than seven thousand mines were laid in twenty-two different fields to the east of the Dover Straits. The effects were disappointing, as the mines were laid at too shallow a depth; not only could submerged U-boats sail safely beneath them, but surfaced U-boats could see them bobbing on the surface at low tide, and steer a course between them. The other problem was the strong tidal streams running up and down the Channel, and more than half of the mines laid either sank to the seabed or were dragged far from their moorings, presenting a real danger to all shipping in these busy waters.[6]

Fortunately, the minefields were backed up by additional lines of defence. One consisted of drifters towing special indicator nets in the hope of trapping a submarine in the mesh. If this happened, the extra pull on the net would cause one of the supporting glass floats to release a carbide flare. Destroyers or armed trawlers would then lie in wait for the trapped submarine to rise to the surface to escape the net, and try to sink it by ramming or gunfire. If the U-boat managed to escape or evade the net while staying submerged, the problem was infinitely more difficult. The only promising weapon was the explosive sweep; towed by a patrol vessel, it was a long wire loop that carried nine small 80-pound explosive charges beneath the surface. If it made contact with a submarine, one or more of the charges would be detonated and the submarine would be sunk. That was the theory, though the huge expanse of water to be covered made it an unlikely prospect.

A much more promising tactic was to hit the U-boat at the time it was doing its deadly work – attacking merchant ships – and this was done in two ways. More and more merchant ships were being equipped with deck guns to defend themselves. With a properly trained gun crew, a merchant ship had a good chance of striking a crippling blow against a U-boat, itself only armed with a single gun, and with a highly vulnerable pressure hull. A more offensive tactic was the use of Q-ships, small merchant vessels with concealed guns on the upper deck. The theory behind these ships was that they would clearly be too small to be worth a U-boat captain using a precious torpedo to sink one. However, if he closed in on the surface to a range that would allow him to finish off an apparently defenceless target with his deck gun, the Q-ship's main armament would be revealed and a powerful barrage would quickly finish off the attacker.

For the idea to work, the Q-ship's camouflage had to be perfect, even when watched through powerful binoculars by a cautious submarine commander. For example, one converted fishing vessel was towing nets in the correct way, but another fishing boat spotted that there were none of the usual swarms of seagulls competing for scraps from the catch. In the case of larger vessels, which *might* attract a torpedo, cargo holds would be filled with empty barrels or baulks of timber for greater buoyancy. Guns were disguised as sheep pens – providing fresh meat for the crew on a long voyage – or as life-belt holders. If a submarine stopped the Q-ship, the cover of a helpless merchantman might have to be maintained up to the crew taking to the lifeboats, leaving enough trained men hidden onboard to man the guns and open fire when the U-boat least expected it.

Another variation on the tethered-goat ruse to lure U-boats to their doom was provided by trawlers towing a submerged British submarine linked to the towing vessel by a cable carrying a telephone link. If a U-boat surfaced and approached the trawler to sink it or capture it, the warning was given to the hidden

A German artist's impression of one of *U9*'s victims: the original caption to this picture identified the cruiser as HMS *Aboukir*, but she was torpedoed on her port side and listed in the opposite direction to that shown here.

(Jak Mallmann Showell)

British submarine, which slipped the towline and torpedoed the German submarine.

All these expedients promised more for the future than for the present. When the Germans opened their first campaign against British merchant ships in February 1915, it lasted to the end of September. In spite of the relatively small number of submarines available, with an average of just over seven U-boats at sea for each day of the campaign, they exerted a steady toll on merchant vessels trading with Britain. In the seven months from March to September inclusive, they sank a total of 480 ships, totalling almost 750,000 tons. Yet as a fraction of the huge resources of the British merchant fleet, which had already been increased by all the German and Austrian merchant ships captured at the start of the war, this would never be enough to make the British release their grip on German trade and food supplies. Only if the sinkings outstripped new construction in British shipyards, and only if more and more U-boats were made available could conditions improve for the Germans.[7]

What finally cut this campaign short was the sinking of two unarmed British passenger liners. The

Arabic was lost on 19 August and the *Hesperian* was sunk on 6 September by the U-boat that had earlier sunk the *Lusitania*, with the loss of many American lives, on 7 May. On that occasion, US President Woodrow Wilson reacted so angrily that he was only diverted from entering the war by a German promise that large passenger liners would not be attacked without warning. Since these new sinkings showed the promise was not being kept, American pressure was redoubled, and on 18 September the U-boats were withdrawn from the ocean routes, and those in the North Sea were ordered to operate within the confines of the Prize Regulations.

For the Royal Navy, these opening skirmishes were mildly encouraging. A total of twenty-two U-boats had been lost, though two of these were due to accidents and another four to 'unknown causes' (possibly British mines). An explosive sweep had accounted for one, two more had been sunk by gunfire from warships, and two more had been rammed. Most promising of all was the fact that three submarines had been sunk by British submarines towed by trawlers, and another three by gunfire from Q-ships. More sobering was the fact that, unlike British merchant ships, the total of U-boat losses was outweighed by new boats leaving the shipyards.[8]

Nevertheless, within months of the end of that first campaign against enemy merchant shipping, Germany was being squeezed ever more tightly by the effects of British attacks on her own trade. During that opening campaign, 743 neutral ships carrying cargoes to German ports had been intercepted by British patrols, accounting for more than three times the cargoes lost to Britain by U-boat attacks during the same period.[9]

Germany's naval commanders now felt that it was time to increase the stakes. If their U-boats could finally begin sinking British merchant ships faster than heavily overloaded shipyards could replace them, perhaps Britain could be forced to relax her blockade. With more of the larger and more effective U-boats being commissioned each month, surely it was reasonable to expect more encouraging results? Meanwhile, the development of effective ASW equipment and tactics by the British had scarcely begun. The most encouraging development had been the introduction of the first depth charges, but it would take time to produce these in the huge numbers needed to be effective, and there was still no way of locating the targets on which to drop the charges. For their part, the Germans hoped that growing American anger would count for little if Germany's aims could be achieved quickly enough.

To achieve their objective, they calculated that they needed to sink 160,000 tons of British shipping each month. In the first two months of the renewed campaign, which began in February 1916, U-boats sank a total of 240,000 tons, a shortfall of 25 per cent. However, as more U-boats joined the fleet, sinkings were expected to increase, and efforts were being made to attack other types of British shipping. These included orders to attack British cross-Channel troop ships, which it was believed would not arouse American anger.

On 24 March 1916, the brand-new *UB29* saw a steamer entering Dieppe harbour. *UB29*'s skipper had been told before sailing that the only civilian passenger ships were those sailing between Folkestone and Boulogne, so that steamers on all other routes could be sunk on sight, without warning. Confident he was watching a troop transport, he sank the steamer. What the Germans did not know was that this was the civilian ferry boat *Sussex*, and that among her

Determined professionals who threatened to overturn the naval balance of power: *U9* and her crew.
(Jak Mallmann Showell)

passengers were twenty-five American citizens, several of whom were killed in the sinking.

President Wilson reacted immediately. He threatened Germany that unless they abandoned their campaign, America would sever diplomatic relations, with the clear implication that a declaration of war could follow. After just two months of the new campaign, it was called off, and the U-boats were switched back to the safer targets – in political terms – of British warships. During that time, only two German submarines were lost to enemy action: one was caught in the indicator nets towed by a British drifter and the other fell victim to a Q-ship. Neither side had much to show for their efforts, but when the U-boats returned to the trade war, in October 1916, it would prove a fight to the finish.

For the time being, both sides could comfort themselves with a relatively low level of losses. In the case of the U-boats, the number of sinkings were deceptively encouraging, though roughly half were only fishing boats.[10] In the meantime, the Germans decided to switch their efforts to the Mediterranean. Because there were virtually no US merchant ships in the area, they could pursue a more aggressive policy without inflaming American opinion, and reassure the German public that they were still striking hard blows against the enemy, to compensate for signs of the growing effects of the British naval blockade at home.[11]

Lacking the weapons and sensors needed to identify, locate and sink individual U-boats, the Allied ASW response was to try to bottle up their access routes into the Mediterranean, through net and mine barrages across the Straits of Otranto and the Dardanelles. This proved almost totally ineffective because of the width and depth of the Straits and only accounted for two submarines, the Austrian *UV1* and the German *UB53*, in the entire war. But German U-boats using Austrian bases in the Adriatic accounted for a rising total of merchant vessels in a worryingly effective campaign.

The next ASW tactic to be tried was the flawed concept of 'offensive patrolling', which turned out to be totally ineffective because of the ludicrously small number of vessels available for the task. The urgency of the problem was reflected in the merchant ship casualties – 153 vessels of a total of 282,925 tons sunk in the three months from June to August 1916 by a force of between three and five U-boats.[12]

Amid the gathering gloom, only one tactic seemed to offer any real hope of entrapping and sinking U-boats: the tactic familiar from the Napoleonic naval wars of assuming a false identity to lure the enemy before revealing the truth at the moment of opening fire. This was the rationale behind the Q-ships, innocuous-looking merchantmen like HMS *Penshurst*.

Penshurst seemed an unthreatening little civilian freighter of about 1,200 tons, with a bridge amidships

A German artist's impression of the triumphant return of *U*9 to her home port.

(Jak Mallmann Showell)

and a single tall funnel aft. Yet an empty lifeboat on deck hid a 12-pounder gun, and her other armament included a 6-pounder and a 3-pounder, all carefully concealed behind her upperworks; her objective was to lure U-boats to their destruction. Early on 29 November 1916, she had been following up a report of a U-boat attacking merchant ships in the Channel when she spotted one in the act of approaching the British steamer *Wileyside*. On trying to intervene, she attracted three shells from the U-boat, but the submarine's skipper obstinately refused to close in and give her a chance of an easy shot. In the end, *Penshurst*'s skipper opened fire, but the U-boat dived to safety before his men could score a decisive hit.[13]

Assuming the U-boat would report her actions, *Penshurst*'s crew worked hard to change her appearance. They painted her funnel a different colour with a white band around the top, lowered her mizzen mast and put up new canvas screens around the bridge. By the following morning she was following up a report of a U-boat seen diving off the Casquets, a lonely group of rocks crowned by a lighthouse off the northern Channel Islands. As she approached the area, she saw a U-boat chasing a British steamer while under attack by a British seaplane, which dropped a bomb close enough to it to persuade it to dive.

The seaplane landed on the water next to *Penshurst*, and her skipper, Commander Grenfell, agreed that the seaplane crew could try to spot the submerged submarine, and lead *Penshurst* to the spot, where she could drop depth charges on the U-boat. These weapons had been developed in two versions: the 300-pound type D and the 120-pound type D*, intended for slower ships unable to get clear of the spot in time to avoid the blast effect of the heavier charges.[14] Enough had now been made available for them to be issued even to the fairly low-priority Q-ships, but because of their chief limitation – that without a way of finding the position of the submerged U-boat – using them was literally a hit or miss affair. In this case, the ingenious attempt to find their target was doomed, as the seaplane hit a rogue wave on her take-off run, and the fragile airframe broke apart. As the ship's boat was rescuing the airmen, the U-boat returned to the surface and opened fire.

The submarine was now a mile away on *Penshurst*'s port quarter, firing at irregular intervals as she approached very slowly and cautiously. At 4.12pm, almost an hour after she had reappeared, she was within a thousand yards of her target, when Grenfell ordered his 'panic party' – members of the crew detailed to abandon ship, leaving only the officers and guns' crews concealed on board – over the side. The submarine then sailed in a wide curve around the stern of the Q-ship before approaching the boats to question the occupants and seize the ship's papers. With the Germans' attention concentrated on the boats, Grenfell opened fire when he was only 250 yards away.

He could scarcely miss. The second shot, fired from *Penshurst*'s starboard 3-pounder, went through the pressure hull into the U-boat's engine room, marooning her on the surface. A succession of hits followed, and she finally sank ten minutes later with the loss of seven of her twenty-three-strong crew. *Penshurst* herself would be in action again off the Channel Islands on 14 January 1917, when another surfaced U-boat, *UB37*, fired a shot across her bows. Once again the panic party took to the boats, while the submarine skipper continued firing, aiming two rounds at the bridge. The shells killed two members of the 6-pounder crew and wounded two more, but the rest of those hidden on board waited for their opportunity.

It came at 4.26pm, with the U-boat broadside on to *Penshurst*'s starboard side. Commander Grenfell gave the order to open fire, and the first 12-pounder shell hit the submarine at the base of her conning tower. Within minutes she sank by the stern, with all her crew. This anonymous and apparently unthreatening Q-ship now had two German submarines to her credit.[15]

Yet, in a matter of weeks, conditions were to change completely. Another Q-ship, the 3,200-ton former Cardiff collier *Loderer*, now serving as HMS *Farnborough* and armed with no less than five 12-pounder guns and two 6-pounders, had sunk *U68* to the west of Ireland on 22 March the previous year, when the

submarine's torpedo had missed and she had surfaced to sink her target by gunfire. *Farnborough*'s firepower had proved decisive, and the shattered submarine sank stern first. The Q-ship had then approached the spot where her target had disappeared, and dropped depth charges. The submarine was blown back to the surface by the explosions before finally sinking to the bottom.

Now, on 17 February 1917, *Farnborough*'s Captain Gordon Campbell was keen to try a new tactic. To convince any attacking U-boat of his ship's complete vulnerability, he wanted to make sure any torpedo aimed at his ship would actually hit it. On seeing a torpedo track, he would speed up or slow down to ensure a hit, trusting in the reserve buoyancy of timber and empty barrels in the holds to keep her afloat until she could reach base for repairs.

At approximately 9.45am, a torpedo hit the ship on her starboard side, with no warning at all. It struck at the bulkhead between two of the holds, an unlucky chance that flooded her more quickly than predicted. As the panic party took to the boat, together with the ship's cat and a stuffed parrot in a cage as additional props, she was already down by the stern. Perhaps because their act was so convincing, the submerged submarine, *U83*, approached so close to the sinking *Farnborough* that, although she was clearly visible, none of the guns would depress far enough to hit her.

Finally, at 10.10am she surfaced and headed towards the ship's boats, whereupon Campbell opened fire. One shell decapitated her captain, and others pierced her pressure hull. Only two survivors emerged from the conning-tower hatch as she sank. For a time it seemed that *Farnborough* would follow her, but other warships soon arrived to take her in tow, and beach

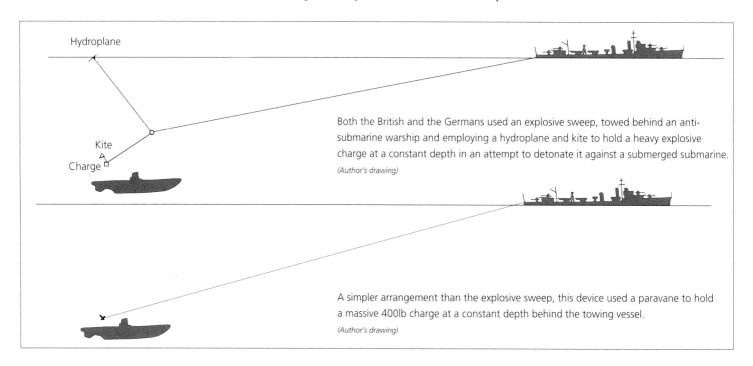

Both the British and the Germans used an explosive sweep, towed behind an anti-submarine warship and employing a hydroplane and kite to hold a heavy explosive charge at a constant depth in an attempt to detonate it against a submerged submarine.
(Author's drawing)

A simpler arrangement than the explosive sweep, this device used a paravane to hold a massive 400lb charge at a constant depth behind the towing vessel.
(Author's drawing)

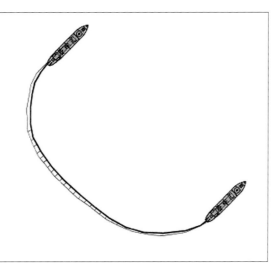

Both sides used towed mine nets to try to trap and sink submerged submarines. The Germans preferred to use a pair of vessels to tow the net between them in an attempt to make entrapment more feasible.

(Author's drawing)

her the following day in Bantry Bay.[16]

The change in German tactics these encounters brought about was no coincidence. By May 1916, when the second German submarine campaign against British merchant shipping had been called off, there was a change in priorities. German U-boats in home waters were to be switched to attacking British warships, which resulted in a major exodus of German submarines to the vicinity of British naval ports, where they would lie in wait for targets responding to a sortie by the German High Seas Fleet. Meanwhile, the successful campaign in the Mediterranean could be left to continue unchecked.

Unfortunately, delays in the sailing of the High Seas Fleet meant U-boats had to wait for just over a week, vulnerable to British patrols. When the German Fleet actually sailed, the code signal to warn the U-boats was only received by four of them. Only one managed to fire a pair of torpedoes at a British cruiser, which missed. As a result, the Grand Fleet emerged unscathed, to attack the High Seas Fleet in the Battle of Jutland.

The Germans modified the tactic just over two months later. U-boats were deployed in a series of patrol lines in gaps in the German minefields laid off England's northeast coast. The High Seas Fleet sailed into the North Sea on 18 August, but intercepted radio signals had warned the British, and the Grand Fleet was already closing the Germans at a range of sixty-five miles. They were spotted by *U53*, which radioed the German commander, Admiral Scheer. He turned for home, and once the British realised that they were too late to catch their elusive enemy, they too sailed back to harbour. The U-boats torpedoed and sank the light cruisers HMS *Nottingham* and HMS *Falmouth*, but their loss was far from the German objective of bringing about parity between the fleets.[17]

These narrow tactical wins for the Germans in terms of ships lost hid a British strategic victory. After August 1916, the German Fleet did not re-emerge for the rest of the war. Though it still presented a threat, requiring British resources to watch it and guard against any attempt to deliver any more attacks, it was in truth a completely spent force.

For the Germans, the unpalatable fact was that the U-boats were now the only part of their navy still engaging the enemy. But if the avenue of sinking Royal Navy units remained almost completely closed to them, their only alternative was to return to the merchant shipping campaign of the previous year. Even before the second attempt to use the High Seas Fleet as a decoy, Admiral Scheer had made the strongest plea yet for a totally unrestricted campaign to break the British blockade finally. Still fearful of the effect on neutral opinion, particularly American, the politicians refused. Scheer was only allowed to sink British merchant vessels according to the old Prize Regulations, but it was clear to everyone that a return to sink-on-sight could not be long delayed.

When the U-boats resumed sinking merchant vessels from October 1916, even under Prize Regulations, losses soon increased to the point of serious damage to the British war effort. One by one, the hopes of finding a counter to submarine attack had been dashed. Even the minefield barrages intended to keep U-boats confined within their bases or restricted to the wider passages around the British Isles proved to be far less effective than hoped. Tests were carried out by running a British submarine into mines with greatly reduced charges, to examine whether they detonated reliably. The results were alarming: only one in three actually went off.[18] Moreover, as more U-boats survived their passage through areas later found to have been mined by the British, less respect was accorded to the minefields, so even their deterrent effect was lost.

Four measures seemed promising: two in the short term, two in the longer perspective. One was the defensive arming of merchant ships, so they could fight back against a surfaced submarine attacking with a deck gun. At first, while U-boats operated under the Prize Regulations, this was reasonably effective. In the last quarter of 1916, 206 British merchant vessels were attacked by U-boats in this way; remarkably, more than half of the targets managed to escape. More significantly, armed merchant ships were three times as likely to escape as unarmed ships. Unfortunately, this would not be effective if the U-boats began a completely unrestricted campaign, but the increase in merchant ships escaping conventional attacks was bound to increase German calls for a switch to more aggressive tactics.

The second measure was the use of British submarines as anti-U-boat weapons. Looking back from a time when the hunter-killer submarine has been developed into one of the most effective weapons against the nuclear-powered fleet submarine or ballistic missile submarine, it is difficult to understand what a revolutionary tactic this was. It proved relatively ineffective at first, partly because of the appalling quality of British torpedoes, but mainly because successes depended on chance encounters between boats that themselves relied on stealth for safety and which were difficult to stalk and attack. In the whole of the war, a total of eighteen U-boats would be sunk by torpedoes launched from Allied submarines, all except one of them British. In nine other cases, U-boat skippers reported actually being struck by British torpedoes that failed to go off. The number sunk was one less than the number lost from accidents, and the fact that the attackers involved were from a number of different classes – three C class, two D class, six E class, two G class, two H class, one J class, one L class and the French submarine *Circe*, in locations ranging from the Orkneys to Otranto – indicated that these were chance encounters of opportunity rather than a deliberately planned and structured tactic.

However, the Admiralty was convinced that it was worth designing a new class of submarine with the express intention of hunting and sinking U-boats. This was the rationale behind the single-hull, low-drag R class, with a high underwater speed of fifteen knots for dashes of up to half an hour at a time thanks to 220 battery cells, and a 12.5-knot high speed cruise for an hour and three-quarters. They were armed with six bow tubes for launching 18-inch torpedoes, and fitted with large rudders and diving planes for fast diving and good manoeuvrability, and had rotatable directional hydrophones for tracking their prey. Like the later generations of hunter-killer boats, the R class were unhappy seaboats on the surface but in their element below it. Twelve were ordered, but of the five delivered before the Armistice, none actually succeeded in sinking a U-boat.[19] Two were cancelled before completion and the rest were sold during the following decade, with only *R4* lasting in naval service until 1934.

The third factor was a result of the Germans' lack of determination over U-boat tactics, see-sawing backwards and forwards between attacking warships and trying to cripple British trade by sinking merchant ships. Having had two years' warning of the storm likely to burst over their heads when the Germans finally decided that the tightening British blockade being imposed on them meant they had nothing to lose, the Royal Navy had begun large-scale construction of their first specialised anti-submarine vessels.

Though these increased resources would eventually prove valuable, for the moment the biggest gap in the British defences remained the impossibility of locating the position of a submerged submarine, or even telling whether or not one was in the vicinity. At the time, the most promising way of detecting a submarine was to lower a sensitive microphone, or hydrophone, into the water to pick up the sounds it made, like the regular throb of its propellers, or the noise of ballast tanks being blown prior to surfacing. In 1915, there were two basic types: one was mounted on the seabed at locations such as the approaches to vulnerable ports, where even the warning of a submarine within a one- to two-mile radius was valuable information. A submarine might be laying mines or simply waiting for merchant ships on their way in or out of harbour, and patrols could be called up to deal with the threat. The other type of hydrophone was used aboard the patrol vessels themselves, and this suffered from two basic limitations. It could pick up the noises of submarines up to two miles away, but it could not detect their bearing from the patrol vessel. Secondly, it could only be used when the vessel was stationary, which left it entirely at the mercy of any submerged U-boat that did happen to be in the vicinity.

By early 1917, the recently-formed Anti-Submarine Division of the Admiralty had sponsored research to produce more effective hydrophones.[20] By April, work at the Hawkcraig Experimental Station near Aberdour on the northern shore of the Firth of Forth had produced two directional hydrophones, which were already being issued to training bases as a preparation for their being made widely available for ASW patrols. There was even a programme to make gramophone recordings of the sounds made by different types of engines and propellers so that hydrophone operators could identify the sources of the sounds they were picking up. This addressed one of the limitations of the original hydrophones, and the other was to be solved by the so-called 'fish' hydrophone, a stream-lined and shielded version that, when slung over the side of a moving ship, could still pick up submarine noises without the need to stop and invite an enemy torpedo. However, by the end of 1917, roughly two-thirds of the 5,630 hydrophones issued to warships were still the old non-directional type and of limited usefulness.

Even as early as June 1917, the device that would finally strip away the cloak of concealment from the submerged U-boat was already being developed. This was an instrument known originally as the 'electrical detector' and later as Asdic (discussed more fully later on) and ultimately as sonar. Ironing out the various difficulties in producing the complex technology involved would delay the introduction of Asdic until the end of the war. For what was coming, the Allies would simply have to manage with what they had.

What was already happening was quite enough to cope with. The existing German campaign against Allied merchant vessels lasted from October 1916 until January 1917, and even under the restrictions of Prize Regulations, the additional number of U-boats at sea was beginning to produce spectacular results. At the time, the pattern of merchant ship losses was relatively concentrated, with lone ships to be found easily at the natural choke points where the trade routes converged on approach to the British Isles. These points were north of the Orkneys for shipping heading around the northern tip of the British Isles to reach ports on the east coast, to the north of Ireland for ports on the Clyde and the Mersey, to the south of Ireland for the Mersey and the Bristol Channel, and the southwestern approaches for the Bristol Channel and the Channel ports proper.

However, some Atlantic U-boats did range further afield. When the larger, heavier and longer-range boats of the High Seas Fleet were sent to join the campaign in October 1916, merchant ships were sunk under Prize Regulations down the western coast of

The British E class of overseas patrol boats were the Royal Navy's most successful submarines in World War One, between them sinking no less than seven U-boats, one battleship, two cruisers, a destroyer, two torpedo boats and countless merchant ships.
(www.navyphotos.co.uk)

France as far as Bordeaux. One U-boat even reached the northeastern coast of the USA – *U*53 blithely sailing into the still-neutral harbour of Newport, Rhode Island, to top up her diesel tanks. After spending a day in port and allowing interested US Navy officers a tour of the submarine, she sailed eastwards into the Atlantic to sink five merchantmen (three British, one Dutch and one Norwegian) off the island of Nantucket, within sight of Cape Cod and the New England coast.

US destroyers were in close attendance, rescuing the survivors and on two occasions actually getting in the way. One almost collided with the submarine, and another had to be asked by the U-boat commander to move, to allow him a clear shot at his Dutch target. It was a remarkable achievement, but one that played extremely badly with American public opinion, since it underlined their vulnerability to similar attacks in their own coastal waters. Another veiled warning was sent by the president to the German authorities that once was more than enough.

The campaign lasted four months, and resulted in the sinking of 768 merchant vessels, a total of more than 1,500,000 tons. Remarkably, almost two-thirds of these ships were neutrals, which imposed an additional loss as neutral countries began to cease trading with Britain. Neutral tonnage entering and leaving British ports dropped by almost three-quarters compared with six months previously. Only the Norwegians defied the trend, accounting for more than 75 per cent of the new reduced neutral shipping tonnage entirely on their own.[21] If all this were not enough, ships that were damaged but survived had to be repaired before sailing again, imposing another temporary loss equivalent to 50 per cent of that lost through sinkings.

When Royal Navy experts studied these losses, they noted that the increased sinking rate was more than double that of the earlier campaigns. This was not because of improved tactics or weaponry, but because of the larger number of German submarines available for duty. The price the Germans paid for this increased success was low; in four months only ten U-boats were lost: two to unknown causes, one from accident, two to mines and one rammed by a Russian trawler. In spite of huge increases in Royal Navy patrol vessels and other ASW craft, only four were sunk by these forces: two by gunfire from Q-ships, one by high-speed paravane (a towed float carrying an explosive charge primed to explode on contact with a submarine) and the last by depth charges.

Underlying all this was a more ominous truth. If this level of damage could be imposed by U-boats operating under the Prize Regulations, how much more could they achieve if let off the hook entirely, to wage a totally unrestricted campaign? The answer would not be long in coming. By the beginning of 1917, the Germans realised that they and their allies were running out of manpower, and events on land must eventually tilt the balance in favour of the Allies. Furthermore, the British blockade was causing severe shortages that delayed the construction of new U-boats. Nevertheless, new contracts were issued during 1917 for almost 150 new boats of different classes.

In these circumstances, German naval commanders could see few real drawbacks to a policy of sink on sight. America remained a problem, but for the time being a distant and long-term one. An unrestricted submarine campaign could perhaps force Britain to the negotiating table before an American declaration of war could bring American forces to the Western Front. Not only would the crippling British blockade on Germany be eased, but Britain herself might be knocked out of the war, ensuring certain victory even if America did join the Allies. France and Italy could only continue fighting with British support, and if deprived of this, then their fighting role would be ended.

Before launching the campaign, the Germans had made more careful calculations. This time, Admiral von Holtzendorff's Naval Staff had calculated a figure of 600,000 tons a month as the losses needed to force a British capitulation. When the drying-up of neutral trade with Britain was factored into the equation (and sinking without warning was almost certain to be more disconcerting than the fairly civilised tactics currently being used), then after five months British imports would fall by almost 40 per cent. This, they were convinced, would force Britain to make peace with Germany.

The final decision was taken at a high-level meeting on 9 January 1917, and the campaign was scheduled to open on 1 February. All Allied and neutral ships were to be sunk on sight, with no warning. The losses rose steadily, increasing from the 328,391 tons lost in January to 520,412 in February (the first month of the new campaign), 564,497 tons in March, and a staggering 860,334 tons in April. While this was to remain the highest monthly loss of all, the figures for May and June of 616,316 and 696,725 tons respectively were little consolation for the British and comfortably over target for the Germans. Experts at the Admiralty estimated that at this rate, Britain could only remain in the war until the end of the year at the very latest. It seemed that the Germans, facing the prospect of defeat on land, had stumbled across a truly war-winning weapon at sea, ironically Britain's principal arena of strength and power. And there was still no effective way of defeating this weapon available to the world's premier navy.

In time, the tactics and weapons being developed by the Allies must be capable of defeating the U-boats. What counted in the terrible months of 1917, however, as losses continued to rise, was whether these developments could be completed in time. It was becoming increasingly clear to both sides that this was a race the Germans were winning. That is, until another tactic from Britain's long naval history was brought to the rescue, slowly and against the determined opposition of many of her own most experienced naval commanders.

During the long struggle of the Napoleonic Wars, Britain's position was surprisingly similar to the situation she faced in 1917. Napoleon's warships were confined to harbour under a tight and effective British blockade, but the maritime trade on which the British economy and her ability to fight depended was highly vulnerable to the contemporary equivalent of the U-boat: the privateer. Effectively, these were licensed pirates, provided with documents called letters of marque, which allowed them to prey on enemy merchant ships, seizing them and their cargoes as prizes of war. They were chosen for their speed and manoeuvrability and were heavily armed with large crews, and were easily able to overcome the resistance of any merchant ships they met on the high seas. And if they encountered a warship, they were usually fast enough to escape.

One tactic above all kept these predators at bay. Since they could not be caught easily in a stern chase, the way for warships to defeat them was to make them

approach to close quarters, and the only reliable way to do that was to assemble as many merchant ships as possible into a convoy, sailing under naval escort. If the privateers kept their distance, and the merchant ships and escorts kept together, then their attacks failed. If they came close enough to attack an individual merchant ship, then they risked being cut off or being battered to pieces by broadsides from the escorts.

Convoy as a tactic dated back seven hundred years, but in 1798 it was made compulsory for ships trading with Britain, and it worked extremely well. In some cases, a convoy might number hundreds of ships, but the chances of every single one reaching her destination unmolested and undamaged were far greater than they were for one sailing independently of convoy. To anyone with a knowledge of naval history, it was clear that the convoy concept would have an effect on German submarines similar to the one it had had on French privateers. Unfortunately, the people least convinced were those at the highest level in the Royal Navy, who viewed the idea as fundamentally flawed.

The reason was a misreading of the history of the Royal Navy itself. Because of the Nelsonian concept that offensive action was the right course to follow in all cases, the idea of convoys was seen by many as defensive and therefore an unworthy admission of weakness. Broadly speaking, the rising losses in merchant ships were forcing naval chiefs to choose one of two alternatives. What a large proportion of naval commanders, led by Admiral Lord Jellicoe, former commander of the Grand Fleet and now First Sea Lord, wanted to do was to increase the size of the forces devoted to ASW. Because these were not sinking enough U-boats on their own, Jellicoe's thinking ranged over other additional expedients, including more and bigger merchant ships that would be difficult to sink, mining German ports to keep U-boats trapped, and even laying in extra food stocks while this was still possible.

Others, including Admiral Beatty, who had replaced Jellicoe in command of the Grand Fleet, were more clear sighted. To them, only one course of action was viable: to take all the ships occupied in hunting down U-boats across the wide ocean expanses, and use them to escort convoys instead. Then, instead of completing countless patrols with never a U-boat sighted, they would have the chance to meet U-boats in plenty.

Both sides used facts and figures to make their cases. To Jellicoe and the anti-convoy lobby, there were four fatal disadvantages. Convoys would take up all the ships then being used on search and destroy missions against U-boats. They would involve delays at ports while convoys were assembled and when they dispersed at the end of their voyage. They would restrict the speed of faster vessels, causing further delays, and merchant skippers could not be expected to keep station accurately. Finally, massing merchant ships together must make them more vulnerable to torpedo attacks.[22]

Only the first of these points proved to be true, and since it resulted in the ASW patrols being moved from where they were achieving little or nothing to where they could achieve a great deal in terms of protecting merchant ships, this was a positive advantage to instituting convoys as soon as possible. The other points could only be demonstrated by experience, and fortunately the necessary precedents already existed.

During the entire course of the war, more than five million men served in the ranks of the British and Imperial armies on the Western Front. All that huge force had to be transported from Britain to the continent, together with millions more sailing home on leave and then returning to combat, through the submarine-infested waters of the English Channel. Because the transports were grouped into convoys and escorted by warships, not one single vessel nor one single man had been lost to enemy attacks. The convoy system had held the line with a spotless record.[23]

Even with this example before them, the anti-convoy faction refused to budge. Finally, an increasingly frustrated Beatty found the situation he needed to force convoying to be given a trial. The trade between Britain and the Scandinavian countries had reached the point where the loss rate was a quarter of the ships making the crossing, a totally unacceptable toll and one that, left unchecked, would see this trade artery severed. Beatty formed a committee to consider what should be done to save the situation, and they recommended trying convoys as a matter of urgency. This gave him the leverage he needed with the Admiralty, and, on 21 April 1917, Jellicoe agreed to the experiment. With the first convoys the loss rate fell to 0.24 per cent, or one-hundredth of the previous level.[24]

The oft-repeated claim that Prime Minister Lloyd George was instrumental in the decision to adopt the convoy system now seems dubious. Lloyd George's description of his role in events, especially after they occurred, has been shown to deviate from the truth on numerous occasions – for example, in recent works like Gordon Corrigan's *Mud, Blood and Poppycock* (London 2003) in relation to the generals on the Western Front, and other naval sources are equally sceptical.[25]

By now, America had joined in the war, responding to repeated provocations of Germany killing her citizens aboard the ships the U-boats were torpedoing. One of the first US Navy admirals to cross the Atlantic was Rear Admiral W S Sims, who would command US naval forces in European waters. He had arrived in England in disguise, wearing civilian clothes and under an assumed name, sailing on an American liner, the *New York* on 31 March 1917. After a fast and untroubled passage, the liner reached Liverpool on 9 April, but as she was approaching the port she hit a mine laid by the U-boat *UC*65. Though she remained afloat, the passengers were sent off in lifeboats to be picked up by an inbound ferry from the Isle of Man. Unruffled by his experience, which emphasised the serious state of the U-boat war, Sims boarded a special train that took him down to London for a meeting at the Admiralty the following day. There, for the first time, he met Jellicoe and was brought face to face with the seriousness of the situation.

Sims was both astute and an Anglophile, and he moved quickly to order as many American destroyers as possible sent to Britain to help hunt U-boats. More importantly, he was a firm believer in the convoy principle, and lent his considerable support to the idea of grouping merchant ships in escorted convoys for mutual protection. In this, at least to begin with, he was out of step with his own service, since US Navy doctrine was firmly at one with Jellicoe and other opponents of the idea. In the words of the British Naval attaché in Washington, 'The Navy Department does not consider it advisable to attempt … convoy … In large groups of ships under convoy, fog, gales, inexperience of personnel, and general tensions on merchant vessels make the hazards of the attempt great and the probability of a scattering of the convoy strong.'[26]

Sims's strongly-worded advocacy of the convoy system began to change American opinion, but the most powerful persuaders were the figures themselves. By the summer of 1917, the cumbersome convoy system was finally operating. Remarkably, 800 vessels were convoyed in July and August 1917, and only five were lost. On the other hand, the overall loss figures only declined slowly, which was used as ammunition for the anti-convoy faction. Only as convoy protection was extended to every stage of an individual merchant ship's voyage between its starting point and its destination, did these too fall away in time. In September 1918, ten U-boats were sunk, more than had joined the fleet in that month, and the tide had clearly turned at long last. But destroying the U-boats on a larger scale, as opposed to merely deflecting their attacks, would call for entirely new weapons.

CHAPTER 3

NEW HOPES FROM NEW WEAPONS
1917–18

Not for the faint-hearted: the cramped and noisy engine room of an oil-burning World War I U-boat

(US National Archives)

O N 24 May 1917, at the height of the unrestricted U-boat campaign against Allied and neutral shipping, a small group of merchant ships, twelve in number, set sail from the anchorage at Hampton Roads in Virginia for the dangerous Atlantic crossing to England. The force of American destroyers that might have escorted these ships had already sailed, heading for Queenstown in southern Ireland to take part in the anti-submarine war. The reason for their early departure was the US Navy's firm and continuing belief that any group of more than four merchantmen sailing together was inviting trouble. This meant that the only protection which could be spared for the dozen ships was the 10,000-ton 6-inch armoured Royal Navy cruiser HMS *Roxburgh*.

Surprisingly for the sceptics, it was enough. On the evening of 6 June, the fourteenth day of their passage, the convoy was met by eight destroyers from the Royal Navy base at Plymouth. The group then split into two sections, one heading for east coast ports and the other for west coast harbours, and, by 10 June, ten of the twelve merchant ships had safely reached their destinations after an uneventful passage. The two that failed to arrive had been unable to maintain convoy speed and had had to make for Halifax in Nova Scotia, the nearest port at the time. One of the stragglers reached port safely, the other did not. As a timely reminder of the dangers of solo passage, she was torpedoed, thousands of miles from the home port of the U-boat which sank her.

In the darkening gloom of increasing and insupportable merchant losses, this first experimental transatlantic convoy flickered fitfully as a beacon of hope. What was done once could presumably be done again and again, and the totals of ships sunk and tonnage destroyed must surely fall as a result. In fact, it had already been done a week before, with the first convoy of all, an eight-day passage from Gibraltar for sixteen merchant ships, escorted by two Q-ships and three steam yachts. It had been met by destroyers from Devonport on 18 May, after some confusion over the rendezvous led to an eight-hour delay, but once again had suffered no losses and no attacks from submarines. The escort officers reported favourably on signals and station keeping. The only potential problem had been the difficulty some of the slower ships had had in maintaining convoy speed.[1]

Yet reductions in the level of losses were painfully slow, testing the faith of even the most fervent supporters of the convoy system. In all, the unrestricted U-boat campaign would finally continue for a year and nine months. An appalling total of 3.75 million tons of merchant shipping was sunk by U-boats in the first six months of the campaign, until the organising of the first convoys. Though these brought about a huge improvement, the fact remains that during the final fifteen months of the war, another 4.5 million tons would be lost. By then, the hidden cost of the unrestricted campaign was a bill being presented to the Germans instead, as the huge increase in US ship-building efforts was more than keeping pace with merchant ship losses, and the tonnage war was being irretrievably lost by the enemy.

While this was taking place, those determined sceptics of the value of grouping ships together to sail them through sea areas teeming with hostile submarines would only yield their entrenched positions with the utmost reluctance. One by one, however, their arguments were discounted. The captain of HMS *Roxburgh* reported after his convoy had arrived safely that the merchant skippers had kept station very well, that alterations of course had been carried out smartly and accurately, and that only the two stragglers had created a problem in not being able to maintain convoy speed.

Careful analysis of continuing losses showed that the vast majority were of ships sailing alone. Some of these were involved in the coastal trade, risking the short trips between one port and another, in areas where the convoy system had not been extended. Others were outward-bound ships, since the system was not extended to sailings *from* Britain until August 1917. Some losses were inbound ocean-going vessels that had been escorted safely across the Atlantic, but which were suddenly open to attack with the dispersal of the convoy's ships to their different destination ports. In the words of a 1956 Admiralty historical review on the efficiency of convoy as a strategy:

> had coastal convoy been developed around the
> east, south and west coasts of England and the
> west coast of France … the large number of
> independent losses would not have occurred.
> As it was, many ships were still being sailed
> independently in coastal waters although the loss
> rate of independent ships on all routes was ten
> times as high as that of ships sailed in convoy.[2]

Yet, in spite of the reluctance of those who refused to believe that convoys helped reduce losses at all, the end result of this policy – once it was carried through to the point of plugging all the potential gaps – was that it would be the most powerful, and with the technology available at the time, the only viable ASW tactic to beat the U-boats. Concentrating the merchant ships into convoys effectively cleared the sea of the U-boats' prey. From this point onwards, the vastness of the sea worked against the U-boats as effectively as it had done against the Royal Navy's offensive patrols. Where their endless searching had spotted only the occasional U-boat, now the submarines searched in vain for merchant ships, singly or in convoy, it mattered little. A convoy of twenty ships, set against the wide and empty ocean, remained only a little larger target than a single ship, but it was twenty times as rare.

It was here that the final bargaining counter of the anti-convoy party was finally lost. It had been advanced by the US Navy Department as an article of faith that convoys could not be allowed to number more than four ships, and that in any case an armed merchant ship was actually safer on its own then when sailing in convoy. The reality was that the larger the convoy, the more ships were able to cross the ocean in safety, and the size limit on convoys from North America to the UK was raised to twenty by the end of June 1917, and three months later the Admiralty only required specific permission to be granted for convoys of more than twenty-six ships. Soon this limit was raised to thirty-six, and the largest Atlantic convoy in World War I, HN73, brought forty-seven ships over safely in June 1918 without loss.

All other things being equal, the size of a convoy was a matter of mathematics. As the number of merchant ships increased, the area occupied by the convoy increased in proportion, but the perimeter of that area increased at a slower rate. The effect of this was that if two convoys of equal size were amalgamated into one, the area occupied by the convoy was doubled, but the perimeter only increased by 50 per cent, so that the gap between each of the escorts was actually reduced by a quarter. This gave the U-boats less opportunity of slipping through the escort screen, and since the presence of warships in close proximity forced them to remain submerged and only able to move at very low speed, their ability to manoeuvre into a favourable firing position was greatly curtailed.

Convoys had another valuable advantage not properly appreciated at the time. Opponents had claimed that regular, well-escorted convoys could not run to schedule because of the shortage of escorts. In fact, the available escorts were squeezed to the limit by shepherding an outward-bound convoy through the U-boat danger zone and then making a rendezvous with an inbound convoy that they would protect on their journey back to base. It was an efficient arrangement, and it brought the hard-pressed escort crews a great deal of experience in a short time, but it was not strictly necessary. At the time when convoys needed as much protection as possible, large numbers of escorts were still being wasted in the demonstrably useless offensive patrols.

The other perceived weakness of the convoy system was its vulnerability to German surface raiders. During the course of the war, these sank some 600,000 tons of Allied shipping. Once again, however, the heaviest losses were suffered by ships sailing independently, but the anti-convoy lobby held that this was a case where sailing in convoy would have made things worse. Instead of sinking or capturing a single merchant ship at a time, the raider could take the pick of the convoy.

The clear answer was to strengthen the escort with cruisers powerful enough to beat off any raider, but the reason for their scarcity was, as always, that they were otherwise occupied. Occupied, that is, on carrying out the endless offensive patrolling that had produced such negligible results.

The shrewd and supportive American Admiral Sims[3] was one of the first to see that the use of convoys was more than a mere inability to pursue offensive warfare against submarines. It actually forced them to fight at a severe disadvantage, which would be reflected in reduced losses and increased U-boat sinkings. He also considered the implications of this shift in fortunes on German strategy. In Sims's view, the only effective German counter move would be to use more powerful forces to break up the convoys, drive off the escorts and sink the ships.

Another weapon that *was* being used against U-boats, more to monitor their positions and their tactics than to sink them, was the combination of radio interception and radio direction finding that would later play a crucial role in the Second World War. Even in the first conflict, U-boats were extraordinarily talkative, using their high-quality transmitters to send a mass of signals backwards and forwards. U-boats reported back to headquarters on a regular basis, and were ordered to particular locations to intercept targets reported by other U-boats. Since a series of fortunate

discoveries (discussed further below) had virtually opened all the German Navy's code books to the Royal Navy, the Admiralty was able to track individual U-boats throughout their patrols, and also pinpoint their positions by taking bearings of their transmissions from different shore listening stations.

In October 1917, with the temporary improvement in losses from convoys appearing to be eroded, the Admiralty decided to try something new. Radio intercepts revealed relatively large numbers of U-boats heading back to their German bases north-about, rounding the furthest tip of Scotland and down through the North Sea. With the luxury of more precise information than usual, the Admiralty planned to attack them, but because their information was still far from detailed enough to direct individual attacks, all they could do was swamp the middle section of the North Sea, roughly equidistant from the British and Norwegian coasts with a series of patrols.

The first was patrolled by four submarines from the Grand Fleet (another of Sims's ideas had been to use submarines to catch submarines, and while some promising results were achieved, the poor quality of British torpedoes prevented this from being a winning tactic). The second was watched by ten Fleet destroyers and a destroyer leader; the next contained a barrage of mined nets, watched over by four destroyers and sixteen trawlers, and the final section by three

Survivors from a World War I merchant ship, torpedoed by a U-boat, row frantically to escape being dragged under as the hull sinks below the waves.
(US National Archives)

uss *Toucey*, one of the 'four-stack' destroyers of the US Navy developed for World War I, would find a new role in both the British and American Navies in the Second World War.

(US National Archives)

destroyers from Harwich.

From the beginning of the operation, which covered the first ten days of October, late equinoctial gales pounded the ships, driving them off station and making careful searching impossible. At the time it was believed that three U-boats had been sunk, but in fact only two were lost during the period of the ambush, and in positions well outside the area it covered. Soon afterwards, radio monitoring revealed that German warships were leaving their bases, and another alert sent out more than eighty British warships in response. Admiral Sims's predictions were coming to pass. German surface warships were being sent to attack British convoys – in this case the convoys between England and the Norwegian port of Bergen.

On 16 October, two fast minelaying cruisers, *Brummer* and *Bremse*, headed for the approaches to Bergen, where they encountered a small convoy of twelve merchant ships, three-quarters of them Scandinavian but escorted by two British destroyers, HMS *Strongbow* and HMS *Mary Rose*. Both British warships were sunk by the German cruisers' superior speed and firepower, and with them went the nine Scandinavian merchantmen. Two British merchant ships and one Belgian survived the slaughter.

This attack had been so successful that on 11 December the Germans repeated it, this time without the radio traffic that had warned of the previous sortie. The Royal Navy had learned that using escorts to attack German warships was a good way to lose valuable destroyers and ensure the destruction of the convoy, so orders were changed to make sure the convoy and its escorts scattered as quickly as possible.

This was another success for the Germans, using eight of their newest and fastest destroyers. Four of them attacked ships off the English coast, and the others headed once again for Bergen, where they met an inbound convoy, once again escorted by a pair of Royal Navy destroyers. Before their new tactics could be used, HMS *Partridge* had been sunk and HMS *Pellew* crippled, leaving the Germans free to sink every single merchantman.

This remained the other side of the convoy coin. Concentrating targets to force U-boats to attack at a disadvantage enabled heavier surface ships to turn the tables and attack with the odds on their side. The British response was swift and effective. The convoy route was shortened by making the departure point Methil on the Scottish coast, and from the beginning of 1918, convoys were escorted by a squadron of battleships, against which the Germans were powerless to intervene without ordering a large part of their fleet to sea – exactly the sort of manoeuvre the British had been praying for since Jutland.

Nevertheless, running merchant ships in convoy continued to prove highly effective when surface raiders were kept at bay. Only one factor was missing. As the U-boats turned up hunting merchant targets, it became very clear that the resources for effective anti-submarine warfare hardly existed. The waters around a convoy might contain German submarines in abundance, but locating them and sinking them was another matter altogether. The only tactic that had worked, on any consistent basis, had been the baited trap of the Q-ship. But disguising a heavily-armed warship as a helpless merchantman had three limitations. It was very expensive; though they sank several U-boats, the Q-ships suffered even higher losses. At its most effective, the tactic accounted for a trifling number of submarines compared with those at sea and those emerging from the shipyards. Finally, it was counter-productive. The more effective Q-ships proved to be, the more reluctant careful U-boat commanders would be to operate under the Prize Regulations. When approaching a potential target, why risk being

bombarded by shells from hidden guns, when a single torpedo from the safety of periscope depth would put the issue beyond all doubt? Whether a ship was indeed a helpless merchantman or a Q-ship waiting to fire, the result would be exactly the same. Consequently, the switch to the unrestricted submarine warfare campaign neutralised the Q-ship concept as a viable tactic. There might still be isolated cases where a U-boat commander had run out of torpedoes, or wished to conserve them for larger and more tempting targets later in the patrol. In these circumstances, he could only sink a ship by surfacing and using his deck gun, but these occasions were increasingly rare. Furthermore, once the Germans realised that the Allies were switching to convoys to protect their merchant ships, any lone merchant vessel came in for even greater suspicion.

If submarines continued to rely on the cloak of invisibility provided by remaining below the surface, there only remained two prospects for the Royal Navy to strike back at these elusive but effective opponents. One was to create a barrier that would deny access to particular areas for submerged U-boats, so making it safer for merchant ships to reach their destinations.

One way of extending the range of vision of a convoy escort was to use a kite balloon carrying an observer – unfortunately they were visible to U-boat lookouts over an equally long range.

(US Naval Institute Press)

One advantage enjoyed by Allied anti-submarine forces in World War I and not available in the Second World War was the use of Irish ports closer to the convoy routes. This US Navy subchaser of 1918 is based at Queenstown (now Cobh in the Irish Republic).

(US Naval Institute Press)

The other priority was the much more difficult one of locating a submerged submarine as a preliminary to attacking it and sinking it.

This was not a new problem for the Navy. One of the earliest references to possible ASW tactics dated back to well before the war. A letter of 29 December 1903, from the Commander-in-Chief of the Home Fleet to the Admiralty, suggested a major fleet exercise should be run to help determine the best way to frustrate submarine attacks against surface warships and, ideally, to sink the submarines responsible.

The only available methods for locating and sinking submarines prior to the First and Second World Wars, and in the early years of the First, had shown the desperate need for something practical and effective. One suggestion was to use a long boat hook to loop a rope carrying an explosive charge round the periscope of a submerged submarine. Another was to simply tow a grapnel with a charge attached. A third depended on finding a submerged submarine and then throwing a net across its probable course. Assuming the prediction was right, the submarine would be caught in the folds of the net, resulting in a red flag being raised on the buoy which supported it. The submarine could then, theoretically, be sunk using something called a 'lasso net' to which an explosive charge was attached.[4]

The Germans developed similar tactics for hunting Allied submarines. The *Spenganker,* or explosive anchor, was a grapnel on the end of a wire cable, towed

between two drifters sailing in line abreast at a depth of up to thirty feet. When the hook hit an underwater object, a line hauled an explosive charge off the deck of one of the drifters and pulled it down to make contact with the obstruction. None were actually known to have been used.

Next came the UD15 explosive sweep, which used a 200-pound charge towed at the end of a 300-foot line that could extend down to depths of eighty feet. It was a simple device in that if it hit an underwater obstruction like a submarine, the contact would set off a detonator and the charge would explode. However, if it was towed at speeds greater than 21 knots, it would tend to rise to the surface and explode from the stresses of crashing through the waves. In other cases, its maximum depth was too shallow to reach submarines, which went deeper to evade those hunting for them.

Nevertheless, the Germans developed tactics for use with the UD15. These involved vessels using it to adopt a line abreast formation and follow a search procedure based on what was called the Berghoff Curve, a spiral pattern radiating outwards from the most likely position of the target. Theoretically, a submarine anywhere within the sweep pattern was bound to be hit by the charge sooner or later. In practice, the lack of high-quality hydrophones meant the data the hunters possessed on the initial position of their target was insufficiently accurate, and only one submarine was known to have been sunk with this device: the Russian submarine *Bars* on 21 May 1917.[5]

What was needed instead, and urgently, were feasible and professional ideas. On 18 December 1916, well before the unrestricted submarine campaign, the Admiralty merged the Operations Intelligence Division and the Anti Submarine Committee to form the Anti-Submarine Division (ASD). This new division would deal with all aspects of ASW, including the conduct of existing and future operations and the development of new scientific counter-measures.

But what form might these take? As far back as 10 May 1915, Vice-Admiral Sir David Beatty, commanding the Battle Cruiser Fleet, sent a circular to all per-

The depth charge became the premier anti-submarine weapon and innovations like the American Y-gun thrower, which could hurl a pair of the 300lb Mark II charges up to 80 yards from the ship carrying them, greatly extended the reach of the weapon.

(US Naval Institute Press)

sonnel inviting them to enter suggestions on ways of combating U-boats for a prize competition. All entries had to use a pen-name and have the sender's true identity attached in a sealed envelope to prevent rank or position affecting the results. In all, sixty-four entries arrived by the deadline of 26 May, and these included sensible but impractical suggestions for kites, balloons, aircraft and ships with special observation platforms.

Others involved ideas far ahead of their time, like the detection of the presence of a submerged submarine by the stray electric fields produced by its electric motors, or by the anomalies it created in the earth's magnetic field, the basic principle of magnetic anomaly detection, which would first be used in the Second World War. Others smacked of desperation, like the suggestion of dowsing for submarines, or using trained seagulls to locate and follow U-boats. Attempts were actually made to train the birds by teaching them to follow a dummy periscope towed by a real submarine, which could be made to eject food when it was felt the seagulls had merited a reward. This proved unsuccessful, as did a follow-up project to train hawks instead.

Finally, more serious efforts were made to train sea lions, much as the US Navy would eventually train dolphins to find submerged mines. Trials began in the Glasgow Corporation swimming baths in December 1916, and moved to the open-air swimming pool at the city's Alexandra Park, then to the pool at Great Smith Street in London's Westminster, then to Bala Lake on the Welsh estate of Sir Watkin Williams Wynn and finally, in May 1917, to the more realistic conditions of the open waters of the Solent. The animals had been trained by a former circus sea lion trainer called J G Woodward, and they showed no difficulty in locating the source of underwater sounds up to three miles away. Unfortunately, the problem was not of ability but motivation, as they were easily distracted by playing or chasing shoals of fish.

For the time being, the hydrophone provided the only promising line of development. To overcome its limitations when used on board ship, different versions were developed for suspending below buoys in areas of dense U-boat traffic, or laying directly on to the seabed to monitor submarines passing above them. Both proved to have their drawbacks: the buoy-mounted instruments picked up a great deal of confusing surface noises and were prone to damage from passing ships, while those on the sea floor had to be strengthened to withstand the increased pressures of greater depths.

Nevertheless, the use of networks of these instruments partially overcame the lack of directional information from a single hydrophone. Groups of between four and sixteen hydrophones might be placed within a minefield, at distances of up to eighteen miles from the coast, with individual sets of mines triggered from shore. Once the hydrophones showed a U-boat was passing through the field, operators at the shore station could detonate those mines closest to the hydrophones picking up the strongest signals.

Though these controlled minefields were used from 1916 onwards, the poor quality of the mines remained a problem. However, by 20 April 1918, no less than fourteen lines of shore-controlled mines had been set up off Cap Gris Nez, on the French side of the Straits of Dover, and just before midnight on 4 May, the noise of submarine motors was picked up on hydrophones. A line of mines was detonated, and when she put into the Belgian harbour of Ostend for repairs, the German submarine *UB*59 later reported she had been badly damaged by two mines. On 16 May she was bombed by RAF aircraft while in dry dock, and she was finally blown up when the Germans retreated from this part of the Belgian coast in the month before the Armistice. However, the truth was that only four U-boats were destroyed by these complex and expensive installations, and something more flexible was clearly needed. One promising omen for the future was the efficiency of the latest generation of mines – particularly the

Depth charges carried in racks, like those aboard this US Navy destroyer, ready to be dropped over the stern to attack a U-boat, were powerful and effective weapons, provided they could be dropped close enough to their elusive targets.

British H2 mine detonated by horns protruding from its casing – as ASW weapons, and these accounted for at least nine of the U-boat sinkings from August 1917 to the end of the year, and possibly as many as sixteen over that period.[6]

Another useful development was the Bragg Loop, developed by Professor W H Bragg, which consisted of loops of electrical cable laid on the seabed. Each loop sent a signal to a sensitive instrument called a galvano-meter in a nearby shore station whenever a steel-hulled ship interrupted its magnetic field. Because the operator of the system could tell which loop had sent the signal, he could then detonate the nearest mines to try to sink whichever ship had triggered the alarm. This was developed late in the war, but on 29 August 1918 the shore operator at Folkestone reacted to an alarm by detonating the mines, and destroyed the *UB*109, leaving nine survivors to be picked up by an anti-submarine trawler. Plans were laid to extend these controlled minefields had the war continued longer. In the meantime, the Germans had produced a version of their own, called the SMP (for *Schiffsmeldepost* or 'Ship's reporting point'), which was an electrical cable

laid from the Friesian island of Norderney to Heligo-land and across to the Schleswig-Holstein mainland. Like the Bragg Loops, this reacted to the steel hull of a vessel crossing the cable, but its usefulness was negated by the fact that it was impossible to tell at which point on the seventy-mile cable the transit had occurred.[7] On the other hand, the Germans had more success with their net barrages across the Dardanelles to stop Allied submarines entering the Sea of Marmara. Using all kinds of scrap from rusty anchors to stone cannon balls, they built a barrier that eventually caught and destroyed one French submarine and one British, though a similar barrier across the Bosporus achieved nothing.[8]

In addition, portable directional hydrophones were finally beginning to prove more capable at finding submarines, and once the problem of noise could be solved, they were mounted on warships. The Ameri-cans went further in developing the hydrophone array, and they supplied hydrophones to both Ameri-can and British warships. Another development was the fitting of multiple hydrophones into tubes that could be towed behind warships. These gave enough information on the position of a submarine to allow it to be attacked, though there was a long interval between losing the contact as the ship approached its target, and the earliest moment for dropping depth charges, enough to allow an alert U-boat skipper to evade the blow.[9]

To make matters worse, German U-boats were being made much quieter by the closing months of the war, effectively reducing the range at which hydrophones could pick them up. In response to this problem, new tactics were developed for the auxiliary patrol forces. These had originally searched for submarines in areas where they posed a threat, but without effective tactics they achieved little. Nevertheless, the strong Admiralty bias towards offensive action of any sort as preferable to the 'defensive' tactics of shepherding convoys safely to their destinations ensured not only their survival but also a huge increase in their numbers.

On only one front were the British making genuine progress at tracking down their elusive adversaries. At the very beginning of the war, on 26 August 1914, the Russians retrieved code-books from the German light cruiser *Magdeburg*, which had run aground on a sandbank off the coast of Estonia, and passed them on to the Admiralty. Just seven weeks later, a North Sea trawler hauled up a wooden chest in its nets. It had been dropped over the side of a German destroyer sunk by the Royal Navy off the Dutch coast and it contained more naval codes. The only gap in the deciphering picture being built up in Room 40, the Admiralty's high-level intelligence centre, related to the German merchant shipping codes, and this was

remedied by papers seized from a German-Australian steamer on 26 October by a Royal Australian Navy boarding party.

As a result of these priceless windfalls, the team at Room 40 were able to read more than 15,000 secret German signals between October 1914 and February 1919.[10] Under the direction of Captain Reginald 'Blinker' Hall, it built up the highest reputation by the quality of the information it produced. With information from a chain of sensitive direction-finding stations, it was able to intercept messages from U-boats to their headquarters, and determine the position of individual submarines from their deciphered call-signs. But its finest hour, and one that was instrumental in turning the German intention to wage unrestricted submarine warfare into a means of bringing the United States into the war and ensuring ultimate Allied victory was its interception of the notorious Zimmermann Telegram, a communication from the German Foreign Office to its embassy in Mexico City, informing the ambassador of the intention to begin the unrestricted campaign. The text of the telegram made it clear that should this bring America into the war, Germany would offer Mexico an alliance to fight the USA and Mexico would be rewarded by the return of their former territories in Texas and Arizona. When the text was leaked to the Americans and shown to be genuine, it was instrumental in persuading them to enter the fighting on the Allied side, and in defeating the submarine campaign that much earlier.

By the end of the war, anti-submarine surface forces numbered more than three hundred destroyers, including fifty provided by the US Navy, together

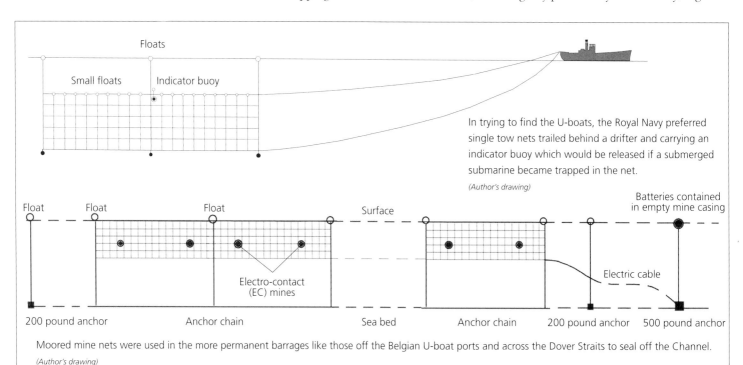

Floats

Small floats   Indicator buoy

In trying to find the U-boats, the Royal Navy preferred single tow nets trailed behind a drifter and carrying an indicator buoy which would be released if a submerged submarine became trapped in the net.

(Author's drawing)

Batteries contained in empty mine casing

Float   Float   Float   Surface

Electro-contact (EC) mines

Electric cable

200 pound anchor   Anchor chain   Sea bed   Anchor chain   200 pound anchor   500 pound anchor

Moored mine nets were used in the more permanent barrages like those off the Belgian U-boat ports and across the Dover Straits to seal off the Channel.

(Author's drawing)

with sloops and patrol boats. These larger units were reinforced by some four thousand smaller vessels, mainly trawlers and drifters taken over from the fishing industry, with five hundred motor launches, seventy-seven Q-ships, forty-nine yachts and twenty-four paddle steamers. Less direct support was provided by sixty-five submarines, in response to Admiral Sims's suggestion that the best way to sink a submarine was to use another submarine. Finally, in a nod to the future of ASW, 550 aircraft were able to help in the search for U-boats, together with seventy-five airships.[11]

This huge force called for 140,000 men to operate it, with another half million building, equipping, maintaining, refitting and supporting it. But this colossal investment in resources could only be justified if it could succeed in sinking U-boats, or at the very least prevent U-boats from sinking Allied merchant ships or warships. So stopgap tactics were developed to make the most of the capabilities of hydrophones and make up for their shortcomings. Air patrols could not only spot surfaced U-boats and call in surface forces to attack them, but seaplanes could determine whether any U-boats were present in any particular area by landing on the water and lowering a hydrophone below the surface to listen for mechanical noises.

Sinking the U-boats, rather than merely forcing them to dive and monitoring them below the surface, was a much more difficult objective. Nevertheless, the eventual power of the aircraft as a submarine killer had already been shown by the naval air service of the Austrian Empire over the Adriatic Sea on the morning of 15 September 1916. A bomber pilot reported seeing an unidentified submarine on the surface close to the Austrian naval base at Cattaro, and two Lohner flying boats were ordered to search for it. It was no longer visible on the surface, but after a careful search they spotted the submerged shape of the French submarine *Foucault* in the clear water. Because it had no idea of their presence, they were able to make a careful and precise attack from low altitude, dropping a pair of bombs apiece.

They were enough to shake the submarine severely, and cut its electric power from the batteries to the motors which drove it. It began to sink, and only surfaced with difficulty half an hour later. The flying boats were still overhead, and they dropped more bombs, which this time stopped the submarine's diesels from working. Its skipper ordered his crew to abandon the boat and it was scuttled. The crew were rescued by the flying boats, which were able to land on the water and let the survivors cling to their hulls and floats until rescue ships had arrived. This was actually the second submarine sunk by Austrian aircraft: a bomb had sent the moored British submarine *B*10 to the bottom of the harbour in Venice a month before.

Finally, a British flying boat sank the surfaced German submarine *UB*32 in the eastern approaches to the Channel almost exactly twelve months later with two heavy 230-pound anti-submarine bombs.

For most of the war, apart from the few chance encounters that predicted the future potential of aircraft as submarine-killers, the value of air patrols was chiefly as a deterrent. Any U-boat spotting an approaching aircraft would dive before its identity could be firmly established. In any case, if it were an Allied air patrol, the weapons it carried were less of a threat than the surface ships it could call in to attack the U-boat directly. In particular, the 'Spider's Web' patrols maintained by the Curtiss Large America flying boats, were laid out on a pattern of concentric octagonal lines centred on the North Hinder light vessel. They used the maximum visibility from each aircraft to cover a wide area sixty miles across athwart the U-boat routes from their bases into the Channel, and it was one of these which had sunk the *UB*32. In fact, within the first two weeks of the patrols being started, eight U-boats were sighted and three of them were attacked.[12]

Surface patrols would commonly follow a patrol route in fits and starts, stopping every twenty minutes or so to lower hydrophones into the water. After dark, the patrols would choose a suitable spot to stop and lie in wait for passing U-boats running on the surface, which could be heard clearly over relatively long distances, and which were vulnerable to gunfire before they could dive to safety.

Later, fast motor launches and trawlers were assembled into rapid response units which could react to signals from aircraft or surface patrols warning of the presence of U-boats. The motor boats had speed on their side, being able to reach a position quickly and force submarines in the area to dive for fear of attack (though they carried relatively few depth charges themselves). The trawlers, on the other hand, could deliver a much heavier punch. Many were armed with a 12-pounder gun, and a depth charge howitzer, which was a long way ahead of its time in that it could hurl a single charge far enough ahead of the ship to cover the gap between the point at which hydrophones could no longer pick up the U-boat, and the point at which it could deliver its own attack.

All these measures between them had produced a remarkable and encouraging transformation in the bitter war against the U-boats. In view of the continuing controversy over the effectiveness of convoy tactics, the remarkable truth is that while hundreds of convoys sailed to and from Britain in the final eighteen months of the war, only eighty-four were even attacked, and in the vast majority of these cases (sixty-four) only one vessel was sunk on each occasion. Another indirect ASW benefit of the convoy system was that the escorts were able to shepherd their charges well clear of the 11,000 mines laid by U-boats in British coastal waters, and which were estimated to have cost almost a million and a quarter tons of merchant shipping.[13]

This was, for want of a better word, the passive side of ASW. The more slowly developing active side was represented by the total of twelve U-boats sunk between August 1917 and October 1918 by the convoy escorts, a total that would almost certainly have been greater if more ships had been made available from the huge number of those still retained for the entirely useless 'offensive patrols'. Yet such was the pernicious effect of the anti-convoy lobby that in March 1918, while the outcome of the unrestricted U-boat campaign still hung in the balance, the Anti-Submarine Division of the Admiralty was calling for the strength of the escort force to be reduced by 30 per cent to return more ships to the offensive patrols.

HMS *Walpole*, a fleet destroyer of the V and W classes built for the Royal Navy between 1917 and 1919, would play a crucial part in the second anti-submarine war two decades later.

(www.navyphotos.co.uk)

Of course, the ultimate solution to sinking more U-boats depended not on listening for the sounds that U-boats themselves emitted, but on generating a pulse of sound that could be bounced off a U-boat's hull to give an echo that could be picked up by the transmitting ship. This was the principle of the device that the British called Asdic (after the Allied Submarine Detection Investigation Committee that sponsored the development). It involved a transducer that could be made to send out a fan-shaped pulse of acoustic energy through the water. If this struck a submerged object, enough of the energy would be reflected towards the transmitting ship to be picked up as a sound echo. The ship's heading gave the bearing of the submarine (later, the transmitter head of the detector could be turned by the operator to cover any direction from the ship carring the equipment) and the delay between the original pulse and the receipt of the echo gave the range of the submarine.

Like the hydrophones, Asdic had its disadvantages,

but they were less restrictive. It could only be used when the transmitting ship was moving at less than fifteen knots, and it tended to produce echoes from many different kinds of submerged objects, only some of which were submarines. It could give little indication of depth, and as the ship closed in on the target, it lost contact when the range dropped to less than 100 yards. It was no use at all against submarines on the surface.

Finally, it was too late for the war – only seven ships were fitted with the equipment by the Armistice, and none used it against U-boats. The result of this last-minute development of the one weapon that would have made a genuine difference was that up to the end of March 1917, British destroyers had made 142 attacks on U-boats, but had only succeeded in sinking half a dozen of them. The chances were therefore 23 to 1 in favour of the U-boat escaping its attackers, though simply forcing it to dive would usually make it lose contact with potential targets.

Yet Asdic promised much for the future. In time, skilled operators could learn to distinguish between echoes reliably enough to be sure when a U-boat was in their sights. They could also estimate its depth well enough for accurate attacks. It could also cause severe damage to the morale of the U-boat crews: the shrill ping of the Asdic pulses travelling through the water and striking the submarine hull told them escorts were searching for them and very probably knew exactly where they were; crippling depth charge explosions could be expected at any moment.

It would be 1920 before warships were equipped with Asdic in quantity. In fact, it was developed at exactly the wrong time for British ASW operations. Too late for the First World War, it was still early enough in service to cause immense and crippling complacency over its effectiveness during the inter-war years. The Royal Navy came to assume that if submarines could not be abolished at the stroke of a pen in the clauses of the post-war treaties, then any resurgent threat could quickly be seen off by Asdic and depth charges. Had there been a chance to use these weapons to a larger extent before the end of the First World War, it would have become clearer how difficult it remained to sink U-boats, even with the aid of these powerful new weapons.

While this undoubtedly promised well for the future, the Germans were already working on tactics of their own to reduce the advantages conferred by Asdic. Since a U-boat's speed and endurance while on the surface were so much greater than when submerged, more and more skippers were choosing to carry out attacks in darkness, when all the enemy would see was the small silhouette of the conning tower against the blackness of the night. At the time, this was advantage enough: when Asdic came into general use, it would be even more powerful a tactic, since Asdic could not pick up the echo of a surfaced submarine.

The fashion spread quickly, even among as individ-

This picture is one of several showing World War I German U-boats washed ashore on the British coast and is captioned as the *U*118, washed ashore near Hastings, though this particular U-boat does not appear on the detailed casualty lists.

(www.navyphotos.co.uk)

ualistic a group as submarine commanders. During the final year of war, more than a third of U-boat attacks in the Atlantic and British home waters were night surface attacks, and in the Mediterranean the proportion was almost doubled. Like Asdic, this was a development that would prove even more effective when the fighting resumed after the uneasy peace.

Finally, what had the U-boats to offer against the stranglehold of the convoy system? Since convoys were as difficult to find as single ships sailing independently, but when spotted offered a wide choice of targets, the clear counter was to group submarines together to increase the force opposed to them. This meant a major shift in German tactics from the individual anonymity of single U-boats operating on their own, but the question was under active consideration from the appearance of the first convoys.

In 1917, when the initial experience with British convoys showed that a single U-boat had only slender chances against the strong defence, the Officer Commanding U-boats in the High Sea Fleet, Commodore Bauer, suggested that several U-boats should operate jointly. For this purpose he wanted to put a flotilla commander on one of the submarine cruisers of the *U*151 class, converted as a command U-boat, and to allow him, as tactical commander, to co-ordinate by radio an attack by several U-boats on a convoy.[14]

This sounded logical, and promising, but the idea contained a practical flaw. In due course, the Americans would try a similar set-up against the Japanese in the Pacific War twenty-five years later, but both the Germans and the Americans found that the idea of a commander on the spot was too restrictive in the fast-moving conditions of a submarine attack. Both would finally come to the same conclusion: what was needed was a way of finding a convoy, of bringing submarines to the spot in large enough numbers to achieve decisive results,

and then to leave the rest to the expertise of the captains themselves.

Not until May 1918 was the idea finally put into practice, and then it proved a failure. From 9 May, Admiralty radio interceptors, reporting to the intelligence chiefs in Room 40 identified the signals from five U-boats in the Western Approaches, thought to be part of a larger force of up to a dozen. Such was the density of convoy traffic at the time, that no less than nine convoys were in the vicinity of four of the U-boats sending the signals, but not one merchant ship was attacked. Only on 11 May was a single steamer sunk on her way into the port of Bristol, having left the convoy that was her protection.

By the following day, five of the U-boats had moved to the slightly more restricted waters at the entrance to St George's Channel, which might have provided more favourable conditions. What happened was much more discouraging. Just before 4am, *U*103 surfaced within sight of the huge troopship *Olympic*, crammed with American soldiers. Sister ship of the ill-fated *Titanic*, the trooper had enough weight and turn of speed to alter course and ram the U-boat before she could dive to safety, sending her straight to the bottom with all hands.

An hour later, the British coastal submarine *D*4 had seen and torpedoed *UB*72, but still no merchant ships had been sunk. Convoy after convoy passed through the danger zone, but not until 17 May did *U*55 manage to sink one small ship from a home-bound Gibraltar convoy and another from a trans-atlantic convoy. On the next day she homed another submarine, *U*94, on to another convoy, where the newcomer sank a 10,000-ton ship, the only truly worthwhile target of the three.

More to the point was the fact that, in the week when so many U-boats were watching convoys sail past, only successfully snapping at their flanks on three occasions, no less than 283 merchant ships had sailed past them in perfect safety. The new tactics would eventually work even more effectively, but it would take another war to show just how effective they could be in the right circumstances and with the right weapons.

So both sides in the submarine and ASW campaigns of the First World War retired to consider the lessons they had learned. Most important of these was the fact that the U-boats had been defeated because of Allied tactics rather than effective new weapons or offensive operations, and their own lack of effective tactics with which to counter them. Unfortunately, the misapprehension, particularly in Britain, that anti-submarine forces had defeated the U-boats by 'offensive patrolling' action instead of escorted convoys was to prove grossly expensive in the Second World War, only twenty-one years later.

CHAPTER 4

NEW IDEAS AND OLD THREATS

1922–39

Another mysterious picture showing a German U-boat carrying the number *U*1 on her conning tower. She cannot be the *original U*1 of 1907, since she is of much more modern appearance. She might conceivably be the *U*1 of the 1930s rearmament, but this normally only carried the number '1' in Gothic script and without the 'U' prior to hostilities, when all identification was removed for security reasons. The third *U*1 in German service was a wartime type XXIII which was scuttled at the end of the conflict and raised and put back into service after the war. This briefly bore the number *U*1 on its conning tower but was soon renamed *U-Hai* or 'U-Shark' and given a NATO S number carried on the tower. If this alone were not enough, the gun adds a further mystery since they were not fitted to type XXIIIs though the conning tower shape suggests one of these boats.

(www.navyphotos.co.uk)

O N the face of it, the transaction was perfectly respectable. A new Dutch company, NV Ingenieurskaantor voor Scheepsbouw, (usually abbreviated to IvS), opened offices in the Hague in April 1922. It was to specialise in the design and building of submarines, an activity prohibited to Germany by one of the specific clauses of the Treaty of Versailles concluded three years earlier. Yet, behind the respectable front, the company was run by one Hans Techel, a German citizen and formerly chief constructor at the U-boat building yard of Germania Werft of Kiel, and had a senior German naval officer, Korvettenkapitan Ulrich Blum as an adviser to the board. The real intention was to maintain German expertise in designing and building submarines, ready for the day when the nation was strong enough to throw off treaty restrictions and re-establish a strong U-boat force as the nucleus of a resurgent navy.

IvS worked through another dummy company called Mentor Bilanz that was set up in Berlin and run by another Korvettenkapitan (Robert Moraht) to act as a conduit to the German Reichsmarine, which provided staff for its technical department, to work on submarine contracts for overseas countries until it was safe to resume U-boat construction once more. These companies and their undercover activities were paid for by the German Navy, with generous donations from German shipbuilders who would be the first to benefit from new submarine contracts once the time was ripe.

Ironically, in view of later events, the first customer for the new companies' expertise was Japan, which as one of the victor nations, had received several First World War U-boats as reparations and been impressed by their quality and ingenuity. Japan bought plans for new boats from the Reichsmarine and negotiated for German engineers to travel to Japan and supervise their construction. A similar arrangement was set up for the Argentine Navy, but this and another proposal for Spain was dropped, though a further contract with Turkey did result in finished submarines. To evade the Versailles ban, two were built by the Dutch shipyard Fijenoord of Rotterdam to a German design for an improved version of the wartime UB-III class. Launched in early 1927, they were tested by a German crew and delivered to the Turkish Navy the following year.

By then the truth behind these activities had emerged, and a political row forced the closure of Mentor Bilanz. In fact, the company simply changed its name and cover story. From 1928 onwards it was known as the Ingenieurburo fur Wirtschaft und Technik GmbH (Engineering Office for Administration and Technology Ltd, usually abbreviated to Igewit) and it remained business as before. Two more wartime U-boat designs were adapted for foreign buyers – three based on the UC-III minelaying submarines for the Finns to build in one of their own yards, and an improved UB-II, again for Finland.

Building new versions of old designs was all very well, but the Germans needed new models to serve as the nucleus for their own navy. A new opportunity arose with a contract for Spain whereby hull sections for the *E1* submarine would be built in Rotterdam, with engines and specialised equipment delivered from Germany to be assembled at a small Cadiz shipyard called Echevarrieta. Catastrophe struck during the assembly process when the yard went into liquidation and the Reichsmarine had to take over financing the project. The boat ran aground after launching, and the Spanish Navy backed away from the deal, which was only saved by selling the completed boat to the Turks. The Germans themselves, pleased with the design, later used it as the basis for the first of the new U-boats, the type IA.

The eventual type II also had a troubled gestation period. The Finnish Navy wanted a small submarine that could be used for laying mines in Lake Ladoga, which, because of treaty obligations with Russia, had to be limited to a displacement of ninety-nine tons. The Germans designed a new small submarine that when completed actually displaced 142 tons, and this was considered the basis for the new coastal U-boats planned for the future, but was rejected as too small. Instead, the engineers worked on a larger 250-ton design that was produced on a speculative basis, to be sold to any interested parties. It was rejected by the Estonians but eventually built by the Finns and tested over a three-year period by the Germans, who cunningly used it as a handy means of training as many potential U-boat men as possible. The design itself then became the basis for the type II U-boat of the Second World War.

Finally, in the autumn of 1932, even before the Nazi takeover of Germany, the decision had been taken to re-establish the U-boat arm. Two classes,

each of eight boats, were to be built – the small type II coastal boats, adapted from the design offered to the Estonians and later built by the Finns, and the larger type IA, based on the design built for the Spanish and sold to the Turks. In fact, the type IA proved a disappointing design from the viewpoint of stability, it was slow to dive and ponderous to manoeuvre and only two were finally built, *U25* and *U26*, both of which were lost on operations early in the new war. The design was eventually developed into the larger, long-range type IX.

To begin with, both designs were constructed under the strictest secrecy, and were only referred to by the misleading description of *Motorenversuchboot* (MVB or Experimental Motor Boat). The biggest change in building techniques had been the switch to welding for the pressure hull, which reduced weight and increased strength. The two classes that were to provide the basis for the whole U-boat war against the Allies were only to emerge once the new inter-war naval treaties had been negotiated, and Germany had once again been left free to construct new submarines openly rather than secretly.

It was an astonishing transformation. At the end of the First World War, German naval power seemed to belong only in the past. The once mighty High Seas Fleet lay on the bottom of Scapa Flow, having scuttled itself in an act of collective defiance on being handed over to the victors under the terms of the Armistice. The clauses of the Versailles Treaty had limited post-war German naval strength to a token fleet of six armoured ships of 10,000 tons, six 6,000-ton cruisers, twelve small (800-ton) destroyers and a dozen torpedo boats of 200-tons displacement apiece, but *no* submarines at all.

Britain's fondest hopes of seeing a worldwide ban on submarine construction were soon to be shattered by the insistence of wartime Allies like France and Italy on developing their own submarines. Worse was to come. The new force arising out of post-war chaos in Germany was the Nazi Party, hell-bent on a massive rearmament programme, with or without the blessing of international treaties. At the end of January 1933 Adolf Hitler was appointed chancellor of Germany, and in just over two years he began tearing up the provisions of Versailles, which he insisted had been imposed through duress on a Germany stabbed in the back by her own corrupt politicians. In March 1935, he announced the establishment of the new Luftwaffe, and three months later it was the turn of the U-boats. To sweeten the pill for the British, whose policy of appeasement still had more than four years to run, he proposed that Germany would build to a limit of 35 per cent of the tonnage of the Royal Navy, though in submarines the limit would be 40 per cent of the tonnage of British submarines, with the right to build up to 100 per cent of British submarine tonnage if circumstances made this necessary.

HMS *Betony,* a Flower class corvette, developed from a whalecatcher design which provided the workhorses of the Royal Navy's escort groups in the Atlantic battle. *(www.navyphotos.co.uk)*

In the event, of course, even these limitations counted for nothing, but in order to allay suspicions and economise on materials, the U-boats that would be built in large quantities for the new war would be modest in size compared to overseas designs. They were constructed from the latest, toughest steel alloys, welded together rather than riveted, enabling them to dive more quickly, because of their lower skin friction and more deeply, because of their greater strength. Both the diesel engines and the electric motors were more powerful than their predecessors', and a clever coupling arrangement enabled a single diesel to drive both shafts for long-distance cruising, greatly extending the range.[1]

Their torpedoes were also greatly improved over the unreliable and virtually hand-built weapons used in the previous war, apart from one almost fatal flaw. They had heavier warheads to inflict greater damage on hitting their target, and the electric versions created no trail of bubbles to reveal the position of the submarine which had launched them. The new generation of U-boats was even able to absorb the bubbles of the compressed air used to propel the torpedo out of its tube when fired. But German engineers had tried to increase the lethal power of this sophisticated weapon by making it run at a greater depth, so that it passed beneath the hull of its target instead of simply striking its side plates, greatly magnifying the effect of its detonation.[2] This was triggered by a magnetic fuse, which could be fitted in place of the old contact fuse, but unfortunately this was to prove chronically unreliable. To compound the submariners' anguish, even torpedoes fitted with the old contact fuses proved to have problems at times.

The most numerous and most successful design, the 800-ton, 220-foot type VII, was designed as an ocean-going boat, with long range and an exceedingly strong pressure hull made from high-quality rolled steel in sections welded together with strengthening ribs on the inside. It was highly manoeuvrable and

could dive quickly in an emergency. It was fitted with an 88-mm deck gun, and four forward torpedo tubes with four reloads, and a single stern tube with no reloads. It had a top speed of seventeen knots on the surface, or 7.6 knots while submerged, though at this speed the batteries would soon require recharging. At an economical cruise speed of twelve knots, the range was 6,500 miles.

In all, 709 type VIIs would be built in a series of different versions intended to improve speed on the surface and seaworthiness in bad weather, and this would be the mainstay of the wolf-packs when the battle between the submarines and the Allied surface escorts reached its peak in 1943. But from the very beginning it was decided that the type VII should be given a larger and longer-range sister that could be used singly (as opposed to being assembled in groups, or packs) on longer-range missions to attack trade in more distant waters.

This was the type IX, which had an original displacement of 1,150 tons submerged, which was increased to 1,800 tons in the later versions, as it was lengthened from 250 feet to 287. It was broadly based on the U-81 class of the previous war, and more than two hundred were built. It was fitted with a 105-mm deck gun and carried four bow torpedo tubes with two at the stern and a total of twenty-two torpedoes, later increased to twenty-four. With a top speed of eighteen or nineteen knots on the surface, and around seven knots submerged, the performance was similar to the type VII, though diving took longer in an emergency. Range increased from 8,100 miles for the early boats to 11,400, with an astonishing 23,700 miles for the final type IXD2.

Both types proved to be an odd combination of dated design with superb build quality. This made them very strong and difficult to sink, but performance and capability that had been highly successful at the start of the war would prove obsolete and limited by the end. Oddly, given German ingenuity

A pre-war picture of *U19*, one of the type II U-boats designed for coastal waters but invaluable as training boats for the crews and commanders of the front line type VIIs and IXs.
(Jak Mallmann Showell)

and engineering quality, little was done to upgrade the designs beyond detailed improvements – for example, the shape of the pressure hull and the square-cut casing built on top with its complex network of drain holes, not to mention the deck gun and anti-aircraft armament, all contributed to a huge hydrodynamic drag factor. This could easily have been reduced by cleaning up the design and a measure of streamlining, while underwater endurance could have been improved by fitting additional batteries long before this was successfully carried out on the tiny type XXIIIs at the end of the long campaign.

Nevertheless, as things were the type IX presented the Royal Navy with a daunting future when, as the 1930s progressed against a background of ruthless and effective German expansion and rearmament, the spectre of another U-boat campaign loomed larger

Pre-war picture of the conning tower of the new type VII *U51* – once hostilities began the clear vulnerability of U-boats to air attack led to much larger and heavier structures carrying more and more anti-aircraft weapons.

(Jak Mallmann Showell)

and larger. What had previously been the largest and most powerful navy in the world was now seriously short of both funds and ships. New construction was severely limited under shrinking defence budgets, and the imposition of the 'five-year rule', whereby expenditure was planned on the basis that no major European war was predicted to occur within the next five years. The problem with what might seem a reasonable assumption is that five years is not an acceptable safety margin where building large numbers of warships is concerned.

Another aspect of a crippling lack of funds was the lack of an operational research department, which would have enabled the Admiralty to understand the full details of the campaign that had been waged against the U-boats in the previous war, and which

would have helped in planning the campaign that would operate in any renewal of hostilities. By the time the new U-boats made their first appearance, it was clear that of all the nations that had fought in the previous war, the Germans were almost the only ones who had decided exactly how their submarines should be used. From the very beginning, the primary targets would be merchant shipping. Warships might be attacked as targets of opportunity, or as obstacles to attacking the merchantmen they were protecting, but this would be a trade war with a vengeance.[3]

Other major naval powers remained unsure how to use their submarines. The old dilemma over whether submarines should operate with the surface fleet to sink major enemy warships or as commerce raiders against enemy merchant fleets returned in full intensity. In the US Navy, peacetime planning of submarine tactics assumed that remaining undetected in the face of newer and more effective anti-submarine tactics would be so difficult and so essential that many attacks were delivered on sonar alone, making sinkings almost impossible. Furthermore, objectives were limited to attacking enemy warships, when the most likely enemy – Japan – depended heavily on imports and presented an ideal target for submarine commerce raiding. Consequently American torpedoes were fitted with magnetic pistols able to trigger an explosion beneath a target's hull, essential to cripple an armoured warship but less valuable against merchant targets.

For the Royal Navy, the problem was different. The ideal escort for the convoys, which would have to be adopted from the start of a future war, was still the destroyer, but these fast and versatile ships would be needed for all kinds of duties, including escorting major fleet units, on every kind of operation. A start had been made during the 1930s to build slower, cheaper and more manoeuvrable ships originally classified as sloops, but which were intended first and foremost as anti-submarine vessels. With a displacement of between 1,200 and 1,400 tons, and a top speed of around twenty knots, these were designed to be fast enough and handy enough for convoy escort work with large stocks of depth charges and a 4-inch gun armament, usually in twin mountings, well able to inflict killing blows to the pressure hull of a surfaced U-boat.

The problem, as always, was numbers. Another attempt to stretch the available budget to produce more escorts was made by designing a mini-destroyer, the Hunt class, with a displacement of around 1,000 tons, a top speed of twenty-seven knots and no torpedo tubes. But boosting the numbers still higher ran into three other crippling limitations on what the Admiralty could do in preparing for a new war. All the naval estimates had to be vetted by the Treasury, who tended to strike out any reference to emotive, warlike words such as 'destroyer', even when Hitler was clearly determined to pick up where the First World War had left off. So the admirals became adept at using new, less inflammatory descriptions of ships like 'fast escorts' and 'sloops' to disguise what they were planning to build, and get the estimates passed by the civil servants through a measure of stealth.

No amount of stealth, though, could cover up two other highly unpalatable facts: naval shipbuilding capacity was too limited to cope with escort building on the scale needed. Even if this were not a problem, existing escorts, like the sloops and corvettes of the First World War, and the new destroyers now on the drawing board, all depended on high-speed steam turbines. This meant they needed another scarce and expensive resource: the high-quality steel and the precise techniques needed to make the blades for these turbines, and supplies of these were even more strictly limited than building berths.

In the end, the Admiralty bowed to the inevitable, and looked for an alternative that could allow them to find a route around these obstacles. What they needed most was an escort vessel considerably smaller and cheaper than a conventional destroyer. Since high speed was not a requirement, nor were batteries of guns and torpedo tubes for attacking surface ships, engines could be less powerful and hulls could be smaller, and the ships could be run with smaller numbers of men. Ideally, what was needed was a simple merchant ship design that could be turned out in relatively large numbers by every kind of merchant shipyard, and which could be made fit for naval use by simply adding the necessary weapons, depth charges, and the rails and throwers for delivering them, and a single gun mounting to deal with a surfaced submarine trying to fight back. The second restriction – the shortage of turbine blades – could be dealt with by using a classic reciprocating engine with no need for scarce or expensive components.

Shipbuilders were invited to send in proposals and drawings, and the eventual design selected was from a small builder called Smith's Dock of South Shields, who had built a 925-ton whalecatcher called *Southern Pride*, one of a series of these tough, manoeuvrable agile and reasonably speedy vessels, mainly for Norwegian customers. She was small, with an overall length of 205 feet, just over half that of the new fleet destroyers that would be her contemporaries. Carrying a single 4-inch gun in a shield mounting, with a sprinkling of small anti-aircraft weapons and a supply of depth charges, her single-shaft triple-expansion reciprocating steam engine could deliver a top speed of between fourteen and sixteen knots, which meant that a surfaced U-boat at full speed could outrun her.

There were other shortcomings in the design. The hull form meant the vessel would roll all too easily in a swell, and the small size and light displacement meant exceedingly tough conditions for the crews.

In the original plan, this would probably not have mattered too much, as, working on First World War experience, it was intended that these escorts should have the major role of protecting coastal convoys or the transatlantic convoys at the very start and completion of their voyages, when most sinkings had tended to occur. It was only when the U-boats extended their operations further and further into the open Atlantic that the corvettes were forced to increase their range in response, taking them into conditions that would impose cruel burdens on those who sailed in them.

Nevertheless, they could be produced quickly and in large numbers. Even the naval estimates provided no obstacles, since the corvettes were referred to originally as 'whalecatchers', a designation that left Treasury prejudices unruffled but made no sense in naval terms. Eventually they were reclassified as corvettes, which made more sense, and for the most critical phases of the anti-submarine war, they would bear the brunt of Doenitz's offensive. The initial order was spectacularly large, at fifty-six ships, but overall, including those built later in Canada, a total of 259 would be built, and their place in the front line of the anti-submarine war would help account for the loss of thirty-three of them.[4] Later, the design was modified by adding a longer forecastle, which improved its seaworthiness and made it slightly more habitable, but it was still rugged rather than restful for the ship's companies. In the end though, they would be just enough, and just in time.

The urgency of the need for the new escorts would be thrown into sharp relief by a highly unequal contest. A small convoy consisting of a tanker and a freighter and a third non-combatant, with a single escort, faced a total of fifteen U-boats, deployed in five packs of three, arranged in a patrol line covering several hundred miles. In spite of evasive action by the convoy and its escort, it was spotted by one of the packs, which radioed the whereabouts of their targets to the others. Over the next two days and nights of increasingly stormy weather, the submarines gathered for a share of the spoils. At the end of the action, all of the boats but two had found and attacked their targets. With odds like these, every ship in the convoy and its escort could have been sunk several times over.

This telling demonstration of the resurgence of the U-boat took place in May 1939, just sixteen weeks before the outbreak of the Second World War. It was the last German naval exercise during the uneasy peace between the two world wars, and it was designed to prove the effectiveness of the wolf-pack tactics that the new commander of the U-Boat arm, Karl Doenitz, would bring to bear on Allied shipping once war began. In the ratio of submarines to targets it had been hopelessly biased in favour of the attackers – never in the real campaign would the submariners

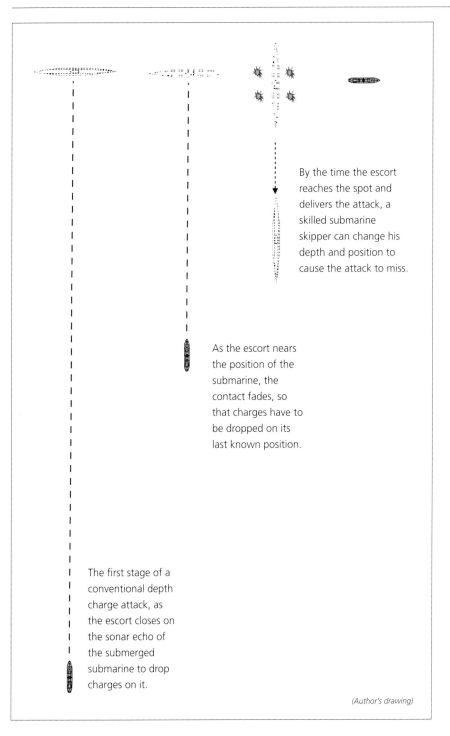

By the time the escort reaches the spot and delivers the attack, a skilled submarine skipper can change his depth and position to cause the attack to miss.

As the escort nears the position of the submarine, the contact fades, so that charges have to be dropped on its last known position.

The first stage of a conventional depth charge attack, as the escort closes on the sonar echo of the submerged submarine to drop charges on it.

(Author's drawing)

achieve odds as favourable as this. Yet as a demonstration of a tactic that would seek to overwhelm convoy escorts by weight of numbers, it was a chilling warning of what was to come.

Already, by the second half of the 1930s, the world's navies were increasingly certain that another world war could not be long delayed. Once that appalling fact was accepted, the most surprising factor was the extent to which most of them seemed dedicated to confirming the famous remark from the philosopher George Santayana that those who cannot remember the past are condemned to repeat it. In this case, the problem was not so much a failure to remember the experiences of the previous war, but a more serious failure to draw the right conclusions from them.

The powerful and frightening German campaign against Allied merchant shipping should have been seen as a lesson written in letters of fire. Instead, many opted for the comforting view that felt the conditions that had made it possible would not recur. Others felt the lesson did not apply to them, or to their opponents. Others saw the power of the submarine campaign as a temporary aberration, whose time had passed, leaving them free to return to the eternal truths of the supremacy of the big gun and the battleship, and the ultimate importance of the decisive encounter between battle fleets in determining the course of a future naval war.

Of all the major naval powers, those with the least excuse for muddled thinking about the implications of unrestricted submarine warfare were those most closely involved: Great Britain and Germany. For the Royal Navy, the huge sinkings of 1917 should have been a final alarm call, to wake them once and for all to the menace of the U-boat, and the need to defeat any of its successors. In one sense, it did the job, but went considerably too far. Because of the huge problem of finding and sinking U-boats, and what was wrongly seen as the narrowness of the margin by which they were defeated, the British tried to head off a resurgence of the problem, not by developing new weapons and tactics to defeat it, but by drawing up solemn and binding treaties to render it illegal.

This was an extreme reaction, based on a misreading of the effects of the submarine blockade. The truth was that at no time had Britain suffered real deprivation, and in that sense the U-boat campaign had been a failure. The British naval blockade of Germany, however, had caused genuine hardship, and the benefits of going for an all-out unrestricted campaign of merchant ship sinkings had seemed clear enough to a nation facing both defeat on the battlefield and slow starvation at home. Faced with this cruel dilemma, the glittering prize of forcing the British to relax their grip by blockading them in turn blinded Germany to the one certain price to be paid for unrestricted sinkings – the entry of America into the war, which would turn their ultimate defeat from a grim possibility into a certainty.

However, while the U-boat force had been comprehensively dismantled and its submarines seized and scrapped, the ban-the-undersea-menace programme was far from secure. Rather like the hopes of the nuclear abolitionists three decades later, the plans of the treaty negotiators would only work if everyone felt the same and agreed to maintain any resulting embargo. Yet it was precisely those aggressive and expansionist powers like Germany and Japan who had the most to gain from a powerful submarine arm, who were ultimately the most likely to tear up treaties once the apparent gains justified it.

In fact, the submarine menace was only one of the problems that exercised the British during the years between the wars. The other crippling lesson of the First World War had been the huge cost of fighting it, and the difficulty of meeting the bills to replace losses and introduce the new weapons that would be needed in an approaching future conflict. The Britain that had cheerfully taken on Imperial Germany in the pre-war arms race to build newer and more powerful battleships now feared a resumption of ruinously expensive competition in warship building, and set to work to persuade the other naval powers they had everything to gain from a set of self-imposed limits on new construction.

This produced a series of conferences and agreements, beginning with the 1921 Washington Naval Conference, and ending with the London Conference of 1930. Britain's objectives were clear enough. Out-building all other navies in the world was no longer an affordable option, but if parity with US naval strength were agreed, and if Japanese expansion could be reined in, then a treaty was to be highly prized. The eventual terms would involve Britain and the USA scrapping battleships wholesale, and aiming to reduce their capital ship tonnage over twenty years to half a million tons each. Japan agreed to a target of 300,000 tons and France and Italy to 175,000 tons each.

The total tonnage of smaller ships like cruisers and destroyers would be allocated in the same proportions, and this would have a major impact on future anti-submarine warfare. Destroyers, the predominant anti-submarine vessels, would be limited to 150,000 tons apiece for the US and Royal navies, 105,000 tons for the Japanese and just over 60,000 tons for the French and Italians. In terms of the latest fleet destroyers, displacing around 1,500 tons apiece, this was equivalent to 100 destroyers each for the US and Royal navies, seventy for the Japanese and some forty apiece for the French and Italians. At this stage no one involved the Germans, officially forbidden anything more than a token navy under the binding provisions of the Treaty of Versailles, which made the whole exercise a little like a production of *Hamlet* without the prince.

Submarines had already created sharp differences of opinion between the different powers. Britain had pushed at the Washington Conference for submarines to be banned, full stop. France led the countries that rejected a ban, and the final result was seen as a compromise, albeit a compromise which let the submarine back into the discussions through a side door. The American delegation suggested a limit of 90,000 tons for Britain and America, then roughly equivalent to a hundred boats, and half this number and tonnage for France and Italy. Once again Germany, the spectre at the feast, was not included in the reckoning.

Only the Americans seemed to think this was a good idea. To British horror, the failure to reach a binding agreement was to result in all the naval powers being left free to develop their own submarine fleets without any formal restriction until the questions was tackled all over again at a conference in Geneva in 1927, called principally to resolve differences of opinion over cruiser limitations. Once again Britain proposed outright abolition, and this time the USA and Japan opposed the suggestion, while France and Italy stayed away.

Only in the London Conference of 1930 did the subject rear its head again, and once again the nations took up their entrenched positions. Britain proposed abolition on humanitarian grounds, but as a gesture to the opposition suggested that submarines be allowed under severe and binding restrictions: that they should only be capable of defensive operations, that they should be limited in size and number, and that they should be constrained by the International Prize Regulations in time of war.

This time the US backed the British and the Italians indicated they would be willing to agree to abolition, provided the other powers did so too. The French, as always, refused to consider a ban, and an agreement was hammered out whereby the major powers agreed to a limit of 52,700 tons overall, with a tonnage cap of 2,000 on any single boat, and no deck gun larger that 5.1 inches, with a few agreed exceptions. France and Italy, with plans of their own, refused to agree. But the one clause on which everyone *was* willing to sign the paper was Article 22, which specified:

> In their action with regard to merchant ships, submarines must conform to the rules of International Law to which surface vessels are subject.
>
> In particular, except in the case of persistent refusal to stop on being duly summoned, or of active resistance to visit or search, a warship, whether surface vessel or submarine, may not sink or render incapable of navigation a merchant vessel without having first placed passengers, crew and ship's papers in a place of safety. For this purpose the ship's boats are not regarded as a place of safety unless the safety of the passengers and crew is assured, in the existing sea and weather conditions, by proximity of land or the presence of another vessel which is in a position to take them on board.[5]

This was an earnest and humanitarian attempt to rein in the lethal abilities of the submarine, but it would be honoured more in the breach than in the observance. Although it was signed by Britain, the USA, Japan, France, Italy, Russia, Belgium, Sweden, Finland, Panama, Albania, Bulgaria, Haiti and even Nepal – and finally, recognising the inevitable, by

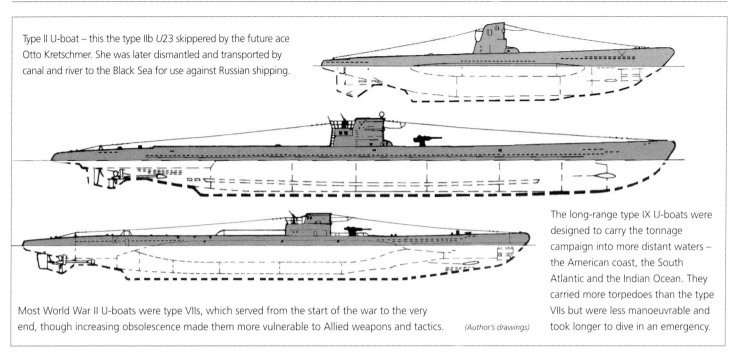

Type II U-boat – this the type IIb *U23* skippered by the future ace Otto Kretschmer. She was later dismantled and transported by canal and river to the Black Sea for use against Russian shipping.

The long-range type IX U-boats were designed to carry the tonnage campaign into more distant waters – the American coast, the South Atlantic and the Indian Ocean. They carried more torpedoes than the type VIIs but were less manoeuvrable and took longer to dive in an emergency.

Most World War II U-boats were type VIIs, which served from the start of the war to the very end, though increasing obsolescence made them more vulnerable to Allied weapons and tactics.   *(Author's drawings)*

Germany too – all the major navies would find its provisions unworkable in the realities of wartime operations and would abandon it sooner or later. Though even tighter restrictions were proposed at the World Disarmament Conference held in 1932 in Geneva, by then the changing political climate made further large-scale disarmament politically inadvisable, and the opportunity of outlawing the submarine through diplomacy – effectively, anti submarine warfare by treaty – was finally dead in the water.

Nevertheless, two unintended consequences resulted from this agreement. Though the submarine remained a legal weapon of war – just – developing the ships, weapons and tactics needed to defeat them was either ignored or severely downgraded in priority, because of a mixture of wishful thinking combined with a yearning for the old realities of naval warfare. And in most cases, those nations that had fought hard for the right to build and use submarines had very little idea of how they would use them if war came.

Unfortunately, Doenitz was one person who was convinced he knew exactly how to use submarines in war, as the man who would command Hitler's U-boats. Not only had he commanded a German submarine in the First World War, but he had earned a reputation among the thinned-out ranks of the inter-war Reichsmarine as an officer who could get things done, and who thought deeply about tactics and operational methods. During the years when submarines were off limits for the German Navy, and when their planning, design and construction were closely guarded state secrets, Doenitz had a variety of jobs. After command of a torpedo boat half-flotilla in 1928, he went on to a succession of staff jobs before a tour as commander of the light cruiser *Emden* in the

mid-1930s. During his time with the torpedo boats he perfected the technique of attacking convoys as a team, the foundation of his night attacks on the surface by packs of U-boats that would be the basis of his Atlantic campaign when war came. As a pointer to the future, the 1929 naval exercises saw his torpedo boats attack a merchant convoy and sink every ship!

From the *Emden*, he moved at last to return to U-boats when Hitler announced the re-establishment of the German submarine arm in 1935. Surprisingly, in view of his later identification with the U-boat campaign of the Second World War, Doenitz had mixed feelings about returning to what might have seemed a backwater in a navy where opinion had mainly swung back in the direction of big surface ships, and where submarines had remained off limits for so long. But the situation was changing rapidly. On the face of it, Hitler had deliberately rejected overt naval competition with the British, which he saw as wasteful and ultimately counter-productive. For the time being, he had been content to shelter behind the provisions of the Anglo-German Naval Agreement, concluded in 1935, restricting Germany to tonnages up to 35 per cent of the Royal Navy.

Behind the scenes, his thinking was very different. Ironically, he made similar assumptions to the British about the likelihood of peace being prolonged, but for entirely opposite reasons. On 29 January 1939, he approved 'Plan Z',[6] a huge expansion of German naval power similar to the plans of the Kaiser, but involving large, powerful, modern ships. By 1945, the Kreigsmarine would include the *Bismarck* and *Tirpitz*, *Scharnhorst* and *Gneisenau* with bigger 15-inch guns for their main armament, and six entirely new battleships, three larger versions of the existing pocket battleships, an additional heavy cruiser, two aircraft carriers, fifty destroyers and 229 U-boats. All this was based on the assumption that war would not come until 1946, and even then the balance of the new force showed outdated thinking in its emphasis on battleships at the expense of carriers. Later, however, he would plan a grandiose and completely impractical expansion into a huge modern fleet, consisting of battleships, battlecruisers and aircraft carriers, all based on the assumption that peace could be preserved into the late 1940s.

In spite of the public accord, the sting in the tail of the agreement was that Germany was allowed for the first time since 1918 to build submarines. Initially she would be limited to 45 per cent of the tonnage of British submarines, but this could be increased up to 100 per cent of British submarine tonnage if outside factors, not defined at the time, made this necessary. Opponents of the U-boats were reassured that this was on condition Germany signed up to the agreed ban on unrestricted submarine warfare and the use of the International Prize Regulations, which also appeared to cause no problems at the time.

The result was that, while working within the terms of the agreement, Germany was building formidable modern ships, though never on a scale to threaten British naval supremacy. The agreed limit for capital ships was 183,000 tons. The first three 'pocket battleships', *Deutschland*, *Admiral Graf Spee* and *Admiral Scheer* had been designed to fit the limits of the earlier Treaty of Versailles, though their actual displacement increased to 12,000 tons on completion. They were fitted with armour, modern diesel engine propulsion and six 11-inch guns to act as formidable commerce raiders, and left 147,000 tons, which was enough – just – for the nominal displacements of the battlecruisers *Scharnhorst* and *Gneisenau* and the powerful modern battleships *Bismarck* and *Tirpitz*.

In the meantime, the agreement had been signed on 18 June 1935 and announced to a startled but hopeful world four days later. A week after that, the Reichsmarine (now formally renamed the Kriegsmarine) announced the commissioning of the new U-boat *U1*, one of six small 250-ton type II coastal submarines that had been built in secret in German yards before the treaty had been negotiated.

For Doenitz the command of the new U-boat arm could turn out to be a poisoned chalice. With most of the agreed tonnage being devoted to surface warships, would submarines ever amount to more than a backwater? Yet all his instincts and all his wartime experience told him the U-boat was the one potentially decisive weapon at Germany's command. All the new surface ships would never amount to more than a commerce raiding force – submarines in large enough numbers could do what their predecessors had narrowly failed to do (in his eyes), and bring Britain to her knees. All he needed to do was ensure that those in charge

of the new resurgent navy shared his ideas and his vision. Unfortunately, this proved to be a long uphill climb to a summit he would never attain, as he was never to feel he had been given the support or the resources he needed to do his ambitious job. For example, having studied the new types of U-boat built for foreign customers and now being turned out by German yards, he had become convinced that the version which met his needs most closely would be the medium-sized ocean-going type VII. But of the first three dozen submarines commissioned, twenty-four were the small type IIs, two were the large but unsuccessful ocean-going prototypes, *U25* and *U26* and only ten were the first type VIIs.

In theory, this left 11,500 tons of construction up to the treaty submarine limit. Doenitz saw this as an opportunity to order another twenty-three type VIIs, but the Navy chiefs disagreed. They wanted eight more type IIs, another eight of the new, bigger type IXs, which were longer in range and building time but shorter on manoeuvrability, and just seven more type VIIs. Doenitz tried with all his might to get this order modified, and failed. To make matters worse, only twenty-one of this mixed bag of twenty-three boats would actually be completed by the outbreak of war.

If construction and commissioning of the new U-boats was beyond Doenitz's powers (and he would have to continue to press for more and more boats throughout the war against official indifference and inefficiency) then at least training and tactics were not. Two flotillas of the small 250-ton type IIs were formed during the summer of 1935, both based in Kiel – one for initial training and the other, later named the Weddigen Flotilla after the First World War ace Otto Weddigen, for advanced training.

Doenitz set up one of the toughest and most demanding training regimes for submarine crews ever developed. From the beginning of October 1935 to a target date of March 1936, the boats were at sea and hard at work almost continuously. The work that had to be covered before they could be declared operational was astonishing. Every submarine crew had to carry out a total of 132 mock attacks – half of them submerged in the daytime and the rest, significantly, on the surface at night – before being let anywhere near even a practice torpedo. Only when this first stage had been finished satisfactorily could the men graduate to firing real torpedoes with dummy warheads at ship targets.

By the time they had completed the course, his submariners were as experienced as it was possible to be, without a war. And the two planks of his future tactics were already well established: surface attacks by individual submarines at night, echoing his own experience commanding torpedo boats during the U-boat embargo, and the assembly of packs of U-boats to attack and overwhelm the escorts of the convoys that had effectively defeated the U-boats of the previous war. Yet his clear vision was still not shared by those higher in the Kriegsmarine command structure. Instead of Doenitz's trade war, official strategy was for the U-boats to gather outside enemy ports on the outbreak of war, to sink warships and troop transports rather than merchant shipping.

Finally, what of the U-boats' most determined adversaries? Where Doenitz had become determined to reverse the previous defeat by developing better training, better weapons, and better tactics, the Royal Navy built on its previous victory by a mixture of hope and complacency. Because Asdic had been developed just too late to come to the rescue in the First World War, its effectiveness had never been tested under combat conditions, which would have revealed its very real limitations. As a result, it had come to be regarded as the panacea for future ASW; sound location and the depth charge were assumed to have virtually rendered the submarine obsolete as a threat.

Nevertheless, some work had been done to develop tactics to use this new combination to sink submarines, and these had been tested at sea, using Royal Navy submarines as targets. The anti-submarine warfare specialists at HMS *Osprey* at Portland, under the direction of 'that devoted father of the Asdic, Professor Jack Anderson',[7] had devised what came to be known as the 'pounce' and 'MRCS' tactics, which set out to reduce the freedom of a submarine to take evasive action during the last stage of a depth-charge attack, when Asdic effectively became deaf.[8] The 'pounce' attack involved the attacking warship moving at slow speed to avoid being picked up on the submarine's hydrophones. In the meantime another escort monitored the submarine's movements. When the time was right, the first escort would accelerate to full speed for the attack, being homed in on the target by its sister ship.

At first this seemed to work quite well, until the skippers of the target submarines realised how the tactic worked and became adept at outwitting it once they realised the high-speed dash had begun. The next step was the Medium Range Constant Speed, or MRCS attack, which involved shadowing a submarine at low speed from half a mile away, and then accelerating to the limiting speed at which Asdic could still hold the echo of the submarine, adjusting the escort's course to match the submarine's movements. This succeeded in reducing the area of uncertainty between the point at which the echo was lost and the dropping of the depth charge pattern to some 250 yards, but this was still ample for a skilled submarine skipper to take successful evasive action.

One of the Royal Navy's particularly strong suits was in the field of training aids, and before the war they introduced an Asdic mobile target and a depth-charge attack analyser, which could be used to assess the success or failure of anti-submarine exercises. The Admiralty Research Laboratories also developed a course plotter as a navigational aid, but it also proved valuable when plotting the course of an anti-submarine attack.

The first attack teaching aid for training officers and ratings in anti-submarine tactics and drills was set up at the Portland Anti-Submarine School by 1925,[9] and consisted of the control equipment of an Asdic set together with a glass-topped attack table covered with a sheet of thin plotting paper. Two spots of light were projected on to this representing the positions of the escort and the submarine, and these were moved independently under the orders of the pupil and the instructor. Each Asdic pulse was represented by beams of light corresponding with the settings of the Asdic controls, and if one of these struck the submarine the sound of the echo was triggered through the pupil's headphones. Other aids trained operators in the techniques of sweeping for a possible target and what to do if a target was lost.

However, the greatest defect of this sound practical training is that so few of the people who would use the equipment in wartime were ever persuaded to specialise in ASW before the war. In spite of the lessons of 1917–18, ASW remained more of a career backwater in the Royal Navy than U-boats in the Kriegsmarine. Captain Donald Macintyre, who became one of the Royal Navy's foremost sub-killers and who sank the *U*99 and captured the ace Otto Kretschmer, spent the pre-war years flying with the Fleet Air Arm and commanding fleet destroyers (apart from a stint running HMS *Kingfisher*, the experimental ship of the Anti-Submarine School). The greatest submarine hunter of all, 'Johnny' Walker, suffered being passed over for both promotion and command for selecting to specialise in ASW in a navy still dominated by the battleship and the big gun.

Ironically, the Germans themselves were to prove they had their blind spots. Since the end of the First World War, they had concentrated much more on passive developments like hydrophones because for several years active sound location methods were seen as being linked to attack rather than defence and were therefore proscribed by the Versailles Treaty. As a result, they had little knowledge of what Asdic and the other ASW weapons could do. Doenitz was firm in his conviction that the British were too complacent regarding Asdic's value and capabilities. Werner Fürbringer disagreed, on the grounds that the Royal Navy's defences would be too formidable to risk wasting U-boats and their crews on a blockade campaign. The problem, from Doenitz's point of view, was that Fürbringer was a rear-admiral, was responsible for submarine planning at the Naval High Command, and was effectively his boss.[10]

CHAPTER 5

NEW FAILURES AND REPEATED MISTAKES

1939–41

Rough weather in the Atlantic made handling heavy depth charges a difficult and dangerous operation. This is the Canadian frigate HMCS *Swansea* off Bermuda in January 1944.

(National Library of Canada)

On 13 October 1939, less than six weeks after the outbreak of the Second World War, HG3, a convoy of twenty-five merchant ships, set sail from Gibraltar for Liverpool. On the fourth day of the voyage, sailing well to the west of the Spanish coast, the ships were spotted by a type VII U-boat, *U46*. The submarine skipper shadowed the convoy through the night while calling in two more U-boats, *U37* and *U48*. When contact with the convoy was lost temporarily, the tactical commander on the spot, Kapitänleutnant Werner Hartmann in *U37*, ordered a search for the morning of 18 October, but the convoy was found again before that became necessary, and the three boats set about carrying out submerged torpedo attacks on as many of these tempting targets as they could.

The eventual tally was three British freighters, one for each of the U-boats. *U46* sank the 7,000-ton *City of Mandalay*, *U48* the 7,000-ton *Clan Chisholm* and *U37* the 10,000-ton *Yorkshire*. After that, patrolling aircraft forced the U-boats to lose contact, and the operation was effectively over. This had been Doenitz's first attempt to put his improved pack attacks into operation, and even though they believed the tally had been four ships sunk rather than three, its context caused the Germans more concerns than celebrations.

Pack tactics depended absolutely on an adequate number of U-boats being available to respond to convoy sightings. Because the worth of using convoys had been well learned in the previous war, the convoy system had been organised from the very beginning, though at times this had been far from a foregone conclusion. In March 1935, Lord Stanley, addressing Parliament as the permanent secretary to the Admiralty, stated 'I can assure the House that the convoy system would not be introduced at once on the outbreak of war'.[1] In fairness to Stanley, the preoccupation at the time was with the threat of German surface raiders, to which convoys would have been particularly vulnerable.

The other reason for inter-war scepticism over convoys was the belief that Asdic and depth charges had virtually eliminated the potential threat of the U-boat, and it remained the case that not one single exercise to practise the defence of a slow mercantile convoy against air or submarine attack was held between the wars.[2] Fortunately for the prospects of defeating the U-boats, more sensible views finally prevailed and from 26 August 1939 the Admiralty took over control of British merchant shipping through its trade division, organising convoys, routes, sailing schedules and escorts. The first Gibraltar to Cape Town convoy sailed the day before war was declared, and the first UK-bound convoys from Halifax in Nova Scotia and Freetown in West Africa had sailed before the month was out.

At this stage of the war, Doenitz had far fewer U-boats available than he would have liked to carry

Once an escort was in contact with a U-boat, delivering a succession of accurate attacks was of paramount importance so racks and throwers had to be reloaded as quickly as possible.

(National Library of Canada)

out his tactics, and the Royal Navy was busy ensuring the numbers were even more restricted. More worryingly for the British, however, was that their adversaries were even at this early stage in the conflict able to read coded signals that tipped them off to convoy schedules, courses and timings.

The first attempt to assemble packs for convoy attacks had failed completely. Originally Doenitz had planned to deploy two groups of five boats each in the Western Approaches, but losses and operational demands whittled down the total to just over half. Gunther Prien in *U47* was occupied with his solo mission to sink the battleship *Royal Oak*, which gave the Royal Navy as unwelcome a wake-up call in the Second World War as the sinking of *Hogue, Aboukir* and *Cressy* in the North Sea had done in the First. Two more U-boats were in dockyard hands for repairs and *U39* had already been sunk by Royal Navy destroyers (as discussed in more detail later).

Even the less ambitious plan of using the remaining six boats as a single pack failed to work properly. One of them, the type IX *U40*, was late sailing for the mission and was ordered to take the short cut through the Dover Straits that the others had avoided by sailing 'north about' around the extreme north of the British mainland. Doenitz believed it was too early in the war for the British to have mined the straits, but sadly for *U40* and her crew he was wrong. She was lost with most of her crew on 13 October.

One down left five to carry out the mission. Another type IX, *U42*, found the 5,000-ton *Stonepool* sailing alone. The skipper of *U42*, Kapitänleutnant Rolf Dau, decided to surface for a gun attack to economise on torpedoes, but to his surprise the merchantman began firing back, while sending out an immediate distress signal. Before he could sink her, two modern

Royal Navy fleet destroyers, *Imogen* and *Ilex*, turned up in response to the call, and he was forced to dive to 360 feet in an attempt to evade their attacks.

He failed. The first patterns of depth charges were right on target, and one of them cracked open the aft ballast tanks, causing a sharp loss of buoyancy at the stern. The bows pitched upwards, and there was a real danger of the submarine plunging backwards to her crush depth. The only way out was to surface by blowing all the remaining ballast tanks and abandon ship. Even so, she was holed by gunfire from the destroyers, and she sank within minutes, taking with her two-thirds of her crew. The remainder, including Dau, were picked up by the ships that had sunk his U-boat.

That left four U-boats. Two of them finally found eastbound Anglo-French convoy KJF3 and attacked independently, sinking four ships from the convoy and two unaccompanied stragglers. The other two arrived too late, one in time to sink another straggler but the other never found the targets at all. The sinkings were encouraging, but in no sense had this been a concerted pack attack and even this off-target blow came at a price. One of the two boats that had found the convoy, the type VIIB *U45*, was pursuing more targets when the signals sent by the convoy warning they were under attack brought four more Royal Navy destroyers, *Icarus, Inglefield, Ivanhoe* and *Intrepid*, from the same class as the pair that had sunk *U42* three days before. The result, too, was much the same. Heavy depth-charge attacks sank the U-boat with all hands.

Only then had the three boats that were the remnants of what had originally been meant to number two five-boat packs been ordered south into sea area Schwarz, where they had encountered HG3. The overall total of sinkings resulting from this messy and un-coordinated operation were seven ships sunk from two convoys (together with three stragglers that were not part of the pack tactical plan). To sink these ten merchant ships, the U-boats had lost three of their number, at this stage of the war an extremely discouraging rate of exchange.

The result was a tactical defeat for the U-boats. Though U-boat headquarters originally professed itself satisfied with the results, 'In spite of its short duration this operation had been successful; at least three or four vessels were sunk,'[3] a later verdict after another attempted pack operation in November where only two U-boats attacked the target convoy proved more sombre. 'This further comparative failure caused the U-Boat Command to defer their attempts at planned concentration and instead to dispatch each boat to the Atlantic whenever it became ready for operations'.[4]

That in itself was worrying enough for Doenitz. Even more depressing was the increasing number of reports being received from U-boat skippers of torpedo failures. These fell into two categories: the first concerned premature detonations of the magnetic firing pistols, which not only caused an attack to fail but which betrayed the presence of the U-boat and in some cases (when the torpedoes exploded before reaching their safety limit of 250 metres after launching) actually damaged it as well. As a result of this, orders were sent out to fit the contact pistols instead, whereupon repeated failures revealed that many torpedoes were

Supplies to Britain to enable the war to continue included weapons as well as fuel and food – these Halifax dock workers are loading Canadian built Handley Page Hampden bombers for the RAF as deck cargo for a merchant ship in 1941.

(National Library of Canada)

running deeper than they should, due to increased air pressure within a submerged submarine leaking into the torpedoes' depth-keeping mechanisms.

This would not have been a problem had the magnetic pistols worked properly, as these were intended to allow a deeper-running torpedo to explode beneath its target and cause much heavier damage as a result, but in this case the U-boats were experiencing the worst of both worlds. Solving these problems on a consistent basis would take longer than Doenitz could have supposed even in his most pessimistic of moments. Even improved magnetic pistols proved to be no more reliable, and on 21 January 1940 he wrote '. . . at least 25 per cent of the torpedoes fired were failures. Statistics up to 6th January show that 40.9 per cent of misses were due to this cause . . .'[5] Finally, on an occasion when at least one of the torpedoes worked as it should, on the very first day of the new war, the *U*30 scored a spectacular own goal when Oberleutnant Fritz-Julius Lemp sank the liner *Athenia* on the premise that it was either a troopship or an armed merchant cruiser. She was neither, and the loss of 118 people, including twenty-two American citizens, reawakened all the problems of the likely US

reaction encountered in the previous war. Lemp was severely reprimanded and the relevant pages of the boat's log were destroyed, but the damage was done. It would be another year and a quarter before America entered the war, but one immediate effect was a shift in political opinion, which allowed President Roosevelt to push legislation for Lend-Lease through Congress, a measure with incalculable implications for the outcome of the war.

Not that the British themselves could afford to be complacent. For the present, the U-boats were only barely showing their teeth. By the end of 1939, after four months of war, 114 ships in all had been sunk, but only twelve of these had been from the convoys that had been organised from the very outset. Another measure that had been put into operation from the previous war had been the resumption of the British blockade of Germany, which had effectively choked off German merchant trade with neutral countries and seventeen German blockade runners had been captured.[6]

The future promised to be much more difficult, however. The relative failure of the U-boats at the start of the war was due more to German mistakes than Royal Navy successes, though it was true that ten U-boats had been sunk during this period, three of them by greatly improved British mines. If Doenitz was fretting for greater numbers to put his tactics into greater use, his adversaries were even more worried about the shortage of escorts. On paper the numbers looked depressing enough, but when winter storms forced more and more escorts to be taken in for repairs, and with the need for time and resources needed to remedy the shortages in the longer term, then the objective of providing each and every convoy with a well-trained and hard-hitting escort was beginning to seem more and more Utopian.

One particular problem would soon make things considerably worse. Already the German B-Dienst decrypting service, set up in reaction to the post-war revelations of the cipher-cracking triumphs of the British Admiralty's 'Room 40' experts in the previous war (see Chapter 3), had broken several British naval ciphers. These would be invaluable in the submarine war, betraying the whereabouts of British warships and making the interception of merchant convoys considerably easier. But their greatest prize came when the German commerce raider *Atlantis* captured the British steamer *City of Baghdad* in the Indian Ocean on 10 July 1940. A boarding party managed to seize documents that the captain was about to throw overboard, and the Germans were delighted to identify . among them the Allied merchant ships' code. Later captures of other British merchant ships brought in more information to make deciphering easier.

The result of this window into British movements and intentions proved almost priceless. Using the

Rough seas made life difficult for the U-boat crews too, and reduced the visibility needed for spotting convoys in the vastness of the Atlantic.

(US National Archives)

code, Doenitz was able to eavesdrop on plans to reroute convoys clear of known U-boat danger zones, and change the dispositions of the U-boats accordingly. By the time of the most crucial stage of the Atlantic battle (see Chapter 12) the B-Dienst was able to decipher the vital 'U-Boat Situation Report' that was radioed to convoy commanders at sea to tell them about the known and suspected positions of U-boats in their area. Finally, the Allies realised what was happening, and the loophole was belatedly closed.

The reason it was closed relates to one of the most spectacular intelligence triumphs any country has been able to win over its wartime opponents. As in the previous war, the whole U-boat campaign was run on constant radio communications between each submarine and Doenitz's headquarters. This time, however, the content of their messages was protected by the complex and sophisticated Enigma system, which the Germans were convinced could never be broken.

The principle behind Enigma was that each machine operated by changing the cipher relationship between the clear text ('plaintext' to the experts) of a message and its ciphered equivalent, with every successive key stroke of that message. As the sender of the message tapped out the plaintext on a typewriter-like keyboard, electrical impulses were sent through a set of rotor wheels to a plugboard rather like a simplified manual telephone exchange. From there they were fed back through the rotor wheels to a set of indicator lamps, each one indicating a particular character of the cipher text. As the operator typed each character of the plaintext, the sequence of indicator lamps that lit up constituted the cipher text, and this is what was then transmitted over the air. At the receiving end of the signal, an operator would then type the cipher text into an identical Enigma machine, and the sequence of indicator lamps revealed the original plaintext.

The cleverness of the system was not merely the huge variety of possible settings: the rotor wheels were chosen from a set of alternatives, all with different internal wiring to link each with the next, and each could be set to a different starting position, while the plugboard connections could be set up in a host of different combinations. What set the Enigma machine apart was the incorporation of a mechanical linkage that caused each pressing of a key to move on the first rotor by one position. This changed the course followed by the impulses through the machine to the indicator lamps, so that if the operator simply typed the letter 't' three times for example, these actions might light up 'r', 'z' and 'q' because of the movement of the rotor. With a reasonably long text, the rotor would carry out a complete revolution, whereupon the second rotor would then move on one position. When the second rotor completed a full revolution, then the third rotor would move on one position, and so on.

This meant that the set of cipher combinations that could be created on a single Enigma machine was estimated to be some 150,000,000,000,000,000,000, a total so vast as to render practically impossible any attempt to decipher the text without the all-important settings. These were essential so that messages could be correctly sent and then read by those for whom they were intended. For a particular day on a given cipher system (for example, the Kriegsmarine had different ciphers for the North Atlantic, for Home Waters, for messages sent by officers only, for weather reports, for minesweepers and coastal forces, and so on), a setting table would show which rotors should be placed into the machine, their starting positions and the plugboard connections, and armed with this information and an Enigma machine, anyone eavesdropping on the messages could read them easily.

Not surprisingly, the Germans guarded these settings with the greatest care. They were printed on water soluble paper so that simply wetting them rendered them illegible, and if a ship were thought to be in danger of capture, the papers were to be destroyed along with any other secret material, since without them any captured Enigma machine was virtually useless. However, brilliant pre-war work on the Enigma machines done by the Poles and later the French was passed on to the British, who developed powerful computers to enable ciphers to be broken in time, even on partial information. This tough protective shell was progressively chipped away by the experts working at the Government Code and Cipher School at Bletchley Park in Buckinghamshire. It was an astonishing achievement, and it would be made possible by a series of captures of information which echoed the achievements of the German surface raiders with the merchant ships' code.

When *U*33 was sunk while trying to lay mines in the Clyde Estuary on 12 February 1941, one of the rescued ratings was searched and a number of rotors for the Enigma machine were found in one of his pockets. On 4 March a German armed trawler, the *Krebs,* was captured as part of commando raids on the Lofoten Islands off the Norwegian coast. Two months later, another trawler, the German weather ship *Munchen*, was captured east of Iceland, and two days later a boarding party from the destroyer HMS *Bulldog*,

escorting a convoy in mid-Atlantic, took an Enigma machine and its rotors, together with masses of tables and other information, from *U*110 before the submarine later sank under tow.

In the end, the Enigma's strength was also its greatest weakness. Because the Germans insisted there was absolutely no chance of the Allies breaking such heavily protected ciphers, they continued to use the system in spite of worrying signs that perhaps messages were being read. Even when U-boats were intercepted by Allied forces too conveniently to be accounted for by the workings of chance, the tendency was to ascribe these to new technology like radar or direction finding rather than cipher breaking.

The power conferred by this information would prove priceless. Once again, individual U-boats would be identified by their messages and their positions pinpointed by shore-based high-frequency direction-finding (HFDF) stations, so a complete picture could be built up of the disposition of the German submarine force in the Atlantic. Furthermore, as orders went out to set up patrol lines for German wolf packs, once the ciphers were broken, Allied convoys could be diverted or rerouted to avoid the U-boats.

For the moment all that was in the future, and the present was daunting enough. To make the most of the relatively small numbers of available escorts, the Royal Navy was using the methods that had worked well enough in the previous war: escorting convoys through the U-boat danger zone as far as – in this case – the longitude of 15° West of the Greenwich meridian. Then the escorts would sail to rendezvous with an inbound convoy and escort it to its safe arrival in UK ports. This saved on escort time and also on fuel, since the range of some of the destroyers used on convoy protection would also become a major cause for concern.

But the biggest blow to British hopes in the campaign against the U-boats would be struck by events on land rather than at sea. With the German triumph in the Battle of France, which began with attacks on 10 May 1940 and ended with the British Army's evacuation from Dunkirk at the end of that month, the whole face of the U-boat war would change beyond recognition, and become dramatically different from anything the previous war had provided by way of experience. When the French surrendered in June, the whole coast of the European mainland was in German hands from Denmark and Holland, through Belgium to France and eventually to the Spanish border. Within weeks of the Armistice, the U-boat flotillas were setting up bases in French ports on the Biscay coast. No more need for the long cruise around the north of Scotland – German submarines could be in among the convoys within days of leaving on patrol. The anti-submarine war was about to become a great deal harder.

CHAPTER 6

U-BOATS TRIUMPHANT – THE HAPPY TIME
1941

Churchill and Roosevelt brokered a deal for exchanging the leases on British bases in the West Indies for fifty of the US Navy's four-stack destroyers – these British and American sailors are taking part in the handover of the ships in September 1940 at Halifax.

(National Library of Canada)

By dusk on 15 March 1941, the fast eastbound convoy HX112 was shouldering its way into a bitter head-wind as it made its long and dangerous crossing between Halifax and Liverpool with forty-one ships. The weather had eased after the passing of a storm three days before, but a different kind of threat now presented itself as the ships entered an area where U-boats were known to be waiting. Sighting reports had revealed to Doenitz that a succession of westbound convoys had been diverted further to the northwards, closer to Iceland, so that from 10 March the few available U-boats had been diverted northwards too, right into the path of HX112.

When one of the earlier westbound convoys, OB290, was spotted on 26 February, it was by none other than ace Günter Prien in *U47*, the man and the boat that had crept into and out of Scapa Flow in October 1939 and sunk HMS *Royal Oak*. Prien's radio calls brought not only *U99*, skippered by his fellow ace Otto Kretschmer, but a succession of FW200 Kondor long-range maritime bombers. Prien himself sank a Norwegian freighter and a Belgian ammunition ship, while the Kondors sank eight more for a total of 48,337 tons – 8,890 to Prien and 39,447 tons to the aircraft. Kretschmer was unable to find the convoy in thickening fog, but finally succeeded in making a rendezvous with Prien, whereupon Doenitz ordered them to join another type VII, *U70*, and the large minelayer *UA* – originally built for the Turks and seized by the Kriegsmarine at the outbreak of war – to form a patrol line and wait for the next westbound convoy, OB293.

On 6 March Prien spotted the convoy's smoke and radioed the sighting report, which brought in the other U-boats. *U99*, *U70* and *UA* were close enough to respond, but this battle was to be no walkover for the submarines. The thirty-seven-ship convoy, which had sailed from Liverpool four days earlier, had an escort of two destroyers and two corvettes. This was a tough and experienced group, led by Commander James Rowland in HMS *Wolverine*, and they knew exactly how to deal with the meagre group of U-boats attacking them. Unknown to the Germans, the two destroyers *Wolverine* and *Verity* were equipped with the early metre-wavelength type 286 shipborne radar. This would begin stripping away the protection previously enjoyed by U-boats remaining on the surface at night where Asdic could not reach them.

The U-boats sank two ships in the early hours of 7 March: the 6,500-ton British tanker *Athelhampton* was hit by three of Kretschmer's torpedoes, but as she was sailing in ballast she proved unusually difficult to sink. At one point, desperate to save torpedoes for future targets, Kretschmer surfaced and fired with his deck gun, but was finally forced to fire another of his dwindling stock of torpedoes to sink her at last. Another tanker, the much larger 20,000-ton converted whale factory ship *Terje Viken*, had proved equally unsinkable. She was first torpedoed by Prien's *U47* and then finally left in a sinking condition by Kretschmer's *U99* before he switched his attention to the *Athelhampton*. Finally, on 8 March, the 5,200-ton British freighter *Dunaff Head* was damaged by *UA*.[1]

But the escorts hit back hard. All four ships picked up contacts and delivered powerful depth-charge attacks. This was one of the escort groups that had already built up formidable experience of working as a team, and they proved an extremely unpleasant surprise even to practised U-boat crews. One that was less experienced was *U70*, which was on her first patrol. She had been taken unawares by her intended target, another almost unsinkable tanker sailing in ballast, the 7,500-ton Dutch *Mijdrecht*. After hitting her with his last bow tube torpedo, Korvettenkapitan Matz was astonished when the tanker turned towards him and attempted to ram his boat. The Dutchman

Britain's V and W classes of World War One fleet destroyers proved excellent anti-submarine ships except for their short range – until many were converted into Long Range Escorts with torpedo tubes removed along with one of the boiler rooms to provide space for more depth charges and additional fuel.

(www.navyphotos.co.uk)

hit the crash-diving U-boat on the conning tower, causing massive damage though leaving the pressure hull relatively intact. The tanker resumed her place in the convoy, and completed the voyage.

Not so the *U70*. Matz carefully surfaced in a patch of mist to check the damage, but was surprised by the two corvettes, *Arbutus* and *Camellia*. Their new tenacious tactics did more than drive the submarine down and out of the attack. After seven patterns of half a dozen charges apiece, two more patterns finally sealed *U70*'s fate. Taking in water aft, she plunged stern-first to more than 650 feet and only regained the surface by blowing all ballast and abandoning ship, losing more than half her crew.

During the evening of 10 March, another U-boat was heavily attacked by the destroyers. At the time it was believed that this was Prien and *U47*, which was thought to have returned to shadowing the convoy. The U-boat blundered into the destroyers with the passing of a rain squall that left the boat completely

exposed. *Wolverine* turned to attack and her target first tried to run at full speed on the surface. With the destroyer rapidly catching up, the U-boat dived, but a prompt and accurate depth-charge pattern damaged its propellers. By now darkness had fallen and the submarine once again tried surfacing and running, but the noise from the propellers betrayed her position. Back came *Wolverine*, the U-boat dived again, and this time another pattern of depth charges brought the vivid glow of an underwater explosion, and traces of wreckage on the surface.[2]

Was this Prien's final demise? Escort commanders insisted it was, and even if the proof was inconclusive, nothing more was ever heard from the ace of Scapa Flow. Now, however, it was HX112's turn to face the tonnage kings. Kretschmer was about to be joined by the two other surviving aces, Johannes Schepke, in the type VIIB *U100* and Fritz-Julius Lemp in the new long-range IXB *U110*, to find the approaching convoy. In the event, it was Lemp who picked up the propeller noises of the convoy on his hydrophones at 10pm on 15 March. He surfaced and followed the bearing of the hydrophone noises, and two hours later he sent a sighting report.

Normal U-boat tactics required the shadowing boat to maintain that role while other boats summoned to the attack homed in on the signals and carried out the sinkings. In this case, with so few boats available in the North Atlantic, Lemp decided to attack straight away. He approached on the surface, out of the darkness on the starboard side of the convoy, and fired two torpedoes at the 6,000 ton British tanker *Erodina*. Both failed to hit the target so that, still unobserved by the escort, he was able to turn around and fire his stern tube at the target. His third torpedo ran true and triggered a lurid explosion.

HX112 was under the protection of the Fifth Escort Group, led by the formidable figure of Commander Donald Macintyre, who would eventually be responsible for the sinking of no less than seven U-boats. However, his Group had only been formed earlier that month, and this was his first trip in command of HMS *Walker*. He had two more V and W class destroyers, *Vanoc* and *Volunteer*, and two corvettes, *Bluebell* and *Hydrangea*, but on this trip they were reinforced by two more small First World War destroyers, *Sardonyx* and *Scimitar*. However, Macintyre was concerned that his group had had no chance to practise as a team before this voyage, and expected the U-boats would give them a hard time. Now, it appeared, the slaughter was about to begin.

When Lemp's torpedo hit the tanker, the escorts were instantly alert, but a hurried search could find no trace of the submarine, either on Asdic (since she was still on the surface) or even on *Vanoc*'s radar.[3] Lemp himself withdrew into the darkness to reload, and then returned and fired five more torpedoes at the convoy

The Royal Canadian Navy, like the Royal Navy, depended heavily on Flower class corvettes for their escort groups. This is the Canadian built HMCS *Forest Hill.*

(www.navyphotos.co.uk)

an hour later. All missed or malfunctioned and the escort remained unaware of this attack. Through the next day no more attacks were made, until at dusk *Scimitar* spotted a surfaced U-boat ahead of the convoy, and she and *Vanoc* and *Walker* headed off at full speed to investigate and drive the submarine under the surface, while the convoy made an emergency turn to starboard to leave the shadower behind.

The U-boat was Schepke's *U100*, which dived before its pursuers could come within gunnery range, and Asdic failed to pick up an echo. Macintyre headed back to the convoy, leaving the other two destroyers to continue the hunt, and was back in the screen at 10pm, six minutes before another ship was torpedoed.[4] This was followed by five more ships being hit by torpedoes in quick succession. Kretschmer had arrived on the scene. After picking up Lemp's sighting report, Kretschmer had searched for the convoy without success. He had dived twice to listen for propeller noises on the hydrophones, and on the second attempt had realised there were ships all around him. Slowly they came to the surface, only to find themselves inside the escort screen and apparently protected by banks of mist. Kretschmer dived again and let the convoy leave him behind as he took up a shadowing position until darkness, when he could catch up again and attack.

Once it was dark, he slid through a gap in the escort screen, and began firing off all eight remaining torpedoes. His first target was a tanker, which burst into flames and lit up the U-boat in its glare. Kretschmer dived, made his way out through the screen, and then back in the darkness, surfaced again and headed around astern of the convoy to creep back into the centre lanes of ships. Then he travelled within the convoy, carefully firing off one torpedo after another, while the escorts, not realising where he was, blazed away with starshells

and snowflake illuminants outside the convoy. He dropped back and let the convoy leave him behind again, before creeping back between the lines of ships for one final shot from his stern tube.

The results of these confident and considered attacks were devastating. For once all the torpedoes but one worked properly, hitting between them six different ships. Kretschmer believed all were sunk; even though this was not quite right, the tally was remarkable enough, including the 5,728-ton British freighter *Venetia*, the 7,375-ton Canadian freighter *J B White*, two Norwegian tankers, the 6,593-ton *Ferm* and the 8,136-ton *Beduin*, and finally the 6,673-ton Swedish freighter *Korshamn*, with the 9,314-ton British *Franche Comte* damaged. Fortunately for the rest of the convoy, Kretschmer now had no torpedoes left, and he began to prepare to leave the battle and head back for his French base.

The escorts were powerless for the moment. Macintyre was convinced the attacks were coming from the port side of the convoy, and, realising the U-boats were running on the surface, kept searching for any sign of the enemy. Finally, he spotted the wake of a U-boat and went after it at full speed. The U-boat dived and *Walker* dropped a pattern of depth charges on the spot, but though the echo faded there was no evidence of a kill. At 1.30am another underwater echo gave them something to aim at, but this was clearly a cool and experienced skipper who seemed to have little difficulty evading their attacks. Only then did their fortunes change at last. Without warning, *Vanoc* rushed off at high speed, only to signal back that she had rammed and sunk a U-boat.

This was Schepke's *U100*. This had been the U-boat that *Vanoc* and *Walker* had been attacking, and in fact the depth charges had severely damaged their elusive target. At one point, the submarine had plunged to the colossal depth of 750 feet, before the crew's frantic attempts to blow main ballast were successful, and *U100* shot up to the surface. The escorts were lucky in two more respects. *Vanoc* was pointing more or less at the U-boat; even though it was more than half a mile away in the darkness, the submarine was right in the arc covered by *Vanoc*'s type 286 non-directional radar array. This was the echo which had sent her steaming off at full speed.[5]

Aboard *U100* they were having trouble starting either the diesels or the electric motors after the pounding the boat had undergone. *Vanoc* came in like an avenging angel and hit the U-boat broadside on, crushing Schepke against the periscope standards and sending the submarine to the bottom with only six survivors. Another U-boat ace gone, and a third was about to realise at first hand how things were changing in the Atlantic battle.

Kretschmer was nearby, heading out of the battle on the surface when one of his bridge lookouts made

Escorts protecting Atlantic convoys had to be able to fight off air attack as well as the U-boat threat.

(National Library of Canada)

a fatal mistake. He failed to spot the two destroyers close by, and when the officer of the watch realised how close they were, he assumed they must have been spotted, and ordered *U*99 to crash dive. In fact *Vanoc*'s crew were busy checking the hull for damage from ramming *U*100, and *Walker* was reloading depth-charge racks and throwers from the magazine ready for more attacks. Only when *U*99 slid below the surface did she produce an Asdic contact once again, and *Walker*'s operator confirmed an echo below *Vanoc*'s stern. At first Macintyre was inclined to assume this was due to disturbed water from their earlier attacks, but the Asdic operator was adamant that it was a good solid contact. With half a dozen charges loaded, *Walker* dropped them on the echo.

It was enough. *Vanoc* reported a U-boat surfacing astern, and both ships opened up with their main armament. A signal lamp on the U-boat sent in garbled English 'We are sunking' and the destroyers ceased fire and began hauling the Germans out of the sea. To Macintyre's delight, the last man to climb over *Walker*'s rail, still wearing his white-covered skipper's cap was the most successful U-boat captain of the war, Otto Kretschmer. Three of Doenitz's most able commanders had been taken out of the fight. With Kretschmer's capture and the sinking of *U*99, all HX112's troubles were over, and the remaining ships reached their destination safely.

For Karl Doenitz, facing the loss of his three greatest

aces in quick succession, this was truly the end of the honeymoon that had begun with his U-boats' move to their French bases in the summer of 1940. For the intervening nine months, his crews had used their superb training, backed by a high degree of confidence, to put his tactics into practice to the utmost of their considerable ability. With some shining exceptions, the escorts had been inexperienced and overwhelmed by the U-boat attacks, and for too long they had remained unaware of three vital points. The reason the U-boats were not showing up on their Asdic sweeps around the beleaguered convoys was that they were manoeuvring and attacking on the surface, where they could move more quickly than the corvettes that formed the backbone of most escort groups. Furthermore, the small silhouette of the conning tower of a trimmed-down U-boat was almost impossible to spot on a dark night. Finally, the coolest and most expert U-boat commanders were able to find their way through the escort screens to the innermost columns of the convoys, where targets were most plentiful and they were safest from the searchlight and snowflake rockets of the escorts desperately searching for them outside the convoy.

At their best, these tactics had served the Germans well. Convoy after convoy was savaged as the escorts had to extend their operations further and further west. At first it had been safe for escorts to leave west-bound convoys and meet eastbound convoys at the

15° West meridian, but with the extra range conferred by the Biscay bases, the U-boats were able to move further into the Atlantic in search of undefended targets. In July 1940, the escort coverage was extended to 17° West, or effectively 300 miles to the west of Ireland, and in October this was extended to 19° West. This had the inevitable effect of increasing demands on the limited numbers of escorts, and in particular on their range. With many of the ships, fuel tank capacity was so restricted that maintaining this kind of coverage prevented them from zigzagging for their own protection and ordering too many drastic alterations of the convoy course to evade U-boats lying in wait along its track.

This meant that tankers had to sail with convoys to top up the tanks of the escort vessels, but the techniques for refuelling at sea were in their infancy and called for careful manoeuvring and good weather. A more effective expedient was the rebuilding of several of the First World War fleet destroyers of the V and W classes. In their original form their range was insufficient to get across the Atlantic without refuelling, since they were designed for operations in Home Waters and the North Sea. Twenty-two of these ships were modified by having one of their three boilers removed and replaced by extra fuel storage. This gave a useful increase in range at the expense of overall speed, but still left them fast enough to cope with convoy escort and hunting U-boats.

Doenitz himself was suffering from the effects of a tonnage war every bit as suffocating as that he was trying to impose on the Allies, except that in his case it was warship tonnage rather than merchant shipping. He still had far too few operational U-boats for the task he had set them. The most astonishing fact about the HX112 battle that saw the end of the tonnage kings was that the entire strength of the North Atlantic U-boat force was down to just six boats. Because the Luftwaffe needed accurate and up-to-date weather reports two of them had had to be detached to monitor weather conditions in the Atlantic, at one point removing between them one-third of the German submarine strength. Though reinforcements had been sent, the loss of four boats sunk and two returning to base heavily damaged meant the U-boat force in the North Atlantic was still a matter of single figures.

When the war first began, Doenitz commanded a force of thirty-nine operational U-boats, which included twenty-two ocean-going type VIIs and IXs. Instead of his target of 300 needed to win a tonnage war, all he had been promised at that stage was an increase in numbers to 162, by Hitler's planned date for the opening of hostilities of the summer of 1948. Although the fact that Germany had been at war with Britain for a year and a half – whatever the Führer's original intentions – had boosted the construction efforts, this would take time to be translated into more operational boats at the Biscay bases.

At the same time the British were increasing their numbers of escorts. During the summer of 1940, it had been all too common for convoys of some thirty ships to be provided with but a single escort.[6] Since

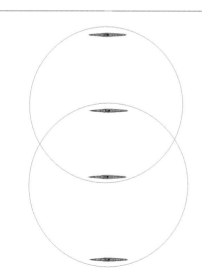 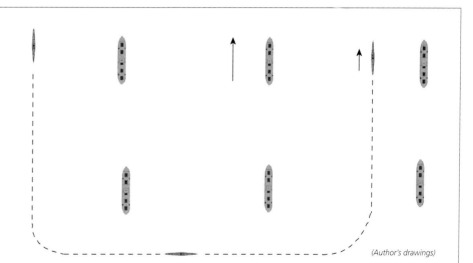

(Author's drawings)

U-boat patrol line (not to scale): submarines patrol in line abreast towards the estimated position of an approaching convoy, with the spacing between different boats governed by the limits of their range of visibility – up to 20 miles in good conditions, but much less in poor weather.

Otto Kretschmer's tactic for infiltrating a convoy for night attacks on the surface. After finding a gap in the escort screen, he would make for the rear of the convoy and then make his way between the columns of ships inside the convoy before firing torpedoes at as many tempting targets as possible. Until they realised where he was, the escorts would assume he was firing from outside the convoy and hunt for him in vain while he simply dived and let the convoy leave him behind while he reloaded, before repeating the tactic to deliver further attacks.

then, more corvettes had joined the fleet and hopes for the future were improving. A deal negotiated between Churchill and Roosevelt had leased bases in the Caribbean to the USA in exchange for fifty old four-stack US Navy destroyers, of similar vintage to the V and W classes that were shouldering much of the burden of the North Atlantic battle. Though extremely welcome at a time when potential escorts were desperately needed, these ships' narrow beam meant they were prone to roll viciously in heavy weather, and their lack of manoeuvrability made them difficult to handle when trying to hunt down a resourceful U-boat skipper attempting to evade their attacks.

Doenitz's submariners achieved a great deal. In the first five months of operating from the Biscay harbours, they had sunk almost 1.4 million tons of Allied shipping. Yet in spite of the quick adoption of convoying from almost the first day of the war, more than half the 282 ships lost had been sailing independently or were stragglers. Only 102, or 36 per cent of the losses, were sunk in escorted convoys using the combination of night attacks on the surface from within the convoy's ranks. Among this total, some convoys had suffered particularly badly: HX72 had lost six ships out of forty-seven for a total of 42,000 tons – all but one of them to the combination of Prien, Schepke and Kretschmer – in September 1940. In the following month, HX79 lost ten, totalling almost 60,000 tons, all but three to the three aces once again. In the same month the slower convoy SC7 lost almost half the merchant ships – fifteen out of thirty-four – for a total of more than 60,000 tons, including five to Kretschmer and one to Schepke.

By this time it was clear to the British that their tactical assumptions were deeply flawed. Instead of the problem being similar to the one they had faced at the worse times in the previous war, where they desperately needed a means of locating and attacking a submerged submarine, they had been entirely wrong-footed. U-boats attacking on the surface in darkness were immune to detection, and too fast for most of the escorts to catch if they did detect them.

In time, faster escorts with heavier weapons and better detection equipment would put matters right. For the moment, there were two urgent priorities: to meet force with force, and to fight back against the groups of U-boats attacking a convoy with an escort group whose ships invariably operated together and who could develop tactics for a faster and more effective response. The second was to produce a means of detecting surfaced submarines at night. Both those factors had proved decisive in ending the careers of the three tonnage kings in the pitched battles of March 1941.

For Doenitz, the job became more difficult too. Even though more and more U-boats began to join the operational fleet from the spring of 1941 onwards, the number of merchant ship sinkings actually fell. Some historians (predominantly British and American) have suggested this was a reflection of a drop in morale and effectiveness that resulted from the loss of Prien, Schepke and Kretschmer. After all, if commanders with this much courage, experience and luck could be defeated by the escorts, what hope was there for those who followed them into the battle? Most German sources deny this was a factor. One remarkable statistical truth remains; for all the U-boat commanders' strong dedication to their duty, which saw them endure a casualty rate of some 75 per cent during the course of the war, it was only a small minority of them who inflicted real damage on the enemy. Thirty U-boat skippers, or some two per cent of the overall total, all of them highly trained and experienced pre-war men, inflicted 30 per cent of the losses. Fourteen of those were responsible for almost 20 per cent of losses between them. Perhaps even more remarkably, at the opposite end of the spectrum, 850 U-boats, or around three-quarters of those commissioned during the course of the war, never so much as damaged a single Allied merchant ship.[7] For Doenitz, trying desperately to turn around a faltering campaign, some new boost was clearly needed. As 1941 reached its end, he and his U-boat men were about to find it.

CHAPTER 7

DRUMBEAT

1941–42

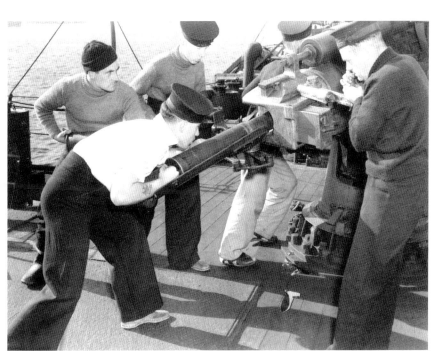

Crew carrying out gun drill
aboard a defensively armed
merchant ship (DEMS) at
Halifax, Nova Scotia, on
29 November 1942.
(National Library of Canada)

THE first of six long-range U-boats to make the long passage from Europe to the eastern seaboard of the United States was the large minelayer *U*151. After a passage of almost five weeks, she began laying minefields off the bays of the Chesapeake and the Delaware to disrupt the vital coastal trade routes. A small tanker hit one of her mines off Delaware, though the damaged ship was later salvaged, and the German submarine managed to sink a total of nine small ships on her way northwards over the next eleven days. By then, however, the American reaction was swift. Within nine days of her first sinking, orders had been sent out to marshal merchant shipping along the coast into escorted convoys, and for all unprotected merchantmen to make for safe ports immediately. Plans were made to extend convoys as far as Florida and the Caribbean, air-raid sirens were set up in New York City and a partial black-out instituted.

Another minelayer, *U*156, joined *U*151 a month later. One of her mines sank the cruiser USS *San Diego* off the Long Island shore, and the submarine later captured a Canadian trawler, put a prize crew on board and used her as an armed tender to help in attacking merchant vessels. Four more U-boats, *U*140, *U*117, *U*152 and *U*155 joined the campaign over the following three months, and between them they sank a total of ninety-three ships, more than half of them American.

The story so far sounds familiar: the German response to the outbreak of war with America being delivered by U-boat attacks and merchant ship sinkings along her eastern seaboard. But this was 1918, not 1942, and it proved a different proposition altogether. Not only were the ships mostly small and not very valuable as targets, two-thirds of them sailing vessels or fishing boats, but the US response was both brisk and effective. Apart from commissioning extra patrol boats and escorts, the institution of convoys quickly and decisively robbed the U-boats of most of their potential targets, and within a matter of weeks, they had been recalled across the Atlantic, back to their distant bases as the war sank into its final phase.

This was another example of how the defeated Germans learned the harsh lessons of war better than the victorious Allies, as they did with the introduction of the tank. When the two nations once again found themselves at war, twenty-three years later, the U-boats returned in force, and with more powerful weapons. America would not merely have forgotten the measures that worked so well before, but her leaders would deliberately set their faces against them, resulting in losses and catastrophe on an appalling scale.

America's entry into the war, when Hitler quixotically decided to support his Japanese allies' attack on Pearl Harbor by a unilateral declaration of hostilities against the United States, gave the U-boats both a new challenge and a new opportunity. Already, Roosevelt's

Tankers like the
uss *Pennsylvania Sun*,
torpedoed by *U*571 on
15 July 1942 were high-
value targets, specially
vulnerable to submarine
attacks – the devoted efforts
of this salvage crew saved
her to be repaired and
returned to service.

(US National Archives)

far-sighted decision to give Britain 'every assistance short of war' had led to US Navy warships escorting convoys over the western part of their route, and there had been several clashes between US destroyers and U-boats, culminating in the loss of the uss *Reuben James*, torpedoed while escorting eastbound convoy HX156 on 29 October 1941, with the loss of 115 of her crew. Now the Allies would enjoy the stupendous shipbuilding resources of the United States, making Doenitz's tonnage war an even more difficult campaign to win.

However, that was still a longer-term objective. For the present, the lack of efficient black-out along the US coast and the absence of a local convoy system, together with a shortage of escorts, gave the Germans their greatest opportunity to cripple Allied merchant traffic.

However, the conditions under which Doenitz was able to mount his carefully planned operation against the US coast in response to the official opening of hostilities against the US on 11 December 1941 was severely limited. The Naval Staff in Berlin had deprived him of U-boats to be sent to the waters around Gibraltar to sink British troop transports rushing reinforcements to the Middle East for an offensive against Rommel's troops in North Africa. He asked for a dozen boats to send to the American coast, but the Staff only allowed him six, of which one – the newly commissioned *U*128 – had to be withdrawn because of mechanical problems. The remaining five – like *U*128 all type IXBs and IXCs and commanded by experienced and successful skippers

– were split into two small groups.

The larger was *Gruppe Hardegen*, comprising the type IXB *U*123, commanded by Kapitänleutnant Reinhard Hardegen, a sister boat *U*125 commanded by Kapitänleutnant Ulrich Folkers and the IXC *U*66, commanded by Korvettenkapitan Richard Zapp. These boats were ordered to head for the US coast while the smaller two-boat *Gruppe Bleichrodt*, consisting of the type IXB *U*109, skippered by Kapitänleutnant Heinrich Bleichrodt and the IXC *U*130 captained by Korvettenkapitan Ernst Kals, were to head further north to strike Canadian waters southeast of the convoy port of Halifax and in Cabot Strait off Cape Breton Island. Another type IXC, *U*502, also set out for the USA, but the boat developed a heavy oil leak that betrayed her position by leaving a huge slick, so she had to return to base for repairs to be carried out.

To make the maximum impact, Doenitz wanted these five remaining long-range boats to start attacks on the same day – later identified as 13 January 1942 – and this was the reason for the operational name of *Paukenschlag*, usually translated as 'Drumbeat', which can imply a repeated beating of a drum. The German term usually implies a single massive blow, borne out by the fact that later attacks by additional boats did not carry the same operational name. However, the planned synchronisation failed to work for two reasons. The Admiralty's Submarine Tracking Room was monitoring the progress of the boats by their radio transmissions, and kept the US Navy informed. The US Navy Commander-in-Chief, Admiral Ernest King, attempted to meet the threat by withdrawing US destroyers from Atlantic waters and stationing them in bases in the coastal areas threatened by the U-boats' approach.

The second cause for the failure of Drumbeat's synchronisation was that the submarines did not all reach their destinations by the appointed day, and in fact Hardegen himself opened the campaign on the 11 January – two days early – by sinking a 9,076-ton British freighter 300 miles east of Cape Cod. Three days later, and 240 miles closer to the US coast, he sank a 9,577-ton Norwegian tanker sixty miles east of Long Island, and at 11pm EST on 15 January he approached the Ambrose Channel Lightship at the entrance to New York Harbor, with seven US destroyers in the port unaware of his presence. He then turned out to sea again, sinking a 6,800-ton British tanker on the way.

So began three weeks of easy targets and little opposition for the three U-boats and their crews, who settled into a relatively undemanding routine of resting on the bottom during the daytime hours and surfacing and heading for the coastal shipping lanes as night fell. They ranged south to Cape Hatteras and marked their targets by seeing them outlined against the brilliant lights of shore communities. Soon they were joined by the other two boats who had found conditions off Canada much less attractive, with cold weather and alert air patrols and surface escorts.

The easiest pickings were found off Cape Hatteras, where the deeper water for daytime refuge was closer to the inshore shipping routes. So many ships were being sunk by this small group of U-boats – smaller than many packs assembled to attack a single convoy in mid-ocean – that Doenitz decided to reinforce success and send every additional boat after them. Three more long-range type IXs were sent to the US coast before the first boats began their return voyage and after two type VIIs succeeded in extending their range far enough to join the distant battle, more were sent as they became available.

Given that the United States had been taken by surprise by Pearl Harbor and the additional twist of being faced with a German submarine attack off their own shores within six weeks of the Japanese strike, it may seem reasonable for their naval defences to have been caught off guard. In fact, they faced many of the same problems as the British, from a combination of lack of resources and wrong tactical decisions.

Like the British, the US Navy had decided before Pearl Harbor that destroyers could only be used as stopgap ASW vessels, as they were expensive, they were

Another US tanker, the *Robert C Tuttle,* torpedoed by *U*701 on 22 June 1942 was saved and repaired.
(US National Archives)

faster than they needed to be, and most important of all, they would be forced to meet too many commitments supporting major fleet units and escorting troop convoys. Admiral King had suggested they produce more of the Treasury class coast guard cutters, but these were turned down by both Roosevelt and the navy as being too big, too slow and too expensive, although several used on Atlantic convoy escorts by both the US and Royal navies proved highly suitable for the job.

For the time being, there was nothing to replace them. Several US historians, including Professor

Morison, have blamed the US Navy for the problem, but Admiral King laid responsibility at the president's door for what he saw as his fixation with small sub-chasers that simply could not cope with tough Atlantic conditions. Fortunately, another option had arisen in early 1941, when one of the senior assistant US naval attaches in London, Edward L Cochrane, an experienced naval engineer, returned to Washington to take over the Bureau of Ships. On 1 February, he asked his design staff to begin work on a larger version of the basic British ASW frigate design, with which he was already familiar. With the overall length increased from 290 feet to 306, and the displacement up from 1,100 tons to 1,400 tons and speed from twenty-one knots to 23.5 knots, this became the basis for the US destroyer escort or DE.[1]

All this boded well for the future. DEs would prove invaluable for both Allied navies, from escorting convoys to protecting the anti-submarine carrier task groups, but none would be completed before 1943. The problem for the present was the large number of valuable and unprotected ships being sunk off America's coastal towns and cities.

Here the Americans repeated another fundamental British error. Given the scarcity of capable escort vessels when hostilities began, they compounded the problem by using many of those they had in the target area for wasteful and unproductive offensive patrols. A second British mistake, dating back to the previous war, had been the reluctance to embrace the restrictions of the convoy system for the protection it offered merchant ships. At the time, a powerful voice in favour of the measure had been the American Admiral Sims, but in this case his countrymen repeated the British mistake of the earlier war, for rather different reasons.

In the US Navy, from Admiral King downwards, the necessity of organising the coastal traffic into convoys was accepted as a vital necessity. Where the mistake seems to have been made was in thinking that, for the time being, an inadequately escorted convoy was worse than no convoy at all. British experience in the previous war had shown that grouping merchant ships into convoys made it much less likely that the U-boats would find them in the first place. Whether or not this inbuilt protection would have been so reliable in confined coastal waters was perhaps arguable, but the fact remains that it took a full four months of steady losses before full coastal convoys were introduced in mid-May 1942.

During that period, various stop-gaps were used. Merchant ships waited in protected anchorages over the dangerous dark hours, used inland stretches of the coastal waterways wherever possible and were shepherded with naval escort past particularly vulnerable stretches like the waters around Cape Hatteras. Air patrols were used to drive the U-boats into deeper

The seas boil under the impact of a depth charge pattern launched in attacking a U-boat. Operational researchers concluded that hundreds were detonated for every submarine sunk.

(US Naval Institute Press)

water, and the arming of merchant ships was quickly organised. The other responses to the proximity of U-boats to the US coast was the formation of civilian coastal picket patrols to give warning of the presence of a submarine in a particular area, reinforced by the sailing vessels of what was officially termed the Corsair Fleet, but which was known to its members as the 'Hooligan Navy', and total black-outs of coastal lights were introduced. But the most eloquent confirmation of the value of the belated introduction of full coastal convoys came with the U-boats' response. They moved immediately to the still relatively unprotected targets to be found in the Caribbean and the Gulf of Mexico, and when convoying was extended to these waters by July, the toll of sinkings dropped sharply as a result.

Throughout this period, Doenitz's hopes had been raised by the successes of his U-boat men, but dashed by the decisions of his own Naval Staff. In February 1942, twenty of the U-boats on which he was relying to maintain the North American campaign at full stretch were taken to form a seaborne defence line

off Norway in response to Hitler's fears that the Allies might try to land on his northernmost possessions. Yet the truth was that even those boats would have made very little difference. The entry of the United States into the war had put the tonnage campaign well beyond the U-boats' capabilities. And even as their numbers climbed, their losses increased too. Thirty-two had been lost during the first seven months of 1942, eleven of them in July alone.

Nevertheless, during that period the total U-boat strength had climbed to almost 350 boats, providing the option of more and more substantial groups to put the wolf-pack tactics into operation against more convoys as more and more of these boats completed their training and arrived at the French bases. Against them were increasing numbers of escort vessels, now armed with better weapons and better tactics. The pace of the Atlantic battle was promising to quicken substantially.

For the British, the U-boat campaign off the American coast had brought a slackening in convoy attacks, which allowed them to set up better training facilities for the new escorts, and develop more effective tactics for new and experienced alike. All newly commissioned escort vessels were now being given a prolonged two- or three-week working-up period at HMS *Western Isles.* This was a shore base at the beautiful harbour of Tobermory on the Isle of Mull, off Scotland's west coast, commanded by the hard-bitten Commodore (later Vice-Admiral Sir) Gilbert 'Monkey' Stephenson. There new and inexperienced ships' companies were challenged by every kind of emergency without warning, to prepare them for the unexpected at sea.[2]

For the escort captains, the establishment of the Western Approaches Tactical Unit in the same Derby House location as Western Approaches Command itself was run by a former destroyer captain and gunnery specialist Commander Gilbert Roberts, who had originally been invalided out of the navy with tuberculosis in 1937. Before this, he had become something of a tactical specialist, and one of his analyses demonstrated the right tactics for a hunting group of three cruisers to deal with a German pocket battleship, which was very much the plan followed by Commodore Harwood in the Battle of the River Plate against the *Admiral Graf Spee* in December 1939.

Recalled to duty in March 1940, Roberts served in a series of low-level jobs until he was ordered in January 1942 to set up a unit to analyse German tactics and advise how best to cope with them. Facing official scepticism at first, he turned for advice to escort commanders about the realities of convoy warfare. He asked them about the tactics they used, and was surprised that only one of those present had a clear idea of what to do when attacked; this commander was 'Johnny' Walker, then on a spell of shore duty between escort commands.

He replied, that on the code-word 'Buttercup' over the radio, all escorts would immediately turn outwards, increase to full speed, fire starshell for twenty minutes, and then return to station if nothing was seen. Walker had in fact sunk two U-boats by this tactic whilst escorting convoy HG76 (see Chapter 8). On this and other occasions, Roberts gathered all the information he could from those with first-hand experience at sea.[3]

In the meantime, the method for teaching tactics was also put together, using the lowest of low-tech materials and equipment. Essentially, a convoy, its escorts and the attacking U-boats would be represented by simple models on a floor display covered by a grid to give distances and bearings, on a scale of ten inches to the mile. Officers under training would be confined to cubicles screened from most of the action to represent what they would actually be aware of during a convoy action, and the battle would be run by a dedicated and increasingly expert team of young Wrens. Each officer was given a plotting table, a bunch of signal forms and chits to order movements and actions, which were passed to the Wrens to put them into effect.

Using these basic arrangements, it would prove simple to create all kinds of tactical situations and even review genuine actions. For the time being, Roberts tackled the other part of his duty, to assess the kind of tactics that should be taught using his war-game setup. They began with Walker's classic action with HG76, and put a series of detailed questions to other officers of the escort on that occasion. Before long, he became aware that the only way of accounting for events when closely analysed was to assume that the submarine had penetrated the escort screen and attacked from inside the convoy, since the limitation of the maximum range of German torpedoes meant this was the only position that would make sense. Nevertheless, this was against all tactical doctrine at the time, and it was only by calling the Flag Officer Submarines in London for advice from a submariner's viewpoint, that his hunch was confirmed.[4]

Once this was assumed, there remained the question of how the U-boat reached this position. Only four possibilities made apparent sense. If it entered from ahead on the surface, the relative speed would be the sum of the convoy speed and the U-boat speed, which would have been too fast for a considered attack. If it had surfaced in the middle of the convoy, it would be too easy to emerge too near an escort where the noise and splash of surfacing would bring swift retribution. If it broke in from the flanks on the surface, the danger of being spotted by lookouts would be too great. Only if it entered the convoy ranks from astern at a slow enough speed to keep the wake to a minimum – say twelve knots – would the chance of being spotted be reduced, since most lookouts

ignored what was astern of them, and this would allow time to plan and launch a series of attacks.

The next question was, how would the U-boat escape after completing the attack? The only feasible tactic was to submerge, dive deep and stay as silent as possible as the convoy passed overhead. Once it was clear, the U-boat could reload torpedoes and catch up the convoy on the surface and then repeat the tactic, exactly as Kretschmer had done with HX211. What could be done to deal with this? Roberts and his colleagues worked through the attack on the plot and decided that the escort ahead of the convoy should remain in position, but the others on a coded word of command should turn through 180 degrees and head for the rear of the convoy at full speed in line abreast before slowing to carry out an Asdic sweep. With luck, this might catch the U-boat responsible for the attack, when conventional tactics of hunting on either side of the convoy would not.

When the escort officers were shown the tactic, they soon realised they had a potential battle winner on their hands. Asked what it should be called, one of the Wrens suggested it was something of a raspberry to Hitler and the U-boats, and the 'Raspberry' tactic it became. On the orders of the commander-in-chief, Roberts was promoted acting captain, and the process of developing new tactical manoeuvres would continue, along with the training of escort commanders.

Another highly successful tactic was the 'Beta Search'. This arose from a conversation with another highly experienced escort officer, Commander Tait of HMS *Harvester* and B3 Escort Group (later killed when his ship was torpedoed after ramming and sinking *U444* in the battle for convoy HX228 in 1943). He had noticed that single U-boats were often sighted ahead of the convoy or on one or other beam, and these would not dive to safety straight away but would stay in view while presumably reporting on the convoy's position, course and speed. Monitoring radio traffic had shown that some two hours after the U-boat finally dived there would be a transmission from close to the convoy prefixed by the Morse character B-bar or 'Beta'.

Roberts's response was that this was almost certainly the sighting report, and if the escorts took care to read a HFDF bearing[5] on the message, they could then follow the bearing at full speed to force it to dive, when the convoy would make a drastic change of course to lose the shadowing U-boat. It might also be also possible to go further and actually sink the U-boat, removing the threat permanently. The Beta Search tactic was calculated to do just this. Instead of responding to the message immediately, Roberts was convinced that it was better if the U-boat commander was unaware that he and his message had been spotted. Instead, Roberts concluded the only logical course for the U-boat was to stay submerged until it was dark enough to catch up with the convoy and penetrate the screen from astern, to save the drain on his batteries.

Therefore all the escorts had to do was to maintain their course until the submarine had dived to make its approach to the stern of the convoy. Once it was below the surface, they could safely turn and head for its estimated position at slow underwater speed, while their noise was masked by the propellers of the convoy behind them. The first the U-boat would realise of the danger it was in was when depth charges started exploding around it. Within weeks the Beta Search tactic had been used successfully, resulting in the sinking of a shadowing U boat, and turning the tables with a vengeance.

One by one other routines and tactics were developed, under names like 'Strawberry', 'Artichoke', 'Gooseberry' and 'Pineapple'. The last named was intended to deal with a group of U-boats lying in wait ahead of a convoy. Once the signs indicated that this was the case, through radio bearings or aircraft reports

or signals from the Admiralty, then the escorts leading the convoy would go to full speed and head out as far as four miles from their usual station, firing starshell all the time. This would drive the U-boats under, though the escorts would be moving too fast to pick up anything on their Asdics. The U-boats would then retire quietly for the time being, scared off by the show of force, but the sterner spirits among them might then decide to attack the convoy from ahead, as they were within the escort screen. But the second part of 'Pineapple' involved turning back towards the convoy and moving much more slowly, to pick up Asdic echoes and sink any venturesome U-boats intending to try to attack.

'Artichoke' was a variation on the theme, in response to a ship being torpedoed. The escort patrolling astern of the convoy was to close the torpedoed ship at maximum Asdic speed, while the escorts ahead of the convoy would turn immediately on to a reciprocal course and head in line abreast at fifteen knots or at the maximum Asdic sweeping speed of the slowest ship. The escorts on the outer wings of this formation would aim to pass just outside the convoy wake, with the inner ships passing between the columns of the convoy, until they reached a line 6,000 yards astern of the position of the convoy at the time the ship was torpedoed, placing them in an ideal position to catch an attacker escaping from inside the convoy.

Even when the Germans introduced their sophisticated *Zaunkönig* homing torpedo,[6] the Tactical School studied the reports of its use, and came up with an effective counter-tactic under the name 'Stepaside'. This was the result of an astonishing process of deduction. Roberts had concluded that the hydrophones controlling the course of the torpedo covered an arc of 60 degrees ahead. Furthermore, he assumed that the U-boat firing the weapon would be aware of the course of the convoy and would therefore aim the torpedo ahead of its target to take this into account, before leaving the homing mechanism to take over. Stepaside simply exploited this. On detecting a U-boat that might have acoustic torpedoes, the escort was to turn back through some 150 degrees to put the U-boat at 60 degrees on the opposite bow. After continuing on this course for a mile at fifteen knots, which experience had shown was too slow to attract a *Zaunkönig*, the escort was to turn on to the initial sighting bearing for another mile, leaving itself outside the acquisition arc of the weapon, and then turn towards the position of the U-boat and attack once its echo was acquired. Once this tactic was circulated amongst the escorts, sinkings by acoustic torpedoes dwindled away, and U-boat sinkings increased still further.

With more and more U-boats at sea, clever tactics and high-quality training for the escorts would be increasingly important. But the escorts' strong suit

US Navy four stack destroyer uss *Roper* on convoy escort duty.
(US Naval Institute Press)

Following America's entry into the war, more convoys were protected by US warships, like this US Coast Guard Cutter uscG *Spencer*.
(US Naval Institute Press)

was that the battle was always primarily between the U-boats and the merchant ships. What this meant in the anti-submarine campaign was that the growing experience among escort commanders was an appreciating asset, while the U-boat commanders with the greatest experience were invariably in the greatest danger. Once they were caught, they were usually killed or taken prisoner, and their knowledge lost to their comrades. As the U-boat war moved into its decisive and critical phase, this would increasingly become a fight to the finish.

Crucial to the outcome of this battle would be the new weapons being made available to the escort forces. Two of those would play a decisive part: HFDF or 'Huff-Duff' and radar. HFDF (high-frequency direction-finding) was simple in principle, allowing a receiver to determine the bearing of any radio signal picked up by the equipment. Every time a U-boat sent a message, HFDF could determine the bearing of the signal. Where two or more HFDF receivers in different locations picked up the same signal, plotting the bearings would give the position from which the signal was transmitted.

At first the bulky HFDF equipment was installed in shore-based listening stations. Paymaster Lieutenant Norman Denning (later Vice-Admiral Sir Norman

Denning, KBE, CD, Director of Naval Intelligence) had been appointed head of the Royal Navy's newly established Operational Intelligence Centre in May 1937, and was instrumental in the setting up of a network that had DF receivers at stations in the UK, at Gibraltar, at Freetown in West Africa, at Cape Town and on Ascension Island, Iceland, Newfoundland and Bermuda. With distant radio transmissions being reflected by the layers of charged particles in the upper atmosphere to the point where they could be picked up by the shore stations hundreds of miles away, this offered the opportunity of pinpointing the positions of any U-boat that transmitted a message back to headquarters.

In practice, it was not that simple. Operators needed training and experience to reduce the initial high level of errors, and it was essential that the chain of stations included those placed to give bearings that intersected at angles to give a precise estimate of the transmitter's position.[7] In time, results improved dramatically, to the point that whenever a U-boat transmission was intercepted, bearings were taken by different stations and relayed to a co-ordinating station at Scarborough, which sent the results to the Submarine Tracking Room at the Admiralty. When the bearings were plotted on a map, using measurements from between three and six stations, the transmitting U-boat's position could be plotted to within twenty-five miles. This produced a picture of where the U-boats were on any given day, and allowed convoys to be given evasive routings, even when Enigma signals could not be read.

Technical improvements made the system still more formidable. Professor Deloraine, a French radio researcher, had developed a means of converting a brief signal intercept into a persistent trace on a cathode-ray-tube screen, and he and two of his co-workers had escaped to America as the Germans occupied his home country. He took with him his work on the display of signal intercepts, and this was used in the setting up of American HFDF stations on both the Atlantic and Pacific seaboards. On the east coast, there were seven stations from Maine down to Puerto Rico. At first, U-boat positions could be fixed to the nearest two hundred miles, but new equipment greatly improved this accuracy.

However, the real breakthrough came with fitting of HFDF aboard escort vessels. This gave real-time information on the whereabouts of U-boats in a convoy battle, and the first shipborne prototype FH1 set and aerial were fitted to HMS *Hesperus* as early as May 1940. Improved versions were being fitted to more and more escorts by 1941, with a faster and more accurate response, displayed on a plan position indicator (PPI) map-type screen giving an instant readout of the transmission's bearing relative to the ship's course at the time.

Once sufficient vessels carried HFDF to have more than one in an escort group, it became possible to plot the U-boat's position as well as its bearing, telling the escort group commander whether it was close enough to make an attack worthwhile. By the spring of 1943, at least two escorts in every group had this equipment,

and were able to monitor the whereabouts of U-boats within a range of up to twenty-five miles, considerably greater than even shipborne radar could offer, though radar could at least keep watch on a U-boat even when it was not transmitting.

There were two supreme advantages to HFDF. First of all, it exploited the U-boat's Achilles heel – its over dependence on radio signals – so precisely. Secondly, the U-boats were not persuaded to change their methods, since they assumed, as with so much other Allied development, from breaking the Enigma ciphers to inventing centimetric radar, that shipboard HFDF was impossible, because their own technical experts had been unable to solve the problems. Initially the Germans were convinced that the Allies could only use direction-finding equipment on medium-frequency signals, so that their own high-frequency signals could not be picked up. Later, when they suspected these might become vulnerable, they briefed U-boat skippers to send brief snatches of a signal in between changes in frequency to avoid allowing eavesdroppers to pinpoint the transmitter. Unfortunately, these changes were announced to U-boats at sea through Enigma-enciphered signals, and when these were being read by the Allies, Huff-Duff operators were able to pre-empt the transmission changes to pick up the whole signal.

HFDF's active stablemate was shipborne radar. The first 1.5-metre wavelength type 286 sets were fitted to escorts in the autumn of 1940. Though its performance was relatively disappointing, sweeping a fixed arc ahead of the vessel carrying it, its successor was a great deal better. Within six months, the type 271 centimetric radar was being fitted to escort vessels. This used the same cavity magnetron valve which was at the heart of the airborne search radar used to find and attack U-boats from the air (and the H2S target-finding radar demanded by Bomber Command) to generate a narrow and extremely precise beam at a wavelength of 9.7 centimetres.

This could pick out a U-boat's conning tower at ranges of between five and eight miles, and could even in the right conditions pick up the echo of a sub-merged U-boat's periscope searching for its prey. An additional and valuable advantage was that, just as with the airborne centimetric radar, the Germans did not realise such technology was possible and therefore did not undertake the relatively easy task of devel-oping a search receiver to warn U-boats when they were appearing on an escort's radar scope. Where Asdic pulses were all too audible to the crew of a submerged U-boat unable to escape and waiting for the charges to be dropped around them, the radar search was silent and unsuspected, but the weapons that were delivered as a result were just as lethal. Now, to this increasingly deadly array of threats to the U-boats would be added the most lethal submarine killer of all, to be reviewed in the next chapters of the book.

The US coast guard cutters – this one is USCG *Spencer* seen from the deck of her sister ship USCG *Duane* on convoy escort duty – proved capable and seaworthy ships which were a much valued asset in the Atlantic campaign.

(US Naval Institute Press)

CHAPTER 8

THE THIRD DIMENSION

1939–42

Early in the war, U-boats were restricted to boarding their merchant ship targets to verify their identity and cargo under the Prize Rules before sinking them. This is a boat from Otto Schuhart's *U*29 carrying a boarding party to a suspect steamer.

(Jak Mallmann Showell)

O N 17 September 1939 *U*29, a type VIIA German U-boat, crept through the cold grey waters of the Western Approaches. Her skipper, thirty-year-old Kapitänleutnant Otto Schuhart, had dived at daybreak to avoid air patrols and planned to spend the day at periscope depth, waiting for an outward-bound British convoy. Already, in the first two weeks of war, Schuhart had proved a quick learner, sinking two large British tankers and a small tugboat.

Unfortunately, the magnetic fuses fitted to his torpedoes had tripped before reaching their targets, and he had had to switch to contact fuses on his remaining weapons. Now, hoping for better luck, he was searching for merchant ships reported by *U*31. Though he would never find the convoy, that very day would bring him astonishing good luck. He would sink one of the Royal Navy's major warships and foil the new British tactics to combat the submarine menace.

Schuhart first spotted a distant aircraft through the periscope lens. As it approached, totally unaware of his presence, he recognised a Royal Navy Fairey Swordfish. This was highly significant. He was south-west of Ireland, more than three hundred miles from the nearest airfield, well outside Swordfish range. It could only have flown from an aircraft carrier, the most longed-for target for any U-boat commander.

Schuhart continued watching for the convoy, but every so often, he would sweep the distant horizon to look for approaching warships. Through the long autumn day nothing marred the distant boundary between sea and sky. Only at 6pm, with daylight fading, did he spot the sign he longed for. A tall column of smoke appeared on the skyline. Still he dared not surface. If this was indeed a carrier, there would be aircraft and surface escorts, all moving far more quickly than his U-boat. Only at dusk could he surface and run on his diesels, but by then his target could have escaped without even knowing he was there.

All he could do was creep along at walking pace, trying to position his U-boat ahead of the oncoming ships. Even when their silhouettes confirmed his fondest hopes, he still faced a formidable challenge. The approaching carrier, identified as HMS *Courageous*, was zigzagging with two escorting destroyers, and trying to head her off was virtually impossible. By 7.30pm Schuhart was losing the race. He wrote in his log: 'At the time it looked like a hopeless operation. Because of the aircraft I could not surface and my underwater speed was less than 8 knots while the carrier could do 26. But we were told during our training always to stay close and that is exactly what I did, following him submerged …'

Just as Schuhart resigned himself to failure, the situation was transformed. To his amazement, the carrier swung slowly around, heading almost straight towards him, as she turned into wind for her returning Swordfish to land on her flight deck. She had

U29's bridge watch. Schuhart himself is not present.

(Jak Mallmann Showell)

placed herself firmly within Schuhart's grasp. At the same time, her escorting destroyers continued on their existing heading, leaving her totally unprotected.

Quickly, Schuhart checked the range and bearing of this priceless target. She was 3,000 yards away, a very long distance for a torpedo attack. Realising she would resume her original course as soon as the plane was safely aboard, he fired a salvo of three torpedoes and then dived deep to safety. At the same moment the pilot of the Swordfish, Lieutenant Charles Lamb, was worried about his plane's almost empty tanks. So concerned was he about running out of fuel on approach that he touched down while the carrier was still turning into wind. In the few minutes it took his observer and himself to climb down from their parked aircraft and walk into the wardroom, two of Schuhart's torpedoes detonated.

As *U29* sank to a safer depth, the crew clearly heard the two massive explosions. In spite of the long range, and the unreliable fuses, this time the torpedoes performed faultlessly. Both struck the carrier on the port side, tearing a huge hole in her hull. The massive warship rolled over and sank in just fifteen minutes, taking with her 519 men out of her crew of 1,260.

The fortunate survivors were rescued by a passing Dutch liner and a British freighter, while the escorting destroyers hunted the U-boat responsible. Over four hours, they expended all their depth charges. Far below, Schuhart feared the conning tower would collapse inward under the remorseless pounding of the explosions,[1] but the severely shaken *U29* survived the attacks and he was finally able to edge away to safety. When Schuhart and his crew finally reached their base, Hitler himself came to congratulate them on their remarkable achievement.[2]

For the Royal Navy, this was a terrible blow. Losing an irreplaceable aircraft carrier and nearly half her crew was bad enough, but their more aggressive anti-submarine tactics vanished with her. Ever since the previous war, naval officers had felt hampered by convoy escort, and waiting for U-boats to attack before fighting back. Naval opinion still yearned for a means of taking more offensive action, and taking the war to the enemy once and for all.

In theory, aircraft carriers promised a possible way out. The much greater speed and range of carrier-borne aircraft suggested that offensive patrols to hunt for U-boats directly might now be a possibility. Now they had to face the sad truth that *Courageous* had found her target all too successfully, but that target had beaten her to the draw.

As a sign for the future, it was deeply worrying. In time though, the Navy's despondency would prove groundless. This apparent dead end would eventually provide a direct route to victory in the anti-submarine war. Nevertheless, at the very time when the Navy had hoped that airborne anti-submarine operations might help them avoid the drudgery of convoy protection, Britain's anti-submarine planes and the weapons they delivered were about as unsuitable for the job as they could possibly be. Rarely was a fighting force so poorly equipped for its task.

Even the RAF's most modern land-based patrol aircraft lacked the qualities they needed most: range and endurance. The weapons they carried were too light to cripple a submarine and were so sensitive that they endangered the planes that carried them. In spite of the courage and devotion of the aircrew, the tactics and training needed to find and sink submarines were also lacking. An air attack on a surfaced U-boat was much more dangerous for the attacking aircraft than its intended target, even if the U-boat failed to fire a single shot in its own defence.

Political pressure for cuts in pre-war defence budgets had put naval aviation under RAF control, an accountant's solution to a military problem. Land based ASW patrols would be operated by RAF Coastal Command. Inevitably, these maritime squadrons had a much lower priority in RAF circles than they would have had they been under the Navy's direct control.

Consequently, when Coastal Command was formed in 1936, its most modern aircraft was the Avro Anson, a twin-engine monoplane carrying far too light a bomb-load over far too short a range. It had originally been designed as the Avro 652 light commercial plane for Imperial Airways in 1933. The first military version appeared three years later, an odd mixture of ancient and modern design. Its wings were made of spruce and plywood, and the fabric-covered fuselage was based on a steel-tube framework with wooden fairings. Two Armstrong Siddeley Cheetah radial engines delivered 640 horsepower between them, enough for a top speed of 170mph at sea level. There was room for a crew of three – pilot, navigator/bomb-aimer and a wireless operator/air gunner.

Total defensive armament was a single machine gun mounted in the nose and firing forward, and another fitted in a dorsal turret. Offensive armament was little better. Though intended to attack submarines, the Anson could only carry a pair of 100-pound bombs in internal racks and eight 20-pound bombs under the wings. It could only patrol for just over four hours,[3] and its short range limited it to the North Sea rather than the Atlantic. Even then, it could not reach the coast of Norway.[4]

Even if it spotted a submarine, its bombs had to be dropped very close to the target to be effective. Anti-submarine bombs were made in 100-pound, 250-pound and 500-pound versions. In each case, detonation was triggered by a contact fuse protruding from the nose of the bomb, or by a time fuse after a short delay. The fuses were armed by the airflow turning a small propeller in the nose of the bomb as it fell.

The fuses leaked, and the explosives often failed to detonate. If they worked properly, even the heaviest 500-pound bomb had to be dropped within *eight feet* of a submarine to inflict lethal damage. Only a direct hit from a 100-pounder would be effective, and this was far from certain. In a mistaken attack on a Royal Navy submarine, HMS *Snapper* on 3 December 1939, a 100-pound bomb exploded against the conning tower. The only damage was four broken light-bulbs in the control room.[5]

The bombs proved far more effective in bringing down the aircraft dropping them. Two days after war began, an Anson from 233 Squadron of RAF Coastal Command had the good fortune to spot a surfaced submarine off the Scottish coast. The crew dived to attack, and dropped their two 100-pound bombs.

The submarine escaped with a severe fright, as the bombs bounced off the surface of the sea. Their time fuses made them detonate in mid-air, blasting a spray of metal splinters through the Anson's fuel tanks. When its engines cut out, the crew had to ditch in St Andrew's Bay, and take to their dinghy. When they were finally brought ashore, they found out that the submarine they had attacked belonged to the Royal Navy.[6]

Yet airborne ASW continued to appeal to naval officers and those directing the war effort. Winston Churchill was then First Lord of the Admiralty; throughout his career, he preferred offence to defence. He was convinced the opening of hostilities would see German submarines escaping through the confined waters around the British Isles to reach the open Atlantic. He therefore ordered the formation of several hunter-killer groups of fleet destroyers, each with a carrier for air support, using an analogy from the cavalry in which he had served as a young man: 'Nothing can be more important in the anti-submarine war than to try to obtain an independent flotilla which could work like a cavalry division on

the approaches, without worrying about the traffic or U-boat sinkings, but could systematically search large areas over a wide front.'[7]

At the time, he was completely wrong. It simply didn't work, and the Royal Navy literally missed the boats. Thirty U-boats slipped out through the English Channel in the last two weeks before war began. With them sailed two pocket battleships, the *Deutschland* and the *Admiral Graf Spee*, surface raiders even higher on Coastal Command's list of targets. At the very moment when the Navy was rehearsing its carefully drawn plans to stop them, the real German warships were slipping past, safely hidden in dense banks of mist.[8]

During the first ten days of war, U-boats sank nine merchant ships. Not until 14 September did the Navy have its first chance to hit back. Another carrier task group, headed by HMS *Ark Royal*, picked up a distress signal from a 5,200-ton freighter, the *Fanad Head*, under attack from a surfaced U-boat near the islet of Rockall, some two hundred miles to the southwest of the carrier. Because her Swordfish biplanes were loaded with torpedoes, a flight of three Blackburn Skua dive bombers carrying anti-submarine bombs was sent instead. The lead aircraft was flown by the CO of 803 Squadron, Lieutenant Commander Denis Cambell with Lieutenant Mike Hanson as observer. It was followed by the Skuas of Lieutenants Thurston and Griffiths, each one carrying a rating in the rear cockpit as air-gunner.

Each Skua carried a single 100-pound anti-submarine bomb, with four of the smaller 20-pounders, a combination unlikely to cause a U-boat serious worries. As a more credible threat, three of the carrier's six escorting destroyers also headed for the threatened merchantman. After their departure, the carrier left her remaining escorts as she turned into wind to launch the Skuas. This was the Navy's first all-metal strike aircraft, a large and ponderous monoplane with a sleeve valve Bristol Perseus radial engine delivering a meagre 620 horsepower in the cruise and carrying up to 500 pounds of bombs. Navy aircrew summed it up as 'Too big, too slow, and too late.'[9] At 187mph, the three bombers would take more than an hour to reach their target.

What no one aboard the carrier realised was that, at the very moment of launching this blow against a distant U-boat, they too were being watched by a second German submarine. As the three remaining escorts receded beyond sonar range, the delighted Germans were already preparing their attack. The type IXA long-range U-boat *U*39, commanded by thirty-year-old Gerhard Glattes, was returning to Germany from its first patrol to form part of a new group being assembled for further attacks. As soon as Glattes sighted the British warships, he had gone to periscope depth to conceal his presence. Just like Schuhart with the *Courageous* a few days later, he saw the carrier turning to place him in an almost ideal position to launch a spread of torpedoes, his first target in the entire patrol.

At 3.07pm, he fired three torpedoes from *U39*'s bow tubes, and waited for results. After an agonising delay, the U-boat men heard several explosions. Convinced they had hit the carrier, they waited for reprisals. In fact, the torpedoes detonated prematurely, almost certainly from faulty magnetic fuses, and too far from the carrier to cause damage. The Navy heard explosions 'in the wake of the carrier'[10] and assumed the Germans had under-estimated the speed of the *Ark*

U29's prime target, the Royal Navy aircraft carrier HMS *Courageous* converted from a World War I battlecruiser and a priceless naval asset.

(www.navyphotos.co.uk)

Royal Navy fleet destroyer HMS *Firedrake*, one of the group hunting *U39* after the abortive attack on the carrier *Ark Royal*, and the ship which delivered the final charges which forced the submarine to surface and surrender.

(www.navyphotos.co.uk)

Royal, then moving at twenty-six knots, so the torpedoes must have passed astern of the ship.

The escorting destroyers, *Faulknor*, *Foxhound* and *Firedrake*, fast modern ships only five years old and fitted with the latest sonar, reversed course to turn the tables on the U-boat. Following rehearsed tactics, they turned into line-abreast formation with a mile between the ships. They then steamed back towards the *Ark Royal* at fifteen knots, the maximum speed for their sonars to detect the submarine without being deafened by the noise of the water against the ships' hulls.

Within minutes *Faulknor* and *Foxhound* had picked up

the echo of *U39*. *Foxhound* ran in and dropped a pair of depth charges, one set to 250 feet, the other to 300 feet. These were close enough to shake the U-boat violently. The lights went out, leaving showers of brilliant sparks from the batteries due to severe arcing. Glattes ordered a deep dive to 230 feet, just as the flotilla leader *Faulknor* dropped another five charges, on shallower settings of between 100 and 150 feet. These shook the battered submarine still further but failed to inflict lethal damage. Both destroyers then lost contact, their sonars deafened by the exploding charges.

HMS *Firedrake*, however, had been far enough away to retain her fix on the U-boat. When she ran in to deliver her attack she too dropped a pattern of five charges, all set to depths of between 250 and 500 feet, closer still to her target. The hapless *U39* was hammered severely enough to allow sea water to reach the batteries. Salt in the water reacted with battery acid, producing clouds of choking chlorine gas.

Battery damage also caused the electric motors to fail and the submarine could no longer steer to avoid further attacks. After almost twenty minutes of bombardment, Glattes, with no realistic hope of escape, decided to surrender. He blew the main ballast tanks, forcing *U39* to the surface under the gaze, and the gunfire, of her attackers. The destroyers opened up with their 4.7-inch main armament, until the Germans began surrendering. The U-boat sank, but her entire crew was picked up.[11]

This was an encouraging victory for conventional ASW tactics and weaponry, even under favourable conditions. But tactics that threatened a valuable aircraft carrier less than two weeks into the war were much less encouraging. Meanwhile, the three Skuas whose launching had so nearly lost the *Ark Royal* had spotted the outcrop of Rockall and began searching for the freighter and its attacker.

When they found them, the merchant crew had abandoned ship. The submarine, the same type VIIA *U30* captained by Fritz-Julius Lemp who had sunk the *Athenia* on the first day of the war (see Chapter 5) had put a two-man boarding party aboard the freighter by rubber dinghy. After setting demolition charges to save precious torpedoes, they were foraging for luxuries like fresh food. Seeing the planes, Lemp ordered the *U30* to dive, leaving his boarding party marooned aboard the freighter. Unfortunately no one remembered to untie the rubber dinghy, leaving it bobbing on the surface. In the absence of any other target, Cambell led his flight to drop their bombs on this mysterious marker, where the submarine had disappeared.

The result was another disaster. Some of the anti-submarine bombs bounced back off the water and exploded in mid-air, fragments hitting those aircraft still attacking. Cambell's Skua pulled out of its dive and circled the area, but the second and third Skuas were hit by bomb fragments and crashed into the sea.

The cumbersome Blackburn Skua carrier strike aircraft. Three of these delivered the attack on Lemp's *U30*, which resulted in the loss of two of the planes but left the submarine undamaged.

(US National Archives)

The pilots survived, one with severe burns, but both gunners were drowned.

Realising the aircraft had dropped all their bombs, Lemp surfaced again to recover his boarding party and sink the merchantman. He rescued his men and both Skua pilots, only to be machine-gunned by the surviving Skua. The bullets hit and wounded the leader of the boarding party as he tried to help one of the Royal Navy pilots through the conning-tower hatch. Lemp then dived and fired four torpedoes from his bow tubes at the *Fanad Head*, but the fuses failed again. As a final throw, he swung the submarine around to fire a fifth torpedo from his single externally mounted stern tube.

To his relief, this one hit its target, and the freighter began to sink. However, all the delays had seen the arrival of a second wave of carrier planes – six Swordfish, now rearmed with half a dozen 100-pound anti-submarine bombs apiece. In the clear water they could see the submarine waiting at periscope depth, but they only managed to shake it up before Lemp made for deeper and safer surroundings.

So slow were the ponderous Swordfish that the three destroyers sent by the carrier group commander were not far behind. They found the freighter sinking. One turned away to rescue the merchant sailors, and the other two began hunting the submarine. Once again they showed the skill of well-trained navy crews. They picked up the U-boat's echo and delivered a series of heavy and accurate attacks that all but sank it. The shocks delivered by the 300 pounds of explosives in each charge cracked open two of the caps protecting the U-boat's bow torpedo tubes and caused a valve to leak and flood the engine room.

Lemp was suddenly in a highly dangerous position. The loss of buoyancy caused the submarine to plunge to a depth of 472 feet, at the time thought to be enough to crush it to death. To arrest the dive, he

ordered his crew to shift water from the engine room in buckets to the bilges where it could safely be pumped out. Even then they had to endure regular sonar searches and deafening explosions for a total of six hours. Only after this seemingly endless ordeal, with dwindling oxygen and battery power, was Lemp able to creep quietly away from the scene and leave his pursuers behind.[12]

The day's events seemed to show that surface escorts were still the most potent threat to the submarine. Aircraft appeared at best useless, at worst positively lethal to their own side. This made it sensible to break up the carrier groups, and release destroyers for convoy escorts. On this occasion, the Navy's luck had held. Just three days later, the loss of HMS *Courageous* would prove these tactics were fatally flawed.

Following the loss of *Courageous*, the Admiralty withdrew the three other Fleet carriers. Two had now been attacked by U-boats in a matter of days, and one had only survived by a combination of German mistakes and her own good fortune. It was clear that both had been most vulnerable when launching or recovering aircraft. It was equally clear that using aircraft in these opening skirmishes would have to depend on land-based patrols. At the time, this was truly cold comfort – yet already there was some hope of eventual improvement in the airborne anti-submarine war.

The key, as in so much else during the Second World War, was radar. Campaigns like the Battle of Britain and the bombing of Germany would rely heavily on the extra information radar provided on the whereabouts and intentions of the enemy. Unfortunately, the first working radar transmitters and receivers were large and heavy, better suited to land-based installations or heavy surface ships.

Yet, as early as 1936, British scientists had begun developing a set for fitting to aircraft. Within a year, the first experimental installation had been fitted aboard a Coastal Command Anson, and in July 1937 it was picking up echoes of large warships up to five miles away. By September, the Anson could find Royal Navy battleships and cruisers exercising off the East coast, including the battleship HMS *Rodney,* the heavy cruiser HMS *Suffolk* and, ironically, the carrier HMS *Courageous.* Even when trials had to be cut short because of worsening weather on 4 September, the Anson crew used radar to navigate back to the coast. But turning an experimental prototype into a weapon would involve costly and frustrating delays.

This radar demonstration was the best service the Anson delivered for Allied ASW in the entire war. After its disappointing operational debut, it moved to training navigators and air-gunners, while a demilitarised version was used by the RAF for transport and communications for almost thirty years. Fortunately, new aircraft soon filled the gap. One of the first was another conversion from a civilian airliner, but this time American, not British.

In the mid-1930s, the Lockheed Aircraft Company developed a medium-sized airliner, the Model 14 Super Electra. In 1938 a maritime reconnaissance version was produced, and bought for RAF Coastal Command as the Lockheed Hudson. This was the first American aircraft used by the RAF, ordered 'in the teeth of furious opposition',[13] but the first Hudson squadron started training just before war began.

Like the Anson, the Hudson was a twin-engined monoplane. In all other respects it was a great improvement, an all-metal, stressed-skin design with twin tail fins and rudders, and bristling with armament – two fixed machine guns in the nose firing forward, two in a power-operated dorsal turret, one on each side and one in the bottom of the fuselage. With a pair of 1,200-horsepower Wright Cyclone radials, it had four times the power of the Anson, it was 100mph faster and had a range of over 2,000 miles – more than three times that of the Anson – staying on patrol for more than six hours. In addition, it carried four 250-pound bombs, which when dropped as a timed 'stick', produced a line of detonations across the track of a U-boat.

Only one other Coastal Command aircraft would

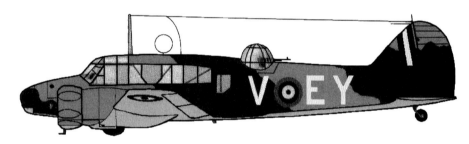

Avro Anson maritime patrol aircraft of 233 Squadron Coastal Command. One of this unit's aircraft attacked a British submarine in error but was brought down by its own AS bombs. (*Author's drawing*)

prove as effective at this early stage of the war. This was even more heavily armed than the Hudson, and in 1939 it equipped two Coastal Command squadrons. The Short Sunderland was a large and relatively modern four-engined monoplane, and yet another warplane derived from civilian origins. It was descended from the great Empire Flying Boats, the supremely luxurious pre-war airliners connecting Britain with distant imperial possessions in Africa, Asia and Australasia. It was a perfect pedigree; power, reliability, range and endurance were inherited from its civilian forebears. To these qualities it added twelve Browning 0.303-inch machine guns including power-operated multiple mountings in nose and tail gun turrets, and a pair of 0.5-inch guns in side mountings. Carrying more than two tons of bombs and depth charges, for more than twelve hours, with a range of almost 3,000 miles, this was potentially a very powerful anti-submarine weapon indeed.

The Sunderland would serve from the beginning of the war right through to the end, and claim second

place in the overall total of U-boat kills from the air. The Germans began by calling them *mude Bienen*, 'tired bees',[14] but after meeting their strong defensive armament, the nickname was changed to the more respectful *fliegende Stachelschweine* 'flying porcupine'. On one occasion a single Sunderland, when attacked by no less than eight fast and heavily armed Junkers 88s, shot down three and drove the rest away.[15]

The first signs of success in the airborne anti-submarine war appeared in early 1940. A 228 Squadron Sunderland, patrolling off northwestern France on 30 January spotted a type VIIB U-boat, *U55*, being chased by escorts from the convoy it had attacked, sinking two merchant ships. The Sunderland forced it to dive. With the submarine trapped, the escorts soon caught up, but once again the U-boat gave them the slip, and once again the Sunderland saw it and forced it to dive. This time the combination of escorts and aircraft kept it under the surface until failing battery power finally forced the skipper, Kapitänleutnant Heidel, to surface and scuttle his submarine.

This was better. Six weeks later, another aircraft accounted for a German submarine all on its own, using ordinary bombs rather than specialised anti-submarine weapons, which may have been a vital advantage. On 11 March 1940 a twin-engined Bristol Blenheim medium bomber of 82 Squadron coded 'O for Orange' was on a reconnaissance flight at 6,000 feet over the Heligoland Bight looking for German shipping. The pilot, Squadron Leader Miles Delap, spotted a U-boat on the surface some ten miles away. He slipped back into cloud before turning towards it, only emerging into the clear with his target in front of him, as he pushed his Blenheim into a dive. It was carrying contact-fused 250-pound bombs, not to be dropped below 1,000 feet, to give the bomber time to get clear of the resulting explosions.

In this case Delap flew much lower, levelling off a few hundred feet above the submarine, and dropping all four bombs at once. His plane was peppered with splinters but he was able to climb away to a safe height, while his rear gunner saw two of the bombs explode on striking the submarine's hull. As the Blenheim circled overhead, the delighted Delap saw the submarine sink, leaving a spreading oil slick.[16] It was the same *U31* that had made the convoy-sighting report that had resulted in the sinking of HMS *Courageous*, now undergoing trials after a dockyard refit. She went down with all hands and a team of dockyard workers, though a salvage team were later able to refloat her and put her back into service.[17]

The special anti-submarine bombs would not prove successful until 13 April 1940, when a seaplane version of the Swordfish, catapulted from the battleship HMS *Warspite*, caught the brand-new type IXB German submarine *U64*. The Swordfish was loaded with 100-pounders, and the U-boat was not only on the surface but actually at anchor in Herjangs Fjord near to the town of Narvik.

Warspite and her escorting destroyers were supporting the Allied landings in Norway, where they would sink no less than eight large German destroyers without loss in the second Battle of Narvik. Though the Swordfish was carrying out a reconnaissance to locate the German warships lying in wait for the British force, this sitting target was too good to miss. The lone biplane dived to the attack and dropped two bombs. One of them hit the submarine forward, opening up a large gash in the pressure hull. She sank quickly, though some of her crew escaped. This gave a third score to air power, although anchored U-boats would be very rare in the coming Atlantic battle.

Four months later a Swordfish struck again, this time at the Italians. Three planes of 824 Squadron, Fleet Air Arm from the carrier HMS *Eagle*, were temporarily based at the desert airfield of Ma'aten Bagush in Egypt. Early on the morning of 22 August 1940, the biplanes were loaded with torpedoes and sent to attack Italian warships in the Libyan anchorage of Bomba Bay.

The Italians were preparing a frogman attack on the Royal Navy fleet anchorage at Alexandria as Captain Oliver Patch, Royal Marines, led the flight parallel to the Libyan coast before turning towards the anchorage, flying just thirty feet over the water. They found the submarine *Iride*, which had been preparing her 'chariots' while moored alongside the depot ship *Monte Gargano* and the torpedo boat *Calipso*.

By the time the Swordfish arrived, the submarine was moving into deeper water for a test dive. Patch, in the centre of the formation, picked the submarine as his target. His two wingmen, Lieutenant Cheesman and Lieutenant Wellman, spread out, aiming for the torpedo boat and depot ship respectively. In spite of the Italians firing with every weapon they could bring to bear, all three Swordfish launched their torpedoes, though Cheesman had to delay his as his observer spotted a sandbank ahead.[18]

The three planes braved intense anti-aircraft fire and returned safely to base. Later reconnaissance confirmed the depot ship sinking in the bay, with no sign of the other vessels, including another submarine thought to be in the bay at the time. The legend grew that four vessels had been sunk by just three torpedoes, but the truth was almost equally remarkable. Instead of a second submarine, there had been a motor fishing vessel, and it and the torpedo boat had escaped. Cheesman's torpedo had actually missed its target, but Wellman had sunk the depot ship and Patch had sunk the submarine with two air-dropped torpedoes.

These isolated incidents showed that aircraft could kill submarines under a range of different conditions. But before air power could become decisive, new weapons and new tactics were needed to improve their chances of doing so in the open sea. Only then could convoys be protected further out across the ocean, into the area of the mid-Atlantic 'air gap'.

Before that, though, there was one other area where air power threatened to play a vital part in the submarine war, this time on the U-boats' side. Once most merchant ships were concentrated into convoys, the Germans' greatest difficulty was in finding targets in the immensity of the ocean. A U-boat might spend weeks on patrol without seeing a single ship or the smoke of a distant convoy. Before the development of the wolf-pack and the patrol line to sweep hundreds of miles of ocean, another way of searching over huge distances for merchant ships was urgently needed.

If aircraft could cover long distances at high speed searching for surfaced submarines, they could easily do the same for the much larger and slower convoys, and relay their positions to U-boats waiting below. All this became feasible after the fall of France. Just as the U-boats' range and time on patrol was greatly extended by operating from bases on the Atlantic coast of France rather than the German North Sea coast, so French airfields gave the Luftwaffe a grandstand seat in the Battle of the Atlantic.

Once again, the aircraft involved were yesterday's airliners, transformed into the latest maritime patrol planes. The massive four-engined Focke-Wulf 200 had been designed as the *Kurier* (Courier or Express) airliner for Lufthansa's long-haul routes. Some were converted to luxury long-distance transports for the Nazi hierarchy, but most were fitted with a bomb-bay containing four 1,000-kilogram bombs, and a series of gun positions using different combinations of cannon and machine-guns to produce the Kondor long-range attack aircraft.

With a crew of eight, including two pilots, a radio operator and flight engineer, no less than four gunners, and a 5-ton maximum bomb load, this formidable aircraft could cruise at 220mph for up to ten hours.[19] From August 1940 until early 1941 one unit in particular, I Gruppe of Kampfgeschwader 40,

The Americans produced a series of tough and capable carrier fighters – one of the first was the Grumman Wildcat, supplied to the Royal Navy under Lend-Lease and known in that service as the Martlet. (*US National Archives*)

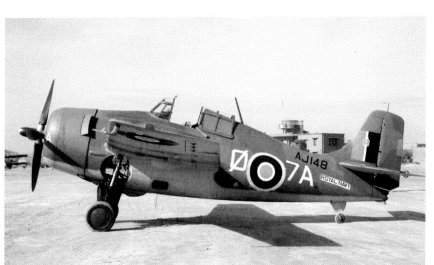

Another Allied tanker falling victim to a U-boat's torpedoes, on fire and with her back broken, she and her cargo become a total loss. (*US National Archives*)

based at Bordeaux/Merignac airfield on the Atlantic coast of France, flew extended long-range missions. They would head westwards into the open Atlantic before sweeping in a huge arc to the west of Ireland and across the convoy routes, before reaching occupied Norway and the Luftwaffe airfields of Stavanger or Trondheim.

During this period, Kondors sank no less than eighty-five Allied ships, a total of 363,000 tons.[20] However, had they switched to reconnaissance earlier, the details they passed to the U-boats might have produced even more sinkings. Only in the late summer of 1941 did Doenitz's frantic pleas for closer co-operation produce changed priorities. The bomb-load was cut to a quarter, and crews ordered to retreat into cloud cover if attacked, so they could stay in contact with a convoy for as long as possible.

This represented a very serious threat. For hard-pressed convoys and their escorts, the drone of a Kondor in the distance was an almost inevitable prelude to an attack by U-boats summoned to the scene. For best selling author and wartime RNVR officer Nicholas Monsarrat, one week-long battle began with the arrival of these patrols.

A couple of long range reconnaissance planes showed up about midday, but as usual they would not come within range: instead they flew round and round the convoy making sure of our

course and speed, and left about four – having no doubt prepared a reliable and detailed report, and having incidentally kept us at action stations the whole afternoon. Some of the destroyers tried shots at them now and then, but it was hardly serious shooting. There was an alarm that night, probably a false one: I don't think the U-boats had picked us up previously, and it takes a little time to collect the pack after it has been put on the scent.

On the following day, the planes returned:

Aircraft came over fairly early, high level bombers that kept us on our toes, but didn't get nearer than a near miss. Nor did we. There were also a couple of Focke-Wulfs playing around most of the day: a routine shadowing, well out of range, but damned annoying all the time. There are thought to be '4 or 5' U-boats in the vicinity. Weather rather too good to be pleasant.[21]

But three days later, the U-boats returned. Several more ships were sunk, including a tanker and one of the escorts, though most were saved by bad weather. On the Gibraltar run, where sunshine and clear conditions usually took the place of rain clouds and squalls, there was often no such protection, and the Kondors, operating close to their Bordeaux base, often proved deadliest.

One southbound convoy, OG71, was spotted by a Kondor on 17 August 1941, then lost and finally spotted again by *U201*, which radioed headquarters, as a result of which relays of aircraft and a pack of U-boats raced to the scene. Using new tactics ordered by Doenitz, the U-boats attacked the escorts first, sinking the ex-US Navy four-stack destroyer HMS *Bath* and the corvette HMS *Zinnia*. In all, a total of eight U-boats made attacks, and claimed a total of sixteen ships sunk for a total of 90,000 tons. The true total, thanks to heavy RAF patrols and reinforcements to the surface escorts was actually less daunting – seven small merchant ships (out of twenty-one) for a total of 11,000 tons.[22]

Incidents like these might have been more bearable if maritime air power worked as well for the Allies. Sadly, progress in airborne ASW was slower, with just a few promising signs for the future. More aircraft were reaching Coastal Command, with better weapons. To begin with, the Hudsons and Sunderlands had been joined by an obsolescent twin-engined bomber, the Armstrong-Whitworth Whitley, withdrawn from Bomber Command. With slab-sided fuselage and drooping nose, the rugged Whitley was no thoroughbred, but a useful addition to anti-submarine patrols.

Earlier Whitleys, fitted with twin 800-horsepower Armstrong-Siddeley 14-cylinder radial engines, had a mediocre performance. Even the later Mark IV and V versions, with Rolls-Royce Merlins, could only cruise at 200mph over a useful range of some 2,500 miles.[23] But a more serious consequence of this limited power, for an aircraft flying over the sea, was the impossibility of maintaining height on one engine. Engine trouble of any kind at all meant the certainty

of a ditching, almost certainly hundreds of miles from any likely rescue.

By now, with the U-boats enjoying the first of their 'happy times' (see Chapter 6), it was clear that air power must play a greater part in the anti-submarine battle. On 1 December 1940, Churchill wrote to President Roosevelt:

We gave orders to the RAF Coastal Command to dominate the outlets from the Mersey and the Clyde and around Northern Ireland. Nothing must be spared from this task, it had supreme priority. The bombing of Germany took second place. All suitable machines, pilots and material must be concentrated upon our counter-offensive, by fighters against the enemy bombers and surface craft assisted by bombers against the U-boats in these narrow waters.[24]

Unfortunately, Churchill was wrong. The bombing of Germany never did take second place. Once the forceful and single-minded Air Marshal Arthur 'Bomber' Harris was put in charge of Bomber Command on the 22 February 1942, Coastal Command would have to fight even harder for aircraft, men and resources against inexorable demands for bombers. Even while still serving as Deputy Chief of the Air Staff, Harris contemptuously rejected the diversion of any of the new Handley Page Halifax bombers to Coastal Command. His comment that 'twenty U-boats and a few Focke-Wulf in the Atlantic would have provided the efficient anti-aircraft defence of all Germany'[25] was a ludicrous exaggeration.

Nevertheless, as 1940 gave way to 1941, the outlook was slowly improving. More aircraft, with better-

Converted from the large *Kurier* civilian airliner, the Focke-Wulf 200 *Kondor* was deadly as an extremely long-range bomber and observation aircraft. (*US National Archives*)

trained and more experienced crews, provided air cover for several hundred miles from bases in Britain, Canada and Iceland. U-boats represented less of a threat in these well-patrolled waters because aircraft forced them to dive even if they could not sink them. But, further into the open Atlantic, where even Sunderlands could not reach, the Germans soon realised they were safe from air attack. In the 'Air Gap'[26] an area in mid-Atlantic some three hundred miles across, they could evade escorts and wreak havoc on any convoy they encountered.

Even in areas where air patrols could reach, there were perils in plenty. Anti-submarine aircrew had one of the hardest duties of the maritime war, lonely, boring, unglamorous and dangerous. The first generation of patrol planes were under-powered and poorly armed. Every mission meant crossing and re-crossing an ocean sometimes calm or sometimes violent, but always hostile. Crews were deafened by the ceaseless roar of engines, shaken by turbulence and numbed by the thousands of different vibrations of the airframe. They were blinded by rain and fog and poor visibility, as time crawled by and concentration drifted. Flying hundreds of miles from base, barometric altimeters often gave inaccurate readings as the pilots flew on instruments through fog-banks or rain-squalls.

Two things dominated their attention. Their eyes strained for a fleeting glimpse of a U-boat, and their ears listened for any missed beat from the engines. A misfire was cause for concern, loss of power a major worry and engine failure a catastrophe. Inability to maintain height meant ditching in the cold and unwelcoming swell, where impact could shatter a fragile air frame like an egg falling on concrete. Even if the crew escaped and reached their dinghy, they might be hundreds of miles from land and far from busy convoy routes, facing a lingering death from exposure and starvation.

Their other enemy was boredom. For hour after hour, day after day, week after week, month after month, they saw only empty wastes of water. Sometimes they might glimpse a convoy or an escort vessel, but almost never a sign of their slim and elusive targets. Yet they could never afford to relax. If the months of searching were to be rewarded, they might glimpse a U-boat for seconds at most. In that time they had to react, turn and attack. The slightest hesitation, from fatigue or anxiety, and it would be too late. The brief chance to hit back at the enemy as payback for the endless waiting might be lost. Small wonder that crews risked so much in attacking, to ensure their efforts were successful.

At this stage, aircraft could only present a real threat to U-boats during daylight. When submarines headed out on patrol or back to base, they minimised their vulnerability. By day they submerged to avoid air patrols, running slowly on their electric motors. At nightfall they would surface, to run on diesel engines and recharge batteries for the next day. It increased the time taken to start and finish a patrol, but almost eliminated the danger of air attack.

Yet changes were on their way. The first American ultra-long-range aircraft, which would transform Atlantic air operations, were already arriving. The relatively slow Consolidated PBY5 Catalina could stay over a convoy for up to two hours at a range of eight hundred miles from its base, and thirty had arrived by summer 1941. In the longer term, the VLR (very long range) version of the B24 Liberator Mark III bomber, with extra fuel tanks fitted in the outer wing sections and an extreme range of some 2,300 miles would help to bridge the Air Gap at last. Even Harris's jealously guarded Halifax bombers would eventually join Coastal Command, as his own night bomber squadrons turned increasingly to Lancasters as their primary weapon.

While new aircraft helped, weapons and tactics

Converted from a German merchant ship seized in the West Indies, HMS *Audacity*, in her short but dramatically successful career as the first escort carrier, showed the value of convoys carrying their own air protection with them. (*www.navyphotos.co.uk*)

to find and sink U-boats were even more important. Fortunately, the unreliable ASW bombs were already being replaced. An effective stopgap had been produced by taking the standard cylindrical naval Mark VII depth charge introduced at the end of the First World War, and fitting it with a rounded nose and a finned tail. This proved a much more effective replacement for the heaviest 500-pound anti-submarine bomb. Thanks to a thinner and lighter casing, it contained no less than 450 pounds of high explosive. The newer, more powerful aircraft could carry these depth charges in larger numbers, for more attacks or for heavier sticks dropped in a single attack.

Tests showed the modified depth charge could survive impact with the sea, provided the aircraft was not flying faster than 100mph or higher than 100 feet when they were dropped. Moreover, the absence of the normal anti-submarine bomb fuses meant the charge would sink to the depth set on its hydrostatic pistol before exploding. For the first time, Coastal Command had a weapon more dangerous to the enemy than its own aircrews, and 700 were supplied by August 1940. Later the same treatment was applied to the smaller 250-pound Mark VIII depth charge, replacing the 100-pound and 250-pound anti-submarine bombs carried by the smaller patrol planes.[27] These new bombs still had severe limitations. The detonation depth had to be set before take off, making it impossible to deal with changed circumstances.[28]

There was still the problem of finding the U-boats at night, in cloud or poor visibility. By early 1941 four Hudsons fitted with Mark I Air to Surface Vessel (ASV) radar had been issued to each of three Coastal

Command squadrons. And a Mark II ASV radar producing a more powerful signal at a higher frequency of 176 megacycles or megahertz (Mc or MHz), was on its way, with a more sensitive receiver, and smaller aerials.

An order had been placed for 4,000 ASV Mark II sets in the spring of 1940, with the first deliveries in August. Unfortunately, the Luftwaffe intervened. Once they switched to night bombing, there was an urgent need for Air Interception (AI) radar to help night fighters shoot down German bombers, and this was given top priority. By autumn 1940, only forty-five Mark II ASV radars had been delivered.

Meanwhile the supreme weapon in the radar battle was already on the laboratory bench. This was centimetric radar, operating at several thousand megacycles. It had already been the target of US Navy researchers, but they had only found it possible to produce relatively low power at these higher frequencies.

The key to producing a viable centimetric radar proved to be a radical new oscillator valve called the cavity magnetron. This was developed in the Nuffield Laboratory at Oxford University early in 1940 by Professor Randall and Dr Boot, who succeeded in generating high-power signals at a frequency of 3,000 megacycles. This would be the basis of the greatly improved ASV Mark III radar, with a much smaller aerial, which could be rotated inside the aircraft for continuous all-round coverage.[29]

Nevertheless, these weapons made it essential to develop the right tactics to use them to their full effect. Coastal Command's Naval Liaison Officer, ex-

Looking like a survivor from the previous war, the Fairey Swordfish biplane won a new role as a capable anti-submarine aircraft. (*US National Archives*)

submariner Captain D V Peyton-Ward RN, began studying all reports of sighting and attacks on U-boats completed by returning aircrew. He developed a series of recommendations, detailed in Coastal Command Tactical Instruction number 15 of July 1941:

- the attacking approach was to be made by the shortest path and at the maximum speed
- the actual attack could be made from any direction relative to the U-boat
- the depth setting of all depth charges was to be 50 feet, the spacing of depth charges in a stick was to be 60 feet and all depth charges carried aboard an aircraft were to be released in one stick
- the ideal was to attack while the U-boat or some part of it was still visible
- in cases where the U-boat had disappeared for more than 30 seconds it was pointed out that success was

The 'Hunt' class of small destroyers – this is HMS *Brocklesby* - were rushed into production to provide increased numbers in the run-up to the outbreak of war, but the weaponry they carried made them top-heavy and difficult to handle in rough weather.

(www.navyphotos.co.uk)

unlikely owing to the progressive uncertainty of the U-boat's position either in plan or depth
- the height of release must not be greater than 100 feet until an aiming sight was provided but the restriction against aircraft carrying depth charges at night was modified (this was because of height uncertainties with barometric altimeters creating a danger of hitting the water)
- great stress was laid on the need for training and constant exercises so as to attain a high standard of attack and aiming accuracy.[30]

In time, the more rigorous findings of operational research teams would revolutionise the tactics and the effectiveness of ASW air attacks. For the moment, though, there remained one more outstanding problem – the Germans' long-range, hard-hitting and ever-watchful Kondors.

A desperate and expensive stopgap would provide a partial solution. The aim was to provide convoys with a token amount of air cover throughout their voyage, to help redress the balance. An initial sugges-

tion had been made in November 1940 to station twin-engined Bristol Beaufighters at airfields in Northern Ireland. By sending a radar-equipped merchant ship with each convoy, it was planned to home in these fast, heavily armed, long-range fighters to attack any marauding Focke-Wulfs and either drive them off or shoot them down.

The formidable Beaufighter was powered by either a pair of Bristol Hercules radial engines or a pair of in-line Rolls-Royce Merlins, delivering a top speed of more than 300mph and a range of 1,750 miles, carrying four 20-mm cannon in the nose and six 0.303-in machine guns in the wings.[31] Unfortunately, the Kondors were most active beyond the range of even the Beaufighters. Even if they could reach the convoy at top speed, the Kondors would probably have departed long before they got there.[32]

Another idea was to make artificial icebergs from a mixture of water and sawdust frozen to order and towed to vulnerable areas of the North Atlantic where they could be used as mobile fighter airstrips.[33] This idea too was dropped, in favour of having fighters on call within the convoy itself. The first expedient was to fit a merchant ship with a catapult to launch a fighter as soon as an intruder aircraft was detected. The fighter could shoot down the raider, return to the convoy and then ditch in the sea so the pilot could be picked up. Where the convoy was close enough to a friendly shore he could head for the nearest airfield instead.

This was the theory behind the catapult armed merchant ship or CAM ship. At the first meeting of the newly formed Battle of the Atlantic Committee in March 1941, Prime Minister Churchill ordered 'extreme priority will be given to fitting out ships to catapult or otherwise launch fighter aircraft against bombers attacking our shipping. Proposals should be made within a week.'[34] With this kind of backing from the top, events moved quickly. A Merchant Ship Fighter Unit (MSFU) was established at Speke airfield in Liverpool. RAF pilots were invited to volunteer and Royal Navy pilots were simply ordered to report for duty. Both groups were given training in catapult launching and ditching in the uninviting Atlantic once the combat was over.

There was a severe shortage of conventional catapults, but the gap was filled by a simple rocket catapult developed at the Royal Aircraft Establishment. The fighter was mounted on a trolley blasted down a pair of rails seventy-five feet long at an acceleration of 3.5g by a battery of thirteen electrically fired 3-inch rockets. If a Hurricane was launched with twenty knots of wind over the deck, it reached flying speed by the time it left the end of the rails, as the acceleration was faster than catapults used on carriers at the time. Furthermore, each new catapult could be built in just three weeks.[35]

By late April 1941, twenty-nine ships had been chosen

to have catapults fitted, and the first one, a freighter called *Michael E*, sailed for New York with convoy OB327 on 28 May. Sadly, the Kondors turned up as expected, but made no attack on the convoy themselves. Instead, they reported its presence to the U-boats, one of which, the type IXB *U108* skippered by Klaus Scholtz, torpedoed and sank the CAM ship on the evening of 2 June, before its fighter could be launched.

However, on 3 August another CAM ship launched its Hurricane as a Kondor approached. The fighter climbed towards its huge adversary only to find the battle was anything but one-sided. The raider's large defensive armament made it dangerous to approach. By the time it was shot down, the fighter had been so badly shot-up that the pilot was only just able to reach the convoy before ditching.

Over the next two years, Hurricanes launched from CAM ships shot down another five Kondors. After that, the KG40 crews changed tactics and treated convoys with more respect. They merely stayed to report the position, course and speed of the convoy from relatively long range. This proved highly effective. As the fighter was a one-shot weapon, it was only launched once the enemy aircraft was close enough to be identified. By then, the damage had been done and the convoy's position reported. Furthermore, the pilots were faced with terrifying risks after returning to the convoy.

> The Hurricane took off in a cloud of steam and a whirl of salty spray, chased its quarry and then lost it, and the RAF pilot then jumped, according to the drill. But a cross-wind carried him into the middle of the convoy, which could not stop for such heroics; and while we waited astern to pick him up his parachute got entangled in the propellers of a small, intent, persevering merchant ship which also could not leave its station, nor alter course, nor slacken speed, nor cut him loose; and he was towed away to a dog's death – but slowly.[36]

Thanks to the Luftwaffe's new tactics, even this kind of sacrifice was in vain, and a new idea was needed. The answer was a more radical conversion of a merchant ship so that aircraft could not only take off, but land on deck as well. The merchant aircraft carriers, or MAC ships, were standard cargo ships fitted with small 400-foot flight decks for the slow but effective Swordfish to operate anti-submarine patrols. In all, fifteen ships were built, nine adapted from tankers and six from grain ships, compared with a total of thirty-five CAM ships.

Using merchant ships as warships created problems of priorities. One proposal to refit the large Union Castle passenger liners – that ran the peacetime UK–South Africa service – as aircraft carriers was dropped, as they were more valuable as fast troop carriers. However, at least one merchant ship had no existing commercial priorities. The 6,100-ton German refrigerator ship *Hannover* had been captured as a prize off San Domingo, and it was decided at the beginning of 1941 to convert her into an auxiliary aircraft carrier. All superstructure above the shelter deck was removed, and replaced by a simple flight deck with no provision for a hangar or lift.[37]

She was sent to Blyth Drydock and Shipbuilding and the job was completed on 26 June 1941, with her first trials on 7 July. The gap between the flight deck and the original hull was plated in, leaving space for the diesel exhaust to be led out through trunking on the starboard side, with platforms alongside the flight deck to control the ship and send and receive signals. The flight deck had just two arrester wires and a rudimentary safety barrier, leaving space for six Grumman F4F Wildcat fighters of 802 Squadron. Not only would they have to land and take off from this deck – at 368 feet long only half the length of that of a fleet carrier like the *Ark Royal* – but all the aircraft not actually flying would have to be kept there, taking up precious space. Repairs and maintenance would have to be carried out in the open, in the worst weather the open Atlantic could inflict on the ship and her crew.

It was equally challenging for the pilots. One of them was the diminutive Sub-Lieutenant Eric Brown, known to his contemporaries as 'Winkle', later to become a captain and a distinguished military test pilot with many feats to his credit, including the first ever landing of a jet fighter on a carrier flight deck. At the time, he was grateful that the Martlet (the RN name for the Wildcat) had the 'best landing characteristics of any naval aircraft that I flew'.

> It offered good forward vision, excellent slow flying characteristics, a robust undercarriage fully capable of absorbing the most punishing vertical velocities and an intelligently positioned arrester hook that could convert a shaky approach into a safe arrival. I had my deck landing baptism in a Martlet Mk1 on the smallest carrier deck ever to serve in the Royal Navy and was to land on that same deck when it was pitching an estimated 65 feet (20m) in the Bay of Biscay … with only two arrester wires, a barrier and its associated trip wire, the test of pilot skill in a rough sea was just about the ultimate. Quite apart from the risk involved, there was the hard fact that any accident to one of our Martlets depleted the convoy's operational air cover by one-sixth.[38]

The new carrier was commissioned originally as a merchant ship, renamed the *MV Empire Audacity*. It

HMS *Stanley*, an ex-US destroyer, lost during 'Johnny' Walker's battle with the U-boats in protecting convoy HG76 which also involved the loss of HMS *Audacity*.

(www.navyphotos.co.uk)

was later decided to man her as a warship, and HMS *Audacity* she became. She sailed on her first convoy, OG74, bound for Gibraltar on 13 September 1941, virtually guaranteed to attract both Kondors and U-boats. Two days later her air patrols saw their first U-boat and forced it to dive and lose contact.

This promising beginning was followed by a hard fight. On 20 September, a fighter spotted another U-boat twelve miles from the convoy and directed surface escorts to attack it without success. Later that evening, another U-boat *(U124)* found the convoy and sank two ships. Another, the collier *City of Waterford* had sunk after a collision, and survivors from all three had been taken aboard the rescue ship *Walmer Castle.*

She was steaming to rejoin the convoy when a Kondor appeared. The bomber made four attacks, finally setting the ship ablaze. As the plane was leaving, two of *Audacity*'s aircraft caught up with it. The Kondor dived to skim the surface of the sea, but one of the fighters pulled off a difficult deflection shot from the beam, and a well-aimed burst hit the rear fuselage. It was enough. Weakness in the tail structure was a design fault of the Kondor and it collapsed, sending the bomber crashing into the sea. With just three more merchant ships lost to later U-boat attacks, this was a successful convoy for the hard-pressed Gibraltar run.

Audacity sailed on another Gibraltar convoy, OG76, on 31 October. Two extra fighters were squeezed in on the small flight deck, but the late autumn weather was appalling. As two fighters returned from a patrol, one landed successfully on the pitching deck, swept by curtains of spray. The other mistimed its landing and bounced over the side, though the pilot was saved by one of the escorts.

A week into the journey, two Kondors appeared,

and two fighters were sent to intercept. One German plane vanished into the clouds but the Navy pilots found the other. One Martlet was shot down and the pilot killed but the other destroyed the Kondor. Three hours later, 'Winkle' Brown tried out an idea of his own. He decided the best idea was a head-on attack to hit the target with a zero-deflection burst, with the majority of the Kondor's guns unable to aim at him. Even so, it was a dangerous and frightening manoeuvre. Both aircraft would be closing at a speed approaching 500mph while firing at one another, and Brown himself was also presenting a zero-deflection target to the bomber's nose gunner – the airborne equivalent of the classic pistols-at-dawn duel. The first one to hit the other would be the only one to survive.

> It proved to be much more difficult than I had imagined to get into position for a head-on attack and indeed, my first such attack was largely the result of a chance confrontation after losing my quarry in cloud. Once committed, the head-on attack is a hair-raising affair, as you close at high speed with a large aeroplane belching fire at you while you are glued to a gunsight. I was fully occupied in sighting, firing and breaking away over my target, but the Condor [sic] pilot must have been going through hell, sitting behind his controls just flying straight and level and praying that his gunners would swat this portly little wasp spitting venom directly at him. One such pass was enough, and my lasting impressions were of the Condor's windscreen crumbling under the weight of lead spewing from my 0.5-inch Brownings and of the very violent evasive action necessary to prevent collision with the monster.[39]

So effective was this action that neither OG76 nor a nearby West African convoy was found by the enemy. Both completed their journeys with no losses, but *Audacity*'s return trip with the homeward-bound convoy HG76 that left Gibraltar on 14 December, proved completely different. Once again, a patrolling fighter forced a shadowing U-boat to dive. Once again a fighter pilot was killed by enemy fire, this time from the surfaced U-boat he was attacking, though the submarine was sunk immediately afterwards by the surface escorts.

Another U-boat was sunk on 18 December, two more Kondors appeared and fighters were sent to intercept. The guns of both fighters jammed and the Germans escaped, and by the following day more and more U-boats followed their signals to reach the convoy, showing how effective these airborne search tactics could be.

On the afternoon of 19 December, Brown brought down another Kondor with a second head-on attack, followed by Sub-Lieutenant Sleigh, who shot another down with similar tactics. More patrols on the following day kept the intruders at bay, and forced more shadowing U-boats to submerge. By the 21st though, the pilots were tired out. Only three of the fighters were serviceable, and flying was made even more dangerous by the carrier pitching and rolling through a heavy swell.

Though junior to the escort group commander, the redoubtable 'Johnny' Walker (Commander F J Walker RN – see Chapter 13), the captain of the carrier, Commander McKendrick RN, had been advised by the Commander-in-Chief Western Approaches to take *Audacity* outside the convoy at night to follow an independent high-speed zigzag course under escort. Unfortunately, the only escorts that could be spared were corvettes, which were far too slow to follow the carrier moving at full speed. In addition, Walker had developed tactics of his own, making sharp changes to the convoy's course after dark, to try to lose the shadowing U-boats. For some of these he ordered the escorts to stage a mock battle with rockets, starshells and gunfire, to cover the fact that the convoy was turning sharply away from known U-boat positions.

On the night of the 21st he was preparing for one of these diversions, where the convoy made a sharp turn to port. He ordered the sloop HMS *Deptford* away to the northeast to stage the mock battle, while the convoy turned from northeast to northwest. Moments before the display was due to start, one merchant ship was torpedoed and another fired a 'snowflake' rocket, signalling another emergency to the remaining merchantmen. As soon as *Deptford* began her demonstration, they all began firing illuminating rockets, turning a pitch-black night into broad daylight.

By then, Commander McKendrick had taken *Audacity* outside the convoy on the starboard side where the attack had been made. Walker had suggested the port side of the convoy would be safest from U-boats, but McKendrick was worried about colliding with a merchantman in the dark during the convoy's sharp turn.

The stage was set for disaster. Oberleutnant Gerhard Bigalk, commanding the type VIIC, *U751*, was amazed to find the silhouette of an aircraft carrier in his sights, against the brilliant flares. As delighted as Schuhart had been to see the *Courageous*, Bigalk responded equally quickly. Just four minutes later, the first of *U751*'s torpedoes hit the carrier. It was followed by two more and *Audacity* finally sank at 10.10pm with the loss of almost a quarter of her crew, a sad end to a promising experiment. However, thanks to her help and Walker's vigorous tactics with the surface escorts, the convoy had survived an encounter with a full-size wolf pack, sinking no less than four U-boats for the loss of two freighters, the ex-US Navy four-stack destroyer HMS *Stanley* and the *Audacity* herself.

This meant the loss of the *Audacity* was a truly bitter blow. The overall picture, though, was now much more hopeful. With more escort carriers being built in American shipyards, air attacks on U-boats would become more widespread and more effective. More plentiful aircraft, improved radar, more powerful weapons and better tactics, made the future of airborne ASW suddenly more promising. To echo Churchill's prophecy about the Alamein victory of November 1942, this was not yet the end, nor even the beginning of the end. It was – just possibly – the end of the beginning.

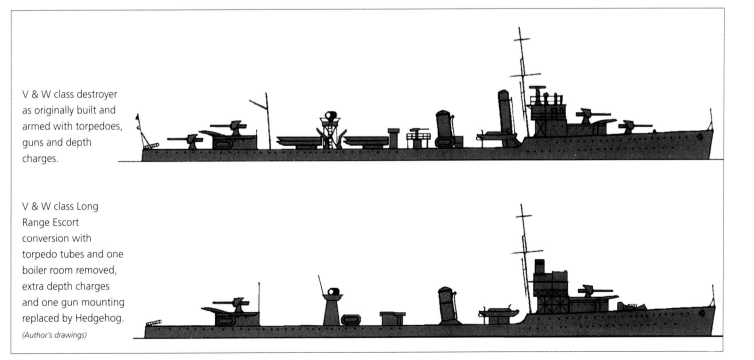

V & W class destroyer as originally built and armed with torpedoes, guns and depth charges.

V & W class Long Range Escort conversion with torpedo tubes and one boiler room removed, extra depth charges and one gun mounting replaced by Hedgehog.
(Author's drawings)

CHAPTER 9

THE AIR GAP AND THE BATTLE OF THE BAY

1942–1943

O n the night of 3 June 1942, the Italian submarine *Luigi Torelli* was outward bound from Bordeaux on her fifth patrol. From mid-1941, the Italian boats had helped make up for the relatively small numbers of German submarines available for operations, though critics doubted their value. Nevertheless, with seven merchant ships to her credit, the *Torelli's* record had been the best of all the Italian boats. Now she had a new skipper, Tenente di Vascello Count Augusto Migliorini.

During the long summer days, the *Luigi Torelli* remained submerged, creeping at little better than walking pace on her electric motors. She surfaced only after dark to recharge her batteries, safe from the danger of air attack. So far, all was well. She had left La Pallice on 2 June with her sister ship *Morosini*. At 3am the following morning, Tenente di Vascello Augusto Migliorini turned his boat on to a heading of 264° for the Bahamas, and by midnight she was cruising on the surface seventy miles north of the neutral Spanish coast.

At 1.27am on 4 June, the bridge watch heard an approaching heavy aircraft at low altitude. Suddenly a brilliant glare lit up the empty sea as the plane roared overhead. In this corner of the Bay, lights suggested a Luftwaffe patrol. Migliorini fired recognition flares, but sent the bridge lookouts below, ready for an emergency dive.

The submarine slowed down, to reduce the phosphorescent wake, and the conning-tower machine guns were manned. By this time the light had gone out, but they heard the plane turn around and fly back towards them, losing height as it approached. Suddenly the spotlight came on again, exposing them like an actor on an empty stage. The aircraft thundered overhead, just fifty feet above the sea, and three violent explosions shook the submarine.

The bridge watch disappeared below as the shock of the explosions released the catch holding back the hatch cover, which slammed shut, trapping the bosun on the bridge. The diesel engines sucked the air out of the boat and then stalled, starved of oxygen, leaving the crew half suffocated. *Torelli's* position was desperate, stopped and down by the bows, stationary with no light and no power. Smoke and chlorine gas poured from the batteries, with fire in a forward compartment.

The bosun watched as their attacker made two more runs, machine-gunning the boat each time, but dropping no more bombs. Meanwhile damage-control parties strove to restore forward buoyancy, dumping extra fuel stowed in the ballast tanks and replacing it with compressed air. The fire was isolated

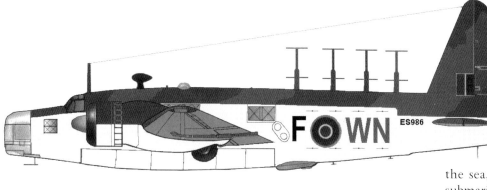

This is the first Leigh Light Wellington Mk III supplied to 172 Squadron Coastal Command and flown by Squadron Leader Jeaff Greswell to attack the *Luigi Torelli*.

(Author's drawing)

by shutting the watertight doors between compartments, but this left the boat without steering compass or powered rudder controls. All the crew could do was use the stars to steer manually on a rough southerly course, heading for the safety of the Spanish coast. Something had gone very wrong that night over the Bay of Biscay – the protective cloak of darkness had developed some very worrying holes.[1]

In fact, this was a major turning point in the anti-submarine war. From now on, boats crossing the bay to and from their French bases would have severe problems; this had taken a huge Allied effort to achieve. Even six months before, hitting U-boats from the air had seemed impossibly ambitious. Yet as the intensity of the U-boat campaign continued to grow and merchant tonnage losses climbed with it, there was a desperate need to hit back. In the longer term, long-range aircraft would cover the Atlantic Air Gap, but until these became available it might prove possible to attack U-boats crossing the more accessible waters of the Bay of Biscay to and from the battle.

Sadly, even this more limited objective was plagued by competition for new technology. Centimetre-wavelength radar was vital, but maritime ASW had a lower priority than night fighters hunting German bombers over England and, as always, the insatiable needs of Air Marshal Harris's Bomber Command. The graphic picture that centimetric radar provided of the ground over which a bomber was flying allowed

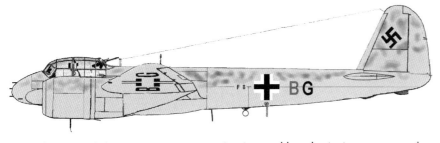

The C6 long-range fighter version of the Junkers 88 which equipped V Gruppe of Kampfgeschwader 40, the unit tasked with shooting down Allied anti-submarine air patrols.

(Author's drawing)

accurate navigation and bomb-aiming, even on the darkest of nights. For anti-submarine patrols, metric-wavelength ASV Mark II would have to soldier on a little longer.

In the meantime, how could U-boats be attacked at night once radar found them? The answer was a simple device, fortunately of no use to Bomber Command. It was devised by a former pilot now at Coastal Command headquarters, Squadron Leader Humphrey de Verde Leigh, who had flown anti-submarine patrols in the First World War, and knew from experience that U-boats tended to surface at night. If the aircraft carried a searchlight, the target could be seen and attacked. Why not simply mount a searchlight on the aircraft, and switch it on during the attack to illuminate the target?

The reality proved much more complicated. On 23 October 1940 Leigh outlined his plan to fit an Army 36-inch searchlight below the belly of a Coastal

Command aircraft. A number of twin-engined Vickers Wellington twin-engined bombers had been used to detonate German magnetic mines in coastal waters by electrical signals, and were fitted with powerful generators that could now be used to provide power for the searchlight. At this stage, Wellingtons (like almost everything else) were reserved for Bomber Command, but these modified aircraft had vanished into the magnetic-mine research programme, and so were easy to requisition.

With Bristol Pegasus air-cooled radials, the Mark 1A Wellington had a useful top speed of 235mph at operational height and an even more useful range of 1,800 miles – or up to 2,500 miles at a stretch. Defensive armament consisted of two Frazer-Nash power-operated gun turrets in nose and tail, each with two 0.303-inch machine guns and a retractable 'dustbin' turret in the ventral position behind the bomb bay. However, several problems had to be solved first. The beam had to be controllable so the crew could avoid being dazzled as they kept the target illuminated during the approach. It needed to be kept at the right temperature, and the whole set-up had to be reliable and easy to use under operational conditions. In addition to all that, Leigh had to see off some infinitely less practical ideas being put up in competition.

Scientists from the Royal Aircraft Establishment (RAE) at Farnborough claimed the searchlight was too big to fit a Wellington. In November 1940 they suggested one aircraft could tow a flare to illuminate the sea, with another free to attack any submarines it revealed. Leigh pointed out that any surfaced U-boat would dive as soon as it saw the aircraft approaching, and would certainly not remain illuminated long enough for a successful attack. Finally, if a submarine was attacked near a convoy, the flare might show the whereabouts of the merchantmen.[2]

Fortunately, Leigh's bosses supported him, and he made one improvement. The Navy's smaller 24-inch destroyer searchlight could fit inside the space left by removing the ventral turret. Using the existing turret-control system, the crew could move the light and keep the target in view until they dropped their bombs. Furthermore, as the light would be in use for such a short time, it could be powered by batteries, recharged from the engines, rather than by a generator.

Flight tests began with a searchlight-equipped Wellington, and a British submarine off the Ulster coast in May 1941. They proved disappointing at first. However, once the crew realised they had to leave the light on for a longer time to pick up the target, results improved dramatically. Then, when success seemed assured, orders arrived to scrap the project and send Leigh back to his office.

What caused this setback? An RAF officer of higher rank, Group Captain Helmore, had devised a searchlight for night fighters. This much more powerful unit was fitted in the nose of a twin-engined Douglas A-20 Havoc attack bomber (known to the RAF as the Boston). Unfortunately, it needed a whole bomb bay full of batteries to power it, leaving no room for weapons. As it was mounted in the nose of the aircraft, the light tended to dazzle the crew operating it; furthermore, it could not be steered to illuminate the target, though it did light up a wider area. For aircrew like RAF night-fighter pilot James Bailey, the project was a dangerous digression, ill-suited even to bringing down enemy bombers.

> The flying searchlight, or Helmore, was a Boston containing in its bomb bay half a ton of batteries. The nose was a searchlight; and the glass face of it being flat the aircraft wandered even on the calmest of days. It was illogical equipment. For if radar could take you within a thousand yards of the target, it could take you the next eight hundred. Once the range was closed, we could always see our targets by the glow of their engine exhausts, however dark the night. On moonlit nights you could see a thousand yards anyway; and on dark nights, which were most frequently cloudy, the difficulty of keeping two aircraft in close formation was excessive, for the Helmore needed another fighter to fly with it, which at the proper time could go forward into the glare to shoot the bombing aircraft down. I believe that someone had sold this foolish idea to the Prime Minister … I wrote a three-line letter to the group officer in charge of postings, saying that I thought the Helmore to be a retrograde step, a waste of time and money, and I asked to be posted to a proper formation …[3]

Helmore's concept was even less suited to submarine-hunting by night, and Leigh was recalled after two months. After fitting a strong and reliable working system weighing just 600 pounds into the old belly-turret mounting, the prototype Leigh Light-equipped Wellington Mark VIII was delivered to 1417 Flight (later 172 Squadron) at RAF Chivenor in Devon early in 1942. It was soon followed by another three aircraft, so the first operational crews could come to terms with the new system. They soon evolved a workable drill. By switching on the light as the aircraft neared the target, and then slowly raising the nose, it revealed the submarine. Because of the danger of the pilot being dazzled by the beam if he watched the target, he would normally fly the final stage of the attack on instruments until it was clearly in view.[4]

Another crucial development was the harnessing of scientific brain-power in a concept known as Operational Research. Here the objective was not to develop new equipment and weapons, but to find better ways of using existing ones. Chief of Coastal Command's Operational Research Section (ORS) was Professor P M S Blackett, a future president of the Royal Society and Nobel Prize winner. He had advised the RAF on pre-war radar development, and after the war began he helped the RAE on new bomb sights and magnetic detection for finding submerged submarines.

From August 1940 to March 1941 Blackett worked on gun-laying radar until called in by Coastal Command's new head, Air Marshal Philip Joubert de la Ferté, who took over in June 1941.[5] Blackett brought with him fellow physicist and RAE colleague Evan James Williams, and between them they began a detailed and objective analysis of all aspects of Coastal Command's operations against the U-boats.

Some of the statistics were highly discouraging; for example it took an average of a hundred reported sightings of surfaced U-boats in daylight to produce a single realistic hope of a sinking. Moreover, a study of the plot at the Western Approaches Operations Room at Derby House in Liverpool revealed the number of sightings was around a quarter of what it should have been. Were the submarine lookouts seeing the approaching planes in time to dive without even being spotted? If so, what could be done about it?[6]

At that time Coastal Command planes still wore standard night-bomber camouflage of dark green and dark earth upper surfaces and matt black undersides. This made the aircraft stand out clearly against a bright or overcast sky, so Blackett and his team experimented with different colours on models and later on full-size aircraft. Finally, they settled on sea-grey upper surfaces and white undersides as the best compromise for different weather conditions. Experiments showed this simple change meant an aircraft could get 20 per cent closer to a U-boat before being seen, and this should produce a 30 per cent increase in the number of sightings by the aircraft.[7]

ORS then turned its efforts to study what happened when the aircraft tried to sink the submarine. They analysed the statistics of U-boats spotted, attacked, and probably sunk or damaged. They concluded that 'under such circumstances, the U-boat is in fact in very little danger from aircraft, which must be regarded as merely moral deterrents, rather than killing weapons,'[8]

ORS then set about putting this right. They calculated the size of the lethal sphere around each current type of depth charge, the distance in three dimensions over which it could cause fatal damage to the U-boat's hull. In the case of the 250-pound depth charge, the sphere was between thirty and forty feet across. They then studied the way the charges were dropped, to determine the ideal spacing between charges in a single 'stick'.

Their first point was that 'the probability that the U-boat will lie partly within the lethal sphere (of a charge) will vary as the cube of the radius, so an

Junkers 88 long-range
fighter-bomber.
(US National Archives)

The RAF's response to the
Junkers 88: the formidable
and heavily armed Bristol
Beaufighter.
(US National Archives)

increase of radius by 20 per cent, say, will raise the lethality by some 75 per cent. ORS pressed for strong action … to produce depth charges filled with the most powerful explosives.' In other words, boosting the explosive power of each depth charge was statistically more effective than dropping more charges in a single attack. After this report, in September 1941, the Air Ministry agreed to use more powerful explosives.

Other ORS conclusions seemed more controversial. Crews attacking a diving submarine tended to aim ahead of it, to allow for the distance it travelled while the charges sank to their detonation depth. Successive charges were timed so the explosions occurred at close intervals, to make it more likely one would detonate close enough to damage the U-boat. Both tactics were wrong, according to ORS. To study daylight attacks, cameras and mirrors were mounted on Coastal Command aircraft, looking back at the target as the charges dropped. These showed pilots were aiming too far ahead of their targets. Professor Blackett

insisted they aim directly at the U-boat's conning tower, giving them a positive mark at which to aim, and results began to improve. The conclusions about depth charge spacing were equally surprising. The timers usually spaced charges thirty-five feet apart, but the ORS found that spacing the charges much further apart would give better results. Though common sense suggested that trebling the spacing between charges would make an attack less effective, the opposite proved to be true.

Finally they turned to the depth at which the charges detonated. Everything depended on the submarine's actual position at the time of the attack, only known precisely while surfaced or diving. Once it vanished below, its position was increasingly uncertain, and attacking it became statistically a waste of time. Yet while the submarine was visible, it was still at the very shallowest depth, so current settings of 100 feet for air-dropped depth charges were totally wrong. What was needed was a compromise setting of twenty-five feet. This would allow the charges to detonate as close as possible to a still diving submarine whose actual position remained visible.

Putting all this into practice was more difficult. By the end of 1941, new hydrostatic fuses made a 50-foot setting possible, and these were followed by 33-foot settings and finally by 25-foot setting fuses, fitted from the summer of 1942 onwards. These different measures between them transformed the effectiveness of airborne attacks on U-boats from that period onwards.[9]

These new weapons and tactics created the hope of a much needed improvement of the ASW situation over the Bay of Biscay. For the wider anti-submarine battle, a single ray of light fitfully illuminated the wastes of the Air Gap in mid-Atlantic. In the summer of 1941, almost six months before America entered the war, another US lend-lease aircraft became available. This was the Consolidated B24 Liberator, a four-engine, twin-tail heavy bomber that would later form the backbone of the US daylight bombing offensive alongside the B17 Flying Fortress.

The two aircraft would become great rivals in the affections of the crews that flew them. The B24 was only slightly faster than the B17 but carried a heavier bomb load, thanks partly to a thinner, high-efficiency

One of the first American aircraft to transform the air war against the U-boats: the Catalina amphibian used by the British, the Americans and the Canadians. This Canso, as the Canadians named the aircraft, is being loaded with depth charges prior to a patrol.

(National Library of Canada)

wing section. Its main weakness showed up when it had to ditch. With a higher-mounted wing than the B17, it tended to finish up a wreck if it was landed heavily or on its belly. If the fuselage took all the stresses, it often collapsed. Ditching in the sea was normally lethal, as the craft broke up and sank before the crew could deploy their dinghies.

But the B24's one supreme quality, which for Coastal Command made it the perfect solution to the mid-Atlantic Air Gap, was its colossal range, almost 50 per cent greater than the B17's. Remarkably, even the B24's endurance was dwarfed by aircraft already

being mass-produced in Britain – the Handley Page Halifax and later the Avro Lancaster. Sadly, these were not initially an option for Coastal Command, as the entire production was devoted to Bomber Command's night offensive over Germany.[10]

On the other hand, removing the Liberator's belly turret, the engines' turbochargers, the armour-plating and the self-sealing lining to the fuel tanks, and storing extra fuel in part of the bomb bay and the outer wing sections, transformed it into the VLR version. This could operate at a distance of 2,300 miles from its base at the low altitudes needed for anti-U-boat patrols. Not only could it reach the Air Gap, but it could stay long enough to attack any U-boats in the area or force them to dive. The other great advantage of this powerful aircraft was that even with additional fuel, it could still carry enough depth charges for a series of heavy attacks on U-boats once it found them.

Nevertheless, the biggest problem was availability. This was not due to reluctance on the part of the Americans. The first Mark I Liberators were assigned to 120 Squadron of Coastal Command, then based at Nutt's Corner, near Belfast. These had not been given the full VLR treatment, so the unit concentrated on solving the technical and maintenance problems that came with the new aircraft, before patrolling out to some 1,500 miles.

Unfortunately, hopes of a fast build-up of VLR aircraft would be frustrated by other priorities, and the opposition of two powerful individuals, one American, the other British. To begin with, progress had been highly promising. B24s of the USAAF's 1st Anti-Submarine (AS) Air Squadron were sent to England in November 1942, to St Eval in Cornwall. The 2nd AS Air Squadron's B24s, followed two months later. Two months later again both units moved to Port Lyautey in Morocco to joint the hunt for U-boats in the Mediterranean, but were replaced in England by the similarly equipped 479th AS Group.

By this time, the RAF's 120 Squadron had six VLR Liberators, with five more shorter-range Mark IIs and IIIs, but then the supply dried up. In the year that followed, with U-boats still ranging freely over the Air Gap, a thin trickle of replacements produced only another dozen VLR aircraft. Even these limited resources were enough to show that more aircraft could properly cover the mid-ocean gap, and make all the difference to the anti-submarine war. But where were the missing VLR aircraft to do this?

Most VLR Liberators were assigned to the US Navy, under Admiral Ernest King, Commander-in-Chief Fleet, after negotiations between the US Army and Navy over anti-submarine patrols. Consequently most US VLR Liberators went to the Pacific. The other powerful obstacle to Coastal Command's VLR aircraft was Air Marshal Arthur Harris, chief of Bomber

The devastating power of heavy depth charges dropped from a Liberator bomber. This type IX U-boat, *U848*, is under attack on 5 November 1943 by US Navy B24s of BV107 flying from Ascension Island. The submarine had sunk a small British freighter, the 4,600-ton *Baron Semple* while she was on passage to the Far East. A series of attacks was pressed home through a furious flak barrage, but the submarine was damaged and an oil leak resulted. Finally, after four hours the submarine broke in half and sank. The B24 crews spotted up to thirty men in the water and dropped three life rafts, but only one survivor was picked up by the American cruiser uss *Marblehead* almost a month later, and he died in hospital.

(US National Archives)

Command. Not content with reserving every Halifax and Lancaster heavy bomber for raids against Germany, he has often been charged with seizing all the B24s for his command too. While this would be consistent with his viewing every other aspect of the war as a diversion from levelling German cities, the exact truth is difficult to determine.

So high were the losses resulting from bombing Germany night after night that the complex training system, including Operational Conversion Units and replacements for individual squadrons, had to be based on aircraft types in common use within the Command. Introducing a handful of B24s into a huge force of Wellingtons, Stirlings, Halifaxes and Lancasters was going to be at best a diversion, at worst a recipe for chaos. The full Bomber Command Order of Battle for January 1945, at the peak of its strength, makes no mention of the B24, apart from the B24 Mark VI, a radio counter-measures aircraft of 223 Squadron, part of the specialist 100 Group ECM unit.

B24s were used as bombers by the RAF, but not as part of Harris's campaign against the German homeland. They flew missions in North Africa and Italy, and later in the Far East during the fighting in Burma. If Harris really had an indirect interest in what happened to the B24s, it could be that he realised that

large-scale diversions to Coastal Command could mean a drain of Halifaxes and Lancasters to meet these overseas commitments.

In one sense, the British were architects of their own misfortune. While the Liberator was in painfully short supply, another ideal contender for the role was under their control. The formidable Avro Lancaster had the range and the lift capacity to make an even better anti-submarine aircraft than the B24. Indeed, several countries, including Canada and France, successfully used it in this role after the war. Even the RAF's post-war anti-submarine Shackleton was directly derived from the bomber, and stayed in front-line service into the 1970s.

Lancasters were already in large-scale production in Britain, with large numbers of crews trained to fly them. Diverting and modifying even a hundred of these aircraft and training their crews in over-water navigation and the techniques of aiming and dropping depth charges could have been done relatively quickly. Bearing in mind that on the catastrophic Nuremburg raid of 30 March 1944 no less than 107 bombers were lost on a single night, a diversion on this scale over a relatively long period would hardly have blunted the edge of the night-bombing campaign. To heighten the irony, later analysis showed this raid caused the deaths of four times as many RAF airmen as it did Germans on the ground.[11]

Unfortunately, hindsight can never fully reflect the conflicts of the time. Churchill was accused of gullibility in believing Harris's claims for night-bombing campaigns. Given the prime minister's eternal enthusiasm for the offensive, pounding German cities into rubble might have had more appeal than searching for the elusive U-boats, but this ignores Churchill's known worries over the submarine threat. A more likely reason was the need to keep Russia in the war as an ally. At the time, Stalin was clamouring for a Second Front to divert the remorseless pressure of the Wehrmacht on the Soviet Union. The bomber offensive was the only hope Churchill could realistically offer to deter the Soviets from opting for a separate peace, a possibility known to concern him deeply.

Furthermore, even if RAF aircraft had been diverted to close the Air Gap, geography meant they could not do this on their own. With the right aircraft they could reach and patrol the centre of the gap, but the other half of the chasm needed equally long-range patrols from North America. Not only were US planes being diverted to the Pacific, but Canadian AS squadrons failed to secure any VLR Liberators directly from American sources. Only when Coastal Command was able to spare some from its meagre and urgently needed stocks of the VLR variant did the RCAF receive any at all..

Apart from the handful of VLR B-24s in 120 Squadron and the few USAAF AS units protecting mid-Atlantic convoys on their own, the only Allied option was to step up attacks on U-boats crossing the Bay of Biscay to and from their French bases. In the early stages of this concerted and deliberate campaign, results had been disappointing. Professor Blackett's statistics showed that, because of poor navigation, a tendency to fly too high for optimum radar performance, and unreliability of the early radar sets, Coastal Command had found too few U-boats in the first place. New measures, including the shallow depth-charge settings and the Leigh Light promised improvements – in time.

The first real successes in airborne ASW occurred south of Iceland rather than within the bay. On 25 August 1941, a 209 Squadron Coastal Command Catalina spotted the new type VIIC U-boat U452 on the surface. The flying boat made a text-book low-level attack, and dropped a stick of four heavy 450-pound depth charges, set to the new shallower settings. Two of them bracketed the submarine and blew its stern out of the water. The U-boat then disappeared, but when an armed trawler reached the position in response to the Catalina's signals and dropped further depth charges, wreckage was blown to the surface. The kill was shared between air and surface forces, but would clearly not have happened without the Catalina.

The second sighting, two days later, had a more remarkable result. Another Iceland patrol by a 269 Squadron Hudson sighted another new type VIIC, U570, which had troubles of its own. The boat had struck bottom crash-diving to avoid a British aircraft off Norway, which wrecked its hydrophones. It suffered loose batteries, badly tuned diesels, a faulty air compressor, one leaking torpedo tube and a badly seasick crew. The skipper, Kapitänleutnant Hans Rahmlow, surfaced to search for a reported convoy, as his hydrophones could give no warning of its presence.

When Rahmlow emerged from the conning-tower hatch, he was appalled to see an aircraft approaching at low level. The Hudson crew had picked up the U-boat's radar echo and attacked immediately. The stick of depth charges on the shallower settings dropped accurately across the U-boat's hull, with two of them straddling it. The effects were catastrophic. Lights went out, instruments shattered and the submarine almost capsized. Someone shouted that the batteries in the after compartment were emitting chlorine gas. The crew rushed forward into the control room and closed the watertight doors, sealing off the rearmost compartments of the boat.

Rahmlow tried to dive, but the boat failed to respond. The controls for motors and diving planes planes remained inaccessible in the after compartments. If the boat filled with chlorine gas, they would have to abandon ship, but in the open Atlantic this seemed suicidal. He decided to surrender to the Hudson orbiting overhead. It had dropped all its depth charges, though Rahmlow did not know that.

The Hudson was joined by another from the same squadron and later by the Catalina that had earlier sunk the U452. Finally a small squadron of destroyers and trawlers, summoned by the aircraft, arrived on the scene. The German crew were taken prisoner and their U-boat towed to Iceland. It was eventually towed to England and commissioned into the Royal Navy as HMS *Graph*.

Though the Germans succeeded in destroying the Enigma cipher apparatus, with the code books and settings tables, the capture proved helpful in another way. Mock-ups were built of the U-boat's interior to train boarding parties searching for vital Enigma data, and show which valves to close to thwart the crew's attempts to scuttle their submarine.[12] To complete this apparent shift in fortunes, Iceland-based aircraft found and attacked two more U-boats the next day and depth-charged them so effectively that one had to return to base for repairs.

After these successes, the spotlight shifted again on 30 November, this time to the Mediterranean,

In the early days following America's entry into the war, aircraft available for anti-submarine patrols along the vulnerable eastern seaboard included these slow and elderly Kingfisher seaplanes manned by the US Coast Guard.

(US Naval Institute Press)

where a U-boat was attacked and apparently sunk in the Bay of Biscay by a 502 Squadron Whitley. In fact, the attack was unsuccessful and it was later decided the submarine had been sunk by a mine off its home port the day before, sinking with its entire crew.[13] Its position had been revealed by an Enigma decrypt, as one of a group of twenty ordered to the Mediterranean, and it was on others from this group that an air attack did finally prove successful.

The obstacle to entering the Mediterranean was the passage through the constricted and closely watched waters of the Straits of Gibraltar, which were patrolled by the antique Swordfishes of 812 Squadron, Fleet Air Arm. A steady west to east current flowed through the centre of the straits from the Atlantic into the Mediterranean. To take advantage of this, the U-boats passing through the straits would surface at dusk, timing their transit of the narrows to take place in darkness, running at their best speed with less danger of being spotted.

However these particular Swordfish carried ASV radar, which could reveal any surfaced U-boat within the straits, and the open cockpits gave an unrivalled view for the final stages of the attack. Furthermore, the Germans could not see the Swordfish against the night sky, so the aircrew could deliver careful attacks, and the results were deadly. During the first twenty days of December 1941, no less than five type VIIC U-boats – *U96*, *U202*, *U432*, *U558* and *U569* were

spotted and attacked with depth charges. All five had to limp back to their Biscay bases for repairs. Finally, on the night of 21 December, 812 Squadron sank their first submarine, when three 450-pound depth charges sent *U451* to the bottom.[14]

Meanwhile, the Leigh Light Wellingtons issued to 172 Squadron were finally making their presence felt. On the night of 3 June 1942, four aircraft fanned out towards their assigned patrol sectors. 'F for Freddie' piloted by the CO, Squadron Leader Jeaff Greswell, headed for the far southwestern corner of the Bay, some seventy miles north of the Spanish coast. There, at 1.27am, they picked up a radar echo, just over five miles away. They turned towards the target, but the first time the light was switched on, it missed the target but the crew spotted a large U-boat pass beneath them. Greswell realised they were flying too high as changes in barometric pressure since leaving base had misled the altimeter.

That submarine was the *Luigi Torelli*. After Greswell delivered his second attack, the crippled submarine tried to head back to Bordeaux on the surface, along the Spanish coast. While mist shielded her from aircraft, it blanked out landmarks, and she ran aground. When her crew refloated her, they took shelter in the neutral Spanish port of Aviles, but were forced to leave or face internment. Without repairs, she could not dive.

On the morning of 7 June she was attacked by two

Mariner flying boats were assigned to the US Navy under the inter-service division of responsibilities for the air anti-submarine war, and their long range and large weapons stores made them very effective patrol planes. This is a variant used for long-range air-sea rescue patrols.

(US Naval Institute Press)

Marlin flying boats reinforced the Mariners in long range submarine patrols.

(US Naval Institute Press)

Sunderlands, which left her with a jammed rudder and losing buoyancy. The crew dropped her deck gun overboard to save weight, leaving her completely defenceless. They sailed into Santander harbour and beached her on a sandbank. She was then transferred to a dry dock for repairs before being taken over by the Spanish Navy.

On 4 July, a month after the original attack, the *Luigi Torelli* was being towed to a mooring at the rear of the harbour. The Italian skipper cut the towlines, started the engines and dashed for the harbour entrance, carrying off the assistant harbourmaster and a naval engineer, under the guns of an escorting Spanish warship.[15] The escape succeeded and the submarine finally reached Bordeaux on 15 July. After

repairs, she carried secret documents and components to the Japanese, and in the Far East she was taken over by the Kriegsmarine and renumbered *UIT25*. After the Germans surrendered, the Japanese commissioned her as *I504*. She was taken over by the Americans after the Japanese surrender, and finally scuttled off the Japanese coast a year later.

For Coastal Command, the lesson of the *Torelli* was disturbing. This large submarine had been caught unawares in the first attack and almost helpless in the second. Why had she not been sunk by three sticks of well-placed depth charges? In addition, the charges used in the original attack were 250-pounders filled with the more powerful Torpex explosive suggested by ORS. Greswell was convinced that many of the fuses were defective.

The truth was more complex. Depth charges dropped from aircraft hit the water faster than those fired or dropped from surface ships, and sank very quickly, dragging down an air bubble with them. This shielded the hydrostatic fuse from increasing water pressure, and delayed the detonation. The solution was to reshape the charge, replacing the original convex nose with a dished or concave nose cap, and fitting a tail unit weak enough to break off on hitting the water. These charges sank more slowly, without trapping the air bubble, so the fuses tripped at the correct depth.

The first successful night-time kill of a U-boat by a Wellington followed only a month later. Another 172 Squadron aircraft, 'H for Harry' was patrolling the central sector of the western approaches to the Bay on the night of 4 July. Appropriately, it was piloted by an American, Pilot Officer Wiley B Howell, who had joined the RAF before the Pearl Harbor attack and was commissioned as a Pilot Officer. At 4.45am the following morning, the crew picked up an echo seven miles away to starboard. They switched on the searchlight a mile from the target. They flew across the U-boat's bows from starboard to port, dropping four depth charges from a height of fifty feet, while the rear-gunner machine-gunned the conning tower.

The Wellington flew back across the area where the U-boat had disappeared, dropping flame floats to light up the sea. There was no sign of the submarine, though the water seemed darker where it had disappeared, suggesting an oil slick. At 5.13am the Wellington headed back to base. The submarine was the type IXC *U502*, returning to base from the Caribbean where she had sunk nine ships, including two US tankers, but she had been sunk with all hands by an impeccably executed attack.

More kills soon followed. Twelve days later an outward-bound type VII, *U751*, was spotted on the surface in broad daylight by a Whitley of 502 Squadron. After the bomber dropped all its charges without success, it radioed for back-up before returning to base as fuel was running low. When help arrived, it was in the unusual form of a Lancaster of RAF Bomber Command, temporarily transferred to the Coastal Command station at St Eval, with a Coastal Command officer flying as a second navigator. First they found an oil slick and later the submarine herself, now back on the surface. The Lancaster dropped its stick of depth charges right across the submarine, which seemed to be making no attempt to dive. Realising it was damaged, the pilot, Flight Lieutenant Peter Casement, climbed to 700 feet and came back to drop his anti-submarine bombs on the target, which began sinking by the stern as its crew struggled to abandon their craft.

In spite of these successes, there were still huge obstacles in the Biscay campaign. Radar and search-lights helped, but success remained difficult and costly to pursue. Long after the war, some thought the whole idea of attacking the U-boats anywhere except around convoys to be 'probably the worst [British] misjudgement of the long Atlantic battle'.[16] To stop it from being merely an expensive mistake, more ingenuity and hard work would be needed. On the other hand, given the Second World War submarine's slow underwater speed, an anti-submarine aircraft was successful if it never even saw its adversary but merely forced it to dive. So long as patrols forced U-boats to spend more time crossing the bay under-water, they were reducing the proportion of time spent on operations – and with it the effective size of Doenitz's fleet.

This was just as well, for the official figures were still discouraging. Between June 1942 and the beginning of 1943, Coastal Command had flown almost 25,000 hours of patrols, and lost some 100 aircraft to accident and enemy action. This huge and expensive effort sank just seven U-boats. In this second stage of the bay campaign, the sad fact remained that more U-boats crossed to and from their bases undisturbed than were sighted, attacked or above all destroyed. In the first two weeks of February 1943 intelligence from Enigma and other sources revealed that forty U-boats crossed the bay between their bases and their operational areas. Only eighteen were sighted and attacked, and just one was sunk.

Significantly, that achievement was down to an American Liberator with centimetric radar. In the second half of the month, a Leigh Light Wellington of the RAF sank one submarine. Finally, in an eight-day blitz on the submarine routes, Wellingtons with centimetric radar looked for the forty-one U-boats known to make the crossing; only thirteen were seen, and only one of these was sunk.[17]

So these first successful sinkings of operational U-boats by British and American aircraft were encouraging, but little more. Yet one person was to change all that. On 16 July Admiral Doenitz ordered U-boats to stay surfaced in daylight, when at least they had a fighting chance of spotting an aircraft approaching, so they could dive to evade it. At night, when they would have no warning, they were to remain submerged. This dramatic change meant sightings in the bay more than doubled in the following two months.

Finally, the Leigh Light had become a temporary victim of its own success. The Germans realised some kind of aircraft-mounted radar had enabled Allied aircraft to find targets at night, and had actually possessed a British ASV set from a shot-down aircraft since 1941. This had been fitted in a Focke-Wulf Kondor for trials, and though it was not developed any further for their own use, they were aware of its capabilities. More importantly, they knew the fre-quencies on which it operated. It proved relatively simple to design a receiver to pick up the radar transmissions at a long enough range for a U-boat to dive before it could be attacked.

In many respects, the Germans showed a strange reluctance to develop new technology to keep pace with increasing Allied technical superiority, but in this case, they moved quickly. Within two months of the first Leigh Light attacks, they produced prototypes of a search receiver, and placed three examples on board U-boats for trials. It was a crude device, with cable wound round a wooden frame in an X-shaped configuration and led through the open conning-tower hatch to a receiver in the submarine's radio room. The radio operator would hear radar signals as a buzz in the headphones, early enough for the aerial and cable connection to be carried below before the submarine dived to safety.

Trials showed the device, the R600A, could detect aircraft radar at more than eighty miles, or about twice the range at which return echoes would alert the aircraft to the U-boat under ideal conditions. The only problem was the shortage of factory space to produce enough sets for the large U-boat fleet. This was solved by ordering two French companies, Metox and Grandin, to make them under licence (as a result the device was normally known as the Metox receiver, though many crews called it the 'Biscay Cross'). Secondly those U-boats first equipped with it escorted less-fortunate colleagues across the bay by night, knowing they could not be attacked without warning.[18]

Introducing Metox also meant that as U-boats could cross the bay on the surface at night, there was now less need to surface during the day. Consequently there were just two sightings of U-boats in August 1942, and one in September. It was time for the Allies to try something new. But for the time being, another German innovation was beginning to complicate life for air patrols over the Bay of Biscay.

Earlier in the campaign, the Luftwaffe used formations of Junkers 88s to attack the anti-submarine patrols. These twin-engined long-range fighters had a top speed of 300mph, a range of 1,250 miles and carried a battery of five forward-firing machine guns in the nose. The smaller and less heavily armed patrol planes like Hudsons and Whitleys proved fairly easy targets, but the redoubtable Sunderlands fought back on at least two occasions.'

In April 1940, a 204 Squadron Sunderland from Sullom Voe in the Shetlands had been escorting a North Sea convoy when it was attacked by two Ju88s from Norway, which it drove off with ease. Later four Ju88s tried bombing the convoy, but were beaten off by naval anti-aircraft gunfire. Finally, six Ju88s returned to attack the flying boat. The pilot, Flight Lieutenant Frank Phillips, dropped down to sea level to prevent attacks from below. As two of the Junkers came in to attack from one side, the others attacked from astern. With great courage, the rear gunner endured the fire from one German aircraft until it came within 100 yards of his turret. Then he fired a short burst at point-blank range. It was enough. The Junkers reared up, burst into flames and crashed into the sea. The gunner, Corporal Bill Lillie, swung his guns across in time to put a burst into the port engine of a second attacker, which retreated leaving a trail of smoke to mark its passing. After trying to drop bombs on the flying boat from above, and missing due to the Sunderland's evasive action, the remaining Junkers returned to base.

The tactics used over the bay proved more formidable. The Ju88s now attacking Coastal Command patrols

The Handley Page Halifax was one of the two most successful heavy bombers used in the RAF's night attacks against Germany, but in time these planes too joined the anti-U-boat patrols.

(US National Archives)

Underpowered, slow and cumbersome, the Armstrong Whitworth Whitley had one advantage for Coastal Command – she was too obsolete to be needed any longer by Bomber Command for raiding Germany.

(US National Archives)

Key to denying the U-boats the protection of the Mid-Atlantic Air Gap, the very long range version of the B24 Liberator helped finally turn the tables against Doenitz's submarines.

(US Naval Institute Press)

The Catalina extended Allied air patrols further into the Atlantic thanks to long range at cruising speed.

(US Naval Institute Press)

were the Ju88C2 fighter version, more heavily armed with a cannon replacing one of the nose machine guns, and grouped in larger formations, sometimes backed up by single-seat fighters. On 13 February 1943, an Australian-crewed Sunderland from Pembroke Dock in South Wales was attacked by two Ju88s and a pair of FW190s but survived the experience. On 2 June, on a daylight patrol over the bay, the same aircraft and crew were set upon by no less than eight Ju88s in a succession of carefully synchronised attacks.

The first onslaught set the Sunderland's port outer engine on fire and shattered the compass, spraying the cockpit with burning alcohol. Another burst wrecked the rear turret and wounded the gunner, and a third wounded the navigator and killed one of the side gunners. Though the pilot, Flight Lieutenant Colin Walker, threw the huge flying boat from side to side in furious corkscrews to throw the German gunners off their aim, more bursts hit their target. The cockpit fire was out but all the instruments were shattered, the intercom had stopped working, the

propeller had fallen off the port outer engine into the sea, and the violent manoeuvres had twisted the airframe out of shape, so internal doors and hatches all jammed.

Not that the attackers were unscathed. By waiting until the last possible moment, with German bullets shredding the metalwork around him, the mid-upper gunner, W O Goode, let one of the attacking Junkers get within fifty yards of his guns. A brief but accurate burst sent it plunging into the sea. When another Junkers tried a similar manoeuvre, Goode and the nose gunner used the same tactics, setting the Ju88's starboard engine on fire. The aircraft hit the sea before cartwheeling and disappearing.

The remaining six German planes continued attacking their battered opponent. By now the rear gunner had recovered consciousness and moved his wrecked turret manually to open fire on another Junkers making a stern attack, which rolled over and plunged into the sea. Within minutes another had been hit by the nose gunner and flew off with its cockpit on fire. Soon afterwards the remaining Junkers disappeared, after a forty-five-minute combat that left the flying boat riddled, and almost uncontrollable.

In an epic of skill and endurance, Walker brought it home to England. He decided to beach the Sunderland off the Cornish coast rather than risk making for Pembroke Dock. On his final approach the starboard inner engine failed, removing any hope of a second landing attempt if anything went wrong on the first. He brought the crippled flying boat down on the water off the long beach at Praa Sands, using the two remaining engines to run her as far up the sand as possible before she ran aground. The crew walked ashore, but the Sunderland was wrecked by the surf before she could be salvaged.

In spite of these amazing examples, other Coastal Command patrols went missing after signals warning they were being attacked. The RAF sent out patrols of their Ju88 equivalents, twin-engined Bristol Beau-fighters armed with a battery of four 20-mm cannon in the nose and half a dozen machine guns in the wings. Unfortunately, these airborne hunter-killer groups could not guarantee to meet the enemy on a given sortie, while the anti-submarine patrols were an almost continuous presence in the skies over the bay.

The Mark III Sunderland anti-submarine flying boat from 461 Squadron Royal Australian Air Force based at Pembroke Dock in South Wales, skippered by Flight-Lieutenant Colin Walker, which beat off attacks from eight Junkers 88 fighters, shooting down three of them, and finally managing to ditch on a Cornish beach.

(Author's drawing)

So ORS scientists were called in. Could the routines of the German fighters be predicted, so the Beau-fighters could find them? All reports of German fighters were analysed, and they showed the probability of sighting German fighters was much greater when Enigma traffic and naval intelligence showed large numbers of U-boats crossing the bay. This made it possible to send out more anti-submarine patrols whenever larger numbers of U-boats were expected, and the RAF then deployed more fighters to fight off German attempts to shoot down the anti-submarine patrols. Later ORS analysis showed interceptions between Allied and German fighters had doubled as a result.

Eventually the Germans changed their tactics. They began flying random patrols across the bay, independent of U-boat activity. By this time, ORS reports showed the higher number of interceptions had persuaded the Germans to assemble fighters in groups of six or even eight at a time, like those trying to shoot down the 461 Squadron Sunderland. Given limited Luftwaffe resources, this greatly reduced the number of attacks. During the entire ASW offensive in the bay, submarine-hunting aircraft made some 9,000 sorties, and just fifty-two were shot down by enemy fighters, a loss rate so low as to make Bomber Command or the Eighth Air Force deeply envious.

One other Allied tactic proved successful during the later months of 1942. Where a U-boat had been seen and attacked unsuccessfully, it was assumed the U-boat would be careful not to expose itself again, and patrols were ordered to look elsewhere. ORS analysis suggested a different picture. They reasoned that a submarine surprised on the surface would have been desperate to recharge batteries and replenish air reserves. This would force her to surface again as soon as possible to complete the task. Furthermore, her course and speed could be predicted reasonably accurately.

This was the theory behind the 'baiting' tactics used as more anti-submarine aircraft became available with the endurance to remain on station for longer. If a U-boat was forced to dive either before or after being attacked, crews were ordered to clear the area for up to half an hour before returning to the search. This greatly increased the number of sightings, compared with patrols searching a wider area of the bay in the normal way.

However, since Leigh Lights and ASV radar had been countered by the Germans' Metox receivers, it became difficult to find and attack U-boats at night. During daylight, tactics were changed to take the new situation into consideration. Anti-submarine patrols flew lower without radar, since they no longer needed to separate the U-boats' radar echo from the background 'clutter' caused by reflections off the sea surface. This also reduced the area of sea they had to search to see their targets. When they spotted a U-boat, they could attack more quickly, while the need to switch from the Metox set to a visual lookout caught some U-boat crews by surprise.

The Germans were also flooded with radar signals. All aircraft were to leave their sets transmitting continuously over the Bay, except for Leigh Light Wellingtons, in the hope of catching a U-boat off its guard. Because a U-boat's radar alarm would be sounding all the time, it should therefore not be aware that it was being picked up by a particular aircraft. Though this appeared convincing in theory, it was not reflected in the results. During January 1943 sightings in the bay hit a new low, with 3,136 hours of daylight sorties resulting in five sightings and 827 hours at night producing just three.[19]

In the longer term, the answer to this German equipment was to be the formidable ASV Mark III centimetric radar, working on frequencies that the Germans could not pick up and having greatly improved performance compared with its predecessor. But before this became available in the spring of 1943, following the inevitable demands for priority from Bomber Command, there remained one area where U-boats were still plentiful: the mid-Atlantic Air Gap.

With many Coastal Command squadrons, and those of the US Navy and Army Air Force concen-

Providing U-boats with warning of the approach of Allied aircraft using metric-wavelength ASV radar, the 'Metox' receiver used an X-shaped aerial on a wooden frame which the U-boat crews called the 'Biscay Cross'.
(Iak Mallmann Showell)

The later versions of the Metox receiver used a dipole aerial (seen to the left of the periscope) but was no more useful against centimetric radar than its predecessor had been.
(Jak Mallmann Showell)

found a particularly valuable type XIV tanker submarine, *U464*. As the Catalina headed for convoy SN73, it passed over a small Icelandic trawler, and when still ten miles short of the convoy the crew spotted a U-boat in very rough seas just under a mile away.

At 6.10am, the Catalina attacked, dropping five depth charges. Two exploded on either side of the conning tower. The submarine remained on the surface, leaking large quantities of oil, and firing back at the PBY. Hopgood flew on to the convoy and signalled a report to the escort commander, who sent a four-stack ex-US Navy destroyer HMS *Castleton* to investigate. When the warship arrived, they found the U-boat crew had boarded the Icelandic trawler from their sinking craft and were trying to use it for a bold attempt to escape to German-occupied Norway. The destroyer stopped the trawler and took fifty-two U-boat men prisoner.

Three weeks later the Iceland-based RAF B24 of Squadron Leader Terrence Bulloch, who became a formidable destroyer of U-boats, was heading for convoy ONS 136. His crew picked up a radar contact, and saw a surfaced U-boat five minutes later. They attacked it, and sank the type VIIC *U597* with all hands, Bulloch's first sinking. Later, he evolved his own personal methods for attacking surfaced U-boats, against the advice of ORS. They recommended dropping a stick of depth charges across the hull of the U-boat, calculating that the length of the stick would compensate for any errors in the timing of the drop, and the length of the U-boat hull would present a suitably wide target.

Bulloch reasoned that the depth charge spacing might allow the U-boat to survive because the charges exploding on either side of the hull might be too far away for fatal damage. Instead, he changed the spacing to bring the explosions much closer together. Then he attacked along the length of the submarine's hull, placing the stick of charges as close alongside the U-boat as possible. This called for very accurate aiming, but if all went well, every charge could contribute to the damage to the submarine's hull. It was a high-risk tactic, but it worked well for Bulloch.

Two more U-boats were attacked by US Navy PBYs during November. One escaped, but on the 5 November 1942, a VP84 Catalina dropped two Mark XVII depth charges with two heavier Mark XXIX charges, and blew the bridge party into the water before the U-boat could dive. The type VIIC *U408* was confirmed destroyed. Air attacks were becoming more formidable, even in the heart of the U-boat's battleground.

For example, eastbound convoy HX217 was attacked by a massive wolf pack with between three and four submarines for each escort, or almost one submarine for each merchant vessel. Yet only two ships were sunk, for the loss of no less than three U-boats, one through collision and two from air attack. The key was constant

trating on the Bay of Biscay, other units with long-range aircraft had continued escorting convoys as far as they could reach. Here, making low-level attacks to drop shallow-setting depth charges proved more successful. Even in cases where aircraft had dropped all their depth charges they could still force shadowing submarines to submerge and lose contact with the convoys.

During the late summer and autumn of 1942, US Navy Catalinas operating from Iceland into the edge of the Air Gap were sinking U-boats regularly. On the early morning of 20 August, for example, a PBY piloted by Lieutenant R B Hopgood from VP73 Squadron

Depth charges dropped in a 'stick' from an attacking aircraft exploded at regular intervals and were timed to maximise the chances of one or more exploding close enough to the target to sink it.

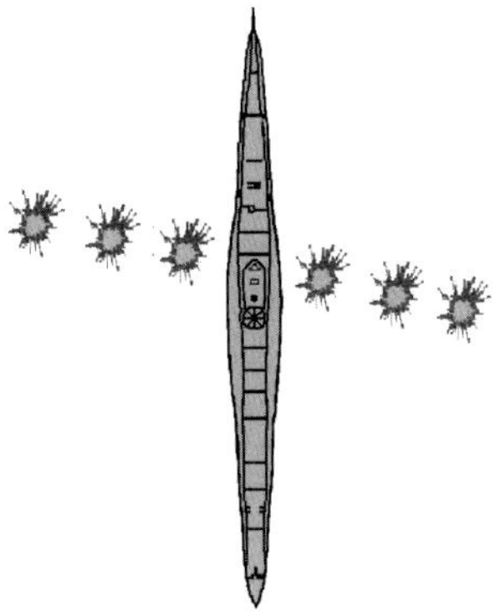

Operational Research Section analyses showed the best chances of sinking a U-boat would result from the timers being adjusted to drop the charges further apart.

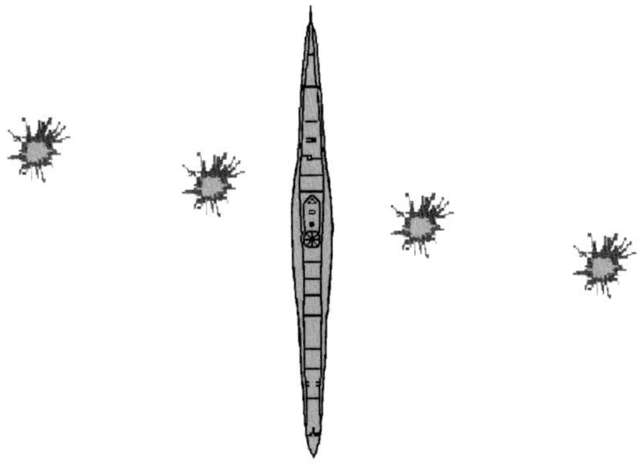

For a very skilled pilot, like Coastal Command's top scoring ASW skipper, Squadron Leader Terrence Bulloch, the best way to maximise the effect of the charges was to drop the entire stick alongside the U-boat's hull, but this called for very precise flying, often into intense anti-aircraft fire.

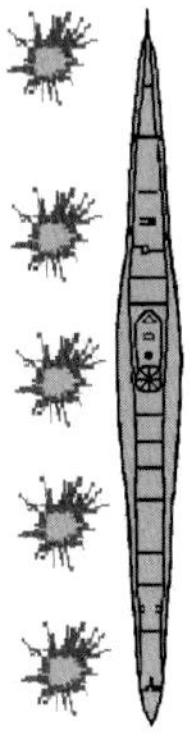

(Author's drawings)

air cover at extreme range, and resolute attacks to sink the submarines or at least drive them under.

Coastal Command had already decided that finding a U-boat shadowing a convoy and forcing it to dive definitely paid dividends over waiting to disrupt an attack actually in progress. Now ORS went a considerable step further. Studying crew reports revealed that patrols that failed to meet their convoys after the long approach flight often did more damage to U-boats than those that found the ships straight away. It appeared that U-boat packs homing in on a convoy's reported position often assembled as much as twenty miles away, and orders to the patrol aircraft were changed to try to find this grouping.

Between August 1942 and May 1943 these more distant patrols attacked 40 per cent more U-boats than the continuous close escort favoured by US forces. The knock-on effects were that daytime sinkings were reduced, but it was the night-time losses which were

cut even more sharply – half as many on the first night of a pack attack and half of that reduced level on the second. More U-boats were found behind the convoy by later patrols, suggesting that the cohesion of the pack had been broken up once the shadowing boat had been sunk or driven below the surface.[20]

The month of March 1943 proved to be the crisis of the whole Atlantic battle (see Chapter 13). Already there was a clear contrast between the fortunes of convoys enjoying air cover compared with those which did not. This resulted in new pressures being brought to bear at the highest level to ensure more long-range aircraft were provided to fill the remaining gaps. According to two historians of the Atlantic battle, one British and one American, President Roosevelt pointedly asked Admiral King to explain where the US Navy's VLR B24s had been during these vital convoy battles.[21]

Whatever his explanation, five squadrons of US Navy B24s being assembled for the Atlantic campaign were quickly sent across the Atlantic, three to be based in southern England and the other two in North Africa. On the western side, one Newfoundland-based squadron of the Royal Canadian Air Force, was equipped with VLR B24s for the first time, using aircraft reassigned from RAF Coastal Command.

In fact, as often happens in wartime, the tables were turned extremely quickly. Just as the U-boats seemed to gain the upper hand, fate handed them a crippling defeat. Many of the reasons had little directly to do with ensuring long-range air coverage across the middle Atlantic. One was the effect of centimetric radar, restoring the ability of Allied aircraft to find and attack U-boats both by day and night.

Another was the introduction of escort carriers in both the Royal and United States navies, which could eliminate the Air Gap by sailing all the way with the convoys they protected. A third was increasingly powerful intelligence, from the breaking of the Enigma ciphers and also the highly sophisticated use of Huff-Duff, or HFDF, to pinpoint the position of U-boats far out in the ocean, and apparently safe from air or surface attack.

One example from June 1942 shows how effective this was. The crew of the type IXC *U158* had sunk thirteen ships in the Gulf of Mexico and off Bermuda. They had boarded and scuttled their final victim, a 4,000-ton freighter, after using all their torpedoes. The skipper, Erich Rostin, reported to U-Boat headquarters on 30 June, but his brief signal was picked up by several different direction-finding stations, including one on Bermuda, to give an accurate position. Bermuda-based US Navy Patrol Squadron 74, equipped with Martin Mariner flying boats, ordered one to the reported position.

After a 50-mile flight, the crew found *U158* on the surface with sailors sunbathing on deck. In waters so close to Allied bases, they paid the price for this criminal negligence within minutes. Before the crew could react, the Mariner dropped two anti-submarine bombs, but not close enough to the submarine to inflict serious damage. The plane turned and delivered another attack, dropping two Mark XVII depth charges with shallow settings on the now rapidly diving submarine. One seemed to jam in the conning tower structure, and when the U-boat finally submerged, it detonated with fatal results. *U*158 was lost with all her crew, in a fast and clinical operation that would become increasingly routine.[22]

In January 1943, the Anglo-American Casablanca Conference had reaffirmed the British preoccupation with winning the Atlantic battle as a first priority. The Americans, anxious as they were to undertake an invasion of Occupied Europe to bring about the fall of Nazi Germany, were finally convinced that overcoming the U-boats to the point where troops, weapons and supplies could be convoyed to Britain in safety and with the minimum losses made perfect sense. With this clear decision, more and more resources would be committed to the anti-submarine war.

The result of all these factors was a dramatic shift in the balance between the submarines and the aircraft hunting them. This would turn U-boats from hunters to the hunted, having to hide from the patrols searching for them in the skies over the Atlantic as carefully as from the surface escorts pursuing them at sea. But could this change have been brought about more quickly, with a better allocation of existing resources?

American historian Clay Blair estimated that switching 100 VLR aircraft like RAF Halifaxes and American B24s would have closed the Air Gap much earlier and defeated the U-boats during 1941. Others have disagreed, on the grounds that the weapons and tactics that made these aircraft such deadly submarine-hunters were not available as early as that. Instead, British historian Dr Alfred Price has suggested that, had a smaller number of these bombers been available a year later, the results in the mid-Atlantic battle might have been very different.[23] What remains undeniable is that the obsession of RAF Bomber Command with night attacks against German cities, and their demands for an ever-greater share of the resources available, made certain that these expedients remained a matter of theory. In the stinging words of British historian John Terraine, 'it is at times difficult, taking into account the ineffectiveness of Bomber Command's "proper" activity, and its strong resistance to all "improper" activity, to decide whether it is more correct to say that Bomber Command was irrelevant to the war, or that the war was irrelevant to Bomber Command.'[24]

Even at the time, Professor Blackett of ORS calculated the value of each long-range aircraft diverted from bombing to maritime patrolling to protect convoys from U-boat attacks was that it saved an average of thirteen ships from being sunk during its operational lifetime. Aircraft used for offensive patrols, like those over the Bay of Biscay, saved approximately three merchant ships by the effects of their patrols and attacks during a single lifetime.[25] Now, with resources, weapons, and tactics being refined to more powerful effect, the Allies were about to demonstrate the lethal capabilities of air power on their courageous but increasingly handicapped opponents.

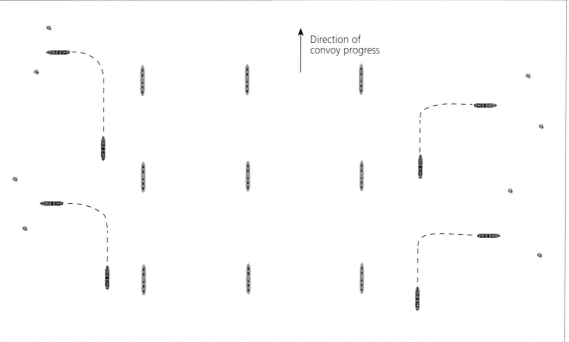

The 'Buttercup' tactic devised by 'Johnny' Walker to trap surfaced U-boats trying to attack a convoy at night. On the code word being given over the radio, all escorts were to turn outwards, increase to full speed and fire starshells for twenty minutes to reveal any targets. If none were seen, escorts would then return to their positions around the convoy. It proved effective against orthodox U-boat tactics, but not against those who, like Kretschmer, were bold enough to attack from inside the convoy.

(Author's drawing)

Direction of convoy progress

Even in the still disappointing Biscay campaign, major changes were overdue. After the meagre harvest of U-boat sinkings during 1942 and the first half of 1943, centimetric radar would greatly increase the number of sightings, attacks and sinkings. So heavy did the toll on the U-boat service become that at the end of the war, two German admirals admitted that the Biscay campaign was 'the most disconcerting offensive that they had experienced because they could not discover how or why their boats were being sunk.'[26]

U-boats attacking from inside the convoy were countered by the 'Raspberry' tactic. Immediately a ship was torpedoed in one of the inner columns, the escorts protecting the flanks of the convoy would turn around and steam to the rear of the convoy. Meanwhile the U-boat would have dived to let the convoy pass ahead of it, hoping thereby to evade the escorts while it reloaded its torpedo tubes.

(Author's drawing)

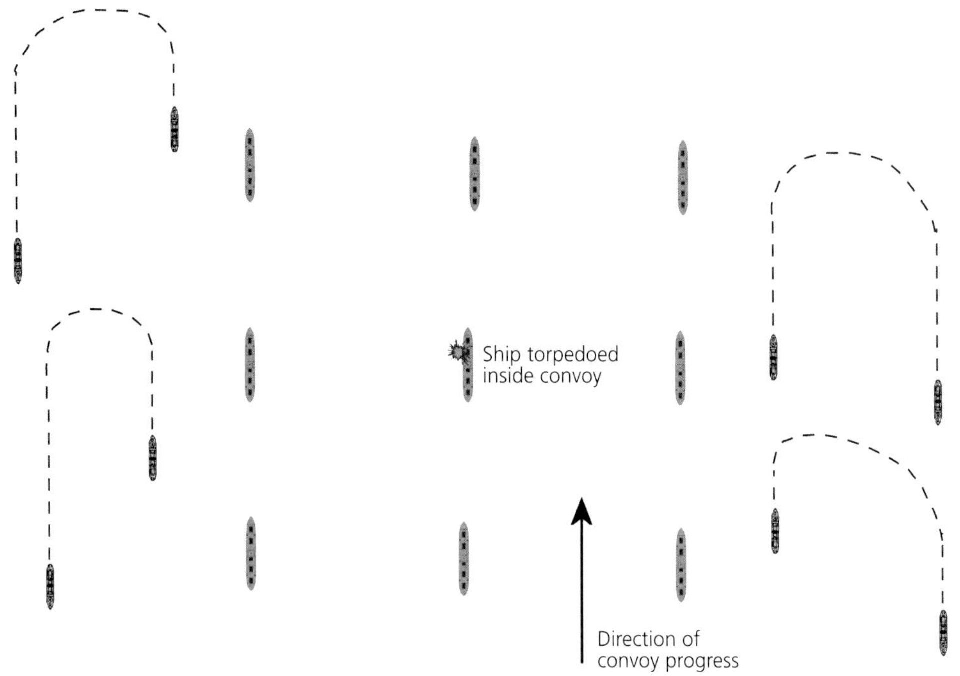

Ship torpedoed inside convoy

Direction of convoy progress

As the escorts reach a point astern of both the convoy and the position of the torpedoed ship which first raised the alarm, they turn back on their original course in a line-abreast formation covering the rear of the convoy. There they carry out a sonar search, placing them in an ideal position to pick up the echo of the submerged U-boat as it emerges into clearer water behind the convoy.

(Author's drawing)

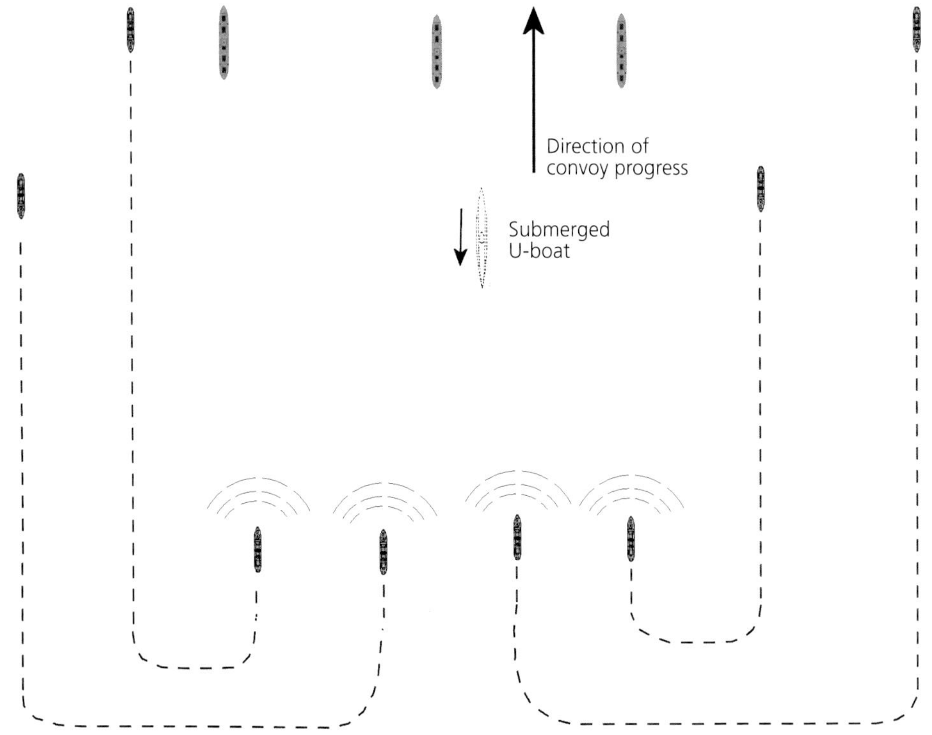

Direction of convoy progress

Submerged U-boat

CHAPTER 10

AIR POWER TIPS THE BALANCE
1942–43

THE Royal Navy's escort carrier HMS *Dasher* was not a handsome ship. Her slab sides and flat flight deck gave her the elegance of a scaled-up house brick, but she and her sisters would make a vital difference to the difficult business of sinking enemy submarines. Unfortunately, as is so often the case with new anti-submarine technology, she posed more of a threat to her crew than to the U-boats she was intended to destroy. Commander R 'Mike' Crosley, DSC RN was a wartime fighter pilot assigned to HMS *Biter,* another of the first trio of diesel powered escort carriers:

These 8000 horsepower opposed-piston engines had eight cylinders, several feet in diameter. If for some reason they had to be started – they were seldom, if ever, stopped – there would sometimes be an explosion of some kind. This would blow some vital bits of the engine up through the exhaust pipe, such as a valve stem or two and would bring the engine to a grinding halt. The engine then had to be dismantled, the loose bits and pieces removed, and the whole thing bolted together again, minus the offending connecting rods and pistons. The engine would then have to run – seriously out of balance – on six cylinders instead of eight until the next start up time, when it would probably have another explosion. Explosions occurred several times in *Archer* and, of course, in *Dasher*.[1]

An entry in Crosley's wartime diary flagged up an early but all too clear warning of *Dasher*'s eventual doom.

Dasher could only make about 12 knots because of her engine trouble. There was a terrible smell of petrol everywhere down below and no-one was allowed to smoke on board. We asked one of the junior engineers who came down to the wardroom for lunch – complete with sweat rags, cotton waste in his overall belt and a dirty, anxious face – what was going on. He said that 'the bloody diesels had thrown another pot' and one engine was only giving half power. That was why the ship was jumping a foot in the air at about 100 times a minute.[2]

Tragically, HMS *Dasher*'s short life came to an end after serving alongside sister ships HMS *Biter* and HMS *Avenger* covering the North African landings and then escorting several Atlantic convoys. From all these operations she sailed home unscathed. But on 27 March 1943 she was sailing the peaceful waters of the Firth of Clyde in Western Scotland while two of her Swordfish anti-submarine aircraft were being refuelled. Without warning the carrier was blown apart by a catastrophic

Following the success of HMS *Audacity* in fighting off the Kondors and forcing attacking U-boats to dive, US shipyards began a major conversion of merchant hulls into escort carriers for both the US and Royal navies. The first RN carriers were the 'Archer' class.

(www.navyphotos.co.uk)

explosion. A huge fireball burst through the after engine room bulkhead and out through the starboard side. All power failed and fierce fires broke out in the hangar and engine room. In less than ten minutes she was gone, leaving a lake of blazing fuel which caused unusually high casualties among her crew – only 149 survivors out of a crew of 526.

This was not an isolated design weakness. By this time HMS *Avenger* had gone too. After sailing with one of the Russian convoys, she was assigned to support the Operation Torch landings in North Africa. With the troops firmly ashore, she was sent back to England as part of the escort for the fast UK-bound convoy MKS1. As with the loss of the *Audacity*, convoy tactics put her in mortal peril. Some eighty miles west of Gibraltar, in the small hours of 14 November 1942, one of the five escorting destroyers, HMS *Wrestler,* picked up the radar echo of a surfaced U-boat some five miles ahead. This was the type VII *U98,* heading for the North African coast.

The destroyer's captain ordered full speed and steered straight for the echo. His first intention was to ram the U-boat, but when he spotted the sleek grey hull only half a mile ahead, he decided to switch tactics and allow the U-boat to dive before launching a depth charge attack. To his surprise, the submarine only slid beneath the surface when the destroyer was a hundred yards away. More than a mere tactical error, this was a suicidal mistake.

With the vortices left by the diving submarine still clearly visible, *Wrestler* steamed in and dropped a

pattern of no less than fourteen depth charges, all at shallow settings, over the spot where she vanished. The result was inevitable: the U-boat sank with all hands. But as an additional safety precaution, the convoy was ordered to make an emergency turn to starboard – right into the path of another U-boat, the type IXC *U155,*[3] skippered by the cautious but experienced Adolf-Cornelius Piening.

Piening did not make the same mistake as his colleague. In fact, he never specifically aimed at the carrier. Seeing lines of ships crossing his bows, including the freighters and troop transports he had been ordered to sink, he fired a spread of four torpedoes at 4.14am and immediately dived deep to escape retaliation. As the depth-gauge needle crept around the dial, the U-boat men listened to the seconds ticking away. Finally, after almost three and a half minutes, they heard a loud detonation. Another explosion followed four seconds later, followed by a third just a second after that.[4]

Piening did not risk returning to periscope depth to see the results. But his torpedoes had hit three separate targets. One sank an 11,000-ton British troopship, while another damaged a 6,000-ton American freighter. The third one hit the *Avenger.* Normally, a single torpedo hit on a carrier meant a reasonable chance of survival. In this case, the torpedo explosion set off secondary detonations and blew the ship to pieces. So violent were the blasts that only twelve survivors remained from more than 550.

The resulting inquiry revealed that fires were

Two early Royal Navy escort carriers, HMS *Avenger* and HMS *Biter*, in heavy seas.
(www.navyphotos.co.uk)

started by the torpedo strike. Some experts insisted this produced a fuel explosion like that which would sink her sister ship four months later. Others suggested the shock of the detonation set off her store of bombs and depth charges, stowed close to the side plating where the torpedo had struck. To guard against this happening to other ships, explosives were moved to the inside of a new internal bulkhead running the length of the ship.[5]

These were discouraging setbacks in a story that had begun so promisingly with the original escort

Pilot's eye view of escort carrier HMS *Battler.*

(www.navyphotos.co.uk)

carrier HMS *Audacity* (see Chapter 8). This had shown very clearly the value of small carriers in ASW, if only enough could be made available. Unfortunately, her conversion was uncharacteristically simple. Following her with a longer production series would prove much more difficult.

Time was the greatest problem, as always. The shift of U-boat attacks to the mid-Atlantic Air Gap meant that escort carriers were at the top of the Allied priority list. By providing air cover throughout the Atlantic crossing, they could transform the anti-submarine war. Later, when better intelligence through Enigma and direction finding revealed the exact positions of individual U-boats, they could do what most naval officers had longed to do from the beginning. They could take the fighting to the U-boats themselves, instead of waiting for the enemy to attack first.

Even before *Audacity*'s conversion was completed, the Admiralty had approached the US Navy for help designing six similar ships, to be built in American shipyards. In October 1940, President Roosevelt had ordered the US Navy to design a merchant ship conversion for a prototype escort carrier in a three-month time-frame, once the plans were finalised. Two months later, with the design under development,

its objectives were extended to cover the conversion of two sister ships, one for the US Navy and one for the Royal Navy.

The American design was based on the Maritime Commission C3 hull for a diesel-powered merchant ship, and two of these hulls, the *Mormacland* (for the US Navy) and the *Mormacmail* (for the Royal Navy) were chosen for the prototype escort carrier (CVE) conversions in January 1941, well before US entry into the war. The American design was considerably more ambitious than the hurried conversion of *Audacity*. These ships were bigger, with a short hangar aft, a lift to the flight deck, a more powerful catapult and improved fuel reserves.

The US Navy took over the *Mormacland* for conversion at Newport News in Virginia on 4 March 1941. Work was finally completed at a cost of $1.5 million by 2 June, two days within the president's time limit, and she was re-commissioned as the USS *Long Island.* She measured 492 feet long with a beam of seventy feet, a displacement of 13,500 tons and a top speed of 16.5 knots. She had a single catapult and a bridge located below the forward end of the flight deck. Later she went back to the yard to have the flight deck extended by seventy-seven feet. This took it over the bridge, so that extra bridge wings had to be fitted to the hull for navigating the ship. These changes increased her weight to almost 15,000 tons but her top speed was boosted to more than seventeen knots.[6]

Her sister ship *Mormacmail* was under conversion at the same time, and was finally commissioned into the Royal Navy as HMS *Archer* on 17 November 1941. Both ships were the first in a long line of small escort carriers that would, between them, help to transform the Atlantic anti-submarine war. At first, though, the technical problems seemed endless. Both the conversions were powered by marine diesel engines, with four power units linked to a common shaft, an arrangement that almost guaranteed a high degree of unreliability. *Archer* was particularly accident-prone. Not long after being taken into Royal Navy service in November 1941, she collided with a Peruvian registered merchant ship. After she became operational, her engines broke down so often that she was finally downgraded to serve as a storeship from August 1943.

The next group of US-built escort carriers supplied to the Royal Navy was based on three more diesel-powered merchant ship conversions, *Rio Hudson, Rio Parana* and *Rio de Janeiro.* These became respectively HMS *Avenger*, HMS *Biter* and HMS *Dasher* and even before the loss of two of the ships, they too were plagued by reliability problems, quite apart from their fatal design weaknesses.

Why did they prove so vulnerable – in one case to a single enemy torpedo, in the other to an accident while refuelling her own aircraft in sheltered home waters? Though each group of escort carriers for both navies were virtually identical, there were still sharp differences of opinion over design details, operating procedures and even the purpose for which the ships would be used. For the US Navy, with a vast construction programme of fast attack carriers, these small 'jeep' carriers were seen predominantly as anti-submarine ships for convoy protection. For the hard-pressed Royal Navy, they would have to be shared between other urgent but conflicting requirements.

From Operation Torch onwards, a succession of seaborne landings on the coasts of North Africa, Sicily and Italy would mean disembarking troops and supporting them against fierce enemy air attacks. Rather than risk valuable but vulnerable fleet carriers close inshore, the Royal Navy would switch escort carriers to providing fighter protection over the beachheads. So although some British carriers helped protect convoys from U-boat attack, this remained an area where the most spectacular successes would fall to US Navy hunter-killer groups.

In particular, the routines followed by the two navies for storing and handling aircraft fuel differed considerably. Normal Royal Navy procedure avoided the build-up of highly inflammable vapour in fuel storage tanks by filling the empty spaces with inert nitrogen gas. US Navy carriers filled the space with water, which risked contaminating the fuel unless it was filtered through layers of chamois leather on its way into the aircraft tanks. Also, the US Navy normally stored fuel in bulk, which was reflected in the design of the carriers. The Royal Navy chose a smaller fuel capacity, with unused fuel tanks filled with water and sealed off from the fuel system.

One method was not inherently better than the other. It was a culture clash, where the US Navy had much stricter fuel-safety procedures as part of the price the service paid for the convenience of storing fuel in bulk. The Royal Navy, on the other hand, normally had a fuel storage system that was inherently safer – if more cumbersome – and which did not call for such strict procedures. So the combination of a ship designed to US standards being operated with Royal Navy fuel safety procedures was an accident almost certain to happen. In the case of HMS *Dasher*, the merest mischance triggered off a fireball which sank the ship. In the case of HMS *Avenger*, a normally survivable torpedo hit produced another fuel explosion with equally lethal results.

In time, all these problems, reliability and safety alike, would be solved for the new batches of escort carriers emerging from the yards. These would finally carry airborne ASW to the enemy wherever he tried to operate. Even by the time HMS *Avenger* was lost, it was clear a complete change of fortune in airborne ASW had been taking place.

While the carrier problems were being sorted out, this improvement was first achieved by shore-based planes, thanks to a huge tactical blunder by the Kriegsmarine's reaction to the North African landings. In a desperate attempt to attack the Allied beachhead, they sent U-boats into confined coastal waters, throwing away their advantages of stealth and dispersion. They were within reach of even short-range aircraft, and their punishment was swift and deadly.

The Germans first realised something sinister was happening on 5 November 1942. An Italian spy reported more than 100 Allied ships, including three carriers and a battleship, leaving Gibraltar and sailing into the Mediterranean. At first they suspected a Malta-bound convoy. Later they realised the danger of a seaborne landing in the rear of Rommel's Afrika Korps. Following their defeat by the British Eighth Army at El Alamein, the Axis armies were retreating westwards towards Tunisia.

They responded quickly. Half the eighteen U-boats already in the Mediterranean went to block the eastern side of the straits and sink any Allied ships they met. Others were ordered to join them as soon as possible. A group of seven type VIIs codenamed Delfin was sent through the straits as reinforcements. By 11 November, three days after the first landings, there were seventeen U-boats in the area, with more on the way.

This should have been a formidable threat. In practice, Allied ships and aircraft along the North African coast were similar in tactical terms to a large but heavily defended convoy. With U-boats flocking to the attack in confined waters crowded with escorts and heavily patrolled by anti-submarine aircraft, the result was a vicious battle, on highly favourable terms for the Allies.

On 11 November, the U-boats sank two Allied troopships, one freighter and the brand-new British destroyer, HMS *Marne*. But heavy depth-charge attacks by well-trained escort crews forced seven of the submarines to pull out of the battle by 13 November for repairs to be carried out. Another five were sunk. One of these was the type VIIC *U660*, which attacked an Allied convoy but was forced to dive by three Royal Navy destroyers and two corvettes. Despite diving to more than 600 feet and firing off bubble decoys to create false sonar echoes, the submarine was so heavily pounded it was forced to surface and surrender.

The relatively short-range Hudsons of RAF Coastal Command, flying from local airfields, accounted for the other four. For the first time, there were plenty of targets in one crowded area. Many were spotted in broad daylight, and the crews could scarcely believe their good luck. One of their victims was the U-boat ace Kapitänleutnant Baron Hans-Dietrich von Tiesenhausen, who had sunk the British battleship HMS *Barham* with heavy loss of life almost a year before.

This determined onslaught delivered a succession of heavy blows to German morale. However the real tactical lesson of this string of successes, several of them involving experienced crews led by highly professional captains with a proven success record, was the folly of operating submarines in coastal waters against massive air cover, a lesson that would be heavily reinforced after the Normandy landings in June 1944.

However, in the wider waters of the Bay of Biscay, results were still disappointing, mainly because Coastal Command was still waiting for centimetric radar. This was now particularly urgent, because of the Germans' ability to detect signals from the older radars using their Metox receivers. Another problem was a difference of opinion among both American and British airmen alike, over the best way to use aircraft to hunt submarines, which mirrored the arguments among naval officers on the most effective way to use surface escorts.

HMS *Battler* from sea level.
(www.navyphotos.co.uk)

Following the loss of HMS *Dasher*, greater precautions to reduce the fire risk included asbestos curtains to divide the hangar deck and prevent the spread of flames.
(National Library of Canada)

The American Admiral King, as befitted a naval officer, was convinced that aircraft would find more targets around convoys, rather than in the wider reaches of the bay. During the first Bay Offensive, it appeared King was right, since four of the five U-boats sunk at that time were destroyed by RAF aircraft on convoy-protection patrols.[7]

On the other hand, the problem with airborne radar meant there was little point in Coastal Command patrols carrying out wider searches. Whenever they did so, the Germans heard their radar transmissions and dived to safety well before they were spotted. Only around convoys were U-boats forced to use different tactics. They had to stay on the surface to trail their targets and move into a firing position. In spite of risking air attack, it remained the only way to sink Allied ships.

For the US air crews already carrying ASV centimetric radar, searching for specific U-boats on the basis of Enigma intelligence was proving a highly effective tactic. In addition, the larger stores capacity of the B24 allowed them to carry the first of the super-weapons to make life even more precarious for the U-boat crews. By replacing small depth charges with the massive Mark 37 650-pound charges, the lethal punch of a single pattern was magnified several times over. The power of each detonation was considerably larger, and the likelihood of the charges detonating in an overlapping pattern to crush a U-boat's pressure hull was that much greater.

On 18 March 1943 No. 2 AS Squadron USAAF moved to North Africa. Just four days later, the B24 coded 'T', known to her crew as 'Tidewater Tillie' was on patrol northwest of the Canary Islands when they spotted a surfaced U-boat. This was the type IXC *U524*, which had already sunk a French freighter and attacked convoy UGS6 using its Metox receiver to avoid attacks by other Allied aircraft. However, they had no defence at all against centimetric radar and the super-heavy Mark 37 depth charges. The pilot, Lieutenant W L Sandford, flew across the submarine and dropped four of the 650-pound charges in a perfect straddle. Their power was unmistakable. Their blasts cracked the pressure hull and the U-boat vanished below the surface leaving a handful of survivors clinging to a life raft.

Aware of the more hostile conditions facing U-boats from greater Allied resources, better tactics and more powerful weapons, the Germans reinforced their passive radar detectors with a positive decoy to mislead enemy radar operators. This was a radar reflector, 'Aphrodite', designed to do at sea what 'Window' or 'Chaff' had done in the night skies over Germany, confuse the enemy by generating spurious radar echoes to distract attention from the real ones.

The reflectors consisted of three strips of aluminium foil four metres (thirteen feet) in length, each fastened at one end to a metre-length cross-bar, suspended below a hydrogen-filled balloon a metre in diameter, itself tethered to a submerged drogue by a 50-metre cable. The idea was that radar signals would be reflected by the foil strips to appear to the receiver as an echo like that of a surfaced U-boat. Under good conditions it remained effective for up to six hours, and in theory large numbers could be launched from a single submarine to confuse enemy forces searching for it.

Unfortunately, as with so many German counter-measures, by the time Aphrodite was available, its drawbacks outweighed its advantages. Because of the size of the balloon and the cumbersome lines and drogues, it could only be assembled on the surface. As Herbert Werner described, it was a frustrating and dangerous business:

Instead of diving instantly, we continued running surfaced at high speed, kept our new anti-aircraft weaponry at the ready, and resorted to a new diversion tactic which, we had been

told, would be very effective. Riedel, in charge of the scheme, filled a balloon with helium gas [sic] stored in bottles affixed to the railing. Then he attached a string of aluminium foils to the balloon, and its loose end to the float, and tossed the arrangement overboard. The float came to rest on the surface while the balloon rose and stretched the string with the foils until it stood like a full-size Christmas tree. The decoy rapidly disappeared astern into the ominous darkness. Five minutes later Riedel repeated the drop, and a second tree floated erect over the waters of the bay. These aluminium trees were supposed to create a stronger image than a U-boat tower on the enemy's radar screen, allowing us to escape in woods of our own making.

Unfortunately, two more balloons became entangled in the railing and three others blew up while being filled with the gas; and in the commotion, the snarled foils made our position amply evident on enemy radar screens. But our luck stayed with us. While Riedel fought with the foils and the balloons, we infiltrated a large French fishing fleet, which gave us more protection than the decoys and the guns. In fact, we discarded the aluminium trees and never used them again. They were more of a hazard than a help.[8]

On some occasions, Aphrodite balloons did allow boats using them to escape attacks. On the night of 10/11 February 1944, the type VIICs *U413*, *U437* and *U731* tried to attack the Liverpool to Freetown convoy OS67. By then the escorts had the upper hand, chasing the attackers off with the aid of their radars, and shepherding the convoy to its destination without loss. Nevertheless, all three boats used Aphrodite decoys and succeeded in evading their pursuers.

Sadly, desperate measures like Aphrodite were mere palliatives, unable to affect the overall situation. Yet the Germans could still have regained the advantage. The longed-for Allied switch to centimetric radar had taken so long to happen that many feared it might only create a temporary ascendancy. With Bomber Command using centimetric H2S to help pathfinders find their targets at night over Germany, it was only a matter of time before one of the radar-equipped aircraft was shot down. Once the enemy picked enough pieces of the radar set out of the wreckage, they would unravel its secrets and realise how to detect its signals.

The inevitable happened on 2 February 1943 when a Bomber Command Stirling from one of the two first H2S Pathfinder squadrons was shot down by a Luftwaffe night fighter over Holland. Though the Stirling was the slowest and most vulnerable of the RAF's four-engined heavy bombers, this was partic-

By the end of the war, the U-boats had belatedly been given extra protection against Allied radar-equipped aircraft – this is the portable radar detector, direction finder and field strength recorder on the bridge of the type IXC/40 *U889* which was commissioned after the war into the Royal Canadian Navy.

(National Library of Canada)

ularly disastrous as it was only the second operation with the new equipment. Even though they had nothing remotely like it, German electronics experts examined the cavity magnetron, and calculated correctly that the set operated on a wavelength in the centimetric range.

Once the RAF realised an H2S-equipped bomber had failed to return, they assumed it was likely that the enemy were picking over its secrets. British radar experts predicted the Germans could have a working search receiver within weeks. For the anti-submarine forces, this suggested that the U-boats would have a defence against the new radar even before they could start using it to search for submarines.

At first, events on the German side moved quickly. Three weeks after the Stirling was shot down, they held the first meeting of the Rotterdam Commission (named after the area where the Stirling had been found). The commission ordered the Telefunken company to reconstruct the damaged set, build six

Even when a submarine hunt proved successful, evidence of the destruction was often hard to find and the smallest items were greatly prized as evidence of a genuine kill – like this small locker door panel from the type VIIC *U247* being shown by Lieutenant Commander Stacey RCN, captain of the frigate HMCS *Saint John* who with her sister ship HMCS *Swansea* sank the submarine in the English Channel on 1 September 1944.

(National Library of Canada)

prototypes of a German version, and to develop a search receiver under the code-name Naxos, which could give warning of these radars being used.[9] Though the set they had found was clearly being used in night raids against the Reich, the Germans did not know exactly how. But it seemed inevitable that they would realise that it could also be used to find U-boats, which made it virtually certain they would develop a naval version of the new search receiver.

However, the resulting delay was far longer than even the most optimistic Allied predictions. Two unexpected factors helped account for this. First, the fact the apparatus had been found and examined by Luftwaffe experts meant, because of the very strong inter-service hostility on the German side, the Kriegsmarine was not informed of this threat for

weeks on end. Secondly, another RAF raid, led accurately to its target by the use of centimetric radar hit Berlin on the night of 1/2 March 1943. One of the factories wrecked by the bombs was the Telefunken plant where the centimetric radar analysis was being carried out. Although another set was salvaged from one of the British bombers shot down that night, a 35 Squadron Pathfinder Halifax, valuable time was lost setting the programme up again.[10]

Yet the Germans' urgent need for counter-measures was underlined within days. In the early morning darkness of 5 March 1943, a veteran type VII U-boat, *U333*, was crossing the Bay of Biscay when she was attacked by a Leigh Light-equipped Wellington, with no warning from the Metox. The submarine crew was alert enough to shoot down the bomber with a burst of cannon fire, but their report caused consternation at U-Boat Headquarters. Already some U-boat crews had had the initiative to search frequency ranges outside those covered by the Metox, as described in the Headquarters War Diary for that very day:

> The enemy is employing very high and very low impulse frequencies which are barely audible. This is substantiated by the experience of *U124*, where the PO Telegraphist, suspecting impulse frequencies beyond the range of the Metox, incorporated the 'magic eye' [oscilloscope] of the general receiver into his apparatus, which enabled him to identify some radar activity. All boats due for sea are to have their receivers fitted with 'magic eye'. A number of oscillographs [sic] are being sent to the boats in the western bases. Used in conjunction with the Metox they should indicate whether the enemy is indeed employing inaudible impulse frequencies. The boats have orders to report results by radio while still at sea.
>
> The enemy is using carrier frequencies beyond the range of the present search receiver. So far the only confirmation of this comes from an enemy aircraft shot down over Holland, which apparently carried an instrument with a wavelength of 5.7 cm. We must therefore assume that the enemy is working outside the range of our instrument.
>
> The enemy switches on his search radar for only very short periods of two to three seconds. This confirms our previous observations of his economic use of radar and makes the identification so much more difficult.

This was ominous news for the submarine arm. The Metox receiver was such a life saver that should a U-boat in distant waters find the receiver was defective, it was ordered to withdraw from operations unless it could beg replacement parts from other submarines or supply ships. U-Boat Headquarters felt that 'by the end of the year [1942] Metox was regarded as essential to the survival of boats.'[11]

Yet there had been no organised attempt to search the airwaves for transmissions on other frequencies. Had they done so, they would have had positive warning that new weapons were on their way. The Luftwaffe listening services would predict the strength of RAF night raids by analysing H2S centimetric signals as bomber crews tested their radars over English airfields, but once again this helpful information was not passed across the inter-service divide. In addition, the reference to radar being used for two or three seconds at a time was false, since this would make anti-submarine radar useless. Possibly this was an attempt to explain why the Germans had not picked up these transmissions before.

In fact, they fell at the final hurdle. The Kriegsmarine predicted the new radar would be used to find U-boats on the surface. They identified one of the earliest occasions when it had been used in attacking a U-boat. Then they became confused over the nature of the threat they were facing, and postponed an effective reaction by more than six months. One reason for this curious lack of urgency was their own scepticism over the Allied achievement. Because centimetric radar was so far ahead of their own research, they assumed there must be other explanations. Gunther Hessler summarised their thinking:

The reasons for their uncertainty and their belated appreciation of [the use of centimetric radar] were that, although well over a thousand of the *Metox* ... observations recorded by the U-boats between March and May 1943 had lain between 120 and 250 centimetres, the number of cases in which U-boats had been approached by undetected aircraft was very small. Thus the non-detection could be attributed either to the dead sectors of the radar search receivers or to intermittent radiations which were difficult and often impossible to register owing to the method of operating the receivers, or to impulse frequencies on or beyond the range of the receivers, which could not be registered at all. Moreover, despite the capture of the *Rotterdam-Gerät* at the beginning of 1943, our scientists still doubted the feasibility of introducing centimetric radar for general operational use because of the great technical difficulties involved.[12]

This complacency would cripple the U-boats. Because they pinned the blame on failings in existing radar detectors rather than entirely new Allied radars, they wasted time developing better versions of the Metox receiver, useless for detecting centimetric signals. The most widely used of these was known by at least three different names. It was developed by the Hagenuk electronics company and was known officially as the Wellenanzieger (Wave Indicator) G1 Zypern (Cyprus). Its official designation was usually abbreviated to W.Anz G1 and it was more commonly known as the Wanze or Hagenuk than by its official code name.

It used a different antenna from the Metox – a pair of small dipoles mounted on a cylinder inside a wire-mesh frame measuring eight inches across and four inches deep. The electronics were more sophisticated, carrying out an automatic sweep over a narrower range of wavelengths (120 to 180cm) than was possible with the manual tuning of the Metox.

At the time, the Allies knew nothing of the relaxed German attitude to anti-submarine patrols using centimetric radar. To try to keep them off the scent, a deception campaign was mounted by sending signals in ciphers that the Germans were known to have broken, and which were read on a regular basis, referring to the detection of U-boats by the infra-red radiation they emitted. Professor R V Jones, wartime head of Air Ministry Intelligence and adviser to the prime minister, had worked before the war on detecting enemy ships and aircraft through infra-red radiation. The genuine theoretical potential of this method might be enough to prevent the Germans suspecting improved radar or Enigma decrypts might be giving the game away.

The scientific background was accurate enough to persuade them to take it seriously. A U-boat painted

The RCN Operations Room in St John's, Newfoundland, in September 1942 – like its British and American equivalents, an essential nerve centre in directing and monitoring the Atlantic battle.

(National Library of Canada)

The final reason why Doenitz's tonnage war was ultimately doomed to failure – the huge shipbuilding resources of the United States – graphically shown by the bows of these Liberty ships lined up in an American harbour.

(US National Archives)

prior to being assigned to a POW camp. This gave questioners a chance to trawl for useful intelligence details, though most captives insisted on giving only names, ranks and service numbers, under Geneva Convention rules.

In this case, the prisoner was much more talkative, and the Germans could scarcely believe their good fortune. When asked how it was that Coastal Command patrols picked up U-boat targets at night without anything showing on the Metox receivers, he cheerfully explained that all the Allied aircraft had to do was home in on the radiation the Metox sets themselves were emitting. Could this actually be true? If the Allies were homing in on signals being transmitted, albeit intentionally, by the U-boats, this would mean the aircraft were using passive homing, which would account for no signals being picked up on the search receivers, as the signals were moving in the opposite direction, from submarine to patrol plane.

As an impromptu explanation designed to reassure the enemy and cause more time wasting, it was perfect. Time and again, the best wartime deceptions proved to be those reinforcing what the enemy already believed. In this case both the Germans and the Allies knew that the Metox search receiver did produce measurable radiation. Allied scientists had actually carried out experiments to see if it might be possible to home in on these signals, but practical difficulties ruled it out as a workable target-finder. The Germans now carried out similar tests with a shore-mounted Metox receiver and an aircraft carrying a specially built search receiver tuned to the appropriate wavelength.

To their horror, they found the emissions could be detected up to twenty-five miles away, at a height of 6,500 feet. Furthermore, a detailed search of the wreckage of a downed Coastal Command aircraft fitted with metric ASV radar revealed that 'an attachment to the ASV equipment … also supported this theory', giving them further corroboration they were on the right track.[14] The German explanation for the reason why the Allied patrols were suddenly more effective was summarised in Doenitz's own war diary: 'The danger of enemy interception of *Metox* radiations exists chiefly when the receiver is kept tuned to a given wavelength and thus radiates at a fixed frequency. The danger appears to be less if the receiver is searching.'[15]

They then ordered that Metox must only be used with the greatest care. Commanders were ordered to switch off the set in areas where visibility was good enough to spot a patrolling aircraft far enough away for the boat to dive in safety. In areas of poor visibility, where radar equipped aircraft could approach without being seen, the sets could still be used providing care was taken to search backwards and forwards through the entire range of wavelengths (from 120cm to

in a standard grey finish would blend in with the normal tones of the sea under ambient light. However, it would stand out very sharply under infrared illumination, continuing to look grey in sharp contrast to the sea, which would now appear black. Though no direct evidence was ever found to prove that the Germans had been led astray by the infrared deception, they spent a great deal of effort developing a portable infra-red detector that was issued to some U-boats.

Furthermore, they also tackled the much more difficult task of developing a paint to camouflage submarines in infra-red illumination as well as normal light. This was an ingenious combination of a black undercoat to allow the boat to merge into the dark background under infra-red light, but covered with a varnish topcoat containing a suspension of powdered glass. This gave enough reflective capability for the overall result to appear grey against the grey sea in normal light.[13]

This example of German technical mastery was totally wasted. But another deception that sent the U-boat service even further up a blind alley was one apparently mounted by a Coastal Command pilot, captured from a crashed aircraft. He had been debriefed at the Durchgangslager Luft reception centre

250cm) to make it more difficult for the Allies to home in on the radiation. At the same time, trials of the Metox replacement, the Hagenuk search receiver were carried out to determine the amount of radiation the new sets produced.

The RAF prisoner's statement had been as effective as a lighted match thrown into a gunpowder store. According to German records, he claimed the radiation used by Coastal Command to find their targets could be detected at ninety miles, at heights of up to 3,000 feet. Furthermore, the system was so reliable that normal ASV radar only had to be switched on at intervals in order to confirm the range. This accorded so precisely with what the Germans already believed that they assumed it was the truth, coloured with an understandable exaggeration of Allied capabilities:

> Related to the results of the latest experiments, and to events and U-boat losses in the Atlantic in recent months, great importance must be attached to this British pilot's statement. Even if this is a deliberate attempt to mislead us, especially as the alleged range seems improbable and could only be achieved by a very sensitive receiver, the statement must be accepted as true in deciding on further measures in the present situation …[16]

So firmly was the story believed by the Germans that Doenitz repeated it to Hitler at a conference five days later. Reassured that they had found the cause of their problems, they remained confident that they had taken the right action to solve them. Trials showed the Hagenuk sets produced only one-fifth of the radiation of the Metox equipment, so in future these would be used instead. The danger that centimetric radar would be seen as the real culprit and remedial action taken quickly had receded, and only in the following year was the truth realised and acted upon.

Nevertheless, the story that an intrepid shot-down pilot had single-handedly decided on such an effective cover story and then used it on his own initiative to deceive the enemy so successfully was a difficult one to believe on the Allied side. Dr Alfred Price, a leading historian of air ASW, concluded that there were only three possible explanations for the situation, which he described in ascending order of likelihood. The first was that the prisoner might have had the technical knowledge to construct such an effective cover story on his own initiative. The second was that a specially trained and briefed officer had been allowed to be captured by the Germans and had passed on the agreed explanation to produce the deception. The third was that German agents inside the UK who had been captured and turned had been used to send the misinformation back to their controllers inside Germany, where it had been accepted as genuine, and the Germans themselves had concocted the captured-airman story as a cover story to protect their agents in Britain.[17]

On the other hand, Professor Jones, who was closely involved in these technically based deception plans and who would almost certainly have been involved in drawing up the cover story for any agent-based campaign of disinformation, was convinced the prisoner story was true. He spared no efforts after the war to discover his identity, admittedly without success, but confirmed that had he found out who the airman was, he would have recommended him for a medal.[18]

In any case, by this time more and more U-boats were being fitted with the Wanze equipment. At first it seemed that fewer submarines were being attacked by anti-submarine air patrols. Sadly, this was another false hope. With more U-boats being attacked without warning in poor visibility when trying to pass through the Straits of Gibraltar, fresh suspicions arose. In October 1943, the number of attacks increased again, but the finger was pointed at the new receivers rather than advanced Allied radar technology.

Further proof of this dangerous mind-set was added when the main counter-move by Doenitz involved an improved version of the Wanze set, rather than a full-scale attempt to check on the centimetric wave-bands. The Wanze receiver was replaced by the FuMB-10 Borkum, a 'new and somewhat primitive replacement' that covered a wider range of wave-lengths, but still in the metric range. Furthermore it had no tuning control, a shorter effective range and simply radiated a warning over the submarine's loudspeakers if it picked up any incoming transmissions. Since it still failed to extend its coverage into the centimetre wavebands, it picked up relatively few of these.

Hessler summarised the thinking at U-boat command:

> October saw a large number of surprise attacks, the symptoms in each case being identical to those experienced off Gibraltar; yet it could still not be decided whether all the *Wanze* failures which had occurred since the spring of 1943 had been due to one and the same cause, namely enemy possession of centimetric radar. We had still not recovered from the shock of the Metox revelations and were disposed to ascribe these phenomena to an enemy location system of a passive nature. On 5th November 1943, Doenitz commented that enemy radar might have developed on lines as yet unknown to us, or that the enemy might be exploiting electrical or thermal radiations emanating from the boats themselves, but since there was a similarity

An Atlantic convoy with merchant ships laden with essential supplies for maintaining the war – despite the dedication and heroism of the U-boat crews, most of these convoys reached their destinations entirely unmolested.

(US Naval Institute Press)

A non-belligerent but war-winning weapon, the Liberty ships were adapted from a World War One British design for toughness, simplicity and ease of construction – this is the Liberty ship *Zoella Lykes*.

(US Naval Institute Press)

between the present phenomena and those observed in the period May to July 1943, the latter possibility was the more likely. That same day, Doenitz, after consulting with the German radar experts, banned the use of *Wanze* and the short-wave W/T receiver, which was also suspected of radiating. Hence there followed yet another period in which the boats possessed no warning equipment against enemy radar.[19]

This picture of the German submarine command almost wilfully blind to the clearest and most obvious conclusion from the equipment found in the wrecked RAF bomber near Rotterdam the previous February

would turn still darker. Allied aircraft were now finding their elusive quarry with greater consistency and even less warning.

Even when they finally realised the nature of the threat being used against them, there was very little the Germans could do about it. Attempts to build new search receivers were hamstrung by the shortage of suitable crystals to suit the high frequency of the centimetric signals. Meanwhile, more and more skippers crossing the Bay of Biscay were reporting attacks by Allied aircraft in darkness or in poor visibility, even though Doenitz was still reluctant to assume that new radar was entirely responsible. Amazingly, it would be almost a year before U-Boat headquarters accepted that

US Navy escort carriers succeeded in taking the war to the U-boats with a vengeance, using patrols of these Wildcat fighters to find their elusive opponents and call up other aircraft to deliver the killing blows.

(US Naval Institute Press)

the Allied anti-submarine aircraft were definitely locating their targets using centimetric radar,[20] an estimation that did little to reinforce the urgency of German developments of passive search receivers to counter this new menace.

In the meantime, whatever the reason for the more frequent attacks on U-boats, Doenitz decided new tactics were needed to counteract the threat. On 27 April 1943 he issued new orders to his U-boat crews,[21] mentioning the threat of a new 'radar device, especially effective in aircraft, against which our U-boats are powerless'. For the time being, they were to cross the bay submerged at night, to avoid the danger of radar-equipped aircraft. Battery charging could only be carried out by surfacing in broad daylight, when at least they would have a fighting chance of spotting the approach of a hostile aircraft and diving before an attack could be launched.

Given the larger numbers of Allied aircraft now criss-crossing the Bay of Biscay on offensive patrols, this was a counsel of despair. U-boat crews were condemned to running on the surface with the eyes of the bridge watch straining to cover the sky and spot the tiny speck of an approaching aircraft. The knowledge that an attack was almost inevitable somewhere on their route

lifted stress levels to new heights and sent morale plummeting. Time and again the shouted alarm would trigger a desperate plunge into the depths, with all hands listening for exploding depth charges as the submarine vanished beneath the surface.

Even if reactions had been fast enough and all was well for the time being, they faced the decision to surface again and resume charging the batteries, or their electric motors would fail to run throughout the coming night. Furthermore, however carefully they scanned the skies through the periscope before surfacing, there were several minutes between blowing the tanks to emerging on to the bridge, when the submarine was totally vulnerable to air attack. Crossing the bay on the way to a patrol or when returning to the safety of a home port became a highly nervous lottery.

Doenitz's decision was to try to provide the U-boats with the means to strike back at their airborne tormentors. From the end of 1942, submarines had been fitted with anti-aircraft armament in addition to the single deck gun for use against unarmed merchant vessels. At first, this was a single 20-mm cannon firing explosive shells with an effective range of about a mile, mounted on a special gun platform abaft the conning tower. Sometimes this would be backed up by additional machine guns, more for their deterrent effect when firing tracer at a plane approaching its target, and intended to put the pilot off his aim. Now, more determined efforts would be made towards a real deterrent by fitting a heavier anti-aircraft battery.

This meant staying on the surface and fighting it out if an aircraft was spotted before the U-boat could carry out an emergency dive in safety. Unfortunately for the Germans, Allied anti-submarine patrols reacted quickly to these new measures. During the

The darkening prospects for U-boats in the Atlantic forced Doenitz to divert his longer range submarines, like these type IXs rendezvousing off the West African coast, to seek targets in more distant waters.

(Jak Mallmann Showell)

first week of May 1943, aircraft flying over the bay from bases in southwest England reported sighting no less than seventy-one U-boats on the surface. In more than half of those cases, the aircraft attacked, sinking three U-boats and damaging three others so severely that they had to return to base for repairs.[22] Most significant of all, though, were aircrew reports that revealed on no less than seventeen occasions – almost 1 in 4 – the U-boats had made no attempt to dive, but had stayed on the surface and fired back at the attacking aircraft.

Sadly for Doenitz's hopes, the tactic soon backfired. With Allied airborne anti-submarine planes now more plentiful, any U-boat tempted to fight it out on the surface gave spotting aircraft time to radio for help. Two or more aircraft could divide the submarine's anti-aircraft fire, leaving one a free hand to deliver an unopposed attack. During the rest of the month, aircraft sank six U-boats crossing the bay and severely damaged another half dozen, at the cost of six aircraft being lost to submarine fire.

The next move was up to Doenitz, who decided safety in numbers might work for U-boats too. Instead of each U-boat crossing the bay on its own, they were ordered to cross in groups, so their combined fire-

power could beat off groups of attacking aircraft. Sometimes this tactic seemed to work. Two pairs of U-boats crossing the bay en route to their home ports in early June reached their objectives without being attacked at all. A larger group of five submarines was spotted late in the evening of 12 June by a single patrolling aircraft, but darkness fell before reinforcements arrived. The same thing happened on the following evening, when a 228 Squadron Sunderland flying boat spotted the group, but on this occasion the pilot, Flying Officer Leonard Lee, decided to attack without waiting for back-up.

Braving the combined firepower of the U-boats, the big flying boat aimed for the type VIIC *U564* and dropped a stick of depth charges close enough to cause severe damage to the target. The Sunderland suffered more severely, riddled with cannon shells, she crashed into the sea and took her entire crew with her to the bottom. By now it was clear that the damaged U-boat was not capable of continuing her mission, and she was ordered back to a Spanish port to carry out repairs, escorted by the type IXC *U185*.

The three undamaged U-boats continued their outbound voyage, but on the following morning a Whitley piloted by Sergeant Arthur Benson of the Royal Australian Air Force spotted *U564* and her escort heading for the Spanish coast. The plane and her crew were part of a force of nine Whitleys loaned to Coastal Command from No. 10 Operational Training Unit, and after two hours of sending radio signals and waiting for reinforcements to arrive, Benson decided to act. Once again the lone attacker opted for the smaller submarine. The Whitley approached the damaged U-boat in the teeth of a furious barrage from the type IX.

At last the plane reached its target and dropped the depth charges in a close pattern around the already partly crippled submarine. It was enough. *U564* went to the bottom, though her skipper and seventeen of her crew were rescued by her consort. The attack proved fatal for the Whitley too; accounts of her fate differ,[23] but the loss of the U-boat was undisputed. The survivors were offloaded on to the large German fleet destroyer *Z24*, and the other U-boat headed out for the Atlantic, this time on its own.

The fight-back tactic had been taken a stage further by this time. Doenitz had decided that U-boats needed even heavier armament, to deal with simultaneous attacks by more than one aircraft, and plans had been drawn up to fit additional multiple anti-aircraft gun mountings. Two designs had been tested, a twin 20-mm cannon mounting and a quadruple mounting. The first two quadruple mountings were fitted to U-boats in May 1943, with twin mountings following two months later. By this time, the anti-aircraft cannon were firing a new more powerful shell called a *Minengeschoss*, which packed three times the weight of a more powerful explosive called *Hexogen*.

Finally, from the end of 1943, boats were also being fitted with a 37-mm gun adapted from an army anti-tank weapon. This fired a projectile more than twice the weight of the 20-mm cannon shell, but at a slower rate and at a longer range – nine miles rather than the seven and a half miles maximum range of the 20-mm guns. Unfortunately, while the gun packed a much heavier punch, the conversion suffered severe problems when subjected to the harsh environment of a seagoing submarine. Because saltwater corrosion caused stoppages, meticulous maintenance and test firings were essential, but this was at a time when surfacing for any reason at all was becoming increasingly dangerous.[24]

While heavier combinations of single, twin and quadruple 20-mm and 37-mm anti-aircraft guns were being fitted to all U-boats to make them less vulnerable to aircraft, a more radical experiment was carried out on the type VIIC U-boat *U441*. She was converted into what was effectively a submersible flak-ship. A bandstand platform was built forward of the bridge in place of the original deck gun, to carry a quadruple 20-mm cannon mounting with the gun crew protected by a shield. A similar platform was fitted abaft the bridge carrying a second quadruple 20-mm mounting, and aft of this was a lower bandstand with a single semi-automatic 37-mm.

These guns and their larger stores of ammunition took up considerable space in an already cramped hull and added a huge weight penalty. This could only be balanced by reducing fuel-tank capacity, and cutting the torpedoes carried to a single weapon in each of the tubes, with no reloads. The true purpose of *U441* was as a specialised escort for groups of U-boats heading to and from patrols, and as such she represented a deliberate escalation in the aircraft–submarine campaign. Her conversion had originally been planned as far back as September 1942, but completion had been delayed for eight months because of shortages of the weapons she carried.[25]

Although her armament was formidable on paper, the flak-boat concept was flawed from the start. Apart from the increase in top-weight, which made her unstable in heavy seas, the additional guns and their protective shields added to the underwater drag. This not only cut the boat's submerged speed but more seriously increased the time taken to dive, already longer than normal owing to all the guns' crews having to clamber through the bridge hatch in an emergency. Even when operating on the surface and fighting back against attacking aircraft, the amount of ready-use ammunition that could be kept on deck was severely limited. In action the guns could only be kept supplied by additional crew members carrying rounds up the bridge ladder, through the hatch and around the gun platforms in a perpetual struggle to

keep pace with the huge consumption of automatic gunfire, and adding even more to the vulnerable personnel above decks.

The new flak-boat sailed on her first offensive patrol on 23 May 1943, with sixteen additional crew members, including extra gun crews and ammunition handlers, a doctor and two scientists searching for intelligence on Allied anti-submarine detection methods. She reached the western edge of the bay proper and then cruised on the surface in broad daylight, waiting for the first Allied aircraft to enter the baited trap. It turned out to be a Sunderland of 228 Squadron of Coastal Command, flown by Flying Officer H J Debnam. As the plane approached the U-boat she made no attempt to dive, but put up a furious barrage before the flying boat could reach the point for dropping depth charges. Nevertheless, all was not well from the German viewpoint either. As they began firing, they realised that saltwater corrosion had caused a weld to fail on one of the quadruple 20-mm mountings and the gun was rendered useless.

Even without this powerful weapon, the lone attacker was raked by German shells. With astonishing courage, the pilot held his course, to the point where he was able to drop a stick of depth charges close enough to severely damage the U-boat. Then the crippled Sunderland crashed into the sea, with the deaths of her entire crew. For *U441*, however, the depth-charge explosions had damaged her steering gear and caused pressure hull leaks at the bows. The damage was so severe there was no alternative but to return to Brest for repairs.

In spite of this, the Germans were greatly encouraged by the results of this fight. They began conversions of six more VIICs into *Unterseebootflugzeugfalle* or 'submarine aircraft traps' – *U256*, *U211*, *U263*, *U271*, *U621* and *U953*.[26] While work was still under way on the first of these, *U441* tried again in July 1943. At 2.05pm on the 12th, she was spotted by RAF aircraft – not a lone anti-submarine patrol this time, but three formidable Bristol Beaufighters.

U441's armament was all in working order this time, but it was still a highly unequal contest. The manoeuvrable Beaufighters approached in line astern and delivered a series of attacks in quick succession. The first sprayed a long burst of cannon fire at the large number of sailors on the deck of the submarine. The second scored a series of hits on the conning tower, repeated by the third fighter while the first and second were manoeuvring to deliver a follow-up attack. The first fighter made a second approach, with the submarine now zigzagging desperately to make a more difficult target. The pilot, Flight Lieutenant C R B Schofield, saw that the guns' crews seemed to have disappeared, and saw one body lying on deck with another in the water. As his cannon fire hit the pressure hull, he glimpsed an explosion and fire abaft the conning tower. Soon afterwards the submarine ceased fire completely and dived to safety.

This time the damage was more serious. The cannon fire of the Beaufighters had killed most of the gun crews and detonated some of the ready-use ammunition. In all, ten U-boat men had been killed and another thirteen wounded, including the skipper and the rest of the watch-keeping officers. The doctor, described as 'a keen and efficient amateur yachtsman'[27] not only succeeded in having the wounded taken below and ordering the boat to dive, but managed to bring her and her crew safely back to Brest, which was reached without incident the following day.

By now it should have been clear the tactic of driving off aircraft attacks by heavily armed flak-

The detecting aerial of the 'Wanze' equipment which was meant to improve on the Metox receivers later suspected of betraying the position of the U-boat to Allied bombers homing on the radiation it emitted – because it too searched on the wrong wavelengths, it was equally helpless against centimetric radar.

(Jak Mallmann Showell)

submarines was doomed. Instead, the policy of providing heavier anti-aircraft armament for all U-boats was followed, which greatly increased the combined firepower of submarines travelling in company without the need for extra crew members or reductions in torpedoes and fuel storage.

Nevertheless there were still cases where single U-boats were able to fight back successfully against relays of attacking aircraft, though not in the heavily patrolled approaches to the Biscay bases. On 28 July 1943, a type VIIC, U615, succeeded in sinking the Dutch tanker Rosalia, 3,200 tons, which had sailed from Lake Maracaibo in Venezuela. Dutifully her

skipper, Kapitänleutnant Ralph Kapitzky, reported the kill. His transmission was picked up by direction-finding stations and air patrols sent to find him. The following day U615 was spotted and attacked by a US Army Boeing B18, patrolling from Aruba, which succeeded in damaging it severely.

As U615 headed for the relative safety of the open Atlantic, more and more aircraft and warships joined the hunt. On the evening of 5 August, she was found on the surface and attacked again, this time by a US Navy Mariner flying boat of VP205. This attack was unsuccessful, but by the following morning more planes from the same unit responded to the Mariner's radio signals. One of them, piloted by Lieutenant A R Matuski, found the target and delivered a much more effective attack.

Headquarters at Port of Spain in Trinidad picked up a signal from the flying boat: 'Sub damaged with bow out of water making only two knots, no casualties to plane or personnel'. The radio operator spoke too soon. Kapitzky was another of the small band of U-boat skippers who had previously served as pilots in the Luftwaffe, and he knew a thing or two about bringing down enemy aircraft. A second signal was picked up a few minutes later saying simply 'Damaged. Damaged. Fire.' The flying boat never returned. The problem of making a tight turn at close range to deliver a second attack against a still-dangerous opponent had claimed the aircraft and all her crew.

Nevertheless, U615 was now in serious difficulty. Another Mariner found her and attacked, and once again the U-boat gunners struck back with formidable skill, setting the fuel tanks in the starboard wing of the flying boat on fire. To escape, the Mariner had to climb above the lethal range of the U-boat's cannon, where the crew could quench the blaze while calling in other aircraft to help. First to arrive was a Ventura bomber – another attack in the face of heavy, well-aimed fire, but more damage to the submarine. Next was another Mariner, which came in to attack while the other aircraft, their depth-charge racks empty, tried to divert the U-boat's fire.

Kapitzky's men realised the most lethal threat was the Mariner that had just arrived. An accurate burst hit the flight deck, killed the pilot and wounded four of the crew before the co-pilot could take control and fly out of trouble. In the confusion, the charges were dropped too soon and the damaged flying boat headed back to base, to be replaced by yet another Mariner. This too delivered an inconclusive attack, though gunfire killed several German gunners and battered the submarine still further.

Before dusk and the chance to repair the submarine undisturbed by air attack, a US Army Bolo bomber turned up, with yet another Mariner from the Navy's seemingly inexhaustible supply of flying boats. Still more damage was inflicted on the U boat, though the Mariner was forced to drop flares to illuminate the target. Finally, even Kapitzky was forced to admit, badly wounded as he was, that there was no chance of losing his pursuers – at one point a Navy airship was shadowing her until it ran out of fuel and had to land on a nearby uninhabited island where it was wrecked by high winds while its crew were rescued. On the morning of 7 August, the U-boat commander sent his crew into their rescue dinghies while he opened the seacocks and went down with his boat. The men were rescued by a new destroyer USS *Walker*, which had been working up in the area and which had been ordered to join the hunt.[28]

Even here, though, the Allied resources, their speed of response, their tactics and their weaponry proved decisive in the long drawn-out battle far from the U-boat's base. In cases where a boat had almost reached the safety of its own home base, and was about to rendezvous with her surface escorts, the constant danger of a lethal air attack was liable to deliver the killer punch far more quickly.

On the 2 August 1943, the elderly type IXB *U106*, skippered by Oberleutnant zur See Wolf-Dietrich Damerow was in trouble just five days into a new patrol. She had been found at 9.30am by a Wellington from 407 Squadron of the Royal Canadian Air Force,[29] which had dropped a pattern of six depth charges, damaging the boat. The aircraft stayed overhead, and the German skipper realised the pilot was calling in supporting aircraft for another attack. Repairs were rushed to restore a measure of diving capability. Meanwhile, U-boat headquarters sent out a surface force of three large torpedo boats to rescue survivors from another group of U-boats attacked by Allied aircraft. As they failed to find any trace of the boats for which they were searching, they were ordered to rendezvous with *U106* and escort her back to base, and were given a rendezvous for a meeting at 8pm.

Damerow and his damaged submarine remained submerged and reached the specified position an hour early. Before long, hydrophone noises revealed the approaching torpedo boats, and the relieved crew felt rescue was imminent. Then, with nine minutes to go, they spotted the bearings of the approaching warships swinging northwards. The submarine could not possibly match their speed while remaining underwater. They had to surface and chase the torpedo boats before contact was completely lost. Less than a minute after the decision was taken and the order carried out, retribution arrived on the scene, and the submarine met its attacker head-on:

> Sunderland approaching from ahead, range 800 metres, medium height. I open fire on her at once and she sheers off to starboard, circling us outside gun range. In order to deny her the opportunity of attacking, I am forced to keep her ahead, so that I gain little on the torpedo boats. Two minutes later a second Sunderland dives out of the clouds and commences to circle us. On reaching favourable positions, they attack from each bow, blazing with their guns. The one to the starboard is engaged by the quadruple 2-cm; the one to port by the single 2-cm and machine guns. The former turns off a little and drops at least six bombs, which detonate about 50 metres astern and cause severe concussion in the boat. The latter, whose fire has knocked out the layer, trainer and two loading number of the quadruple, dropped her bombs almost simultaneously on the port quarter. The port engine room switchboard is torn from its securings and catches fire. The starboard diesel stops. Thick smoke fills the boat, which lists to port with a bad leak. Five minutes later the aircraft return to the attack. We engage them as before. The single 2-cm is shot out of action. The bombs fall very close and cause further damage. The port diesel stops. Both electric motors are out of action. The boat is out of control and settles appreciably by the stern because of the inrush of water. Chlorine gas is coming from the batteries. At 2008 [16 minutes after the boat surfaced] a third attack is made and, since casualties among the guns' crews have been replaced by non-gunnery ratings, our fire is less accurate. The aircraft, engaging with all her guns, drops four bombs which detonate about 10 metres away. The boat continues to settle and the Senior Engineer reports that she can no longer be kept afloat.
>
> 'Abandon Ship !' Rafts are manned and inflated. The crew spring overboard with them, except five men manning the AA armament.
>
> 2015: Fourth attack. Aircraft repeatedly attacks with gunfire, wounding several men in the water and shooting up a number of rafts. My guns have run out of ammunition, and I jump overboard with the last five men. Shortly afterwards, there is a heavy explosion in the boat and she sinks rapidly, stern first, to the cheers of the remaining crew.
>
> The aircraft flies over us several times without shooting and then drops two smoke-floats. I and 36 of the crew, clinging to lifebuoys and a rubber dinghy, are picked up at dusk by the three torpedo boats.[30]

Incidents like this resulted from deliberate Coastal Command policy, with carefully planned patrols searching for submarines crossing particular areas of the bay, so they could be concentrated very quickly once a group was spotted. This assembled large groups

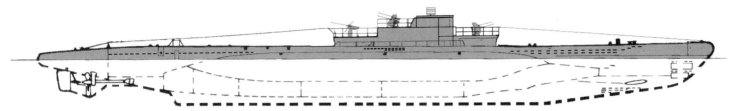

The modified type VII *U441* was equipped with a heavy anti-aircraft armament of two quadruple 20mm cannon mountings and a single 37mm cannon and intended to escort operational U-boats across the Bay of Biscay while protecting them from air attack. The tactic failed as Allied aircraft meeting the formations of submarines were able to call in reinforcements and divide the U-boats' fire by attacking from different directions.
(Author's drawing)

of aircraft to overwhelm even the combined firepower of the largest U-boat groups, and exploit the inherent vulnerability of submarines trapped on the surface. As Alfred Price has pointed out, the tactics were an aerial equivalent of Doenitz's own wolf-pack tactics for attacking convoys. It was simple but effective, and proved immensely successful.[31] In place of the patrol line of U-boats searching for convoys, patrols of seven aircraft were sent out three times every day, flying on parallel tracks across two sea areas straddling the main U-boat transit routes, ready to radio headquarters to call in support. The areas covered stretched more than 115 miles east to west, as this was calculated to be the maximum distance a U-boat could cover in a single 24-hour day, spending four hours on the surface and the rest submerged, giving the maximum chance of spotting any group crossing the area.

In fact, the sinking of *U106* was decisive. On that same day, Doenitz issued orders to cancel the sailings of all U-boats from the French bases, while those who had sailed the day before were recalled. In Hessler's words, reflecting the official German viewpoint:

> Groups in transit were disbanded and returning commanders were recommended to keep close to the Spanish coast, if necessary disregarding territorial waters. Losses in the Bay since 20th July had not then been established, but a few days later, the absence of boats' routine reports revealed the melancholy truth – of the 17 which had sailed, 10, including three valuable U-tankers, had been lost and one severely damaged. Once again the ratio of losses in groups compared to that among boats proceeding independently pointed in favour of the group procedure, but it would have been wrong to continue with it, since the groups, despite their higher fire-power, were unequal to the enemy's combined attacks and, *above all, were an inducement to the enemy to concentrate strong air and surface forces against them.* Hence it followed that, even with the addition of the twin 2-cm guns, the boats would be unable to fight their way through the Bay against the enemy air patrols and would have in future, to sneak through on widely dispersed routes with the aid of a good radar search receiver. Sailings had therefore to be suspended until the *Wanze* radar search receiver became available at the end of August.

Returning U-boats kept close to the Spanish coast. The enemy, soon realising this, instituted a close watch here and to the westward, and it was only due to the protection afforded against radar by a steep coastline and numerous fishing vessels that all the boats passed here without loss [emphasis added].[32]

This was a perceptive analysis of the problems the U-boats faced, but the picture was bleaker than Hessler realised. Because the reason for the ability of Allied aircraft to find targets at night and in poor visibility still eluded the Germans as their radar detectors searched in the wrong part of the frequency spectrum, they looked for other explanations. They had noticed that U-boats suffering deadly night attacks without warning had been in the Bay of Biscay, where Metox was heavily used, rather than around convoys. U-boats in convoy attacks did without Metox, so they could dive as quickly as possible in any emergency. Moreover, many air attacks over Biscay were carried out by twin-engined Wellingtons. The Germans believed these were too small to carry the fairly bulky radar apparatus found in the wreckage of the four-engined Stirling near Rotterdam.

As a result of these assumptions, and a deliberately planted deception, the Germans were now falling victim to one of the oldest traps in analysing information. This was the logical fallacy of *post hoc, ergo propter hoc*, 'after this, therefore because of this'. Because U-boats had been ordered to discontinue the use of Metox, it was all too easy to conclude the resulting drop in U-boat losses was because of this action. In reality, it had no effect at all, but the other measures instituted at the same time – like hugging the Spanish coast – were the true cause of the drop in the casualty rate.

Had the Germans but known it, the real situation was far worse than they suspected. The temporary fall in U-boat casualties, far from being a new source of hope, was a final glimmer of light before deeper darkness closed in. Even when the truth finally dawned that Allied airborne anti-submarine patrols were using centimetric radar to find and attack the U-boats, and even when they overcame their own supply and production problems to make a reliable detector, it was already too late. Waiting in the wings was an arsenal of new weapons and new tactics that would tilt the balance of life and death still further against Doenitz's brave but beleaguered submariners.

CHAPTER 11

MEDITERRANEAN SIDESHOW

1939–44

The amphibious version of
the Catalina was a highly
effective anti-submarine
aircraft, particularly in more
restricted waters.

(US Naval Institute Press)

S EEN from Doenitz's point of view, the message from the Italian spy that had triggered the powerful German response to the Allied landings in North Africa described in the previous chapter had the unwelcome effect of intensifying what he had always seen as a pointless distraction from what he was convinced was his primary and overriding objective: the tonnage war against the merchant ship convoys in the North Atlantic.

Doenitz was as single minded about the Atlantic battle as Air Marshal Harris was about the importance of bombing Doenitz's homeland into submission. Just as Harris loathed having any of his bombers diverted to attacks on resources like transport, fuel production and the aircraft industry, which he dismissed contemptuously as 'panacea targets', so the head of the U-boat arm was always bitterly aware of the limited numbers of submarines he could bring to bear on attacking Atlantic convoys.

The irony contained in his attitude to the diversion of effort into the Mediterranean was that in the First World War, this was the area where U-boats had been most successful, on an individual basis. The greatest U-boat ace of both wars, the resoundingly named Kapitänleutnant Lothar von Arnauld de la Periere, had wreaked havoc with Allied shipping in a series of cruises in the Western Mediterranean. In just three weeks in the summer of 1916, his *U*35 sank fifty-four steamers for a total of 91,000 tons. Remarkably, most of these sinkings were carried out on the surface, with the aid of his 4.1-inch deck gun, firing a total of 900 rounds during a patrol when he launched only four torpedoes. He went on to sink a total of 194 merchant vessels for a total of 453,716 tons.

This was no fluke. Two more First War U-boat skippers, Kapitänleutnant Walther Forstmann and Kapitänleutnant Max Valentiner, sank 146 ships of 384,304 tons and 141 ships of 299,326 tons respectively, also in the Mediterranean. For comparison, the highest scoring Atlantic U-boat skipper was Otto Kretschmer, who up to his capture in 1941 had sunk forty-four ships of 266,529 tons.

However, the Mediterranean in the First World War was a very different proposition to the Second World War from the U-boat point of view. In the first campaign, Germany's opponents included both France and Italy, and many of their victims were lone merchant vessels sailing between the coasts of southern Europe and North Africa. In spite of occasional successes, Allied air patrols were no hindrance to de La Periere carrying out a whole succession of gun attacks on the surface, and there was the overwhelming advantage, in German eyes, that there was almost no American shipping in the Mediterranean at all. As a direct consequence, an unrestricted warfare campaign could be maintained throughout without the need to worry about inflaming public opinion in

Merchant seamen, like these British officers being rescued by an American warship, bore the brunt of the anti-submarine war, seen by the enemy as their primary targets, but unable to strike back in retaliation.
(US Naval Institute Press)

the United States.

In 1939, the Mediterranean was a much less inviting target, with Italy an ally and France neutral after the first year of conflict. Nevertheless, Doenitz did experiment with sending some of his meagre force of U-boats to one of the natural choke points where targets could be expected in abundance – the approaches to the dangerous and heavily patrolled Straits of Gibraltar. As early as 1 October 1939, he decided to send the two reasonably long-range type I U-boats, *U25* and *U26* together with the type VIIB *U53* to the straits. *U26* was ordered to lay mines off the entrance to the British harbour and then all three boats were to sail into the Mediterranean and search for targets. After this patrol, they were supposed to sail back through the straits, an altogether more difficult undertaking, and return to their bases in Germany.

The operation was a failure. *U53* met a convoy on her passage to Gibraltar. The submarine shadowed it without any other U-boats coming to join the attack, and she eventually returned to Germany with

dwindling fuel reserves. Her skipper was sacked and posted to a billet on a training cruiser. In the meantime, *U25* met a French merchant ship that was part of an unescorted convoy, and he fired four torpedoes with contact fuses at the target. Ominously, none of them detonated. He then surfaced and sank the ship with gunfire, but when he dived afterwards he found that firing the gun had damaged the forward torpedo-loading hatch so that water leaked into the pressure hull on every dive. Unable to force the passage of the straits in this condition, he too was forced to return to base.

Only *U26* made it. Bad weather and heavy British patrols forced the minelaying to be aborted, and the submarine only found and claimed to have sunk a single ship, which can not be found in Allied losses. Her disappointed skipper turned back and succeeded in passing through the straits from east to west, a difficult proposition since the surface current through the passage runs from west to east. The balancing stream in the opposite direction flows below the surface and when it encounters a submerged ridge to the west of the narrows, creates a stretch of confused layers and counter-currents. *U26* finally reached her Wilhelmshaven base on 5 December 1939. She would be the only U-boat to return from the Mediterranean into the Atlantic in the whole of the Second World War.

This reinforced Doenitz's growing conviction that the Mediterranean could be little more than a pointless sideshow. Any U-boats successfully running the gauntlet of the Straits of Gibraltar – itself an increasingly difficult achievement as British sea and air patrols were stepped up – would be lost to the main Atlantic campaign once and for all. Unless they could sink similar amounts of Allied shipping before they fell victim to anti-submarine patrols, sending U-boats to the Mediterranean station would be a gross waste of resources.

Apart from the relative lack of targets, there were other factors that, given the huge developments in ASW tactics and technology since the previous war, made the Mediterranean a much more hostile place for submarines. The clear and relatively shallow waters allowed boats to be spotted by aircraft even when they were submerged below periscope depth, when they would be unaware of any imminent attack.

Because of factors like these, and the relative dearth

of merchant shipping targets, the U-boats did far more damage to warship targets than they did to trade in the Mediterranean. This in itself struck another blow against Doenitz's Atlantic strategy: Naval Headquarters (OKM) was delighted at the sinking of the battleship HMS *Barham*, and the aircraft carriers *Eagle* and *Ark Royal*, all of them grievous losses to the Royal Navy, along with four cruisers, eight destroyers, one fast minelayer, five destroyer escorts, three minesweepers, one frigate, one submarine and one sloop. In addition, they sank a French cruiser, a Dutch destroyer, two US destroyers, a destroyer escort, one patrol craft and a minesweeper.[1]

This had two consequences. OKM was happy to accede to demands from Hitler for more and more U-boats to be sent on the one-way voyage into the Mediterranean, and their successes against naval targets meant they were often subject themselves to attacks from well-drilled escort crews charged with protecting the major warships. This meant that even if they survived, they invariably suffered considerable damage, which meant a spell in dockyard hands having that damage repaired.

Here too, they found fighting the submarine war in the Mediterranean imposed additional demands of its own. Their main bases of La Spezia in northern Italy and Salamis in Greece had restricted capacity for berthing and repairing U-boats and, in Italy at least, priority tended to be given to their own warships. As a result, repairs and maintenance that could have been carried out quickly in dockyards in Germany or Occupied France usually took much longer, further diluting U-boat strength in the area.

Even when all went well, Mediterranean conditions imposed extra stresses on the submarine crews. Like their British opponents, they found the warm climate sent conditions of heat and humidity inside the pressure hulls of their boats to barely endurable levels. When patrol time was spent predominantly underwater, health and morale suffered, especially when subjected to long and terrifying hunts by Allied anti-submarine craft. Even the marked changes in diet caused sickness and other afflictions that sapped the crews' resolve and impaired their efficiency.

Torpedoes – a severe problem for German submarines through most of the war – also met additional limitations. Air reconnaissance had shown that many tempting targets in Mediterranean harbours were protected by torpedo nets. Only with reliable magnetic pistols could torpedoes be set to run deeply enough to slip under the nets and explode under the hull of their targets. To make matters worse, the extra time spent under water caused air pressure to build up within the pressure hulls. During the course of a patrol air leaked into the pressure-sensitive torpedo depth-setting equipment and made them run inaccurately. Finally, a high proportion of the few

In the more confined waters of the Mediterranean, 'swamping' tactics using heavy air patrols closely co-ordinated with massive depth-charge attacks soon made life extremely difficult for the U-boats.

(US Naval Institute Press)

The Lockheed Hudson, another patrol plane adapted from a pre-war airliner, proved particularly successful in sinking U-boats trying to attack the Allied landings on the North African coast.

(US Naval Institute Press)

worthwhile merchant targets were too shallow in draught for the torpedoes to hit them, but surfacing to carry out a gun attack was often lethally dangerous in areas covered by Allied air patrols.

However, all the difficulties and limitations suffered by U-boats in the Mediterranean were eclipsed by their losses following the North African landings. From the point of view of the Naval High Command in Berlin, the U-boat losses were a harsh though necessary price to pay for opposing the Allied landings, since most navies accepted that submarines were expendable weapons, and tended to build them in large numbers for that reason. On the other hand, from Doenitz's viewpoint, each of the losses had a negligible effect on the peripheral North African land fighting and was a criminal waste of a boat and crew that could have been sinking Allied ships in the Atlantic.

As the war progressed, and the balance of resources in the Mediterranean was tilted even further in favour of the Allies, U-boat losses mounted still further. More and more escorts became available as necessary protection for the convoys needed to mount landings in Sicily and on the Italian mainland, and to keep them supplied once the leading troops were ashore. Because U-boats were frequently operating close to the limits of their endurance in air and battery power, through having to stay submerged to avoid air patrols, they were particularly prey to small hunter-killer groups of destroyers – often small Hunt class destroyers or US-built destroyer escorts – sent to investigate a sighting or contact, and with the time and weaponry to hold the U-boat down below the surface until dwindling reserves forced it to surface and fight or surrender to Allied gunfire. Another Allied tactic used with great success in the Mediterranean was 'swamping': responding to a contact by putting heavy air patrols overhead until the U-boat was eventually forced to surface, an option made possible by much shorter distances than those facing Atlantic air patrols to and from the mid-Atlantic Air Gap.

In all just over a hundred U-boats were ordered to the Mediterranean during the course of the war. Thirty-nine failed to make it past the obstacle of the Straits of Gibraltar: nine were damaged by enemy attack, two suffered technical problems and two more had to return to base because of illness among the crew. U-boat Headquarters recalled nine of the boats, while the remaining seventeen were sunk trying to complete the passage through the narrows. The remaining sixty-three boats reached their area of operations, but once there they became prisoners in an almost landlocked sea; armed and dangerous prisoners admittedly, but confined in a sense that did not apply to Allied warships or merchant vessels.

By the end of the war every one had been lost. Twelve were sunk on operations by Allied aircraft, and another twenty-five by surface escorts, with one sunk by a combination of air and surface attack. Two more were sunk in accidents, two due to unknown causes, three were scuttled at the end of the war and three more seized by the Allies when their bases were overrun. Five were torpedoed by Allied submarines (one Dutch and four British) while the remainder – ten in all – were sunk at their moorings by bombers attacking their bases.

This was particularly ironic since, following the North African landings by the Allies, the Germans occupied the remainder of France, which enabled the U-boats to use the major French naval base of Toulon, where dockyard facilities were much better. By this time, though, Allied air raids were much more damaging, and to the end of the war Toulon lacked the bomb-proof submarine pens of the Biscay coast dockyards. Consequently, many of the losses of the Mediterranean boats in the closing stages of the war were suffered in harbour.

In terms of Doenitz's objective of sinking Allied merchant ships, the Mediterranean U-boat force had proved an expensive luxury. From October 1941, when the first group of submarines had been sent through the straits to the final sinking in May 1944, they had sunk a total of 156 merchant vessels, with a total of 555,121 tons. When compared with the damage done by the Atlantic force (which at times was actually smaller than the Mediterranean force) over that same period, this was less than a quarter of the damage inflicted, and one which made little impact on Allied resources. In contrast, the much smaller group of Royal Navy submarines based on Malta had – thanks to poorer Axis anti-submarine resources (the Italian Navy was dependent on hydrophones to locate submerged submarines until their allies provided sonar equipment) and the advantages of Ultra intelligence[2] – a much greater effect on sinking tankers and troopships ferrying supplies and reinforcements to Rommel's Afrika Korps. It was an expensive and unsuccessful sideshow to the Atlantic battle, but one that showed up very clearly the increasing capabilities of Allied ASW tactics and technology.

CHAPTER 12

THE ATLANTIC CRISIS – THE CRUCIAL CONVOY BATTLES

1943

In the last resort, when faced with a U-boat surfacing to try to escape, escort commanders often tried to ram their enemy, risking damage for the virtual certainty of sinking a U-boat – this is HMS *Hesperus*, returning to Liverpool port with a badly crumpled bow after sinking the type VIIC *U357* on Boxing Day 1942 – she had already rammed and sunk another type VIIC, *U93* eleven months earlier.

(www.navyphotos.co.uk)

I T was the blackest time of the North Atlantic night, in the small hours of 16 March 1943. Spread out across this huge arena, beyond the range of land-based patrol aircraft were the ships of three eastbound convoys, the slow SC122 convoy and the faster HX229 and HX229A convoys from New York to England,[1] and the U-boats of three different wolf packs. The western-most of these was code-named *Raubgraf* (Robber Baron) and further to the east were the packs *Stürmer* and *Dränger* (from Sturm ünd Drang, or 'Storm and Stress', a popular theme in German literature). By a combination of good luck and clever evasive routing, the convoys had missed the *Raubgraf* group, but it was now becoming increasingly clear that both HX229 and SC122 would eventually encounter the patrol lines of the two eastern U-boat packs.

For the moment all was well for the convoys, with a bout of terrible weather giving way to easier conditions. So bad had the storms been that one of the *Raubgraf* U-boats, the type VIIC *U653*, had lost an officer and four ratings washed overboard from the bridge, and a petty officer had later fallen ill. Added to these problems was a temperamental starboard diesel engine, low fuel reserves and a torpedo comple-ment of one single weapon which was itself defective. The skipper, Kapitänleutnant Gerhard Feiler, had radioed headquarters and been given permission to leave the pack and head eastwards on the surface for a rendezvous with a tanker U-boat to top up his tanks ready for the long voyage home. The petty officer in charge of the bridge watch, Obersteuermann Heinz Theen, was peering into the darkness when he suddenly spotted a pinpoint of light dead ahead for just a couple of seconds.

> I think it was a sailor on the deck of a steamer lighting a cigarette. I sent a message to the captain and by the time he had come up on the bridge we could see ships all around us. There must have been about twenty, the nearest was on the port side between 500 metres and half a sea mile away. We did an alarm dive … after about two hours we surfaced behind the convoy and sent off a sighting report. Then we took up a shadowing position at a distance from which we could see the masts of the ships and when we were taken up by a high wave we could see the bridges and funnels.[2]

The ships were those of HX229. and no one aboard either the merchant ships or their weak escort of just five warships had spotted the submarine. But by now, U-boat headquarters knew exactly where they were, and orders were being sent out to ten of the *Raubgraf* boats to make for the convoy, reinforced by eleven boats from the two eastern groups, while the remainder kept watching for another convoy that the Germans knew was also somewhere in the area. The scene was set for one of the greatest of all convoy battles, and one that was both highly encouraging for the Germans and deeply dispiriting for the Allies.

In fact, the Germans overestimated their success. For the Allies, the truth was bad enough. The first U-boats reached the area at midday on 16 March, and by the evening seven were in contact and preparing to attack. To make matters worse, Escort Group B4 was by now down to five ships, led by an elderly 1918 destroyer HMS *Volunteer*, commanded by a regular Royal Navy officer who was an ASW specialist but who had direct personal experience of only one uneventful Atlantic crossing, Lieutenant-Commander Gordon John Luther. Both Luther and his ship had been temporarily transferred from another escort group to make up the strength of this one.

The other ships consisted of two corvettes, *Anemone* and *Pennywort* and two ex-US Navy four-stack destroyers, *Mansfield* and *Beverley*. Another V and W class destroyer, HMS *Witherington*, had been forced to drop out the previous day with damaged deck plating resulting from the storm. The commander of B4, Commander E C L Day RN in the modern destroyer HMS *Highlander*, was late leaving St John's because of urgent repairs to leaks and the need to fit a new Asdic dome, and was still trying to catch up and resume

Later wartime escort groups were equipped with the larger and more heavily armed frigates like HMS *Loch Fada*

(www.navyphotos.co.uk)

command.

Before he could do so, things had begun to go wrong. Just before midday, HMS *Volunteer* had picked up one of *U653*'s shadowing reports to U-boat headquarters on HFDF. Because *Volunteer* was the only ship in the convoy with this equipment, there was no chance of a cross-bearing, so Luther ordered HMS *Mansfield* to head out from the convoy on that bearing to see if she could locate the U-boat. Ironically, *Mansfield* had earlier almost run down *U653* when the convoy made an abrupt change of course, but, because her radar was inoperative, had failed to spot

the submarine. This reduced the number of escorts to four, and when the convoy later made another change of course, the inexperienced Luther forgot to keep *Mansfield* informed. By the time she failed to find *U653* and tried to resume her place in the screen, the convoy had moved off on a different course, and catching it took her until early in the morning. In the meantime, expecting action that night, *Volunteer* tried to refuel from the oiler sailing with the convoy, but was unable to do so.

Later the sinkings began. Seven different U-boats sank ten ships that night from the beleaguered convoy. To make matters even worse, HX229 had sailed without a designated rescue ship, and an attempt had been made to remedy the omission by instructing the rearmost merchant ship in each column to take on this highly dangerous job. When some of them failed to do so, escorts did so instead, saving the survivors but leaving the convoy almost completely unprotected. Nonetheless, the escort crews fought back as hard as they could and two of the attacking U-boats suffered damage from depth charges.

At 11.00pm *Mansfield* was still trying to rejoin the convoy after its change of course, three escorts including *Volunteer* were busy picking up survivors and *Anemone* was attacking an Asdic contact astern of the convoy, leaving it completely without protection for ninety minutes. This was a temporary respite as the *Raubgraf* boats withdrew because many of the undamaged U-boats were now running short of fuel. In the meantime, the boats released from the *Stürmer* and *Dränger* groups were approaching from the east to take up the fight.

One of them, the new type VIIC *U338*, skippered by Kapitänleutnant Manfred Kinzel was amazed to find itself approaching another group of merchant ships that same night, while he was still more than a hundred miles northeast of the position reported by U-boat headquarters. His reaction was immediate. Rather than worry about the identity of the convoy he had found, (it was actually SC122, the convoy the U-boats thought they were attacking 120 miles to the southwest, which was really HX229) he reported it to headquarters and then attacked. Launching four torpedoes from the bow tubes and one from the stern tube before the escort could react, he sank three merchant ships and severely damaged a fourth.

Other U-boats from the eastern groups did manage to find HX229 and resume the attack on the second day. Three more submarines sank another three ships under the noses of the hard-pressed escorts that were still having to cope on their own while reinforcements were on their way from Iceland and from Halifax. In the meantime, SC122 – though having a numerically stronger escort, but also awaiting reinforcements – lost four more ships after two additional U-boats had joined Kinzel's *U338* in the attack.

During the following day, 18 March, the battered and depleted convoys were approaching the limit of Allied air cover, and reinforcements arrived by sea and air. It was just in time for the remaining ships: thirteen U-boats had now found SC122 and with the escort now comprised of nine ships there was time to subject the attackers to crippling depth-charge attacks that lasted in two cases for eight hours and nine hours apiece. Kinzel's *U338* suffered heavy damage from depth charges and was forced to withdraw, as was another type VIIC, *U665*, which was finally sunk with all hands by a Whitley from an Operational Training Unit that was crossing the Bay of Biscay on its return to base. Nevertheless, three other U-boats managed to sink two more ships from the convoy.

Between them, the two convoys had lost a total of twenty-two ships totalling 146,000 tons, compared with German claims of thirty-two ships sunk for a total of 186,000 tons. Only one of the attacking U-boats had actually been sunk; a B17 from 206 Squadron Coastal Command had arrived over convoy HX229 and started to patrol around it at a range of thirty miles. Seeing a local squall, the pilot had flown into it, to find type VIIC *U384* shadowing the convoy from astern. Taken completely by surprise, the boat was fatally slow to react and the aircraft dropped four depth charges that exploded alongside. The submarine disappeared, leaving only a vast and expanding lake of oil from shattered tanks, the only German loss in the battle, though many of the boats returned to base with severe damage.

Nonetheless, the convoy losses represented almost a quarter of the ninety ships originally making up the two formations, and there were undoubted lessons to be drawn from what the Germans saw as a victory and the British as a defeat. There were clear errors made: a lack of designated rescue ships and insufficient escorts, combined with sailing two convoys close together and on almost the same track, which caused U-boats heading for one to stumble into the other. Yet the escorts had fought back hard, inflicting heavy damage on seven U-boats (five by HX229, two by SC122) and with better luck several of these badly damaged U-boats might have been sunk.

For the time being, the Germans were free to celebrate what they referred to as 'the greatest convoy battle of all time'. Yet this would be the last of their real successes in the Battle of the Atlantic. Already changes were under way in both technology and tactics that would completely alter the balance between the opposing forces, some of them as a direct consequence of the lessons learned in the HX229/SC122 battles.

Part of the reason for the lack of escort vessels was that the Atlantic weather had been so bad that many urgently needed escorts were being repaired. Because they were under strength, the escort commanders could not afford to have ships leave the screen to attack U-boats for long enough to ensure kills, and when the HX229 escorts had to rescue survivors as well, they became grossly overburdened. The shortage of VLR aircraft, which could have closed the Air Gap and made life much harder for the U-boats is dealt

Based on escort carriers like the uss *Santee*, the US Navy carrier groups proved efficient U-boat killers.

(US National Archives)

with in an earlier chapter, but historian Martin Middlebrook has already pointed out[3] that if an ordinary B24 was able to reach HX229 after flying a thousand miles from its Northern Ireland base, why could similar aircraft not reach it from Newfoundland, which at that point was 160 miles closer?

As far as surface escorts were concerned, the overriding requirement was for more ships, which could be formed into support groups, trained and prepared to rush to the aid of convoys threatened by U-boat wolf packs, quickly enough to turn the tables. Ironically, the decision to form these groups had been taken the year before, but from the autumn of 1942 the demands of the convoys supplying the North African landings had taken precedence.

The difference that these groups would make in future convoy battles would be proved over and over again, and are covered in the next chapter. The difference that might have been made to the recent battle for HX229/SC122 was shown by a remarkable exercise in what would eventually come to be known as 'virtual reality' carried out by a duty captain at the Derby House headquarters of Western Approaches Command. A former First World War submariner, Captain Neville Lake had become a tactical expert on ASW operations in the Second World War, and had been carrying out a number of war-game exercises based on actual events, using three notional support groups formed from new frigates and sloops, at the operational plot at Derby House.

Lake's analysis started on 18 February 1943 and everything was done to make it as realistic as possible. Not only were the genuine movements of U-boats and convoys alike taken from the plot, but weather conditions were also factored into the equation to determine as precisely as possible the outcome of events using these virtual support groups. The groups themselves were monitored for consumption of fuel and depth charges, and the ships were sent back to harbour to rest the crews or repair damage at regular intervals, corresponding to the practice with genuine escort vessels.

Even bearing these practical considerations in mind, Captain Lake's exercise produced some surprising outcomes. Without over-extending any of his support groups, it proved feasible to keep two out of the three at sea at any one time. More importantly, had the three groups been available in reality, then every single convoy that was attacked by U-boats during the period of the exercise would have been reinforced by one of the groups.

What would have happened when Lieutenant-Commander Luther's five escorts were trying to rescue survivors from torpedoed merchantmen at the same time as they were endeavouring to attack U-boats and prevent them from inflicting additional casualties? The records of the exercise show that

Support Group 'C', which was assumed to consist of three Black Swan class sloops, HMS *Whimbrel*, HMS *Wild Goose* and HMS *Woodpecker*, and a pair of River class frigates, HMS *Tweed* and HMS *Ness*, would have been dispatched to join HX229 at midday on 16 March, soon after the interception of *U653*'s original sighting report. They would have reached the convoy in the early evening, more than two hours before the first ship was torpedoed. This would have more than doubled the escort force, and if the support groups were assumed to be manned by experienced and able crews (as they were to be in practice) then the effect of these reinforcements on the battle would have been dramatic.

Captain Lake's analysis was invaluable in another way too. Such was the severity of the shock administered by the U-boats on HX229 and SC122 at a time when the escorts had seemed to be gaining the upper hand, that it produced a great deal of alarm at the highest levels of the Navy. Once again, reactions showed there were murmurings that indicated the old innate hostility to convoys had never quite gone away, and suggestions were made that perhaps losses could be reduced by allowing ships to sail independently, in the hope they would manage to elude the wolf packs. Such an expedient would have been a terrible mistake, but great concern was indeed being expressed at the morale of the merchant sailors, who frequently felt that membership of a convoy was a trap rather than a protection.

At this point Admiral Max Horton, Commander-in-Chief Western Approaches, was due to attend a meeting of the Anti-Submarine Committee. There he would have to explain to the Prime Minister his proposals for maintaining supplies to the UK, particularly in view of the tanker shortage, which was then seen to threaten oil reserves needed for future operations. Lake gave him the report of the exercises he had carried out to test the value of support groups, in the hope that it would be useful.

It was. Quizzed by Churchill on how he proposed to defeat the latest tactics being used by the U-boats, Horton showed him the report. After the Prime Minister had studied it in detail with the American Admiral Stark, Commander of US Naval Forces in the European Theatre of Operations, he told Horton he could have the extra ships he needed to form the support groups. Destroyers would be made available by releasing them from the Home Fleet, and other escorts would be released by temporarily calling a halt to the supply convoys to North Russia, at a time when the Soviets were clamouring for every kind of Western assistance.[4]

The results of Churchill's decision were rapid and effective. In a matter of days, five support groups (rather than the three envisaged by Lake) had been formed or were in the process of being assembled.

Two of them were made up of new, or fairly new, sloops and frigates that were more effective anti-submarine ships than the ageing corvettes, two more were made up of former Fleet destroyers, and the last contained the new aircraft carrier HMS *Biter*. Together with US Navy groups based around their own escort carriers, these were the forces that would transform the Atlantic battle and quickly drive the U-boats from the ocean they now seemed to dominate.

Another change being introduced at the time was a switch to larger convoys as a result of the work of the ORS. In the previous autumn, Professor Blackett had been carrying out a detailed study of the convoy statistics covering 1941 and 1942, when he had been struck by a perplexing fact which seemed to defy explanation. Common sense suggested that if two convoys of different sizes were both attacked by a group of U-boats, their losses would be roughly in proportion to the number of merchant ships they contained. A larger convoy would contain more potential targets and this would result in more sinkings.

In fact, the opposite was the case, and this proved to be consistently true, rather than a singular quirk of statistics. Smaller convoys, which were made up of an average of thirty-two ships, when attacked by U-boats, suffered an average loss of 2.5 per cent of the ships they contained. Larger convoys, which contained an average of fifty-four ships suffered an average loss of 1.1 per cent of their ships. What this amounted to was an average loss per convoy of approximately 0.6 ships, and this was independent of the size of the convoy, and that each of the ships forming a larger convoy therefore had a smaller chance of becoming a victim.

Further studies showed that the chance of a convoy being spotted by a U-boat in the vast spaces of the Atlantic were roughly the same whatever the size of the convoy. Whether that U-boat, or any of the others it called up from nearby groups, managed to find its way past the escort screen to torpedo the merchant ships depended on the spacing of the escorts and the width of any gaps. In other words, the vulnerability of the convoy could be expressed as the perimeter of the area covered by the convoy divided by the number of escorts protecting it.

More surprising was the outcome if a submarine did manage to evade the escorts long enough to start sinking merchant ships. The number of sinkings achieved by that submarine was not affected by the size of the convoy, since even a small convoy represented more targets than the U-boat could take advantage of. Consequently, the figures suggesting that the average number of ships sunk from a convoy attacked by U-boats was more or less the same, whether the convoy was small or large, were explained by the mathematics of the situation. The conclusion to be drawn from this was a simple one: if roughly the same number of ships was to be lost from a large

convoy as a small one, then it made the best sense to group merchant ships into the largest convoys practicable. If a given number of merchant ships was divided into a smaller number of larger convoys, then the losses should be substantially reduced.[5]

Calculations and predictions were relatively easy to make. Much more difficult was reassuring the admirals that these larger convoys would not be specially vulnerable to new tactics adopted by the U-boats, like attacking the convoys from ahead. Studies of recent German attack methods showed that the U-boats were tending to concentrate more on eastbound convoys, carrying valuable cargoes, rather than westbound convoys, where the benefits of sinkings were largely limited to the ships themselves. They were also tending to begin group attacks from ahead of the convoy, and this was seen as a means of hedging their bets: that if the escorts' response showed that surface attacks were too dangerous, then they could submerge and attack as the convoy passed by. The other advantage, from the U-boats' viewpoint, was that early attacks en masse tended to disrupt the cohesion of a convoy, which helped them make follow-up attacks with greater ease. If one U-boat attacked successfully from a particular direction, it was often followed by others, and if a submarine was driven off by the escorts, it tended to remain out of the action until at least the following night.

The Germans were also becoming more careful about selecting their battleground. The advantages of attacking a convoy as it entered the Air Gap were clear enough, since they would be less likely to be caught unawares by Allied aircraft. The pattern was tending to show that the most favoured part of the Air Gap was that closest to the limit of air coverage from Newfoundland. This might have been partly because these were seen as less of a threat than those launched from Iceland or the United Kingdom, but another factor must surely have been that this would also give the maximum time when an eastbound convoy would find itself without protection from the air, as it made its painful progress towards the limit of patrols from the north and east.

Blackett's proposals were finally accepted by the Cabinet Anti U-boat Warfare Committee, which met on 3 March 1943,[6] and agreed to try running larger convoys whenever a case could be made for sailing them. As a first step, a New York to Liverpool convoy (HX231) departed with sixty-one merchant ships on 29 March 1943, with an ocean escort of one frigate, one destroyer and four corvettes from Escort Group B7. It was reinforced by four destroyers. *Eclipse*, *Fury*, *Icarus* and *Inglefield* (all transferred from duty with the Home Fleet to form the 4th Support Group), which had paused at Iceland to refuel. Delayed by heavy weather, they were three days late adding their

The US destroyer escorts designed on similar lines to the RN's Hunt class destroyers quickly proved their worth. uss *Bronstein* took part in the sinking of three U-boats in three weeks in Spring 1944

(The Floating Drydock)

weight to the escort, though air cover from Iceland- and Northern Ireland-based VLR B24s added their strength to the battle after the first of those days.

Though the Germans mounted an attack with the *Löwenherz* group of seventeen submarines, two of them were sunk by B24s and five more badly damaged. Even with these odds the merchant ship losses from the convoy proper, one on each of the first three nights before the support group joined, amounted to a 7,000-ton tanker, a 5,500-ton freighter and another freighter of 9,400 tons. This confirmed Blackett's predictions, though another three ships that were also sunk by the pack were actually stragglers and did not fall within the convoy's protective screen.[7] Doenitz believed, from the reports made by individual U-boat skippers, that they had sunk a more encouraging total of eight ships totalling 54,000 tons.[8]

The figures were rather better from the Allied point of view. Five per cent of the ships within the convoy was an acceptable rate for an attack by a large U-boat pack. Furthermore, no ships were sunk after the arrival of the support group and had it not been delayed by the weather, the casualty rate may well have been lower. Ironically, given that half the boats sunk were stragglers, Doenitz criticised the pack for spending too much time signalling to one another and on chasing stragglers rather than attacking the convoy. More

puzzling was the assessment in German eyes suggesting that 'in this case U-boat numbers were adequate, but the relatively small result was ascribed to difficulty in attaining attacking positions owing to the presence of carrier-borne aircraft' when no carriers of any kind were actually involved.[9]

Clearly, support groups were likely to make a great deal of difference to the battle between surface escorts and U-boats, but another question that was exercising the minds of Allied commanders at the time was whether or not it was better to devote the greater part of shipbuilding capacity to replacing merchant ship losses, or to build larger numbers of escort vessels. The ORS tackled the problem by examining the value of each additional escort in terms of the merchant ship sinkings it prevented by its presence in the screen of the convoy(s) it was protecting.

Figures showed that from summer 1942 to the end of the year, 210 merchant ships had been lost to U-boat attack, at a time when the average escort strength was about one hundred. Examining the detailed convoy statistics showed that increasing the number of escorts present in the convoy screen from six to nine tended to reduce losses – all other factors being more or less equal – by a factor of about a quarter. Extrapolating this effect across the statistics for all convoys suggested that an extra fifty escorts, repre-

Beta Search pattern 1. On sighting a shadowing U-boat ahead of the convoy, the escort maintains course and speed to reassure the submarine skipper he has not been spotted. As soon as the U-boat dives, the escort turns towards her last known position and increases speed, safe in the knowledge that the noise of her propellers is masked by that of the convoy behind.

(Author's drawing)

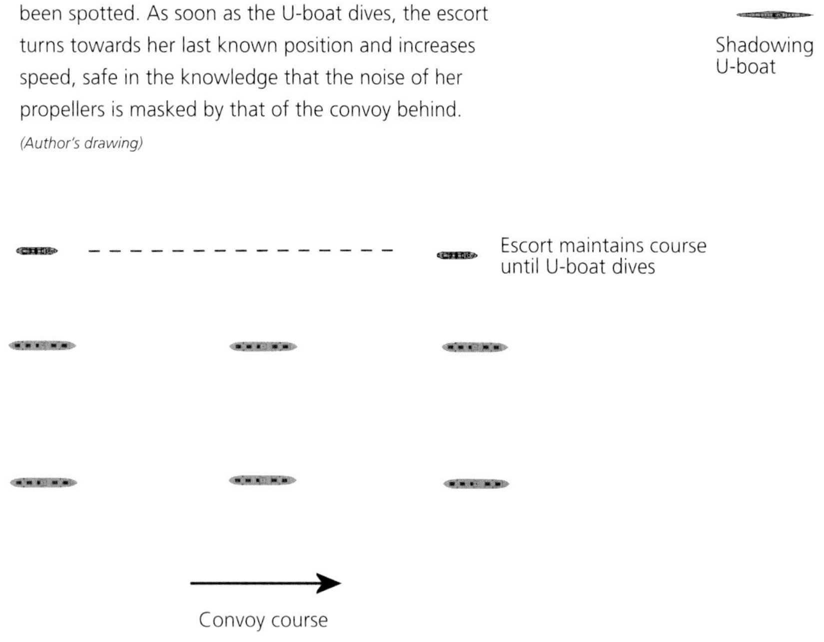

Shadowing U-boat

Escort maintains course until U-boat dives

Convoy course

Beta search pattern 2. Masked by the noises of the convoy on the same bearing, the escort approaches the last known position of the U-boat while the circle of uncertainty is still small because of the submarine's low underwater speed. This makes it highly probable the escort can pick up a solid echo and deliver a successful attack.

(Author's drawing)

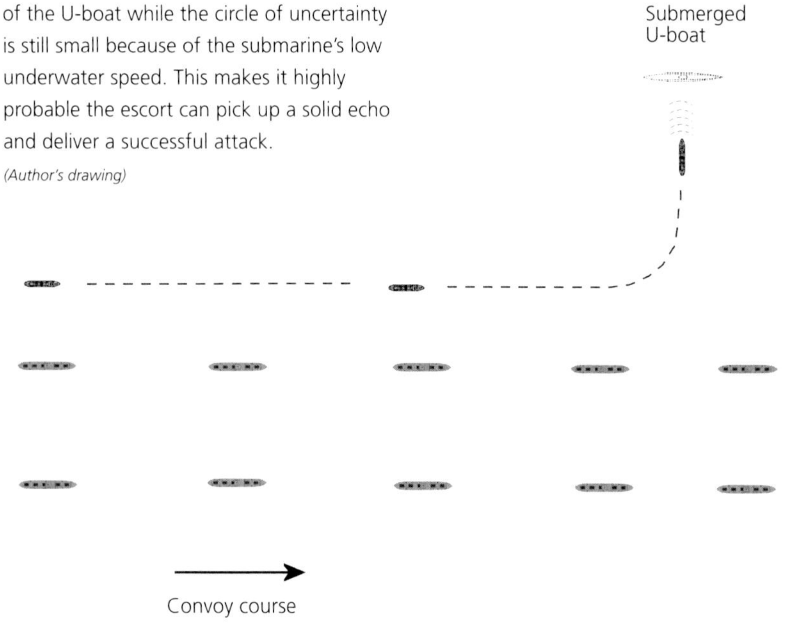

Submerged U-boat

Convoy course

senting an additional 50 per cent over and above the existing force, would also have cut losses by approximately a quarter, and in that case each additional escort vessel could be expected to save one merchant ship being sunk in a year. This was the so-called 'defensive' value of additional escort vessels making it more difficult for U-boats to mount successful attacks on more heavily defended convoys.

There was also the offensive role of escorts in actively sinking submarines, since each submarine sunk could be considered to save all the merchant ships which that U-boat might have gone on to sink in its subsequent career, had it survived. Again using the statistics for the second half of 1942, it appeared that sinking a U-boat saved an average of 3.6 merchant ships, and in helping to sink U-boats an escort vessel could be expected to save 0.7 of a merchant ship each year.[10]

The point was that the new support groups would allow the surface escorts to pursue both objectives. Until this point, the convoy escorts had an unenviable choice to make. When U-boats attacked the convoy in their charge, the escorts could attack in turn and drive them under, but unless that attack was successful in a relatively short time, they could not afford to remain on the spot and risk leaving a gap in the escort screen shielding the convoy from further attacks, as had happened with HX229. Support groups, on the other hand, had time on their side, and could afford to remain on the spot, provided they were still in contact with the U-boat, until cumulative damage from successive depth-charge attacks, or dwindling reserves of air and battery power forced it to surface and face the gunfire of its enemies.

New escort vessels were being built in larger numbers on both sides of the Atlantic. In Britain, frigates designed from direct experience in fighting U-boat packs in the great convoy battles were beginning to take over the brunt of the battle from the corvettes. Larger, heavier, faster and better armed escorts of the Loch, Bay, Castle and River classes, together with the modified Black Swan class – which was developed from the earlier sloops – were armed with ahead-throwing weapons like Hedgehog and eventually Squid, and larger numbers of depth charges to exploit the more profligate but more successful tactics being developed by ASW aces like 'Johnny' Walker (see Chapter 13).

In the USA, a different solution to the same requirement was the escort destroyer, or DE (later DDE), a smaller and cheaper version of the fleet destroyer that had previously been seen as the mainstay of the US Navy's anti-submarine campaign. Though the need for specialised and capable escort vessels had been appreciated as early as the spring of 1939, it took two years for the first design to be approved, and the first vessel was commissioned in February 1943. This was destined for the Royal Navy

The 'Pineapple' tactic was used when a U-boat was suspected to be in the path of a convoy, either as the result of a signal from the Admiralty or from a HFDF fix from the U-boat's own transmissions. On the order 'Pineapple', the escorts ahead of the convoy would increase to full speed, firing star shell to illuminate the area where the U-boat was thought to be. This would force it to dive as the escorts passed by at speed, unable at that stage to carry out a sonar search, and deliberately allowing it to approach the convoy.

(Author's drawing)

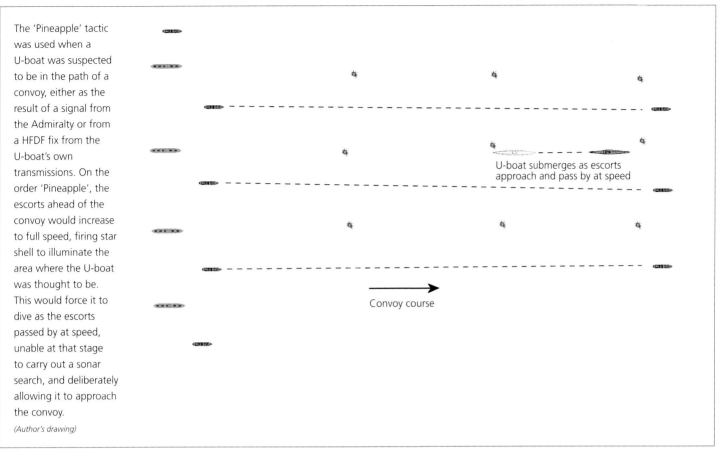

U-boat submerges as escorts approach and pass by at speed

Convoy course

After 15 minutes, the escorts reverse course and head back towards the convoy without firing star shell, to catch the surfaced U-boat unaware of their stealthy back-tracking.

(Author's drawing)

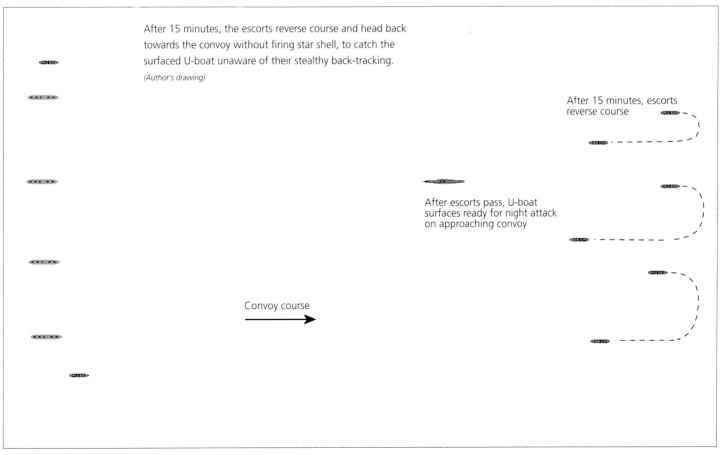

After 15 minutes, escorts reverse course

After escorts pass, U-boat surfaces ready for night attack on approaching convoy

Convoy course

as HMS *Bentinck*, the first of what became known as the Captain class. By July 1943 sixteen US shipyards would be devoted to DE production, and a total of 563 were built by the end of the war.

There were detail differences between sub-types of DEs. They were all some 300 feet long and displaced between 1,400 and 1,750 tons fully loaded, and while they were slower than fleet destroyers, with a top speed of between nineteen and twenty-six knots, they were much more manoeuvrable and quite capable of dealing with a U-boat at full surface speed. They had the latest sonar with a maximum detection range in good conditions of 4,000 yards, carried 100 depth charges and a main armament of either three 3-inch guns in single shield mountings, or two 5-inch guns in enclosed turrets. Propulsion was by diesel engines, diesel-electric drive or steam turbines, and ships were usually grouped together in divisions according to their propulsion systems to simplify handling, speed and requirements of fuel and spare parts.

As an indication of the increasing technical sophistication of the anti-submarine campaign, two

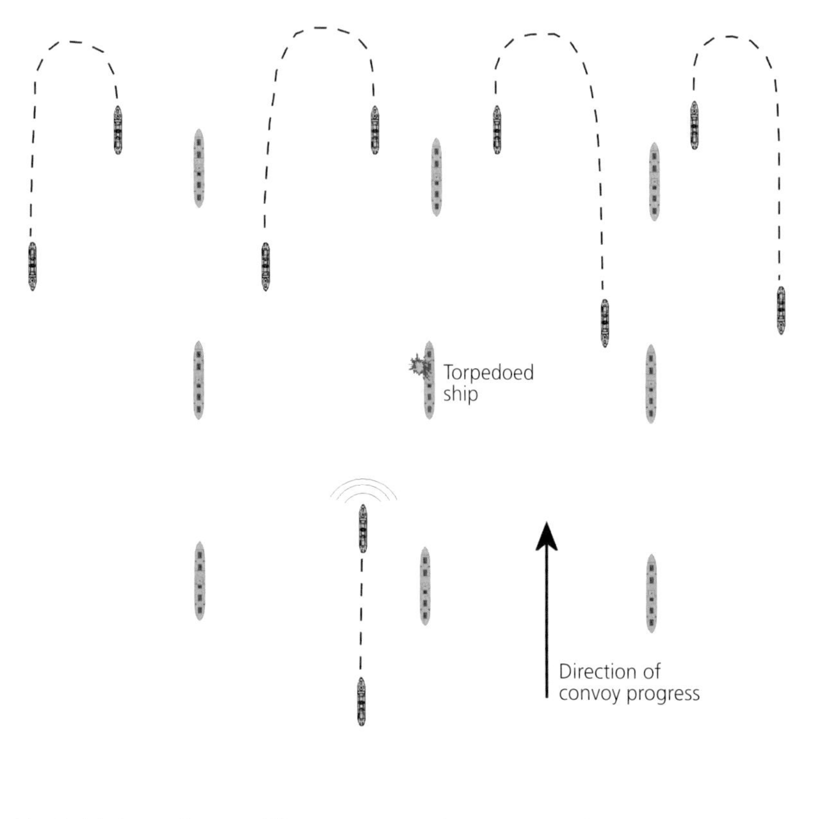

The 'Artichoke' tactic was a different response to the torpedoing of a merchant ship in the middle of the convoy. On the order being given over the radio, the escort stationed astern of the convoy made for the position of the torpedoed ship at maximum sonar speed, searching for the echo of the U-boat responsible for the attack. At the same time, the escorts ahead of the convoy reversed course and headed at maximum sonar speed through the columns of merchant ships to reach the rear of the convoy.

(Author's drawing)

DEs in each division were fitted with HFDF, to enable U-boats sending radio messages in their vicinity to be pinpointed in terms of both bearing and range. They also carried long-range radio telephony equipment, and navigational direction finding systems, including the latest Loran receivers, which could fix their position with considerable accuracy in any weather.

Perhaps the most innovative feature was a combat information centre (CIC) similar to those carried aboard major units like carriers. In a space behind the bridge, all incoming data from radar and sonar, look-outs and members of the bridge watch, radio and signals would be processed, evaluated and plotted. This became a tremendous help to a commanding officer trying to keep ahead of a quickly changing situation around a convoy under attack, perhaps at night and in heavy weather, when it was all too easy to miss something vital.

However, the US Navy had one drawback that their comrades in arms in the Royal Navy (not to mention their opponents in the Kriegsmarine) had encountered earlier with the huge wartime expansion in warship building. Finding the resources and the berths to turn out the ships so badly needed by both sides was a difficult enough assignment, but finding the crews with the training and expertise to put the new ships to the best use was an even more difficult conundrum. On both sides of the U-boat war the inescapable fact was that the toughest, most experienced and most highly motivated crews and commanders were those out in the Atlantic doing the actual fighting. How could their know-how be transferred and shared by those now joining the battle in increasing numbers?

Like the Royal Navy, the US Navy depended heavily on its reservists. Once the first DEs had been brought into service using serving officers from the regular navy to train those serving under them, most of the ships were commanded by reservists who had some recent seagoing experience on minesweepers or small patrol craft and sub-chasers, and who therefore knew something about the basics of the U-boat war. Much depended on the calibre of the warrant officers – chief petty officers and petty officers, first class – who had mostly served aboard larger ships during wartime operations, but very often the captain and the executive officer would be the only ones with the experience to allow them to stand watches at sea. Until the others gained the necessary knowledge and experience, the skipper and the executive officer would have to stand alternate watches for the whole of an Atlantic crossing, which proved a formidable strain with very little sleep.

DEs were used as convoy escorts and later as protection for the small escort carriers that would make such a vast difference to the U-boat war. Their anti-submarine training was carried out at a specially

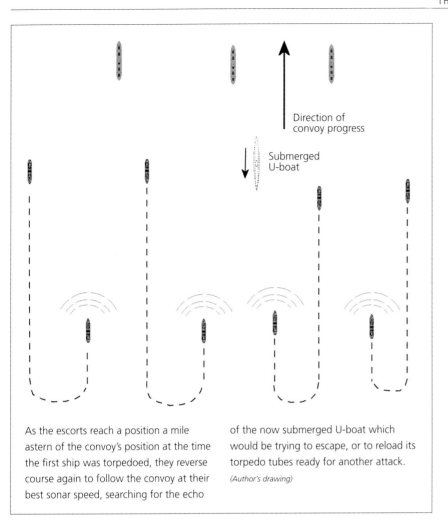

Direction of
convoy progress

Submerged
U-boat

As the escorts reach a position a mile astern of the convoy's position at the time the first ship was torpedoed, they reverse course again to follow the convoy at their best sonar speed, searching for the echo of the now submerged U-boat which would be trying to escape, or to reload its torpedo tubes ready for another attack.

(Author's drawing)

commissioned centre in Miami – the Subchaser Training Centre, or SCTC – which was directed by the formidable Captain 'Mac' MacDaniel. He was reputed not to be a sufferer of fools, like his Royal Navy equivalent, Vice-Admiral Sir Gilbert Stephenson, who ran the training school at HMS *Western Isles*, based at Tobermory on the Isle of Mull, where all Western Approaches escort crews were mercilessly put through their paces before being judged fit or unfit to join the convoy battles.

By now there was a huge amount for prospective escort commanders to learn, and for existing escort commanders to re-learn. The Western Approaches Tactical School, run at Liverpool by Captain Gilbert Roberts from early 1942, worked with experienced escort group commanders to ensure its teaching reflected the latest experience and the most effective tactics in defeating each new German move in the campaign. Careful study of earlier convoy actions had resulted in the development of new manoeuvres for dealing with specific situations as quickly and effectively as possible, and skippers were put through detailed and elaborate war-games using models and a specially marked floor to represent the turbulent and dangerous waters of the North Atlantic.

With the onset of heavy German pack attacks attempting to overwhelm the escorts and reach the vulnerable merchant ships, escort commanders had the difficult task of deciding how far to maintain an attack on a solid Asdic contact, or when they were needed back in the convoy screen. Simply chasing one contact after another could easily last a whole night, and the Tactical School had studied the problem, noticing that the U-boats preferred to attack downwind wherever possible, for better visibility, a steadier platform and to minimise the chances of their bow-wave being spotted by the escorts. Consequently, escort commanders were advised to concentrate most of their strength on the windward side of the convoy and dispose themselves in an outer and inner screen to provide defence in depth for up to four nights while a convoy had to fight its way through the Air Gap.[11]

Just how well these tactics worked in the most threatening and discouraging of circumstances was to be shown by a westbound slow convoy that ran into what is possibly the greatest concentration of U-boats of all time. This was ONS5, which began its running of the gauntlet on 22 April 1943 when Escort Group B7, commanded by Peter Gretton, one of the rising stars of the anti-submarine war joined the forty merchant ships in their charge. Quite apart from the gathering packs of U-boats, they would face appalling weather and a shortage of fuel, which would rob them of nearly half their escorts while the battle was still at full intensity.

The voyage was quiet enough for the first four days. The escorts numbered two destroyers, HMS *Duncan* (Gretton's ship) and HMS *Vidette*, then about to sail from Iceland to join the convoy with three more merchantmen. There was also one River class frigate, HMS *Tay*, and four Flower class corvettes, and it was already clear that the destroyers were all too likely to run seriously short of fuel during the journey. To economise as far as possible, the convoy was steering a Great Circle course as the shortest route to its destination port of Halifax, and HMS *Duncan* took up station in the centre of the convoy.[12] Already the weather was worsening which, with many of the ships lightly loaded, made it difficult for them to keep station and slowed the convoy down below its nominal speed of 7.5 knots.

'One night we could see no less than eight sets of "two red lights vertical" from ships out of control due to the weather. On 26 April, the inevitable happened and two ships collided with each other.'[13] One of the victims was able to remain in the convoy, while the other was forced to run unescorted for the safety of Iceland, where it successfully made port. Later that day, *Vidette* and her charges joined ONS5, and the convoy continued its painfully slow progress into the rising storm. All that was missing in this apocalyptic scenario was the presence of the U-boats.

On 27 April the weather eased sufficiently for *Duncan* and *Vidette* to top up their fuel reserves from the escort tanker, *British Lady*, which was equipped to trail a heavy rubber hose astern to be picked up by the ship needing to refuel. Once the hoses were connected – a daunting task in rough weather –

High Frequency Direction Finding (HFDF or Huff-Duff) proved a priceless asset to escort group commanders faced with an assembling wolfpack approaching their convoy.

(National Library of Canada)

normal refuelling took a couple of hours, though station keeping called for a lot of care and could be interrupted at any time by a submarine attack. A second tanker, the *Argon*, was fitted with equipment for refuelling a ship sailing alongside, but due to an oversight her hoses were canvas rather than rubber. Though this was faster in theory than refuelling astern, the fragile canvas hose meant it was only possible to make the connections in a flat calm.

The first U-boat appeared the following day. On 28 April 1943, the group *Star* had been ordered to disperse following an unsuccessful attempt to find the eastbound convoy SC128. One of the boats, the type VIIC *U650*, was heading for the new Fink patrol line of thirty-four boats for another attempt to find the convoy when she heard convoy noises on her hydrophones. She shadowed these sounds until they reached the Fink patrol line, whereupon U-Boat headquarters realised the magnitude of the prize. '*The initial conditions for a convoy battle had never been more favourable.* Thirty boats of the Fink group were in a patrol line, with gaps of only eight miles, and the convoy was sighted in the centre of this line. Moreover, 11 boats of Amsel 1 and 2 were ahead of the convoy [emphasis added].'[14]

Fortunately, they were not alone in seeing their opportunity. Though this was one of the periods when changes to the German Enigma system meant that Bletchley Park could not read full signals quickly enough for completely accurate warning, they were aware of another patrol line, Amsel, ahead of ONS5. Now at last they had the luxury of a support group that could be sent to redress the rapidly worsening balance between the convoy and its assailants. This was the 3rd Support Group, four modern O class ex-Home Fleet destroyers that were ordered to sail from Newfoundland, while another, HMS *Oribi*, would sail to join them from Iceland.

The convoy escorts realised the peril they were facing on 28 April, when around noon they picked up a transmission on HFDF just ahead of the convoy. Gretton headed out along the bearing of the signal but found nothing. Meanwhile a total of fourteen other U-boats had been called in by the shadower and were closing with the convoy. The next sign of their presence came as the afternoon light was beginning to fade, when *Duncan* spotted a surfaced U-boat on the port bow of the convoy, approaching downwind. As Gretton headed straight for it, the U-boat vanished beneath the surface, though the rough weather made an Asdic attack extremely difficult.[15] Worried about the convoy, he ordered *Tay* to maintain the attack while he returned to his position in the screen.

Gretton's tactics were in perfect accord with the advice from the Tactical School. Deprived of the ability to evade the U-boats by altering the course of the convoy, since the fury of the storm would have made the manoeuvre lethal, he reasoned the U-boats would also be unable to attack from the leeward, starboard side. He therefore positioned his escorts on the port, windward, side of the convoy, leaving none to starboard.

He was right. At 10pm the corvette *Sunflower* picked up the radar echo of a U-boat approaching the port side of the convoy. She opened fire with her 4-inch gun to force it to dive, then made for the spot where it disappeared and dropped a depth-charge pattern. She was back on station within half an hour, and another thirty minutes later *Duncan* picked up a further radar echo, and rushed in to drop more depth charges. While heading back to her station in the screen, the crew picked up yet another radar echo, this time to port and up wind. *Duncan* turned to intercept, but this meant plunging into steep head seas, with flying spray betraying her presence even in the darkness. There was no sign of the submarine, but they dropped charges to try to keep it from surfacing again.

So the attacks went on, with the hard-pressed escorts parrying each blow. At dawn on the following day, 29 April, HMS *Tay* was sent astern of the convoy to drive down any shadowing U-boats. Later a torpedo hit the US freighter *McKeesport* but for half an hour she was able to maintain her speed and her position in the convoy until the overstrained bulkheads collapsed and she sank quickly.

That night HMS *Oribi* reached the convoy from

Iceland, but HFDF signals showed there were still at least four U-boats in the vicinity, and the weather had worsened again, preventing any attempts at refuelling. On the following morning, *Oribi* was able to refuel, but in doing so she damaged the oiler's equipment so no one else could refuel that day. By the evening the weather deteriorated once again to a full gale, forcing the convoy to reduce speed but preventing the U-boats from attacking, apart from one attempt to penetrate the escort screen, which was deflected by the corvettes *Snowflake* and *Sunflower*. As Asdic could not detect a submerged submarine in such violent seas, the escorts were limited to plotting the position of each transmission and dropping a depth-charge pattern on the spot to keep the submarines from surfacing again until the convoy was safely past.

On the following day, 1 May, the convoy was almost stationary, and two ships had to turn and run before the wind to survive, luckily reaching Iceland without foundering or being torpedoed. By that evening, the weather was moderating slowly, though the convoy was badly scattered, and *Duncan*'s oil tanks were leaking into the forward boiler room, which depleted reserves still further. On the afternoon of the next day, 2 May, the four Home Fleet destroyers, led by HMS *Offa*, also arrived.

Extra escorts allowed new tactics to screen the convoy. In the early evening, the support group

destroyers were placed on both bows of the convoy, and at midnight they moved ahead into a line abreast formation seven miles ahead of it. At daybreak, two ships of the support group covered each side of the convoy at maximum visibility distance, while *Duncan* swept ahead of the convoy and *Offa* patrolled astern, to force any shadowers to dive and lose contact. The night was quiet, but on the morning of 4 May *Gretton* was forced to pull *Duncan* out of the escort and head for Newfoundland.

Worse was to come. By the same afternoon, three support group destroyers also had to leave for shortage of fuel. Meanwhile the convoy and its attackers blundered into the next German patrol line. Soon thirty submarines were moving into attack positions, and on the following day, 5 May, the weather began to improve at last.

During that night and the following day, 6 May, repeated attacks by U-boats claimed eleven of the merchant ships. By dusk it seemed certain that more would be lost, as the 1st Escort Group, sent to protect the convoy, could not reach them until the following morning. But as night fell, a thick curtain of fog came rolling in, the one piece of genuine luck enjoyed by the defenders. Not that the U-boats gave up: no less than twenty-four determined attacks were made during the hours of darkness. Astonishingly, every one was driven off, and not one single ship was lost. The U-boats, on

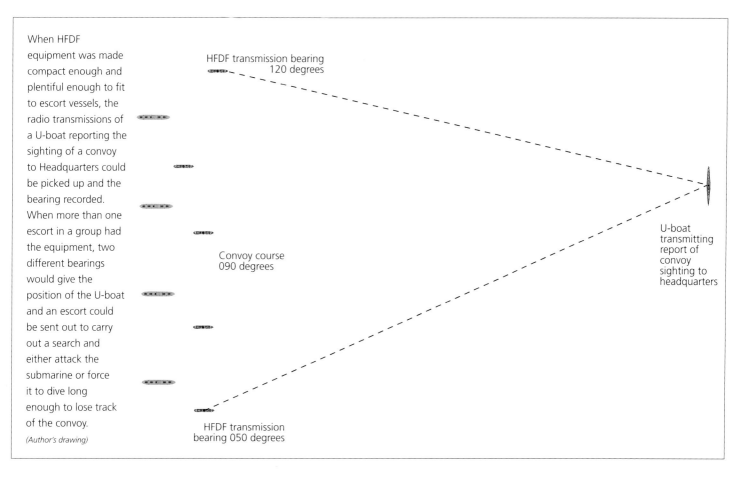

When HFDF equipment was made compact enough and plentiful enough to fit to escort vessels, the radio transmissions of a U-boat reporting the sighting of a convoy to Headquarters could be picked up and the bearing recorded. When more than one escort in a group had the equipment, two different bearings would give the position of the U-boat and an escort could be sent out to carry out a search and either attack the submarine or force it to dive long enough to lose track of the convoy.
(Author's drawing)

HFDF transmission bearing 120 degrees

Convoy course 090 degrees

U-boat transmitting report of convoy sighting to headquarters

HFDF transmission bearing 050 degrees

Relatively small convoy of thirty-five ships (not drawn to scale). At 1,000 yards between columns and 600 yards between successive ships in each column, the total perimeter of the convoy patrolled by the escorts amounts to some 16,000 yards.

Large seventy-ship convoy (not drawn to scale). With 1,000 yards between columns and 600 yards between successive ships in the same column, the total perimeter of the convoy would amount to some 26,400 yards. If these ships had sailed instead as two thirty-five-ship convoys, their combined perimeter would total some 33,600 yards, an increase of 27 per cent quite apart from the greater statistical risk of one of two convoys being spotted and attacked over that of a larger single convoy.

(Author's drawing)

the other hand, suffered much more severely: four were sunk and three heavily damaged during that violent night, two of them were sunk by ramming and the others by depth-charge and Hedgehog attacks.

This had promised to be a major convoy disaster, with masses of U-boats, a depleted escort, a raging storm and weather that prevented air patrols from playing a major role in the battle. Nevertheless, on the morning of 6 May the 1st Escort Group arrived, catching some of the U-boats unaware and sinking one. The final total was eleven merchant ships lost, but five U-boats sunk by surface ships, two lost due to collision and another sunk by air attack, making eight lost with others badly damaged. It was an unac-

ceptable rate of exchange and at 9.15am Doenitz ordered his wolf packs to call off the fight. Estimates of their total numbers range from between fifty-one to more than seventy, but their achievements were so disappointing that they showed how completely the balance of power had passed to the Allies.

The Germans realised only too well what the high cost of the operation meant. If the U-boats could not triumph with numbers so much on their side, what hope was there in actions under less favourable circumstances?

> ... boats participating in this operation had sent a number of radio reports which showed FO U-boats how dangerous the situation had become during the night fog, and he anxiously awaited the short signals indicating the further state of readiness of our boats. Four of them reported heavy damage necessitating a return to base, while six were silent – they had been destroyed. In spite of the claim of 16 ships sunk, totalling 90,000 tons [British records show twelve ships (55,000 tons) sunk] and probable damage to several more, *the heavy loss of* U-boats *compelled us to regard this operation as a reverse* [emphasis added].[16]

The grim truth was that continuing losses were reducing the experience and expertise of the U-boat arm. The month of May 1943 saw a total of forty-one U-boats sunk for the loss of just fifty merchant ships, a staggering and sudden reversal of fortunes. As a measure of pure survival, the U-boats were withdrawn from the Atlantic, to search for less well-defended prey in more distant waters. By July, merchant shipping tonnage built in mainly American shipyards passed the total of tonnage sunk by U-boats since September 1939, and the Atlantic battle was effectively won.

Over the course of the war as a whole, the remarkable fact was that more than three-quarters of all U-boats completed and commissioned never so much as damaged a single Allied merchant ship or escort vessel. And it was those skippers with experienced crews and the skill and determination to brave the defences and make successful attacks whose numbers would dwindle most quickly, as the defences continued to grow stronger. Under these conditions, Doenitz's continued pressure for more and more U-boats would achieve little. Without a more efficient organisation for distilling the experience of the most successful crews and spreading it among their newer colleagues, this dilution of quality would continue, to the ultimate advantage of their Allied adversaries.

CHAPTER 13

ASW TRIUMPHS IN THE WEST

1943–45

The greatest submarine hunter of them all – Captain 'Johnny' Walker seen conducting a hunt from the bridge of HMS *Starling* while finishing a hurried sandwich.

(www.navyphotos.co.uk)

O N the morning of 1 June 1943, the North Atlantic weather was uncommonly sunny and warm, with blue sky and a gentle breeze. The frigates of the 2nd Support Group were searching south of Iceland for convoy HX241, to help escort it to Liverpool. This was the group's first operational patrol, commanded by an officer who had blighted his career by specialising in ASW between the wars. As a result, he had been repeatedly passed over for promotion, but in the short time left to him, he would become one of the greatest submarine killers of all time.

Captain Frederic John Walker RN was known throughout the navy as 'Johnny' Walker after the famous Scotch whisky. After a succession of shore-based posts in a navy still dominated by the battleship and the big gun, he had not been awarded his first seagoing command until September 1941, when he was appointed captain of the anti-submarine frigate HMS *Stork* and leader of the 36th Escort Group. Sailing on the Gibraltar convoys with the escort carrier HMS *Audacity*, Walker had begun his combat career with a spirited fight against a large wolf pack (see Chapter 8).

Other convoy battles followed, allowing Walker to weld the crews under his command into a tight professional team. After just over a year, he was brought ashore in October 1942 to join Admiral Sir Max Horton's staff directing the Atlantic battle from Western Approaches Headquarters in Liverpool. It was a vital role, but Walker longed to return to action, and in March 1943 he was given command of the brand-new anti-submarine frigate HMS *Starling* and the equally new 2nd Support Group.

Support groups were very different from the escort groups that Walker knew. All his ships were new Black Swan class frigates, faster and more heavily armed than the corvettes of most escort groups. Displacing almost 1,500 tons, they carried three twin 4-inch gun mountings and relatively large stocks of depth charges, with all the increasingly complex equipment needed to hunt and destroy submarines, and had a twenty-knot top speed.

They also had different priorities. Escort groups ensured 'the safe and timely arrival of the convoy'. In Walker's view the objective of his support group was to sink submarines and that was clearly expressed in the instructions he wrote for those he commanded: 'Our job is to *kill*, and all officers must fully develop the spirit of vicious offensive. No matter how many convoys we may shepherd through in safety, we shall have failed unless we can slaughter U-boats. All energies must be bent to this end.'[1]

Like all good ideas, the logic behind support groups was simple. Using the greater numbers of new escorts and the temporary cutback on the heavily escorted convoys to Northern Russia, these new groups could be sent wherever the fighting was fiercest. When they detected a U-boat, they could continue the hunt, long after escorts would normally have gone back to defending the convoy from other attackers. This meant they could use the U-boat's weakest point – its limited underwater endurance – to destroy it, by waiting until its air or battery power ran out, forcing it to surface and face them. It proved a powerful and effective tactic, and would solve one of the three persistent problems facing submarine hunters. The other two would take longer.

At 9.30am, the operator monitoring the HFDF equipment on HMS *Starling* picked up a strong radio transmission on a bearing of 311 degrees, some twenty miles away. The group responded instantly: engine-room telegraphs rang 'full ahead' and all six ships swung on to a new course of 311 degrees. Crews ran to action stations, guns were loaded and engines strained to reach the U-boat's position before it could run for safety on the surface. If they could bring it within gunnery range and force it to dive, cutting its speed to walking pace, they would have ample time to sink it.

The signal was from the type VII U-boat *U202*, commanded by twenty-seven-year-old Günther Poser. He had taken command in September 1942; in February 1943 he sank an American tanker and damaged two British tankers in convoy UC1, but suffered torpedo problems. Now he was returning from his fifth patrol, after four frustrating weeks, harried by frequent air attacks. He had been bombed three times and forced to dive on twenty-nine occasions to avoid Allied aircraft.[2]

Because there were relatively few U-boats in the Atlantic at the time, captains were ordered to send more messages than necessary, to convince the Allies it was business as usual. The tactic proved fatal for many. In sending a report that he was down to his last thirty tons of diesel fuel, Poser betrayed his position. At the time, he was unaware of what was heading his way, and he was resting on his bunk when the bridge lookout reported seeing the mastheads of a convoy on the horizon.

Pleased by this new chance to improve his score, Poser pulled on his boots, reached for his binoculars and clattered up the bridge ladder. On the way, he shouted to the helmsman to steer to intercept this target. It was only when he emerged into the brilliant sunlight and turned his binoculars towards the approaching ships, that he spotted his lookout's terrible mistake. These were no merchantmen, but the taller, slimmer masts of approaching warships. *U202* and her crew were in appalling danger.

At first, it seemed the enemy ships were too far away for their lookouts to spot the submarine's conning tower. The correct tactics were clear. Poser must take the *U202* deep, before the approaching ships could see him. By reaching a depth of some 500 feet

and shutting down all non-essential machinery, he had avoided escorts on five previous occasions. Why should this be any different?

The difference this time was in the quality of his opponents. In spite of his hopes, they already knew where he was, and exactly what to do about it. By 10.05am, Walker's ships reached the position where *U202* had vanished half an hour before, and they reduced speed to fifteen knots to improve sonar reception. Within five minutes, *Starling*'s chief sonar operator picked up an echo 20 degrees on the starboard bow. This was the U-boat, almost immediately recognised as the quarry they were hunting.

On other occasions, two or more U-boats operating together had thwarted an attack on one of them by the other's launching torpedoes against the escorts. So as Walker took *Starling* to open the attack, he ordered sister ships *Kite* and *Wild Goose* to continue listening. The remainder of the group, the frigates *Woodpecker*, *Cygnet* and *Wren* began a square search around the target's position to watch for other submarines.

As the range closed and the sonar contact faded, *Starling* dropped her depth charges, six over the stern rails and four from the upper-deck depth-charge throwers. Some were set to explode at 350 feet, the remainder at 550 feet. Between them, the ten charges made the sea boil in a series of vast explosions, and the guns' crews waited impatiently to open fire if the submarine should break surface. For the moment, they were disappointed. Nothing emerged as the detonations faded, and the sonar once again picked up the echo of *U202*.

However, for those on the receiving end, this was a crippling first blow. That single pattern of depth charges exploding at close range shattered fragile items of equipment. The lighting circuits failed and water poured in through a leak at the stern. Trying to out-guess his adversary, Poser ordered the submarine to float upwards to a depth of 400 feet as they waited for the next hammer blows to fall.[3]

As attack succeeded attack, Walker realised this was a clever adversary. As each attack was delivered and just before charges were dropped, the U-boat would make a sudden sharp turn or a change of depth, to avoid the worst. So far, it was working well. It was clearly time to try something else. That something else would be Walker's cleverest gambit, responsible for the death of a string of brave and experienced U-boat crews.

As an ASW specialist, Walker had long ago realised that each depth-charge pattern might not sink the submarine on its own, but their cumulative damage would either sink it or force it to surface and face the escorts' gunfire. Unfortunately, great pressure was applied during pre-war ASW exercises to show the submarine threat had been contained, and it was assumed a single, five-charge pattern could sink a

Walker's ship, the formidable HMS *Starling*.
(www.navyphotos.co.uk)

HMS *Woodcock*, another Black Swan class sloop and member of Walker's group.
(www.navyphotos.co.uk)

U-boat. While this might be true of the smaller type II U-boats or against crews learning their trade, it was also true there were mistakes in placing the patterns. This was a problem that would become more acute as large numbers of new escorts with less experienced crews joined the battle.

Statistics showed thirty-three U-boats were sunk by depth charges in the first six months of war.[4] This took an astonishing 4,000 depth-charge attacks, or roughly 120 attacks per submarine sunk. Unfortunately, delivering these attacks took time that could ill be spared when escorts had to prevent other submarines exploiting gaps in the screen. These attacks were also less effective against more experienced skippers operating

at much greater depths. This was the second problem facing the escorts.

The Navy made two moves to solve it. The existing Mark VII depth charge was fitted with a cast-iron weight, to make it sink at sixteen feet per second rather than ten, and a new setting was put on the hydrostatic pistol that detonated it, so that it exploded at a depth of 550 feet. Furthermore, by combining old and new charges in a single pattern, a U-boat might be trapped between them in three dimensions rather than two, causing greater damage.

Because this used more charges, 10- and 14-charge patterns were introduced, needing greater stowage capacity. Furthermore, using evidence from trials and tactical studies, the spacing between charges was widened to make aiming errors less important, and the original Amatol explosive was replaced by the more powerful Minol, all of which improved depth-charge performance, and these were the weapons Walker was using.

Nevertheless, the massive problem of the final 200-yard run to the target still remained, while the attacking ship's sonar was too close to hear the U-boat, and be aware of any last-minute evasive action. Only when the escort was over the probable position of the U-boat could the charges be dropped. In that time-lag of up to a minute, a clever skipper could move to leave the charges exploding in the wrong place. Because he could clearly hear the propellers of the escort heading for him, he had a far better idea of his opponent's position and could time his evasive action precisely.

Eventually new ahead-throwing weapons would

eliminate this blind spot altogether. For the moment, Walker's team had a plan devised to counter the U-boat's evasions. They called it the 'plaster' attack and they proceeded to deliver it. As *Kite* and *Wild Goose* took up positions either side of *Starling*, Walker set all three ships moving slowly towards the submarine's position at five knots. As the range shortened, they began dropping strings of depth charges at intervals of five seconds, set to detonate at 550 feet. The ships were close enough for the explosions to overlap and create a huge single pattern, covering an area too wide for the U-boat to escape. It used up seventy-six charges in a single attack, and made the sea boil, but this time it failed to destroy their target. Once again, Poser had dodged the approaching blows by timing his boat's movement as the attack was delivered.

Then Walker had his inspiration. He realised the best way to trap the German skipper was to stop him guessing when the charges were being dropped. He ordered *Kite* and *Wild Goose* to repeat their previous attack at slow speed, without using sonar at all. Instead *Starling* stayed further back, guiding the other two ships. For Poser, they would approach too quietly for his hydrophones to reveal their position. The only sonar pulses he would hear were from *Starling,* too far away for an attack to be imminent.

This was Walker's 'creeper' tactic. He had already noticed that the U-boat was using compressed air in changing depth at each attack. Air reserves were being depleted still further by launching SBTs – submarine

bubble targets – to confuse the attackers by mimicking sonar echoes.

There were several different types of SBT: the basic version, codenamed *Bold*, appeared in 1942. It consisted of a small metal can filled with calcium hydride, which reacted strongly with seawater. The can was expelled by compressed air from a special launcher, and a pressure-sensitive valve opened to admit seawater. The resulting reaction released bubbles of hydrogen gas, and the valve opened and closed to keep the can and cloud of bubbles at a depth of around a hundred feet, giving a stronger sonar echo than the submarine for almost half an hour. This allowed the U-boat to escape, while the escorts attacked the decoy instead.

This worked well at first, but skilled sonar operators spotted the decoy, since it remained relatively still while a real U-boat would take evasive action. More convincing versions appeared later, operating at greater depths. *Sieglinde* used a stream of bubbles to propel it forwards at around six knots, resembling a submarine trying to escape. *Siegmund* generated a succession of sharp explosions to deafen enemy sonars while the submarine made a speedier getaway.[5]

In this case, though, using decoys reassured Walker that the U-boat must eventually surface for lack of air and battery power. All he had to do was keep up the pressure for long enough for this to happen. Walker estimated this would probably be around midnight.

As night fell, the light breeze dropped to a flat calm. The ships waited as the summer day faded. Alan Burn,

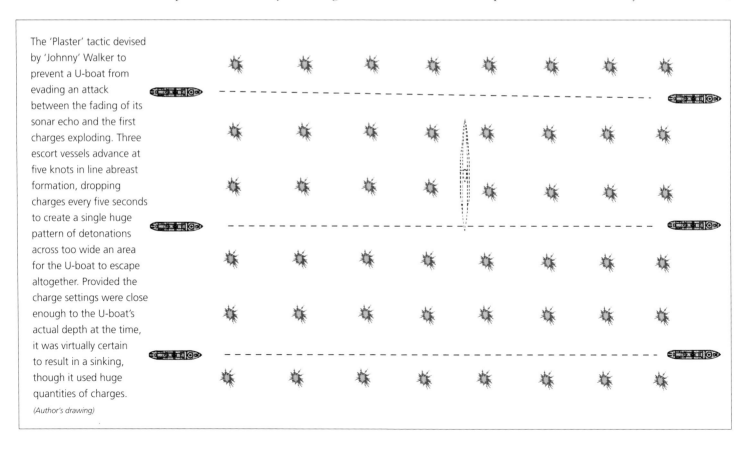

The 'Plaster' tactic devised by 'Johnny' Walker to prevent a U-boat from evading an attack between the fading of its sonar echo and the first charges exploding. Three escort vessels advance at five knots in line abreast formation, dropping charges every five seconds to create a single huge pattern of detonations across too wide an area for the U-boat to escape altogether. Provided the charge settings were close enough to the U-boat's actual depth at the time, it was virtually certain to result in a sinking, though it used huge quantities of charges.

(Author's drawing)

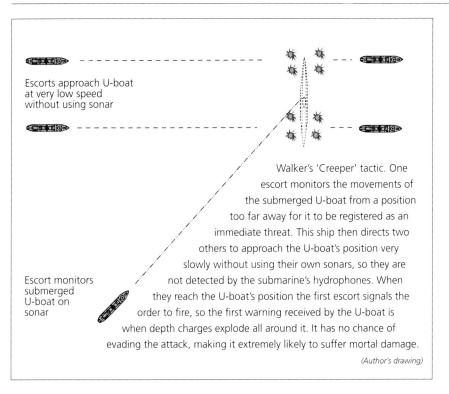

Escorts approach U-boat
at very low speed
without using sonar

Escort monitors
submerged
U-boat on
sonar

Walker's 'Creeper' tactic. One
escort monitors the movements of
the submerged U-boat from a position
too far away for it to be registered as an
immediate threat. This ship then directs two
others to approach the U-boat's position very
slowly without using their own sonars, so they are
not detected by the submarine's hydrophones. When
they reach the U-boat's position the first escort signals the
order to fire, so the first warning received by the U-boat is
when depth charges explode all around it. It has no chance of
evading the attack, making it extremely likely to suffer mortal damage.

(Author's drawing)

Walker's gunnery officer, felt a mixture of tranquillity and anxiety:

> Backwards and forwards down the starboard side of the bridge paced Captain Walker. The shapes of the ships on either beam began to merge into the surface of the sea and a blue haze settled slowly down, blending the horizon and the darkening sky. The night grew dark; the faint murmur of conversation died. All was quiet, except for the soft creaking roll of the ship, the hum of the fans and the muffled reports of the lookouts changing watches. Eight bells came and went. Tucked up in the starboard forward corner of the bridge, the signalman rested his elbows on the wind deflector and swept his binoculars towards the starboard bow. It was two minutes after midnight.[6]

At that moment, the bridge lookout spotted a submarine surfacing off *Starling*'s starboard bow. Immediately, B 4-inch mounting, its twin guns already loaded with starshell, fired to light up the sea. As the shells exploded high above, their intense glare revealed the silhouette of the U-boat and the white wake unrolling behind it as Poser ordered full speed on the diesels to try to outrun the escorts.

His escape attempt was doomed. *Starling*'s other forward twin-gun mounting, loaded with high explosive, was training on to its target. Shells were soon bursting around the submarine, and the rate of fire increased as the guns of the other frigates joined in. Now and again, a brief red glow showed a direct

hit as a shell struck the conning tower or the casing. Walker ordered full speed and turned to ram the U-boat. At the last moment *Starling* sheered away to starboard, as the damaged submarine had stopped, emitting clouds of smoke, and clearly unable to fight. As the frigate passed close alongside, bursts of cannon fire swept the U-boat's deck clear and two final depth charges, set to shallow settings, were fired from the port side throwers. They exploded closely on either side of the submarine.

U202 took fully forty minutes to sink, even after Poser's scuttling charges detonated. Four officers and twenty-six ratings were picked up by *Starling* and *Wild Goose*. In keeping with normal routine, rescue only began when survivors gave the U-boat's number and the skipper's name, essential intelligence that survivors often refused to give once safely aboard. Several U-boat men were badly wounded, but fourteen hours of surgery by *Starling*'s doctor saved all but one, including her badly shaken skipper.

Walker's tactics had succeeded through attrition rather than direct action. How had Poser been able to escape long enough to deplete his reserves of air and battery power? Walker suspected U-boats must be diving to still greater depths, well below the new depth-charge settings. His report to the Admiralty showed that both 'creeping' and 'plaster' attacks could be successful on two conditions. First, charges had to be set to detonate at still greater depths. Secondly, escorts would have to maintain the hunt long enough to force the submarine to surface, even if the depth charges did not cause fatal damage.

The *U202* sinking was, in the words of the Navy's monthly Anti-Submarine Bulletin, '. . . an outstanding operation. A perfect example of locating, hunting and destroying a U-boat.' Later, in operations ranging from the Bay of Biscay to the Arctic convoy route to Russia, Walker's group would show it was no fluke. He was sometimes criticised for his vast consumption of depth charges – some 250 over fifteen hours in hunting the *U202* – but no one could argue with a lengthening record of sinkings.

Even as Walker was developing better tactics to exploit existing anti-submarine weapons, Allied experts were developing new ones to make life even harder for U-boat crews. Walker's methods cancelled out the effect of an attacking ship losing target information as it headed for the U-boat's position before dropping depth charges. Others tackled the same problem in a different way. While an escort retained a clear sonar contact before attacking the U-boat, then the best weapon would be one that could be thrown ahead of the escort, before the submarine could carry out any evasive action at all.

Ironically, this need had been apparent well before the war. During the 1930s, the Royal Navy worked on a mortar capable of flinging an anti-submarine bomb ahead of the ship using it, but this project became a casualty of the drastic cuts in pre-war defence estimates. Not until 1939 was it resurrected, spurred by the threat of a new war.

The first outcome was a rather different weapon, given the codename Hedgehog, after a competition offered a bottle of Scotch for the team member who chose the best name. The main problem faced with any ahead-throwing weapon was making it throw a charge heavy enough to be effective. Anything powerful enough to do this risked imposing colossal stresses on the bows of the vessel firing it. Even if it worked, it could only launch one charge at a time, so that depth-charge patterns would be impossible.

The problem was solved by scientists at the Admiralty Department of Miscellaneous Weapons Development (DMWD). Their pre-war parents, the Royal Navy Anti-Submarine Experimental Establishment (RNASEE) decided to resolve these difficulties by replacing the single heavy charge with a set of smaller and lighter charges, fired in a pattern and fitted with contact fuses. Unless one or more of the charges hit the target, there would be no huge blasts to deafen the ship's sonar for minutes on end.[7]

After DMWD had taken over, they found that a small group of Royal Engineers had invented a charge-throwing projector as part of a new anti-tank weapon, the Blacker Bombard. When the army engineers were asked to assemble an array of projectors to fire a pattern of small charges, their design fitted each projectile around an electrically actuated spigot, or peg, which fired it when the device was triggered.

In the meantime, however, the RNASEE worked on the Fairlie Mortar, a similar idea with an array of charges, each one having a cast-iron nose for greater stability and just twenty pounds of explosive, detonated by a fuse carried in the tail. This had several shortcomings. Unless the projectile hit the target at exactly the right angle, the fuse would fail to detonate the explosive, and it was thought unlikely to deliver a large enough punch to be effective even if the fuses did work.

Although DMWD's design was simple in principle, getting it made was anything but straightforward. Because of the cost of developing both weapons, DMWD had to prove Hedgehog was more effective. Each projectile carried a 30-pound charge, with a fuse in the nose, and a tubular tail for stability. Dummies were fired off the end of the disused Birnbeck pier at Weston-super-Mare (commissioned as the 'stone frigate'[8] HMS *Birnbeck*) to check their flight dynamics. They found the bombs needed a flat nose to enter the water cleanly rather than skidding along the surface, and their explosive power was tested by dropping them on steel plates like those of a U-boat's pressure hull.

One unknown remained: the gap between the outer casing of a U-boat and the pressure hull. Since the bombs exploded on hitting the casing, a heavier charge would be needed if this distance was too great. Happily, Naval Intelligence found an Italian magazine with a feature on naval dockyards. One picture showed a man standing on the pressure hull of a U-boat while working on the outer casing. Estimating the length of his legs produced the required information, showing a 30-pound charge might work, but confirming the Fairlie Mortar's 20-pound charges would not.

The next step was to determine the most lethal pattern of charges. Scale models were used to determine the trajectory of the bombs and the elevation of the launcher. Full-size charges were fired at the outline of a U-boat laid out on the ground at the government research station at Whitchurch in Buckinghamshire. The ideal proved to be a group of twenty-five charges in a rough circle, with the distance between their points of impact being smaller than a U-boat's beam, and the diameter of the circle shorter than the U-boat's length. If the aim was good, at least two of the charges must hit the submarine and their explosions should sink it or at least severely damage it.

The final requirement was to design and build the mounting for the launcher array. The prototype was built by a Bristol boilermaker – the bomb casings were made by musical instrument makers Boosey and Hawkes, with machines that once made dance-band trumpets. The launcher mounting transmitted the thrust of the recoil down into the ship's hull structure rather than the deck plating, and the shock of firing was reduced by firing the projectiles two at a time in quick succession.

To stop a bomb detonating on hitting the water, the fuse was armed by the turning of a propeller in the nose of the projectile. This provided extra safety if the bombs were launched by mistake. One Hedgehog-equipped escort was moored to a jetty in New York harbour when the weapon was fired by accident. A full salvo fell on to a nearby quayside, but because the propellers had not armed the fuses, not a single bomb exploded.[9]

The first sea trials were carried out in May 1941 aboard the destroyer HMS *Westcott*. The target was a submerged wreck in Liverpool Bay, and the destroyer picked up its sonar echo before steaming straight towards it and firing Hedgehog. The cluster of bombs lifted off two by two on a curving trajectory before plunging into the water. After a long pause, there was a deep rumble and clouds of spray rose from the sea.

The production version of the Hedgehog bomb held thirty-five pounds of high explosive in a total weight of sixty-eight pounds, enough to sink a submarine with a direct hit. The whole mounting could be swung to aim at the target, and the spigots were angled so the bombs fell in an ellipse some hundred feet across. They entered the water roughly fifteen feet apart, more than

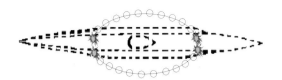

The pattern of Hedgehog charges aimed at a U-boat, with 25 charges arranged around the edge of an ellipse some 100 feet across, or approximately half the length of a U-boat's hull, at 15 feet intervals. Since the U-boat's beam was wider than this interval, then if the pattern fell across the U-boat several charges would detonate on impact. More than one hit was usually fatal, and if the pattern missed altogether the U-boat remained unaware of the attack.

(Author's drawing)

Hedgehog attack. The escort fires the weapon at the submarine's sonar position before its echo fades as the range closes. As the bombs sink through the water, those which strike the submarine's hull detonate, while the others sink harmlessly to the sea bed. If the salvo misses altogether, another attack can be launched once the weapon has been reloaded, with the U-boat remaining unaware of the first attack.

(Author's drawing)

200 yards ahead of the ship, bridging the gap where sonar was temporarily deaf.

Because Hedgehog bombs only detonated on contact, if the attack missed the submarine, there were no loud explosions like those of a depth-charge pattern, and the U-boat was unaware of the threat. If, on the other hand, one or more of them hit the target, there would be an unmistakable underwater detonation, and the submarine was almost certainly sunk. As each broadside was fired, the recoil reset the spigots ready for reloads to be carried out, and a series of attacks could be delivered in fairly rapid succession.

Compared with the depth charge, Hedgehog had both advantages and drawbacks. All the escort crew had to do was aim the array of bombs as accurately as they could at the known position of the U-boat in two dimensions. As the bombs sank through the water relatively quickly, the depth of the submarine was almost immaterial. Sooner or later, if the target's position was correct and the aiming accurate, the bombs would sink far enough to hit it and success was assured.

On the other hand, it was an all-or-nothing weapon. Either there was a hit, and the U-boat was probably destroyed, or the bombs missed, in which case it was completely unscathed. For the escort

crews, there was no encouraging crash of depth charge after depth charge, or the progressive sapping of the submariners' morale by the pounding of incessant explosions. In the same way, near misses with depth charges might eventually build up damage to force the U-boat to surface and take on the escorts. Near misses with the Hedgehog had no effect at all.

By 1942, Hedgehog was in full production, though the secrecy shrouding the project made escort crews wary when they found the cumbersome frame being fitted to the bows of their ships. At first, little training was given, and results were disappointing. Trials with dummy projectiles against British submarines showed roughly half the attacks should have succeeded, but operational results showed a tenth of this level, only a small improvement on conventional depth charges. The situation only improved when an officer from DMWD was sent to Londonderry to train escort crews in operating the new weapon. As more crews went through the training process the kill rate rose. By the end of the war, fifty enemy submarines had been destroyed by Hedgehog.[10]

Why were initial results so poor? Possibly due to poor maintenance, some bombs failed to leave the spigots when the weapon was fired, leading to gaps in the lethal pattern. For most escorts, the weapon was issued on a take-it-or-leave-it basis. Commander Reginald Whinney, an Atlantic veteran, took command of the old First World War destroyer HMS *Wanderer* in March 1943. She had recently been refitted with a strange new weapon.[11]

At more or less the last minute, the bits and pieces for an ahead-throwing anti-submarine mortar code-named 'Hedgehog' arrived. It was put together and then a four-stripe Captain arrived to look at it.
'How does this thing work, sir' I asked, 'and when are we supposed to use it?'
'You'll get full instructions' he said, and disappeared. I was mildly suspicious.

Soon, he realised what the weapon would mean for anti-submarine tactics.

In the previous, established method of attack with depth charges, the ship held contact with the submarine and approached with the Asdic [sonar] control equipment computing to allow for movement of the submarine in the final stages of the attack and also to give the time to fire. To defeat this, the U-boats had taken to diving deep when under attack so that, when the ship got close, the cigar-shaped Asdic beam would go over the top of the U-boat and the attack would thus be blind – or rather deaf – for several hundred yards and would thus be inaccurate.

With the Hedgehog, the surface ship would come in slowly, at eight knots and, when the range was about 250 yards, the mortar would be fired and the bombs would go rippling off through the air landing on the perimeter of a fair-sized ellipse ahead of the ship; quite spectacular this looked. The idea was that one or more of the bombs would hit the U-boat and the explosions would cause all the other bombs to countermine. The nice healthy explosion would finish the U-boat off. Later, we tried this for real![12]

The crew of HMCS *North Bay* reloading Hedgehog charges on to the spigots of the mortar ready for firing another salvo.

(National Library of Canada)

Nevertheless, Whinney remained wary, after one text-book attack produced only a small 'pop-gun' explosion and no sinking. He remained convinced that the ammunition was of poor quality, and others were equally dubious. 'Over 100 ships had been fitted with Hedgehog by the end of 1942, but what with minor faults, poor maintenance and inadequate documentation the weapon was little used if depth charges were available. British commanders eventually had to be ordered to use the weapon, but it was long before its deadly potential was fully exploited.'[13]

More serious problems remained. In September 1943, the pre-war Fleet destroyer HMS *Escapade* picked up a sonar contact and fired her Hedgehog. A charge exploded on leaving the launcher and set off the rest of the pattern, causing carnage. The destroyer's bows were wrecked, her captain was severely wounded and twenty-one crew were killed. She had to be sent back to Northern Ireland, taking no further part in the battle.[14]

Fortunately this was the only incident where bombs went off prematurely. In time, the Hedgehog success rate improved until it rivalled those of depth charges,

and advances in sonar made it even more effective. The eternal problem of finding a submarine's depth from a sonar echo was to be made easier by the 'Q attachment' – a second transducer producing a narrower beam at a steeper angle than the main beam. Not only did this give a more accurate estimate of the depth of the target, but it maintained contact right up to the delivery of the attack. This was later developed into the type 147 sonar, 'which produced a series of thin, fan-shaped beams which could be tilted through a vertical 45 degrees'.[15] With this precise target information, Hedgehog finally came into its own.

The 147 prototype was first tested aboard the destroyer HMS *Ambuscade* in May 1943. It enabled the operator to monitor the echo of the submarine, its wake and the explosions of the depth charges. It had a two-ply steel transducer eighteen inches long and one inch wide, protected by a thick rubber sheath and secured at a permanent 9-degree tilt from the keel, operating at 60kHz. In the new prototype (type 147XB) the transducer was moveable and the depression variable from the vertical to forty-five degrees. This allowed the depth of the U-boat to be determined from the time of the initial contact at a range of about 800 yards until the ahead-thrown weapon was fired.

As it happened, the convoy battle where *Escapade* was crippled was highly significant for quite another reason. After reeling under successive blows from improved Allied technology and tactics for almost six months, the Germans began hitting back with a new weapon of their own. For ten years they had been working on new types of torpedo to improve the chances of hitting a target in spite of poor aiming or firing at relatively long range. The first FAT *Feder Apparat Torpedo* (Feather-Apparatus Torpedo) weapons were designed to be launched in the general direction of a convoy. Once the torpedo had run straight for a preset distance, its internal guidance system turned it on to a new course followed by a series of zigzag manoeuvres designed to cover the area occupied by the convoy, improving the chances of it finding a target.

The zigzags or 'ladder' patterns followed by these torpedoes looked vaguely similar to the plumes of a feather, which may have accounted for the name. The first FAT weapon was adapted from a G7a steam-driven torpedo that left an obvious wake of bubbles in its track, and so was only to be used at night, or in emergencies. Another problem was the danger of it hitting another U-boat in the case of a wolf-pack attack on a convoy, though no cases of this ever happening appear in the records.[16]

The FAT succeeded on several occasions, but the ultimate aim was a true homing torpedo, which would correct its course to hit the target without being aimed accurately – later to be known as a 'fire and forget' weapon. This would be a godsend for a

Hedgehog charges fired by the Canadian corvette HMCS *Kootenay* in the action which resulted in the sinking of the type VIIC *U621* in the Bay of Biscay on 18 August 1944.
(National Library of Canada)

it) and less than nineteen knots (to give it a chance of catching up before it reached its range limit).

Though the design was ready for testing in 1940, sorting out the complex control system meant it could only be tested at sea in early 1943. It was passed for operational use at the beginning of July 1943, but only a few U-boats were given the necessary adaptations to use it. Around a hundred Falkes were produced, of which no more than thirty were launched in earnest, and by this time it had been replaced by a more formidable version.

This was the T5 *Zaunkönig* ('Wren'), which was a true homing torpedo. Instead of the target's propeller noise triggering a mere course change and a preset search pattern, the T5 picked up the cavitation noise and adjusted its course to home in on it directly. Its sensors were more receptive to the high-frequency sound of an escort's screws than they were to the slower rhythm of a merchant vessel. Once again the limitations caused by its own propeller noise and its restricted speed of just under twenty-five knots meant it could only be used at targets moving at speeds between ten and eighteen knots. But because it was electrically driven, it left no discernible wake, and could be used at any time.

The T5 was armed by a small propeller near its nose. To allow its use in emergencies, it was given a short arming distance of just 250 metres, after which it might home in on the U-boat instead. To avoid this, skippers were ordered to launch the torpedo at periscope depth in the normal way, and then dive deep immediately afterwards.

In comparison with other German torpedo developments, the introduction of the T5 was spectacularly fast. Doenitz hoped to have it ready for early 1944, but after the turning of the tables between U-boats and escorts in May 1943, he brought the date forward to early October 1943. Two months later, rising U-boat losses caused him to bring it forward again by two months. This seemed hopelessly optimistic, but no less than eighty T5s were ready. By September 1943, seagoing U-boats carrying the weapon were at sea searching for convoys, and more particularly for the warships escorting them.

U-boat headquarters had great hopes for the T5s. They were to be used to blow gaps in the protective escort screen through which the U-boats could then attack their primary targets, the merchantmen. By this time, also (as described earlier) Doenitz was convinced that stopping the use of the Metox radar receivers had made crossing the bay safer, so his boats could mount the mass attacks that the new weapon would make possible.

Recent months have brought severe reverses for the U-boat campaign. Inexplicable losses have occurred among boats in transit and in waiting

harassed U-boat commander beating off an attack or seizing a chance to sink a tempting target.

As with all ambitious new weapons, achieving that simple aim proved highly complicated. It worked on acoustic principles – the torpedo heard the noise of the target ship's propellers and altered its course so as to close the range and eventually collide with it. In its first form, the T3 or *Falke* was a modified G7e electrically driven torpedo. When launched against a ship, it ran in the usual way until close enough for its sensors to hear the target's propellers. This triggered the control system to steer it into a tight circle, to improve the chances of it hitting the target it might otherwise have missed.

The main problem was – as with the Allied air dropped homing torpedo Fido – making the torpedo ignore the noise of its own propellers. Though improvements were made to their blade shape to reduce noise, the torpedo had to be limited to a top speed of twenty-five knots. It could only be used against targets moving at speeds greater than twelve knots (so they would generate enough noise to attract

The US Navy found Hedgehog highly successful in the Pacific and continued to use the weapon after the war – the destroyer uss *Sarsfield* fires a double Hedgehog pattern in an ASW exercise in June 1950.

(US National Archives)

areas. Our U-boat dispositions have been circumvented by the enemy and our successes have declined. This we attributed to enemy location gear of a new, undetectable type. It has now been established by experiment and confirmed by the statements of prisoners of war, that it was due to the enemy's interception of strong radiation from the *Metox* radar search receiver. This instrument is now being replaced by the non-radiating *Hagenuk*,[17] with which it is possible to detect intermittent radar emissions on all principal frequencies. The radar question thereby undergoes a decisive change.[18]

In this, as in much else, he was wrong. The Wanze receiver could pick up emissions from the original Allied centimetric radar operating in the 10-cm band, but failed to detect the new higher-frequency Allied radar used by both aircraft and surface escorts. The tactics for massed attacks on escorts using the new torpedoes were also seriously flawed.

> Should a large bunch of U-boats be located by several escort vessels, all would be forced temporarily to withdraw from the battle. On the other hand, the location of, say, six well separated boats, or of several groups of two or three, would draw at least six escort vessels from the convoy and thereby attenuate the convoy escort … Two boats in company are better able to protect themselves against air attack, besides providing mutual support in engagements with destroyers …[19]

The idea of U-boats staying on the surface and using their anti-aircraft armament was one whose time had gone, and losses proved surprisingly heavy. Still, the acoustic torpedo would make an apparently spectacular debut in the fighting around convoys ONS18 and ON202 in late September 1943. To Doenitz's delight, news came in from the *Leuthen* wolf pack claiming a string of successes from their T5s against the escorts.

The two convoys followed the latest doctrine by combining into one very large assembly of sixty-eight merchantmen, escorted by five destroyers, three frigates, eleven corvettes and two anti-submarine trawlers, together with a MAC ship carrying Fairey Swordfish anti-submarine biplanes, so there were plenty of potential targets. Although two U-boats had been sunk by VLR B24s of Coastal Command and the Royal Canadian Air Force, the others claimed no less than seven destroyers sunk, with another three 'probably' sunk.[20]

Had this been true, it would have been grim news for the Allies. Fortunately, the truth was quite different. The U-boats' need to dive deep immediately after launching the T5 was bound to produce exaggerated claims, as any detonation after roughly the right interval would seem to be a hit. The reality was therefore less damaging, though still worrying for the escorts. *U270*, the boat that had first reported the convoy, had already blown the stern off the frigate HMS *Lagan*, shortly before the self-inflicted damage of a premature Hedgehog detonation (see earlier) had crippled the destroyer HMS *Escapade*.

After that, two T5s sank the Canadian four-stack destroyer HMCS *St Croix* and another the corvette HMS *Polyanthus*. On the following night, the U-boats claimed another five escorts sunk. In fact, the only casualty had been the River class frigate HMS *Itchen*, hit by another T5. The ship's magazine exploded, sinking her with the loss of most of her crew, together with survivors from those escorts sunk earlier.

In addition, the U-boats sank six merchant ships rather than the nine they claimed. The price was the loss of two U-boats to air attack at the start of the battle, another depth-charged by the destroyer HMS *Keppel*, and four more so badly damaged they took no further part in the fight. Yet this was to remain the largest single success for the Germans' new wonder weapon. The reason was partly that the Allies already knew that something like this might be made available to the U-boats. In fact, simple decoys had been made to detonate acoustic mines in harbour areas, and a counter-measure for the new German torpedo was modified from one of these. This 'pipe noisemaker' contained a pair of hollow pipes held loosely in an open frame that was dragged through the water, allowing them to hammer against one another and create random high-frequency noise.

This was developed into the 'Foxer', to be towed by the escorts whenever U-boats were in the vicinity. Although it effectively decoyed the German torpedoes, it deafened the escorts' sonars when in use, and 'Johnny' Walker decided his ships were largely immune to homing torpedoes anyway, moving at the slow speeds used in his stealthy approach tactics. He soon stopped using the Foxer, while destroyer skippers, used to rushing at a target at high speed, also found the decoys a hindrance. Equally, moving at low speed with U-boats in the area would leave any escort deeply vulnerable to an accurate shot with a conventional torpedo, a weakness underlined on several occasions.

Even Doenitz himself was not completely convinced that the new weapons could genuinely turn the tables, and the reality was much bleaker than he realised. Yet more powerful weapons were soon to be issued to the escorts to find U-boats, attack them and send them to the bottom. While Hedgehog filled an important gap, an even more powerful ahead-throwing weapon was about to enter service, returning to firing single heavy charges rather than a pattern

Hedgehog imposed heavy stresses on the bows of the vessels fitted with it, so the US Navy also used a rocket powered alternative called Mousetrap – here fitted to the destroyer-minesweeper uss *Trever* in the dockyard at Mare Island.

(US National Archives)

of smaller ones, and only carried by destroyers and larger frigates.

This was the Squid anti-submarine mortar, with three tubes, each loaded with a massive 350-pound charge. When the weapon was fired, these could be hurled a full 700 yards in quick succession – three times the range of the Hedgehog – in a pattern designed to destroy any U-boat within its spread.

In the end, it was to be a combination of new tactics with well-drilled ships, powerful new weapons and a more capable system for sharing intelligence that finally finished off the U-boats in the surface anti-submarine war. One campaign in particular would show what the Germans were now up against. At the beginning of 1944, the 2nd Support Group made its rendezvous with two escort carriers, HMS *Nairana* and HMS *Activity* off the Orkneys, to support a series of Atlantic convoys under threat from wolf-packs.

They faced the job with mixed feelings. An earlier patrol with an escort carrier, HMS *Tracker*, showed that these large ships were highly vulnerable. The need to protect them properly cut the offensive power of the group by half, and the cost of a single mistake, with U-boats in the vicinity, harked back to the loss of HMS *Audacity* in convoy OG76 two years earlier. To make matters worse, it was clear as they met the carriers on the night of 29 January that both could be seen clearly in semi-moonlit conditions more than five miles away and easily identified as the high-priority targets they were.

Ultra intercepts showed three wolf packs searching for convoys in the central Atlantic. At 10.15am on 31 January, the carriers were launching air patrols, while Walker's group sailed ahead of them in line abreast at twelve knots, his five ships spaced out at one-mile intervals. Four had recently returned from repairs to leaks caused by constant pounding from heavy depth-charge patterns for hours on end. HMS *Starling*, *Magpie*, *Wren* and *Wild Goose* had strengthened sterns and HMS *Kite* was rejoining the group after her refit, while HMS *Woodpecker* had yet to go for repairs.

Kite was rejoining the formation when *Wild Goose* picked up a contact to starboard, between herself and *Magpie*. The U-boat had almost passed through the group's line and could be aiming at one of the carriers, or sending a homing torpedo at one of the frigates.

There was no time to delay. The standard response was to slow to seven knots to lose any homing torpedo while the ship was beam-on to a contact and therefore most vulnerable. *Wild Goose* slowed and turned to starboard under full helm. Once the target was dead ahead she increased to full speed to attack and force the U-boat to dive deep to survive.

Meanwhile Walker signalled the rest of the team. *Magpie* and *Starling* joined *Wild Goose* to attack the U-boat, while the convoy's own escorts closed on the carriers. Walker estimated that another minute or two could have seen torpedoes striking the *Nairana*. As things were, he and *Wild Goose* were able to use a clever twist on the creeping attack.

Most of his ships now had the Q attachment, given priority as U-boats were diving deeper. Operational Research showed persistence mattered in sinking U-boats, and the probability of a kill rose sharply after the sixth attack. By then, there was a real danger that the submarine would dive as deeply as possible, and sonar contact might be lost.[21]

By keeping the installation as simple as possible the first depth-finding equipment was available from April 1943, and the time needed to fit it was reduced to less than a week. Sometimes this meant a dockyard visit, but all the 2nd Support Group ships but one had recently been in dock anyway. The result of this modification was to take away one of the U-boats' most effective evasion tactics and make it easier to hunt them to the death.

The U-boat that had nearly outflanked Walker's group now faced a creeping attack. This had been spelled out in detail in the group's Operation Instructions:

The creeping attack will normally be used against a deep U-boat, as follows:
- The directing ship (normally [that of] the Senior Officer) is to take station astern of the U-boat at convenient range for keeping Asdic [sonar] contact, i.e. about 1,500–2,000 yards. She is to keep astern and pointed at the U-boat.
- When ordered by the directing ship, the attacking ship is to proceed at about five knots and to take station about 1,000 yards ahead of the directing ship, i.e. between the latter and the U-boat. She is then to attack at about five knots. She is NOT to operate Asdic.
- Meanwhile the directing ship is to pass ranges and bearings of the U-boat continuously to her by R/T, and is to inform her exactly when and what courses to steer; in other words the directing ship cons the attacker over the U-boat …

- When the attacking ship is over (or preferably just short of) the U-boat, the directing ship is to order her to 'stand by' and then 'fire'.
- The attacking ship is then to fire 26 depth charges setting as previously ordered; distance between dropped charges 25 yards, i.e. 9 seconds at 5 knots.
- Immediately the attacking ship has fired her pattern she is to report by R/T and clear the range at full speed. The directing ship is then to increase to full speed and drop a pattern of 22 charges spaced 25 yards apart setting 'E for Easy' over the U-boat or over the area of the first attack if the U-boat's position is not known. This pattern is to be eighteen charges from the rails and four from throwers.[22]

With the Q attachment, Walker knew the depth of his opponent. Any moves to evade the next attack would be exposed with pitiless clarity, and the inevitable end should be achieved far more quickly. In this case, *Starling* was the attacking ship, with *Wild Goose* acting as director. Once Walker reached the position of the U-boat the first depth-charge pattern, set for 700 feet, began detonating at precise 5-second intervals. Charge number 14 had gone off, and charge number 15 had just been fired.

Suddenly the frigate was shaken by a huge explosion thirty feet off her starboard quarter. It shattered the bottles in the wardroom wine store and tripped the main switchboard circuits. In spite of being swamped by tons of water, the crews dropped the rest of the pattern. *Starling* drew clear for *Wild Goose* to drop a pattern in turn, when sonar reported a large underwater detonation, followed by tapping sounds and two smaller explosions. Finally, after that one pattern, a mixture of oil, timber, books, clothes and body fragments bubbled to the surface, evidence of the loss of the type VIIC *U592* and every man aboard.

During the week that followed, each frigate refuelled from HMS *Activity* before being sent to support another large combined convoy made up of SL147 and MKS38. Intercepts showed U-boats

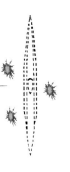

In a 'Squid' attack the escort approaches the position of the submerged submarine and before the contact fades, fires the Squid mortar, hurling three massive 350lb charges a full 700 yards, a range more than three times that of the Hedgehog and correspondingly difficult for the submarine to evade.

(Author's drawing)

The Squid in action: A Canadian warship, HMCS *Lanark,* fires a three-charge pattern on an ASW exercise in July 1956.

(National Library of Canada)

gathering, and after making contact with the local escorts, the carriers moved within the convoy for greater safety. This left Walker's ships unfettered by escort responsibilities. On the night of 8 February, the sea was blanketed in mist and a sinister quiet settled. It was only broken when the port lookout on *Wild Goose* saw a U-boat in the act of diving, a mile ahead. The captain, Lieutenant-Commander Wemyss, slowed to seven knots in case of an acoustic torpedo and steered for the spot where she vanished.

The lookout then saw the U-boat's periscope sliding through the calm water just twenty yards away. Apart from emptying a 20-mm magazine at it, they could do nothing until *Woodpecker* arrived to launch an attack on their target information. Walker was heading for the scene in *Starling,* when the twenty-two charges in that first attack finished exploding. Immediately, *Starling*'s hydrophones picked up the noise of the submarine blowing its tanks and then a series of sharp explosions. Wreckage bubbled up to the surface and *Starling*'s seaboat discovered tins, paper, clothing and human remains, whereupon Walker sent the classic signal to *Woodpecker*'s captain, telling him to 'come over here and look at the mess you made'. The wreckage was tribute to the final fate of the type VIIC *U762*, sunk with her crew in that brief encounter.

The mist persisted until, early the following morning, two more U-boats were detected. Walker and *Starling* were astern of the convoy when *Wild Goose* picked up the radar echo of a submarine some two miles away, trying to creep through the gap in the screen left while they delivered the previous attack. At the same time, HMS *Kite* was steering for the

position of a HFDF transmission nine miles ahead of the convoy. Suddenly the U-boat that had sent the signal appeared, heading for the convoy at full speed out of a mist-bank half a mile ahead of her.

Walker ordered *Magpie* to help, while he responded to *Wild Goose*'s sighting. In the meantime, Wemyss had again slowed down to avoid acoustic torpedoes, while firing starshell to make the submarine dive. He watched its radar trace finally disappear at a range of just over a mile and a quarter. Immediately, a sonar echo was picked up, together with the noise of a bubble decoy being launched and later the explosion of an acoustic torpedo at the end of its run, having missed the now slow-moving escorts.

Wild Goose's first attack produced no apparent effect. When Walker arrived on the scene, he directed Wemyss in a different form of creeping attack using flares to show the enemy's position and firing the charges by eye. After a second attack an hour later, during which strange underwater noises had been picked up, the U-boat fired a torpedo at Walker's ship, now moving too slowly to take evasive action. When his lookouts spotted the torpedo, all Walker could do was fire a depth-charge pattern at the shallowest settings. The roar of the charges detonating was followed by a heavy explosion as the torpedo went off fifteen feet from *Starling*'s stern. After this narrowest of escapes, the third creeper attack was delivered, producing a very heavy explosion followed by surface wreckage, evidence that the type VII *U734* had now also vanished with all hands.

Ahead of the convoy, *Kite* had seen her target disappear too, and her skipper, Lieutenant-Commander

Eli Whitney, another of the ubiquitous Liberty ships which helped make Allied victory in the tonnage war a certainty.

(US Naval Institute Press)

Segrave, thought the U-boat might fire an acoustic torpedo. As a precaution he dropped a single shallow-setting depth charge, and its detonation was echoed by a much larger explosion far too close for comfort. For the second time a shallow-setting charge had counter-mined an oncoming torpedo a split-second before it would have wrecked one of the escorts. Now, with *Magpie* joining the hunt, the U-boat was facing a desperate situation.

First, it survived a series of creeping attacks. *Kite* was left with just seventeen charges, so that Walker, who had moved from astern of the convoy to ahead, ordered *Magpie* to attack. *Magpie* was one of the first to be armed with Hedgehog, which just might help turn the tables on their opponent. Walker began vectoring *Magpie* towards the position of the U-boat that his depth finder recorded at the colossal depth of 700 feet. His navigating officer calculated the point where it would be in range of *Magpie*'s Hedgehog, and once it had been fired, Walker ordered her to drop a normal depth-charge pattern on the same spot, after which he would deliver a full pattern of his own.

Slowly *Magpie* crept up to the vital spot, and the order to fire was given. A full salvo of twenty-four bombs arced out over the sea and plunged below the surface. To everyone's joy, two clear underwater explosions were heard, followed closely by the thunder of the two depth-charge patterns. Then came the usual jumble of shattered wreckage surging upwards from the depths below, evidence of the destruction of the submarine.[23]

Walker himself was delighted at this success. 'I was highly tickled by all this hedge-hoggery,' he wrote later.

Complicated instruments are normally deemed essential to score an occasional hit with this weapon. But under my orders over the R/T,

Magpie steamed in to attack and fired off her bombs when told as if firing depth-charges for a creeping attack. The result was an immediate double explosion which shook both ships. To score two bulls-eyes like that first shot with someone else's Hedgehog 1,000 yards away was, of course, a ghastly fluke, but amusing considering no instruments at all were used.[24]

So perished the type VII *U238* with her entire crew, making a total of three U-boats sunk in a single violent night.[25] Two days later, *Wild Goose* and *Woodpecker* sank another type VII, *U424* and her crew. Finally, on 19 February, *Starling* and *Woodpecker* between them sank a fifth type VII, *U264*. The hunt was long and difficult, and sonar conditions poor. Contact was lost, once for an hour, and again for forty-five min-utes, and when regained, reception was too fuzzy for the operators to reliably distinguish the U-boat from a succession of bubble decoys.

At last, after six hours, *Starling* had used her re-maining charges. The only encouraging sign had been an underwater detonation two hours before, but with the echo still present, the U-boat remained a threat. The two ships searched on, watching for their oppo-nent to turn and follow the convoy. Finally, to their surprise, at 4.59am, after a seven-hour hunt, the U-boat surfaced. Both escorts opened fire, and the submarine finally sank beneath the waves, leaving her entire crew to be rescued by the men who had finally beaten her into submission.

The record of six U-boats sunk by a single support group in quick succession was never bettered, but it came at a price. When the search was resumed after sinking *U264*, all seemed well. Then at 10.16pm, Walker's crew heard an explosion and saw flares out to port in the vicinity of *Woodpecker*. A signal con-firmed she had been torpedoed, just after picking up

Large numbers of the simple but capable escort destroyers for both the Royal and US navies equipped more and more of the escort groups – this is uss *Raby (DE-698)* departing from Pearl Harbor with the uss *Marsh (DE-699)*.

(US Naval Institute Press)

another contact. Walker took her in tow, but her wrecked stern made it almost impossible and a naval tug took over. Later she capsized and sank, but by good luck and good seamanship her crew was saved, along with her share of U-boat prisoners.[26]

In addition to the effectiveness of Walker's tactics, and the lethal power of the new weapons, operational research by Professor Blackett's team ensured escorts would be better deployed to protect still larger convoys (see Chapter 12).

However, while the future was bleak for the Germans, it would be all too brief for 'Johnny' Walker. The man who persisted in his conviction that ASW

would be supremely important in a new war, and who became the most effective escort commander of all time, was now worn out. He took his group after U-boats sending weather details back to Germany from the Western Atlantic, and sank the type VII boat *U653* with a single depth-charge pattern. He then escorted convoy JW58 to North Russia through the most dangerous waters in the world. The ships under his command sank two more U-boats and not one ship from the convoy was lost.

Walker's last duty was protecting the Normandy landings from U-boats. He was overdue for promotion and command of a carrier in the Far East, but after news of the death of his eldest son in the submarine HMS *Parthian*, he went on leave. A week after *Starling* docked in Liverpool, he suffered a stroke and died within hours. The Commander-in-Chief Western Approaches, Admiral Sir Max Horton, gave a moving address at his funeral and eight captains followed his coffin to the destroyer HMS *Hesperus*, and the burial in the grey waters of Liverpool Bay. He had sunk twenty U-boats during the course of the war. Two weeks after his death, his group was back at sea, and went on to sink another eight.

By then, some of his methods had been improved, using new weapons. In particular, his combination of creeping and plaster attacks, expensive in depth charges, was overtaken by the Squid, which gave a sub-killing punch at almost a single blow, with no warning at all for the unfortunate submarine at the receiving end. Not only was this an attack of devastating power, but thanks to new sonar equipment it was delivered with unprecedented accuracy.

The type 147 sonar equipment with the Q attach-ment described earlier was to be just as useful with Squid as it was with Hedgehog. It was relatively simple to use. Once a U-boat was found, all the operator had to do was sweep the beam across the target to find the strongest echo. The axis of the sonar beam was then pointing at the U-boat, and the data was fed to the depth recorder, while a cursor was lined up with the echo to display the depth on an indicator on the bridge and automatically set the correct depth on the Squid charges. The data was also sent to a new range recorder, which converted the slant range into the horizontal range (the range setting for the launcher) and the vertical range. This information was also relayed to an improved bearing recorder that incorp-orated an optical cursor able to cancel out the effect of the ship's own speed, to give a more accurate mortar bearing.

This new sonar combination of the type 147 sonar with the Q attachment (depending on the type of ship carrying it) and the Squid mortar was widely fitted during the last two years of the war in the Royal Navy's Castle and Loch class frigates. By May 1944, these were proving highly successful. Walker's old group now included a Squid frigate, HMS *Loch Killin*, and on patrol off the Scilly Isles, they detected an old Atlantic veteran, the type VII *U333* formerly commanded by Peter Cremer in the original Drumbeat attacks on America's eastern seaboard two and a half years earlier. She was now commanded by Hans Fiedler, who had already lost two earlier commands, *U564* and *U998*, the first to an RAF plane from a training unit that forced her to be scuttled off the Spanish coast and the second to a Norwegian Mosquito armed with a 57-mm

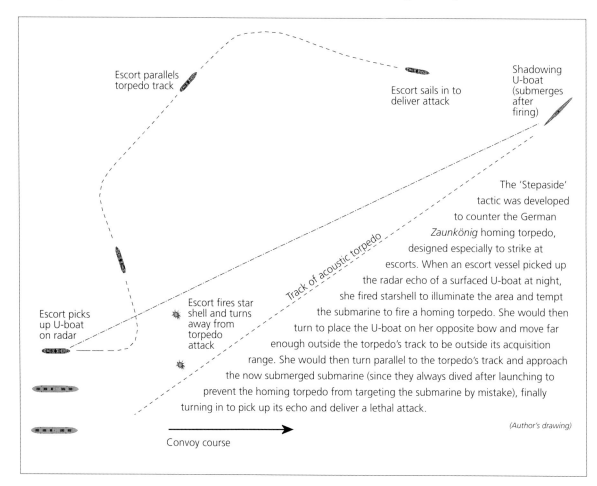

(Author's drawing)

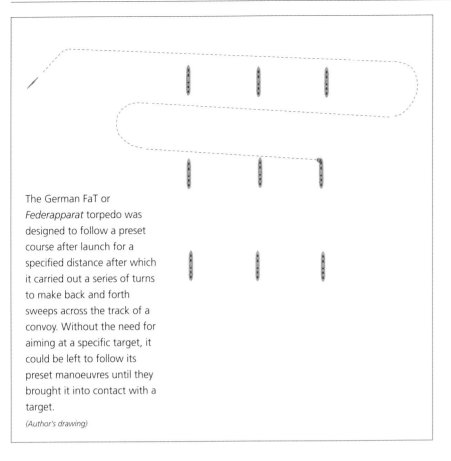

The German FaT or *Federapparat* torpedo was designed to follow a preset course after launch for a specified distance after which it carried out a series of turns to make back and forth sweeps across the track of a convoy. Without the need for aiming at a specific target, it could be left to follow its preset manoeuvres until they brought it into contact with a target.

(Author's drawing)

The LuT torpedo was a development of the FaT weapon, which allowed the U-boat crew to vary the length of the initial run, the length of each run in the sequence of sweeps and the change of course at the end of each sweep. This made it a more flexible weapon which could be tailored to suit the nature and position of the convoy being attacked.

(Author's drawing)

anti-tank gun (see following chapter).

U333's former skipper described how Fiedler's luck finally ran out:

> At 1700 on the 31st July, the listening room in *Loch Killin* reported the Asdic echo of a U-boat. The group leader was informed and with *Loch Killin* began a systematic search. At 1727 *Loch Killin* fired a Squid salvo. The depth charges were set for 40 metres. When *Starling* passed over the site of the attack, oil was seen everywhere on the surface. The U-boat had probably been hit. Twenty minutes later it was again attacked with Squid, whereupon wreckage and oil came up. The ships waited patiently.
>
> At 1806 *Starling* threw a series of ten heavy depth charges set to depths of 80 to 130 metres. They were heard to explode. Then there was silence.
>
> Just when it was all thought to be over, there was an unusually heavy explosion in the depths. More oil kept coming up.
>
> *Starling* and *Loch Killin* continued to throw depth charges and Squid projectiles until the whole surface of the sea was covered with wreckage and objects of all kinds. But the U-boat stayed down.
>
> It was the fifteenth U-boat *Starling* had helped to sink, and the 538th U-boat which the British Admiralty claimed as destroyed.[27]

Other experienced escort groups had equally remarkable results in the dying phases of the war. The 22nd Escort Group was patrolling north of the Shetlands, hunting for U-boats sailing between Germany and their Norwegian bases in early 1945. Two ships, the frigates HMS *Loch Dunvegan* and HMS *Loch Eck*, were armed with Squid and the other two, US-built DDEs HMS *Bayntun* and HMS *Braythwaite* were armed with Hedgehogs.

On 3 February, sailing through the eastern end of the straits between the Shetlands and the Faeroes, *Loch Eck* sank the type VII *U1279* with a single Squid salvo. On 14 February they picked up another echo, and both types of weapons were used. The final sinking of the type VII *U998* was mainly due to the Squid of *Loch Dunvegan*, but three days later it was the turn of HMS *Bayntun* to sink *U1278* with her first Hedgehog salvo. In one more case, another Squid-armed frigate, HMS *Loch Glendhu* fired a single salvo so accurately that the type VII *U1024* was blown to the surface and abandoned.

To the bitter end though, one area where U-boats still scored occasional successes was against the convoys to northern Russia, now guarded by strong escorts and anti-submarine carriers. Even then, deception could still be useful. When convoy JW61A left the Clyde on 29 October 1944 and JW62 a month later, both escort commanders avoided U-boat attacks by sending some escorts on different courses, making as much noise as possible by towing Foxer targets and tempting the Germans to search the wrong area.[28]

Nevertheless, U-boats were still sinking ships on Russian convoys as late as March 1945 on the approaches to the Kola Inlet. Returning convoys were in great danger here, so escort groups would sweep the area the day before departure to drive the U-boats away, but some used snorkels to avoid discovery. This led the escort commander for convoy RA65, due to sail at midnight on 23 March 1945, to try a new tactic.

Instead of sending out escorts the day before, he assembled the convoy in three columns rather than two to speed up leaving harbour. Just before sailing, four destroyers left on the usual route at high speed, dropping depth charges and firing starshell, to simulate a sweep of the area, suggesting that the convoy would sail next day. In fact it left hours later, using a new channel, and by the time the U-boats realised that the convoy had left, it was well clear of danger. When this trick was tried again with RA66 on 29 April, the U-boats were not fooled, and T5s exploded in the wake of HMS *Alnwick Castle*, while HMS *Loch Inch* detected U307 on sonar and blew her to the surface with Squid before sinking her by gunfire. Nevertheless U968 torpedoed the DDE HMS *Goodall*, which exploded when the torpedo set off her magazine. This was the last Russian convoy attacked by U-boats.

In the face of this overwhelming Allied superiority, there was precious little consolation for the Germans, not even the desperate expedient of the schnorkel, adapted from a Dutch invention that allowed a submarine to run on its diesel engines while hidden just below the surface. In essence, it was an air pipe with its upper end above the water and fitted with a float valve to prevent water getting in should it dip below the surface, and the lower end feeding air into the submarine. The Dutch had developed it to allow their submarine crews to remain cooler below the surface while operating in the stifling heat and humidity of the East Indies, but when the Germans captured Dutch boats fitted with the device, they realised it might offer them the chance of avoiding detection by air or surface radar, though it proved potentially lethal for the crews depending on it. The first two boats carrying the device failed to return. The second, U575, sent an enthusiastic signal, but noted the schnorkel should not be used when a hunt was in progress because the noise of the diesels made it impossible to listen through the hydrophones. Finally, the third boat to try the equipment, U667, returned after sailing underwater for nine days in succession.

Normally, boats used the schnorkel for three to five hours during the night, schnorkelling being interrupted every 20 minutes, when the diesels were switched off and all-round listening carried out. If the U-boat proceeded with one diesel on screw and one on pure battery-charging, at a speed of three to four knots, then in three hours snorting the batteries received a sufficient charge to operate for one day submerged.

The schnorkel was also very useful for ventilating the boat. To accomplish this the outer diesel air-intake valve was closed slightly, so that some air was sucked out of the compartment by the running diesel; then, as soon as pressure dropped sufficiently, the air was renewed from outside by re-opening the air-intake valve. If the interior of the boat became foul as a result of heavy seas or bad depth-keeping causing the schnorkel head to dip below the surface for any length of time, escape apparatus was donned at once, while the boat was brought up to periscope depth and ventilated by the method just described. If the presence of the enemy made this impossible, the crew was gravely imperilled by the foul air, and it is fairly certain that one or two boats were lost in this way.[29]

This problem was confirmed by serving U-boat officers like Herbert Werner. Prior to leaving Norway on their final wartime patrol, one of his machinists wrote 'The Schnorkel Lament' an eloquent complaint about the agonies of the miracle-working new equipment:

With jitters and fears and lamentation,
We drag ourselves often to 'Schnorkel station'.
When the vacuum happens to rupture our ears,
We writhe on the deck in torture and tears.
Our eyes go jumping from out of our heads;
To see, we take them in our hands instead.
To ease our pain and distorted poses,
We equalise pressure by squeezing our noses.
Everyone swears – it will go down in history –
'The Schnorkel float should have stayed a
    mystery'.
But we were born to Schnorkel till very late,
And we were chosen to suffer this nightly fate,
And we will depend for the rest of our lives,
On the eardrums and eyeballs of our faithful
    wives.[30]

Wolfgang Hirschfeld on U234, reported in his diary the first acquaintance of his crew with the vagaries of the schnorkel at Kiel in December 1944:

The boat dived and was trimmed at periscope depth. The schnorkel exhaust and air intake masts were raised and the boat ran submerged on the diesels. We progressed smoothly and conning tower was clear of the sea, he carefully turned on the test-cock and jumped smartly clear. The air came whistling in, but it was some time before the air intake masts could be reopened. When they were, a storm-wind swept through the boat, followed by a strange mist. Our ears 'popped' as their drums adjusted to the change in the pressure.

It had all been the fault of the Chief Engineer. Instead of giving the order to cut out the diesels, he had got confused and given the order to put the diesels into neutral, in which state they continued to consume the air in the boat. Lt-Commander Ernst was brought before the assembled crew and given the severest possible reprimand. It was his first schnorkel attempt and a complete disaster …[31]

It was clear the schnorkel was far from the miracle on which Doenitz and his staff had based their hopes. All it could do was extend the hem of the cloak of invisibility, always the submarine's chief protection, a little further than before. But the latest centimetric radar could pick up the tiny echoes of the schnorkel heads, and reveal the whereabouts of a U-boat already blinded and deafened to approaching attackers until too late. To redress the balance slightly, the Germans coated the schnorkel heads in anti-reflecting materials and on the final generation of U-boats the schnorkel carried a centimetric radar detector.

Overall, German technology failed against more inventive opponents. The U-boat crews fought a hard but relatively humane campaign. They showed real bravery facing one of the most awful deaths twentieth-century warfare could inflict – drowning in the darkness far below the surface as their craft was crushed under appalling pressure, intensified by the shocks of larger and heavier depth charges. If this were not enough, they endured a fearful casualty rate. More than three U-boat men out of four were killed in action, a higher loss rate than elite infantry, paratroops or Panzers, fighter pilots or bomber crews.

Yet the devotion of the submariners was badly served by those in command. Doenitz used his weapons skilfully enough to cause the Allies the deepest anxiety at times. He fought hard to counter indifference and lack of understanding at the highest levels, but rarely looked beyond the figures of Allied merchant tonnage sunk, the only measure of his command's effectiveness.

Against the highly effective combination of tanks, dive bombers and motorised infantry in the 1940 Blitzkrieg, the Anglo-French alliance had little to offer. But in air and naval warfare, the boot was firmly on the other foot. The British air defence system was far more professional than the tactics the *Luftwaffe* used against it, and the forces fighting the U-boats

The chaos of victory: a Royal Navy officer surveys the wreckage of Wilhelmshaven dockyard after the German surrender.

(National Library of Canada)

Captain Valentiner asked Lt-Commander Ernst to have the schnorkel cut under the waves.

Initially there was no noticeable effect even though the diesels were consuming the air from the interior of the boat. After five minutes the diesels were still running and this created a partial vacuum which was particularly unpleasant on the eardrums and rapidly became intolerable. Peter Schölch, the Boatswain, found that two fillings in his teeth dropped out.

Suddenly all the men in the diesel room collapsed over the machinery, but fortunately the last man on his feet, Warrant Officer Winkelmann, still had the strength to disconnect the diesel – and without receiving the order to do so. The tanks were blown and the boat rose, but the vacuum remained. The control room petty officer went up to the tower and, when it was reported to him that the

The threat that came too late – the type XXI U-boat *U3008* lying alongside in Wilhelmshaven after the surrender.

(US Naval Historical Center)

to achieve their objectives.

In contrast, the Allies explored every avenue open to them to improve both weapons and tactics, from centimetric radar to operational research, from more powerful depth charges to more effective ways of launching them like Hedgehog and Squid, from airborne rockets and cannon to sonobuoys and magnetic anomaly detectors, and of course, Enigma intercepts to reveal the intentions and whereabouts of U-boats. The Germans, in contrast, hardly realised how much their enemies achieved, what new challenges were about to face them, and how much was known about their own plans or intentions. Doenitz continued using wolf-pack tactics, decided his signals were proof against Allied decrypting teams, and assumed his crude and outdated methods of detecting Allied radar signals were effective against a weapon that made life impossible for his crews.

Even where German technology did provide improvements, in most cases these were in response to new Allied equipment already far ahead in capability and availability. Where scientists and engineers should have been improving their main weapon – the U-boat itself – development was too slow, and when the possibilities of final defeat began to emerge, it was too late to put that right.

Yet the final months of the long U-boat campaign provided evidence that things might possibly have been different. From the beginning, the basic weakness that Allied tactics had been able to exploit was that the U-boat was no genuine submarine. Because its main diesels could only run on the surface, it was always a submersible. When forced to dive, its speed and endurance were crippled. It could move at little better than walking pace, for a few hours at most before battery power and oxygen ran out.

Once escorts could be spared for a long hunt, and once aircraft used 'hold-down' tactics, handing over to others once fuel ran short, even the best handled U-boat would have to surface eventually. Then, faced with their attackers' superior firepower, she was effectively doomed. Only a true submarine could have escaped in safety.

So could the Germans have developed a genuine submarine, given the limitations of Second World War technology? One option was to make strenuous efforts to improve underwater speed and endurance, so the U-boat could evade her enemies before the inevitable shortages of air and electrical power forced her back to the surface. The more radical, and more difficult alternative was to modify the propulsion system so the U-boat could cruise for long distances, attack, escape and return to base without ever having to surface. Sadly, though the Germans made efforts to attain both these aims, they began so late in the war that only their opponents enjoyed the benefits. (see Chapter 17).

learned and developed their tactics and technology far faster than the Germans had done, an omission for which the U-boat crews paid the price.

Doenitz started the war with submarines closely similar to those of the First World War, while many of the British and US destroyers used as Atlantic escorts also dated back to that time. German engineering was still of very high quality, building strong pressure hulls, sensitive hydrophones, high-quality periscope optics and excellent torpedo aiming equipment. But there was a lack of commitment to new ideas that limited German performance and made it impossible for them

CHAPTER 14

AIR POWER INVINCIBLE

1943–45

Wildcat fighter being
launched from the ASW
carrier USS *Core*

(US National Archives)

On 27 July 1943, the American escort carrier USS *Card* sailed from Hampton Roads, escorted by three old flush-deck four-stack destroyers, USS *Barry*, USS *Borie* and USS *Goff*. The small task force sailed southwards to Bermuda, where they stopped to refuel. They sailed again on 1 August to join the convoy UGS13, heading from the Caribbean to North Africa. The intentions of the task force commander, Captain Arnold J 'Buster' Isbell, USN were clear. He would patrol ahead of the convoy, looking for U-boats lying in wait. Instead of helpless merchantmen, the U-boat would receive the most lethal of surprises.

The carrier had eleven Grumman TBF-1 Avenger strike planes, and six Grumman F4F-4 Wildcats. With these aircraft hunting up to a hundred miles ahead of the convoy and far out to each side, submarines could be attacked with little or no warning, in the most radical development in ASW. Offensive tactics that had failed so spectacularly for the Royal Navy at the outbreak of war could now work at last. For the very first time, effective hunter-killer groups would become a reality, thanks to new ships, new weapons and above all new information to find their elusive targets in the vastness of the ocean.

Although the Wildcat had already proved its value in the anti-submarine war when operating from HMS *Audacity* (as described in Chapter 8), the Avenger was something entirely new. Originally designed as a torpedo bomber to a 1939 requirement for a replacement for the obsolescent Douglas Devastator TBDs then serving aboard US carriers, it was rushed into service, with the first production examples reaching the Pacific in time for the Battle of Midway in early June 1942.

It had a faint family resemblance to the tubby but tough Wildcat, but its larger and longer fuselage carried three crew members and a large internal weapons bay. Its streamlined all-metal structure and 1,700-horsepower Wright 14-cylinder R2600 radial engine blessed it with a top speed of 278mph. Even better for ASW operations, it could cruise over a range of 1.100 miles at 150mph, carrying a weapons load of up to 2,000 pounds. It had a useful defensive armament, with two .50-inch calibre forward-firing machine guns in the outer wing sections, a .30-inch calibre machine gun at the rear of the weapons bay and a .50-inch calibre machine gun in a dorsal power turret. To fill its capacious weapons bay, more powerful weapons were being made available, including heavier depth charges and a sophisticated acoustically guided homing anti-submarine torpedo codenamed 'Fido' or the Mark 24 mine.

This was the product of an ambitious US development programme. It was a compact weapon, to fit the restricted space of an aircraft bomb bay. Its 21-inch calibre was the same as a standard torpedo, but it was only seven feet long, less than a third the size of the torpedoes carried by the U-boats. Early trials with two different passive sensor systems had used four acoustic sensors mounted around the body of the torpedo, with signals fed to its guidance system. Differences in inputs from sensors on opposite sides of the torpedo sent commands to the rudder actuators to turn the torpedo until the signals were equal in amplitude, whereupon it would be steering straight at its target.[1]

Early trials were promising, with two limitations. The need to hear its target clearly made the British prediction of a twenty-knot top speed hopelessly optimistic. The Mark 24 mine could manage twelve knots, though its makers were sure this would be more than enough to catch a submerged U-boat. Much more damaging would be the effect of the U-boat slowing down after submerging. This would reduce the cavitation noise on which the homing system depended, and could cause the weapon to miss its target altogether.

However, so long as the Germans were unaware of how the new weapon worked, they were almost certain to dive at full speed when evading an air attack. Under these conditions, the torpedo could pick up the noise of the submarine's propellers at ranges of up to three-quarters of a mile. The submarine skippers would only slow down after diving if they knew what kind of new weapon was being used against them, and how they could throw it off the scent once safely below the surface. So convinced were the Allies that the Germans would realise the truth that they planned to stop production by the end of 1943.

The homing torpedo still had to be proved under operational conditions. The first weapons for UK-based aircraft were shipped aboard the Canadian Pacific liner *Empress of Scotland*, which was fast enough to sail independently of either convoy or escort between New York and Liverpool. Jeaff Greswell, the RAF pilot who had made the first successful Leigh Light attack on the Italian submarine *Luigi Torelli* (described in Chapter 9), was now an acting group captain, returning from a liaison visit to the USA. He was ordered to see the torpedoes safely to their destination. He did this so discreetly that British Customs chased him for importing mysterious boxes without declaring their contents.

Those first Fidos went to 86 Squadron of 15 Group, Coastal Command, at Aldergrove in Northern Ireland flying B24 Liberators. To prevent the Germans from deducing what Fido was and how it worked, it could only be dropped when the target submarine was submerged. It could not be launched near the coast, or where any other German ship or aircraft in the vicinity could see what was happening. Nevertheless, there was always the faint possibility that the submarine under attack might escape to tell the tale.

Incredibly, during the very first attack, on 12 May 1943, that unlikely outcome actually happened.

It was a textbook launch, with Flight Lieutenant John Wright's crew spotting the type VIIC U-boat *U456* in showery weather while guarding the fast eastbound convoy HX237 in the Southwestern Approaches. As they turned to attack, the U-boat dived, and at 1.13pm, the first Mark 24 mine to be launched in anger was dropped close to the swirls where the submarine had disappeared. There followed an anti-climax, compared with the instant response of shallow-setting depth charges. The limited-speed weapon had to search for, acquire and then chase its target, which often took more than ten minutes. In this case, after two minutes there was a small underwater explosion, more than half a mile away from the launch point. Soon afterwards they were amazed to see the submarine surface again. The gun crews emerged and opened fire on the aircraft. With no weapons remaining, and fuel reserves almost exhausted, Wright headed back to base. All they could do was radio the escort commander and suggest he sent a destroyer to chase the U-boat in the hope it could no longer dive.

What the submarine skipper, Kapitänleutnant Max Martin Teichert could still do, though, was radio Doenitz's headquarters to tell them what had happened. The admiral's war diary revealed a confusion over the weapon that had struck such a crippling blow: 'Between 12.00 and 13.00 *U456* reported that she had been hit from the air, she is in no condition to dive and is in urgent need of assistance. Later she reported, several times, that she is leaking badly at the stern, presumably as a result of an aerial bomb hit . . .'[2]

Teichert and his crew managed to survive until the following morning, when their luck finally ran out. A Sunderland from 423 Squadron RCAF emerged from cloud cover a mile away, and the U-boat crew strove to beat off its attack with another furious barrage. At first they seemed to force the flying boat to turn away. What they could not have known was that its radio operator was signalling HX237's escort commander to send a corvette to deal with the U-boat. Once the surface escort turned up, the U-boat's fate was sealed. Again she managed to dive, whereupon the Sunderland crossed her track and dropped two shallow-setting depth charges on the turbulence left by her disappearance. Two warships then took it in turns to deliver a series of depth-charge attacks. Finally Teichert and all his crew went to the bottom, taking the secret of their ultimately fatal encounter with the Mark 24 mine with them.[3]

Had the experienced Teichert returned to base, expert debriefing might have revealed the nature of this powerful new weapon. As it was, the time elapsing before the explosion and the relatively small disturbance at the surface suggested he had probably

gone deep after diving, and the torpedo had followed him down to detonate far below the surface. This was clearly different to normal depth charges, which might have given the game away to other U-boats in the vicinity. Nevertheless, maintaining strict rules of engagement preserved the weapon's secret to the end of the war. One of the few references to it in German sources merely mentions U-boat crews being 'baffled by what they believed to be a system of under-water location using some explosive body'.[4]

Another type VIIC U-boat, *U266*, was attacked by an 86 Squadron Liberator on the following day, this time while protecting the slow convoy SC129. At first the result seemed inconclusive in this case too. No water disturbance at all was seen, though the submarine never returned to her base, and was recorded as sunk with her entire crew.

Then US Navy squadron VP84, operating Catalinas from Iceland, achieved its first homing torpedo sinking on the same day, protecting westbound slow convoy ONS7. One Catalina was vectored by the escort commander to a point sixteen miles from the convoy, where the type VIIC *U640* was sighted three miles away. Confusingly, the official US Navy report described how the Catalina dropped three depth charges from a height of seventy-five feet, with two of them straddling the boat and causing it to stop before sinking slowly under the surface. In fact, the weapon used was the Mark 24 mine.

To compound the confusion, the submarine was

Type VII U-boat *U664* under attack from aircraft from escort carrier uss *Card* on 9 August 1943. On the previous night the submarine had passed close to the carrier without being spotted and fired three torpedoes, all of which missed or malfunctioned. Forced to dive by the escorts, she had surfaced the following day to charge batteries and was attacked. Two attempts to dive were frustrated by damage and the picture shows the crew preparing to abandon ship as she begins to sink for the third and final time.

(US National Archives)

U118, a type XB minelayer serving as a refuelling boat under attack from aircraft from uss *Bogue*, after betrayal by Enigma decrypts, as the depth charges fall into the water alongside her hull – their explosions would sink her.

(US National Archives)

originally thought to be the *U657*, with the *U640* sunk by depth-charge and Hedgehog attacks from the frigate HMS *Swale* three days later. Later it was revealed that the identities of the two U-boats had been transposed, the homing torpedo had sunk the *U640* and the surface escort the *U657*. The US historian Clay Blair pointed out that the sinking of a single merchant ship from this slow and potentially vulnerable convoy had cost Doenitz the loss of no less than four type VII U-boats and one type IXC, showing how far the tables had been turned.

The *Card*'s planes found their first victim two days later. On 3 August, Isbell received an Enigma decrypt, revealing the type IXC *U66* was ordered to rendezvous with a makeshift tanker submarine, the big XB minelayer *U117*, in a position well within range of the carrier group. *U117* was to lay mines off New York harbour, but had been switched to top up *U66*'s fuel supplies first. *Card* launched an Avenger strike plane and a Wildcat fighter, to look for *U66*. At almost 4.30pm they found her some 450 miles west-southwest of the Azores, totally unprepared for what was about to happen.

The tactics, like the planes, were new. Ensign A S Paulson, flying the fighter, dived to machine-gun the submarine to persuade her skipper to dive, while the Avenger held off for the moment. The Wildcat's bullets killed the second watch officer and two sailors as the boat began to submerge. At that moment the captain, Kapitänleutnant Friedrich Markworth, countermanded the order from below. U-boat tactics were to stay and fight back under air attack, but he arrived on the bridge just in time to be hit by the Wildcat's second firing pass. He was badly wounded in the stomach, and his first watch officer, a midshipman and five other sailors were also hit. Once again the order was given to dive.

As the casualties were dragged below, the Avenger finally swept in to attack. The first pass failed, as the weapons failed to release. The aircraft banked and returned, and this time both depth charges fell into the water along with a Fido. Some forty seconds later a large underwater blast sent out a shock wave on both sides of the submarine, just forward of the conning tower, followed by a huge column of water more than a hundred feet high. The submarine was heaved upwards by the blast and heeled over to starboard before she disappeared. The planes turned back for the carrier, confident they had sunk the U-boat.

In fact, *U66* was badly damaged and severely shaken from the blast of the depth charges, but the Fido had missed and her pressure hull was still intact. The first watch officer, wounded but temporarily in command, surfaced after dark and radioed headquarters, who repeated the order to rendezvous with *U117*. These messages were decrypted by the US Navy's 10th Fleet

American ASW carrier USS *Bogue*.

(US Naval Institute Press)

The Grumman Avenger first appeared at the Battle of Midway. This aircraft landed back at base as the only survivor – the type was named in honour of this initial sacrifice.

(US Naval Institute Press)

Headquarters and details relayed to the *Card*. This time, there was only an approximate position for the two submarines to meet, and it took them three days to find one another in the immensity of the ocean. When they made contact at last, just after midnight on 6 August, the big minelayer sent over her doctor to tend the wounded and her first watch officer, Oberleutnant Paul Frerks, to take temporary command. After daybreak, hoses had been connected up, and fuel was being pumped between the boats.

Card launched follow-up patrols at first light, and Lieutenant (jg – junior grade) Asbury H Sallenger USNR, flying an Avenger in clear but hazy conditions some eighty-three miles to the west of the carrier, spotted what he thought was a large white object twelve miles away to starboard. He turned to investigate and as he approached he realised the mysterious object was two submarines running side by side on the surface, about two hundred feet apart. He turned so that the rising sun was at his back, while radioing for reinforcements, and then dived towards the U-boats. For precious seconds the German sailors failed to see what was heading their way. Finally, with less than a quarter of a mile to go, they saw the threat roaring towards them and manned their anti-aircraft guns. Both crews opened up with 20-mm and 37-mm cannon, sending a barrage of shells towards the approaching bomber.

Miraculously, the Avenger suffered no hits at all, as Sallenger skimmed over the U-boats at a height of 125 feet. Two depth charges fell into the sea, one on either side of the big minelayer, as the Avenger rear-gunner hosed bursts of machine-gun fire at the gunners to stop them correcting their aim. The first charge detonated some eight feet off the starboard quarter of the U117, close enough to cause real damage, and the second went off eighteen feet on her port side, just ahead of the conning tower. It was a well-nigh perfect straddle, and the minelayer began to follow a twisting course, giving off clouds of smoke and apparently unable to dive.

Bravely, Sallenger returned through the flak to attack again. The refuelling hoses had been cast off, and U66 was now beginning to dive. Only U117's gunners were still firing, but the barrage was intense. The Avenger swept over the U-boats a second time and Sallenger dropped his Fido fifty yards to the right and 150 yards ahead of the disturbance in the water left by the diving submarine, but there was no detonation. Once again, U66 had been extremely lucky, and survived her second near-miss in four days.

Not so the hapless U117. Having expended his weapons, Sallenger climbed to 6,400 feet, well out of range of the U-boat's guns, to vector the next wave of *Card* aircraft to the target. In the meantime the stricken submarine tried to dive and failed, and was now lying helpless on the surface. At 7.30am, just forty minutes after the Avenger's first attack, two more Avengers arrived, escorted by a pair of Wildcats. The fighters dived to machine-gun the anti-aircraft gun crews once again, and one by one the bombers followed them down to the attack. The first Avenger planted depth charges close to the U-boat's port bow, and the second dropped two charges about twenty-five feet off her port quarter.

The blows added to the suffering of the crippled U-boat. She turned in a tightening circle to starboard, slid below the surface and then surfaced again, now apparently losing way. For five minutes there was an impasse, and then slowly and painfully the battered U-boat finally vanished below the surface, with first the stern and finally the bow disappearing from view. As soon as she was gone, both Avengers approached and dropped their torpedoes, one from port and the other from starboard.

Once again five long minutes crept by, while the planes orbited the spot and waited for something to happen. At last a wide area of turbulent light blue water, sparkling with air bubbles, spread over the surface. This time, at least, one or both of the Fidos seemed to have done their deadly work.[5] From the U-boat service's point of view, this was a particularly crippling blow. Although *U66* had escaped, admittedly badly damaged, it was the loss of the big minelayer that threw into jeopardy the plans for refuelling more than a dozen other U-boats to allow them to return to the safety of their Biscay bases.

These highly encouraging events heralded a radical shift in the anti-submarine war. On the rest of her opening cruise, *Card's* planes sank two more U-boats, one of them another of the badly needed supply boats. Nor was she alone. Other US Navy task forces based around her sister ships, USS *Bogue*, USS *Core* and USS *Santee* were also busy hunting and sinking German submarines, delivering a series of devastating blows to Doenitz's tactics of long-range operations backed up by distant resupply from submarine tankers. By this time, the Air Gap had finally been bridged by the increase in numbers of VLR aircraft like Halifaxes and B24s on both sides of the Atlantic, but already the small carriers made them almost irrelevant. By accompanying convoys which needed protection, they were completely turning the tables. No longer were merchantmen the hunters' defenceless quarry. Now the beleaguered and battered U-boats were finding themselves the targets.

The Mark 24 mine achieved its greatest successes when used by patrols from the US escort carriers. Time and again a fighter and an anti-submarine attack plane would find surfaced U-boats, singly or in company. They developed a cruelly effective routine. The fighter would strafe the submarine, and the anti-submarine plane would drop bombs or depth charges to persuade it to dive. Once it disappeared, it would drop the homing torpedo. On most occasions the only indication of the U-boat's fate, and a fearful death for her entire crew, would be a slight disturbance of the water as the Fido detonated far below.

How well these tactics worked was written in the blood of the U-boat crews during the summer of 1943, when the US carriers *Bogue, Core* and *Santee* joined the USS *Card* in sinking thirteen U-boats between them in a two month campaign. These crippling losses were inflicted in the waters of the central Atlantic where Doenitz had withdrawn his wolf packs to escape the carnage of the main North Atlantic battlefield.

When USS *Card* sailed into Casablanca to replenish her stores, Captain Isbell expressed delight with his effective new tactics and new weapons. In a report he emphasised the '500 pound bomb breaks enemy's morale and at the same time improves ours'. He went on to say 'It is believed that the Mk.24 Mine is far more effective than commonly given credit. It is acknowledged that our eggs are in one basket. However, when the mine functions as it is supposed to, the show is over, and there is no further argument from either the enemy or ourselves.'[6]

With the Mark 24 mine, American weapons engineers produced a formidable weapon. Its self-homing capacity took the need for careful aiming out of the equation altogether. In post-war jargon, it had become a 'fire-and-forget' weapon. Even the tactics followed to protect the secrecy of its weakness worked in its favour. On many occasions, even experienced U-boat commanders assumed the reluctance of a plane to attack them on the surface was because it had no more depth charges or was marking the position of the submarine for airborne or surface escort reinforcements. In either case, the sensible action was to dive to safety, the one move that made their destruction virtually certain.

Though the long-suffering U-boat men had enough to cope with, worse was heading their way, in the shape of the anti-submarine version of the 3-inch aircraft-launched ground-attack rocket used for destroying tanks and fortifications. Once fired, the rocket neared the speed of sound at its impact point, where it penetrated the thickest tank hull with ease. If it could pierce the front armour of a German Tiger, (a task beyond the guns of most Allied tanks at the time) it could easily punch its way through a U-boat's pressure hull, where even a small hole would render the vessel unable to dive to escape further attacks.

The rocket was modified by replacing the normal explosive warhead with a solid version made of mild steel and weighing twenty-five pounds out of a total weight of sixty-six pounds. It was carefully shaped to impose a specific path on the rocket when it hit the sea. Provided it struck the water surface at around 13 degrees to the horizontal, the shaped warhead would

Compact and capable: the Grumman Avenger could carry depth charges and torpedoes in its compact internal weapons bay.

(US Naval Institute Press)

Avengers being loaded with weapons on an American carrier flight deck. Compact torpedoes like the 'Fido' or 'Mark 24 Mine' homing torpedo were able to fit the restricted space of its internal bomb bay.

(US Naval Institute Press)

make it level out and travel almost horizontally for around eighty feet, losing half its impact speed in the process. If it was correctly aimed, to hit the water around sixty feet short of the submarine (the best way to attack it was from the beam) it would almost certainly penetrate the pressure hull at least once. Usually, one hit was enough.

For the RAF's strike fighters, the twin-engine long-range Bristol Beaufighter and its faster and more powerful replacement, the de Havilland Mosquito, it was simple enough to fit a battery of eight rockets, four under each wing. Similar installations were fitted under the wings of carrier-borne aircraft, from the venerable but still effective Fairey Swordfish biplane to the modern Grumman Avenger, and to additional stub wings projecting from the fuselages of anti-submarine B24 Liberators.

The first appearance of this awesome weapon showed exactly how effective it was. It also showed how the Allied efficiency in other areas was able to work together to strip away the cloak of secrecy under which the U-boats had been able to operate during the early days. In this case, the victim was a veteran type VIIC, U752, on her eighth patrol on the morning of 23 May 1943. Her skipper, thirty-year-old Karl-Ernst Schroeter, spotted the fast east-bound convoy HX239 and radioed the good news back to Doenitz's headquarters. In doing so, he signed his own death warrant.

The brief radio transmission was picked up on the HFDF of the Royal Navy destroyer HMS *Keppel*, leading the 3rd Escort Group protecting the convoy. This particular convoy had a much more powerful asset of which Schroeter was almost certainly unaware – the escort carrier HMS *Archer*, equipped with a mixture of Martlet (Wildcat) fighters and Swordfish strike aircraft. One of the slow and archaic Swordfish biplanes was sent along the HFDF bearing, where the crew found the surfaced U-boat and dropped depth charges. The pilot radioed the carrier, which launched a second Swordfish, with a battery of under-wing rockets. Forewarned of the exact position of the U-boat, the pilot approached in cloud cover, while a Martlet fighter followed in support.

The Swordfish emerged into clear sky to find the submarine back on the surface and unaware of its approach. The pilot dived to the attack and, to avoid the fierce anti-aircraft fire expected at any moment, he fired all four pairs of rockets in quick succession. The first two pairs missed, one of the third pair hit the target and the final pair passed right through the plating of the pressure hull ahead of the conning tower, close to the radio room. No longer able to dive, Schroeter called for anti-aircraft fire, but before his men could open up on their attacker, the fighter arrived on the scene in time to blast the deck of the submarine with machine-gun fire. One of the rounds caught Schroeter in the head and killed him instantly;

others killed several of the gun crews. The chief engineer gave the order to abandon ship, and the first lieutenant deliberately chose to go down with the stricken U752.

In time, the equipping of a wide range of units with rocket-armed aircraft would extend this terrifying weapon across the whole range of U-boat operations. Under air attack, the skipper of a German submarine now had a truly appalling choice. If he dived, he risked being blown to pieces by a homing torpedo (even if he had no idea what a Fido was, or what it could do, he would know how many of his comrades had dived only to disappear for good). If he stayed on the surface to fight it out, his craft might be holed by salvoes of rockets. The only way of avoiding the choice was to spot the aircraft and dive before it noticed his presence. This made it less likely an attack would be made at all.

Those boats that were sent, under Hitler's direct orders, to run the gauntlet of the Straits of Gibraltar to attack Allied shipping in the Mediterranean, had found the narrow choke point between Europe and Africa the most dangerous of obstacles. However, from February 1944, it would be made even more perilous by another ingenious American invention. To be strictly accurate, this was not a completely new device, but a clever adaptation of a civilian instrument used in aerial prospecting for minerals. A sensitive magnetometer could be used aboard an aircraft flying a regular search pattern to reveal the presence of metallic ores underground, through the anomalies they created in the earth's magnetic field. This suggested it would also be possible to reveal the presence of the large mass of metal represented by a submerged submarine in the same way, and this was the thinking which eventually produced the magnetic airborne detector (or MAD).[7]

Work on an operational set began early in 1942, involving Western Electric and the Airborne Instruments Laboratory, and by the late spring of that year prototypes were tested in airships and aircraft against submarine targets. Results were promising enough for the device to go into production, and the first examples were fitted to patrol aircraft flying over the east coast of the USA. Certainly MAD had a number of advantages. One was the stealth factor, since the target submarine had no idea it was being monitored, whereas sonar pulses could be heard for miles and gave the crew valuable information on the bearing and range of those hunting them.

MAD also had severe limitations, which greatly reduced its usefulness. Since the effect on which it depended was only measurable over a relatively short distance, the submarine had to be at a shallow depth and the aircraft had to fly at very low altitude, in most cases only detecting its quarry as it passed over it. Unfortunately, it was then too late to drop conventional bombs or depth charges, as the momentum

An ingenious solution to maintain mass production in the teeth of Allied bombing – the modular construction of the Type XXI U-boat.

(Author's drawing)

IX: Bridge

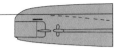

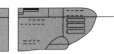

I: Stern section – steering and aft hydroplanes

II: Electric motor room

III: Diesel engine room

IV: After accommodation room

V: Control room

VI: Forward accommodation

VII: Topedo stowage

VIII: Bow section

By the time the type XXI construction programme was into its stride, bombing had become so effective that many of the completed sections languished uselessly in the assembly yards.

(Jak Mallmann Showell)

given them by the aircraft would carry them well clear of the target.

This was solved with in an ingenious way. What was needed were bombs that dropped vertically from the point of release. This was achieved by rocket-propelled bombs developed at the California Institute of Technology. These Mark VI 'retro-bombs' or 'retro-rockets' were fitted facing astern on racks beneath the aircraft's wings. Once the firing button was pressed, the rockets ignited and blasted the bombs backwards, so that if the aircraft was flying at 100mph, their speed cancelled out that of the plane which fired them, leaving them free to drop vertically into the water.

This called for extremely careful and accurate flying. To make the task a little easier and to compensate for the time taken to react to the detection of the submarine and press the firing button, the twenty-four retro-bombs carried on the PBY Catalina, for example, were fired automatically in three timed salvoes. The wiring of the firing circuits and the alignment of the launching rails resulted in eight bombs falling in a 100-foot line abreast formation, followed by another pattern ninety feet further on, and a third ninety feet beyond that.

In addition, MAD patrols were trained to use their

stealth advantage to the full. Instead of attacking as soon as the submarine was spotted, they first had to track its progress. They flew backwards and forwards across its apparent track, dropping a smoke float each time they detected its presence beneath the surface. Once the line of floats showed its course, they could come in for the kill, this time aiming their attack so they passed along the length of its hull. With three salvoes of retro bombs covering an area 180 feet long by 100 feet across, there was a good chance of at least one direct hit.

With its range limitations, MAD was not suitable as a primary search weapon in open waters. In areas like the Bay of Biscay it could only pick up the trace of a U-boat that had just submerged under conventional air attack. The only location where MAD-equipped aircraft could be left to hunt on their own was the one natural submarine choke point, which could have been created with MAD in mind.

U-boats sailing through the Straits of Gibraltar used an eastbound current through the narrows to carry them through to open water. They could only dive to some 150 feet, as below this depth a strong westbound current would prevent them making progress. On the other hand, a channel only four miles across with a depth of more than 600 feet meant there was little chance of the equipment reacting to wrecks on the sea bed.

So good was MAD hunting around Gibraltar that it transformed the success record of US Navy Squadron VP63, which had been equipped with 'Madcats' – PBY Catalinas fitted with MAD detectors and retro-bombs – at the end of 1942. Because of target scarcity off the US east coast and later off Iceland, and a disappointing role in the Biscay campaign, they were finally moved to Port Lyautey in Morocco on 14 December 1943, to maintain close patrols over the Straits of Gibraltar. From then on, VP63 met a very different kind of anti-submarine war.

Maintaining an airborne magnetic barrier across the straits meant a pair of Madcats flying a slow series of long and narrow orbits across the straits just 100 feet above the sea.[8] Each circuit took approximately six minutes, but the total duty lasted for ten gruelling hours, out and back a hundred times over the same unchanging stretch of ocean. Once the watch was over, two more aircraft would take over and complete the day's patrolling, and the following morning it would start all over again. The patrols began early in February 1944, but on 24 February, Lieutenant T Russell Wooley flew right across the track of a type VII U-boat, *U761*. This was one of a batch of five ordered by Hitler into the Mediterranean, despite Doenitz's bitter opposition to wasteful diversions.

The weapon demanded the fiercest concentration. Even on a perfect interception, the sensitive magneto-meter needle would only react for a fraction of a second. Fortunately, Aircraft Radioman J Cunningham saw the needle kick across the trace roll of paper emerging from the instrument, and called the pilot. Wooley banked the Catalina into a tight circle centred as closely as possible on the spot where the instrument had reacted. This was a standard tactic, aimed at producing a second fix, whatever the direction the submarine was steering. Again they crossed its track, and again the needle shivered. This time they dropped a smoke float and repeated their search, joined by their fellow Madcat, skippered by Lieutenant H Baker.

The two planes circled backwards and forwards over the hidden target, still totally oblivious to the threat overhead. At each interception they dropped another smoke float, revealing that their target was heading eastwards at around two knots. No underwater wreck this, but clearly an enemy submarine. Identifying its speed and track made an attack possible. However, the crowded conditions of the straits soon resulted in a Royal Navy destroyer, HMS *Anthony*, picking up a sonar contact and joining in the fray. Because sonar conditions were patchy, due to different density layers below the surface, the contact faded before she could drop depth charges, but her presence forced the Catalinas to break off their low-altitude search, and they lost contact too. Back they went to the circular search around the point at which contact had been lost, and after half an hour of anxious orbits, they picked up the trace once again.

Signalling the surface ships to keep clear (*Anthony* had now been joined by HMS *Wishart*), they laid another trail of smoke floats. By the time a trail of ten had been dropped, Wooley had a close enough idea of the position of his quarry to deliver an attack. At precisely 100mph he followed the trail of smoke floats, flying just 100 feet above the water. As the needle kicked to show they were passing over the U-boat, he hit the bomb release button. In quick succession, the three salvoes of retro-bombs – twenty-three in all, as one misfired – shot backwards along the launching rails and fell vertically into the sea.

The result was exciting to begin with, though something of an anti-climax in its results. Four of the bombs hit their target and exploded. Apart from telling the Germans that someone was looking for them, they did little lasting damage. Instead, the most obvious effect of the MAD attack was to warn the U-boat men they could expect something a lot more powerful before long. First in line was Lieutenant Baker in the second Catalina. Second were the Royal Navy destroyers. HMS *Wishart* had now picked up the echo and came in at high speed to drop a pattern of depth charges, followed by HMS *Anthony*.

If the U-boat men had congratulated themselves on escaping the retro-bombs without their boat being damaged, the conventional destroyer attack soon brought them back to the grim reality of what professional escort crews could deliver. In a series of powerful detonations, *U761* was turned in moments from an operational warship into a wreck. Her electrical system was shattered, with batteries, motors, radio, hydrophones and other equipment rendered useless. With the clutch connecting the diesels to the electric motors jammed, so she could not make her escape, water was seeping in through holes in the pressure hull and as the sea water reached the batteries, there were signs of chlorine gas.[9] There was little the crew could do but surface and abandon ship.

Three weeks later, the combination worked again. The crew of a US Navy B24 from VPB112 spotted a submarine periscope, and an echo was later picked up by a Leigh Light Wellington from Gibraltar. Three VP63 Madcats joined the search, and at 7.53am one picked up the signature of the type VII U-boat *U392* creeping eastwards through the straits. The PBY called in two more VP63 aircraft, and all three trailed their target with smoke floats and sonobuoys (air-dropped expendable hydrophones that could be used to track the progress of a submerged submarine, though these early models were relatively crude). After losing and retrieving the trace, all three aircraft attacked in succession.

Type XIV tanker U-boat. Known to submariners as *Milchkuhe*, or 'Milk Cows' these were specially capacious boats loaded with extra fuel, torpedoes and food to replenish the stocks of the operational boats and enable them to stay on patrol for longer. However, the signals they sent to organise rendezvous points and the time taken for their large hulls to submerge in an emergency made them fatally vulnerable to air attack.

(Author's drawing)

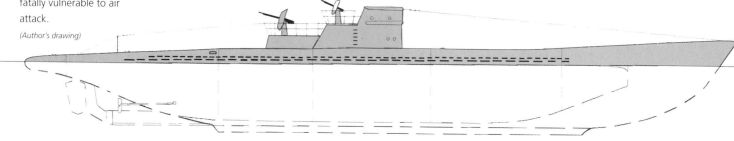

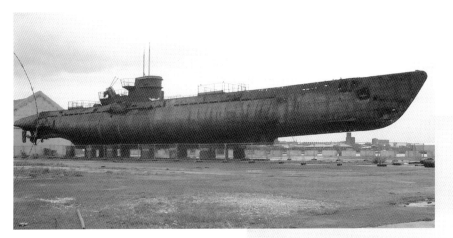

LEFT This type IX *U534* was sunk by Allied aircraft off the Danish coast in the last days of the war, and raised and brought to Birkenhead in England to be put on display. Currently her fate remains uncertain as the Trust maintaining her has gone into liquidation.

(Author's photo)

BELOW Eloquent testimony to the power of air-dropped depth charges – the pressure hull of *U534's* starboard quarter, forced inwards by the blasts which finally sank her.

(Author's photo)

RIGHT The silhouette of *U534* stands against the docks which handled the merchant ships she once hunted in the open Atlantic.

(Author's photo)

The destroyer HMS *Vanoc* reported that each salvo of retro-bombs produced two or three distinct explosions showing direct hits, followed by louder explosions some half a minute later, which were probably the remaining retro-bombs detonating as they hit the seabed. Once again, the surface escorts decided the issue once and for all. *Vanoc* and the DDE HMS *Affleck* used depth-charge attacks and Hedgehog salvoes to blow the damaged submarine to pieces and she sank with her entire crew.

Almost two months later, on 15 May 1944, VP63 struck again,[10] picking up a MAD contact at 3.20am. After twenty minutes, two PBYs dropped retro-bombs, and wood fragments floated to the surface, and their sonobuoys detected underwater noises. The aircraft radioed the position of the submarine to HMS *Kilmarnock*, which then made a Hedgehog attack, causing oil and bubbles to come to the surface. This was the type VIIC *U731*, on its way into the Mediterranean, also lost with all hands. Five days later, U-boat Command cancelled orders for any more submarines to go through the straits because of these losses.

VP63's hat trick was a dramatic setback for Doenitz's reluctant attempt to boost U-boat numbers in the Mediterranean. Even though the retro-bomb salvoes had not sunk the U-boats on their own, on at least two occasions they had provided the trigger for the killer punch from the surface escorts. In post-war years, when magnetic anomaly detection was refined to cover longer ranges and given potentially much more powerful weapons, MAD could have proved to be one of the most effective airborne ASW techniques of all.

Sadly, the lack of U-boats trying to force the straits removed the best opportunity for VP63 to find and attack more U-boats in such a favourable location. Only on the last day of April 1945, in the dying hours of the conflict, would the unit add another to their score. A PBY was patrolling southwest of Ushant in the approaches to the English Channel, when the crew spotted a plume of white spray thought to be produced by a schnorkel head at a range of two miles at 6.08pm. This time, they would need no markers to plot the course of their U-boat.

They attacked from the stern of the boat to the bow, at 100 feet. As they passed over the U-boat the planes picked up a strong MAD signal, and dropped three salvos of retro-bombs. As they flew back over the spot, no further MAD traces resulted, but a few minutes later oil and debris bubbled up to the surface. The aircraft laid a wide pattern of sonobuoys, but no more sounds were picked up. Finally the 1st Escort Group arrived, took oil samples and picked up a sonar contact lying on the sea bed, the last resting place of type VIIC *U*1055, sunk on her second patrol from Bergen, and the last German submarine to be sunk by Coastal Command's 19 Group in the whole of the war.

In terms of its effect on the U-boat men, wartime magnetic anomaly detection had one advantage and one closely allied drawback. Until the retro-bombs hit the pressure hull and detonated, there was none of the morale-sapping sense of approaching doom that submarine crews had to endure in a creeping depth-charge attack. Only if they had spotted the approaching aircraft and dived to safety would they even suspect they were being hunted. Even then, wartime MAD interceptions were so relatively rare that the absence of depth-charge explosions would convince the crew they might have made a successful escape.

The opposite end of the threat spectrum was that an attack by an aircraft armed with rockets usually rendered even the most courageous and experienced submariners almost helpless. Stealth and evasive action were useless. Their only tactic was to fire all anti-aircraft weapons as accurately as possible to put the attacking aircraft off its aim and to cause it to run out of its limited supply of ammunition. Soon, even this forlorn hope would be banished by a yet more powerful new weapon.

This was the deadly Mark XVIII or 'Tsetse' Mosquito. The twin-engined de Havilland Mosquito was the first true multi-role combat aircraft, designed and developed in the face of supreme official indifference, verging on hostility. Because of a chronic shortage of aircraft alloys, the de Havilland company could only bid for a contract to produce a light, fast reconnaissance bomber by designing an aircraft made mostly from wood. Its structure was made up of box sections and a stressed skin in a complex three-layer sandwich of tough marine plywood protecting a centre of soft but exceedingly light balsa wood. By the time of its design, the Rolls Royce Merlin engine that powered the RAF's Spitfires and Hurricanes (and later the Lancaster bomber and the USAAF's P51 Mustangs) had proved its reliability and was becoming more plentiful, so the new design was built around a pair of them, one on each wing.

It went into production in July 1941 as the Mosquito Mark IV bomber, which could lift 2,000 pounds of bombs (one-third of the maximum bomb-load of the B17). It had a ceiling of 36,000 feet, could cruise at 315mph for up to 3,500 miles and had a flat-out speed of 425mph at 30,500 feet – faster than most enemy fighters, which meant no need for defensive armament.[11] Performance on this scale was the Mosquito's trump card. The bomber version was given

a bigger bomb bay, to carry the 4,000-pound RAF 'cookie' for blowing large buildings apart. Another variant flew high-speed photo-reconnaissance missions for both the RAF and the US 8th Air Force, and yet another became a highly effective night fighter.

Mosquitoes delivered precision attacks on individual targets, bombing from treetop level in broad daylight. Two flew all the way to Berlin without fighter escort to bomb the broadcasting studios at 11.00am on 30 January 1943 to disrupt a speech by Luftwaffe commander Hermann Goering. Others wrecked Gestapo headquarters in Holland, Denmark and France, and a larger force smashed the guards' barracks and the outer wall of Amiens Prison to allow captured Resistance agents to escape to freedom.[12]

In June 1941, official approval was given for a fighter version and the first long-range fighter/intruders, combining the functions of fighters and bombers in one compact airframe also provided the basis for anti-shipping versions. These could put down a devastating barrage as an overture to a rocket attack, to knock out the target's anti-aircraft fire with four 20-mm cannon and a quartet of machine guns in the nose of the aircraft.

The Mosquito would approach its target at around 2,000 feet, and the pilot would pitch the plane forward into a 45-degree dive. He would open fire with machine guns at 1,500 feet and with cannon at 1,000 feet, before easing out of the dive and letting go the rockets at 500 feet. Following the flight of the tracer bullets and cannon shells made it easier to aim for a direct hit with the rockets.

The final logical step in making the Mosquito's bite as lethal as possible was to replace the four 20-mm cannon with a single 57-mm anti-tank gun. In the Mark XVIII 'Tsetse' version (named after the African fly responsible for sleeping sickness), which appeared in October 1943, the cannon was modified to fire a solid 6-pound shot once every second and a half. The gun had a maximum range of more than a mile, well outside the range of the U-boat's own anti-aircraft weapons, but if the Mosquito could approach within 1,000 yards of its target, it was powerful enough to punch a series of holes right through the pressure hull.

Here the tactics were slightly different. The pilot approached the submarine at around 5,000 feet, and then dived at around 30 degrees in an absolutely straight line – if the aircraft drifted even slightly, the gun tended to jam. Provided it worked properly, a single short burst could turn a fighting and still formidable submarine into a leaking and helpless hulk in seconds, unable to dive to safety or to evade further attacks. Even if the Mosquito missed on its opening attack, there was enough ammunition for another pass, and another, until the U-boat was crippled or sunk.[13]

So far as existing convoy battles were concerned, this arsenal of anti-submarine weapons provided the

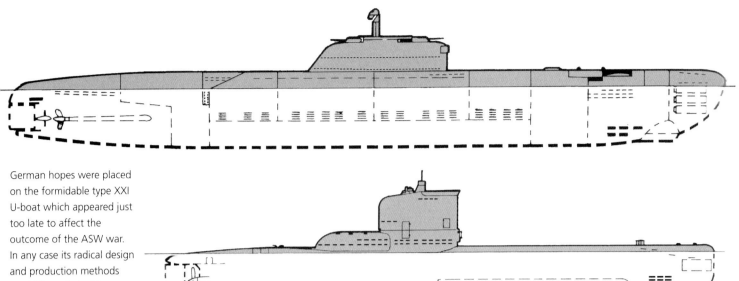

German hopes were placed on the formidable type XXI U-boat which appeared just too late to affect the outcome of the ASW war. In any case its radical design and production methods would have limited its usefulness even if it had appeared earlier.

(Author's drawing)

The type XXIII coastal submarine, with a remarkable performance but too small a weapons load to present a serious threat.

(Author's drawing)

strongest argument for the U-boat crews to leave enemy shipping well alone. But at the very time when air power seemed to have them at its mercy, the next stage of the war threatened to hand the German submarine force one last opportunity. The whole Atlantic battle had been fought to keep Britain fed and armed, but the ultimate objective was to make it possible for the Allies to land in Occupied France and finally defeat the still-formidable German Army. This would call for huge numbers of ships in narrow and confined waters vulnerable to submarine attack.

Everyone knew the landings were coming, but not exactly where or when. Summer 1944 became clear favourite, and the confined waters between the southern coast of England and the northern coast of France the chosen arena. Once the invasion armada was launched, the Germans planned to send every available U-boat to inflict all the damage they could. Some would sail northwards from the French bases, others westwards from Norway and the German homeland. While much of the Allied defences would depend on surface warships, much would be expected from the airborne weapons and tactics that had proved decisive in the Bay of Biscay and the Atlantic. Could they prevent the invasion being thrown off balance at its most vulnerable time, as the leading troops were storming their way ashore?

The chief problem was the western opening to the Channel. The narrow and relatively shallow Dover Straits at the eastern end could be blocked by dense minefields and surface escort forces, and were extremely dangerous waters for U-boats in any case. But the opposite end of the invasion coast opened into a much wider area, much more difficult to seal against determined submarine assault. Allied intelligence estimated the Kriegsmarine might have as many

as eighty type VII U-boats available in France and the Western Approaches, and up to three-quarters of these might be sent into the Channel during the first few days of the landings.

On the face of it, any torpedo launched from a U-boat in the invasion area was almost bound to hit a valuable target. On the other hand, the confines of that target area also worked in the Allies' favour. This would be like a convoy battle on a large scale, since the U-boats could do nothing without approaching dangerously close to the defences.

For conventional U-boats, this would have been virtually impossible. Surfacing to recharge batteries would mean they would be sunk as soon as they emerged from the depths. Only those boats equipped with schnorkel could possibly survive a difficult and uncomfortable trip to reach their targets. The brutal realities of the situation were spelled out in an often-quoted signal from U-boat headquarters to the commanding officers of the boats involved:

… every enemy vessel supporting the landing, even though it may be carrying only 50 men or a tank, is a target. Press home your attack, even at the cost of your boat. Should it be necessary to close the enemy landing fleet, pay no regard to the danger of shallow water, mines or other hazards.

Each soldier and weapon destroyed before reaching the beachhead diminishes the enemy's chance of victory.

A U-boat which inflicts losses on the invasion forces fulfils her highest mission and justifies her existence, even though she herself may be destroyed …[14]

Thanks to a cunning and effective deception campaign, the Allies achieved complete surprise with the initial landings. The two principal German commanders were away on leave: Rommel celebrating his wife's birthday at the family home near Ulm, and Doenitz holidaying in the Black Forest. Many army commanders were attending a war-game exercise based on the unlikely (to them) assumption that the Allies had landed in Normandy. But the dispositions of the U-boat fleet had already been set out, to be put into effect once the alarms were sounded.

The *Landwirt* group included all the forty-nine type VIIC submarines in the Biscay bases, thirty-five of which were ready to sail, and the *Mitte* group numbered twenty-one boats based in central and southern Norway. But, thanks to heavy Allied bombing, only eight *Landwirt* boats and five *Mitte* boats had been fitted with schnorkel. Without this additional advantage, attacks were almost certain to be one-way trips. To ensure this was the case, Allied air crews had to cover some 20,000 square miles of sea from the southern Irish coast to the northwestern coast of France and eastwards into the Channel to the narrows between the Isle of Wight and the Cotentin peninsula, at the western end of the invasion beaches. There were twenty-five squadrons with a total of 350 aircraft, but careful tactical planning was needed to create a reliable safety cordon.

The basic objective was to keep thirty aircraft on patrol over this huge expanse of sea at any time. A series of rectangular boxes were drawn up, each representing the area that could be covered by one patrol aircraft of a given type in thirty minutes, using its particular variant of radar. These boxes of different sizes were fitted into an overall pattern like pieces of a vast jigsaw covering the whole area. The result was that any U-boat surfacing anywhere to recharge batteries or replenish its air supply would have only a maximum of half an hour before being spotted and attacked. Because the idea was to impose a bottleneck to keep U-boats out of the Channel, these patrols were known as 'Cork' patrols and they proved extremely effective.[15]

Just how effective was shown by a small British submarine, HMS *Viking*, ordered to run the gauntlet of the patrols on the night of 6 April 1944. With an hour and a half head start while fog blanketed the airfields and delayed the patrols, she was soon hunted to exhaustion. In twenty-eight hours, she could only surface briefly nine times in the gap between one patrol and the next. The total time was some two hours, far too short to recharge the batteries, and she finally had to abandon the test five miles short of her objective.

So it proved for the U-boats. When the *Landwirt* group headed for Normandy the night after the landings, air patrols spotted twenty-two boats, and attacked seven of them. Two of these were sunk and

four damaged so severely that they were forced back to base. One more was too slow in diving at daybreak and was caught by two Tsetse Mosquito XVIIIs. Before she could dive to safety, 57-mm anti-tank rounds had punched holes in her tanks, letting in six tons of water and forcing her to follow the rest back to port.

Those evading the patrols on the first night were closer to their targets by the second night, but the end result was the same. A Liberator crew from 224 Squadron Coastal Command found and sank two U-boats in half an hour – one lost with all hands, the other leaving forty-four survivors. Others were forced to return to base, one was damaged by another Tsetse Mosquito and later sunk with depth charges, and finally *U441* was caught and sunk in clear moonlight by an aircraft with radar failure but a keen-eyed crew.

U-boats trying to reach the invasion from Norway faced a similar fate. On two occasions, schnorkel-equipped boats were attacked, and the small remnant that evaded the air patrols met the fury of the escort groups patrolling off the landing beaches. The final account was deeply discouraging for the U-boats. Out of some 7,000 ships, from warships to landing craft and supply ships, they sank two frigates, HMS *Blackwood* and HMS *Mourne,* one tank landing craft *LST*280, and three Liberty ships off the English coast, with another heavily damaged. The cost to Doenitz's submariners was a dozen U-boats sunk in the Channel or the approaches to the Biscay bases, and another thirteen in more distant waters. Such an unequal exchange in waters abounding with targets was ample proof that the anti-submarine war was all but won by the Allies.

The basic limitations of what was still a submersible rather than a true submarine had been cruelly exposed in the confined waters around the invasion fleet, to an even greater extent than in the trackless waters of the open Atlantic, and the titanic struggle was now almost at an end. By 15 September 1944, with Allied armoured spearheads hounding the *Wehrmacht* back to the German border, it was clear that the last great effort of Doenitz's men had failed. Despite a horrific loss rate of U-boat crewmen of 75 per cent, they had failed to prevent the triumph of the Allied air and naval forces, and it was time to acknowledge that unpalatable fact, however reluctantly.

Our U-boat effort in the Channel is thereby terminated, and the old fighting spirit of the U-boat arm has again magnificently stood the test. A comprehensive survey of operations shows that, contrary to our initial misgivings and the doubts that assailed us during the course of the operations, we were right in employing the U-boats. Considering the extremely difficult operating conditions, the results achieved were good and losses tolerable, though heavy. Despite the fact that our blow at the enemy's supplies

was indecisive, it was certainly severe and helped relieve pressure on our troops ashore. Besides achieving tangible results, we also gained experience and knowledge of continuously submerged U-boat warfare which will be of great value, particularly for the new-type boats. We also tied down considerable sea and air escort forces, which would otherwise have been able for purposes such as the disruption of our supply traffic off the Dutch and Norwegian coasts, as well as for intensive air attacks on our lines of communication on the Western Front. Results would have been better and losses certainly lighter, had the boats been possessed of higher submerged speed and a greater endurance; the fact that these very qualities have been highly developed in the new-type boats gives us good hope for the future.[16]

A final effort against merchant ships around the British coast in September sank eight freighters, two warships and a small tug for the price of six boats, a terrible price by the standards of 1942 but one now considered not only acceptable but actually encouraging. Just one advance worked to the U-boats' advantage. At last they had a reliable radar-search receiver able to pick up

Close up of the nose gun, backed up by four machine guns, and the anti-tank shell fired by the 57mm cannon which could penetrate a U-boat's pressure hull. (*Philip Jarrett*)

centimetric radar transmissions. This not only meant that U-boats would be aware of the approach of a radar-equipped aircraft, but they could pick up these transmissions at a range where the aircraft could not pick up the radar echo (or the visual sighting) of the schnorkel head itself.

Apart from the alarm call of a torpedo hit, which gave the nearest escort group a positive point from which to start their search and destroy mission, the truth was that the situation was becoming a stalemate. Escorts could not find and sink U-boats in confined inshore locations unless they launched an attack. But because the U-boats had to stay submerged most of the time, they were simply not finding targets worth the expenditure of their torpedoes, let alone the lethal attacks that would inevitably follow. Further analysis by Doenitz's staff showed that targets often passed while boats were resting on the seabed and were only heard over hydrophones when the ships were over-head, and it was too late to rise to periscope depth to mount an attack. Doenitz then ordered boats to

stay at periscope depth during daylight to watch for potential targets, they then still saw so little that luck played a huge part.

In the five months from the beginning of November 1944, a total of 101 sorties were mounted to British waters. Between them they sank a total of thirty-seven merchant vessels, many of them small coasters, and five small warships. This cost the Germans no less than fifty U-boats, a rate that was completely unsustainable. By the closing weeks of the war, all that remained was a final gesture to point to the achievements of the past.

A scratch patrol line of seven type IX U-boats was assembled, under the nostalgic title of *Gruppe Seewolf*: *U*518, *U*546, *U*805, *U*858, *U*880, *U*881 and *U*1235. They were ordered to rendezvous in the open Atlantic more than 600 miles north of the Azores and to patrol to the westwards in a north–south line, using schnorkels during daylight to look for Allied convoys. The plan was doomed from the start. The Allies were now reading Enigma decrypts of U-boat signals on a routine basis, and knew exactly where the U-boats were, and what they were looking for. They diverted the convoys out of danger well to the south and sent heavy escort forces, including four US Navy carrier task groups, to take their place.

Four days after the U-boats began their sweep on 11 April 1945, the carrier groups found them. Over the next three and a half weeks, all but two of the group were sunk by US Navy ships and aircraft. All they achieved was the sinking of the DDE USS *Frederick C Davis* by blowing her stern off with a homing torpedo, and a failed attack on USS *Card*.

All this time the Germans knew nothing of the fate of the group, and were still sending orders even after most had been sunk. Finally, on 6 May another type IX under separate orders from the *Seewolf* group was found off Block Island, south of Cape Cod on the American coast. She had sunk a collier and the resulting alarm brought no less than eleven warships from destroyers to corvettes to join the attack. One frigate concentrated on maintaining sonar contact, while others formed a line to prevent the submarine from escaping into the relative safety of deeper water. Then a destroyer escort delivered a Hedgehog and depth-charge attack, and the two ships then reversed roles until the ensuing attacks produced oil leaks and items of clothing and equipment.

Two airships with MAD gear confirmed the presence of the U-boat's hull on the shallow seabed. When a diver went down to check, he found the U-boat was split open, with the bodies of her crew strewn about the site. And so perished the last German submarine destroyed by American anti-submarine forces in the Second World War. Following this, the surrender of the remaining *Seewolf* boats, part of the general U-boat capitulation, was ample recompense for all the effort, all the casualties and all

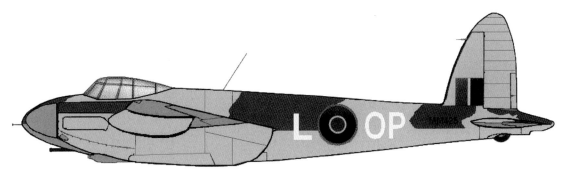

Even more deadly was the Mark XVIII 'Tsetse' Mosquito armed with a 57mm anti-tank gun in the nose of the aircraft. This aircraft from 618 Squadron sank the type VIIC *U*976 as it was returning to Saint Nazaire escorted by a destroyer and two minesweepers on 25 March 1944.

(Author's drawing)

Mark XVIII 'Tsetse' Mosquito in flight.

(Philip Jarrett)

the hard fighting of a long and bitter campaign.

In the three years from the outbreak of war to September 1942, including the first 'Happy Time', the figures confirm these conclusions. To the end of 1941, some 900 convoys crossed the Atlantic. In only nineteen cases were losses truly heavy, defined as six or more merchant ships sunk. In all, only 2 per cent of merchant ships – 1 in 50 – heading for British ports failed to arrive because of U-boat attack.[17] Granted, losses in men, material and ships were grievous and the fighting cruel, but on this evidence it seems clear that German war aims could never have been realised. Moreover, this would have remained materially unchanged, even if their hopes of more formidable submarines in larger numbers had actually come to pass.

On the eve of the German surrender, Doenitz ordered all U-boats to cease attacks. Plans were laid for a mass scuttling of all submarines in the Wagnerian traditions of the German Navy, but in this case the intention was partly thwarted. Under the surrender terms, U-boats were ordered to sail to Allied ports,

flying plain black flags. Only 174 did so. The remaining 222 went to the bottom at the hands of their crews and commanders.

Doenitz's final valediction stressed the courage of his men without dwelling on the reasons for their defeat.

My U-boat men!

Six years of war lie behind you. You have fought like lions. An overwhelming material superiority has driven us into a tight corner from which it is no longer possible to continue the war. Unbeaten and unblemished, you lay down your arms after a heroic fight without parallel. We proudly remember our fallen comrades who gave their lives for Führer and fatherland. Comrades, preserve that spirit in which you have fought so long and so gallantly for the sake of the future of the fatherland. Long live Germany !

Your Grand Admiral

Last act in the Atlantic battle. The type IXC/40 *U*889 surrenders to Canadian warships off the coast of Nova Scotia on 13 May 1945.

(National Library of Canada)

The truth was rather different. Driving the U-boats into a tight corner, in the sense of overrunning their bases, may have owed much to the Allied material superiority, but in spite of the Germans' undoubted heroism, they had been well and truly beaten long before that. Not by the Allies having more ships, more men, or more weapons, but by the overwhelming superiority in their tactics and their technology, and how they put those ships, those men and those weapons to the best and most effective use.

The Type XXI U-boat *U*2540 was, like many of her fellows, scuttled at the end of the war. In 1955 she was raised and put back into service as the *Wilhelm Bauer* as an experimental boat for the Federal German Navy.

(www.navyphotos.co.uk)

CHAPTER 15

JAPANESE CATASTROPHE

1941–44

The battered wreck of the Japanese submarine *I1* being examined by a team of US intelligence experts landed from a PT boat off the coast of Guadalcanal.

(US National Archives)

O<small>N</small> the evening of 29 January 1943, submarine *I1* of the Imperial Japanese Navy was creeping at periscope depth through the Sealark Channel off Kamimbo Bay, close to Cape Esperance on the northern coast of Guadalcanal. The island had been the scene of an epic struggle for supremacy between Japanese and American troops for possession of the Solomon Islands. More than five months of fierce fighting had caused terrible loss of life. Slowly but inexorably the American grip had tightened, and so many Japanese supply ships had been sunk by American aircraft that two months earlier, the emperor had ordered that the submarines of the 6th Fleet should be modified for new duties. They would be used to deliver essential supplies on to the beaches still held by Japanese forces, running the gauntlet of reefs and Allied warships to do so.

I1 was hardly ideal for the job. She was the first of four large Junsen oceangoing submarines built by Kawasaki of Kobe between 1926 and 1929. She measured 320 feet from stem to stern and displaced 2,791 tons submerged, much bigger and heavier compared with the Kriegsmarine's largest type IX U-boat, which measured 250 feet long and displaced a mere 870 tons. This was partly due to a double hull construction, with the main pressure hull surrounded by a thinner outer hull, and the intervening space filled with water at the same pressure as that outside. Her speed was almost identical to the type IX at eighteen knots on the surface and eight submerged, but her original deck armament was much heavier, two single 5.5-inch guns rather than a single 4.1-inch mounting, and her safe diving depth of 265 feet was only around a third that of the German boat.

This meant that, like most of the larger Japanese boats, she was slow to dive and difficult to manoeuvre, and she could not escape the enemy by diving deep. Because the Imperial Navy had intended their submarines for attacking enemy warships, little or no attention had been paid to surviving anti-submarine attacks. Fortunately, her war service so far had been relatively uneventful. She had been sent to watch the approaches to Pearl Harbor during the original Japanese air attack, but had been allocated the outermost position off the island of Kauai, where she was left largely undisturbed. On 11 January 1942, she was assigned to a new patrol area, 500 miles southwest of Pearl Harbor, but because of problems with her diesels, she had to be replaced by *I9*, which became famous in Japan for torpedoing the carrier U<small>SS</small> *Saratoga*.

Later, *I1* had taken part in the invasion of the Dutch East Indies as part of Submarine Group C (Hei). She had originally been stationed along the eastern coast of the island of Celebes and had then patrolled between Java and Australia without any success. Early in 1942, the submarine was ordered to patrol off the northwestern Australian coast where, on 3 March, her lookouts sighted smoke from the 8,667-ton Dutch freighter *Siantar* en route from Tjilatjap in Java to Australia. The *I1* dived and fired a spread of torpedoes, all of which missed their target. The submarine then surfaced and opened fire with the 5.5-inch deck gun. Though the merchant ship fired back, *I1*'s heavy gun scored between thirty and forty hits and set the steamer ablaze. The *I1* fired a last torpedo and the steamer finally sank some six hundred miles off Shark Bay. This remained *I1*'s only success.

After a patrol supporting the Japanese campaign in the Aleutian Islands in the northern Pacific, *I1* returned to Yokosuka dockyard, where she had her aft 5.5-inch gun mounting replaced by fittings for carrying a 46-foot landing barge, to be used in resupply operations. In October 1942, she evacuated Japanese troops from Goodenough Island in the Admiralties to Rabau; at the end of the month her captain, Commander Eitaro Ankyo was diagnosed with dengue fever and he was replaced by Lieutenant Commander Eiichi Sakamoto. Finally, the *I1* was sent to carry out a resupply mission for the beleaguered Japanese garrisons on Guadalcanal. On 10 January 1943 she picked up her landing barge at the Japanese base on the island of Truk. Arriving at Rabaul ten days later, she was loaded with rice, bean paste, curry, ham and sausages, all packed into rubber containers and loaded into the barge.

Finally, early on 29 January, she entered Kamimbo Bay off the northern tip of Guadalcanal, diving to avoid the fast US PT-boats making regular sweeps of the area. As she approached the shore through heavy rain squalls, the *I1* failed to spot two Royal New Zealand Navy warships, HMNZS *Kiwi* and HMNZS *Moa*. These were small 600-ton corvettes, classified officially as minesweeping trawlers. Each one was less than half the size of the *I1* and armed only with depth charges and a single 4-inch gun, but they packed a punch totally out of keeping with their small size. Now *I1* would pay dearly for her inexperience of modern anti-submarine warfare.

At 9.05am, the officer manning *Kiwi*'s Asdic set, Sub-Lieutenant D H Graham, picked up a contact at 3,000 yards, the set's maximum range. As the range closed, it became possible to see the submarine's silhouette, outlined in brilliant phosphorescence, below the surface, and *Kiwi* dropped a pattern of six depth charges at shallow settings. The power of the explosions wrecked *I1*'s port electric motor, all her lighting failed and she began taking on water aft. She plunged down towards the seabed and finally hit bottom at 595 feet, more than twice her test depth, violently enough to damage her forward torpedo compartments. Another pattern of six depth charges shook the submarine violently, and it became obvious that her attackers knew exactly where she was. Reluctantly, her skipper decided to fight it out on the surface and try to escape.

As the battered submarine emerged from the

The American carrier USS *Yorktown*, sunk by a Japanese submarine after the battle of Midway.

(The Floating Drydock)

The American carrier USS *Saratoga*, which survived being torpedoed twice by Japanese submarines. On each occasion she was able to return safely to port for repairs to be carried out.

(The Floating Drydock)

depths, both attackers opened fire with their 4-inch guns. Under return fire from *I1*'s massive 5.5-inch gun, *Moa* fired starshell to illuminate the scene as *Kiwi* steamed in to ram the submarine. As *I1* swung to starboard, running at eleven knots under one of her diesels, *Kiwi* collided with her pressure hull just aft of the conning tower and bounced off the thick plating. She turned and tried again, knocking several of the submarine crew overboard. As she backed away a second time, her gunners turned their fire on to the supply barge, setting it ablaze, and then shifted their aim to cut down the submarine's captain and the crew of the 5.5-inch gun.

The *Kiwi* rammed the *I1* a third time, and two of the submarine's officers, the first lieutenant and the navigating officer, armed with samurai swords, tried to scramble aboard their attacker. Only the navigator, an expert Kendo third-dan swordsman, managed to make the jump, but the corvette's rail was too high so he was left hanging from it, sword waving helplessly as the two ships separated. Meanwhile the first lieutenant took command of the submarine and ran *I1* hard aground on a submerged reef close to the shore, more than two hours after the attack began. By then, the *Kiwi*'s gun barrel was too hot to continue firing, and *Moa* was driven out to sea by gunfire from Japanese army artillery on the island.

Two-thirds of the submarine's eighty-one crew survived the attack and managed to scramble ashore, carrying the boat's vital current code-books, which they destroyed to avoid capture by the Allies. But when US divers inspected the wreck, they found immensely valuable material, including the past and future codes, charts, manuals, the ship's log and other secret documents. The Japanese changed the current code settings, but continued to use the existing code, even though they were certainly aware of the dangers.

Later they made several attempts to destroy the wreck. Four days after the battle, five members of the crew with eleven Japanese soldiers tried to set off a pair of depth charges, but the explosion failed to destroy the boat.

Eight days later, the Japanese sent an air strike of dive bombers with fighter escort to bomb the remains. Though they scored a direct hit close to the conning tower, the boat remained largely intact. Finally, her sister boat, *I2*, was sent to the spot with *I1*'s first lieutenant as guide, but on two visits they failed to find her in the dark. At last, on 1 April 1943, her number was taken off the official list of the Imperial Japanese Navy.

In fact, the inglorious loss of the *I1* summed up the Pacific anti-submarine war surprisingly well. Remarkably, neither side originally profited from the German experience in the previous war, and the lessons it should have made clear to everyone. The Germans knew from the beginning of the Second World War that the primary objective for their U-boat fleet was to sink merchant ships and cripple the supply lines carrying troops, weapons, stores, ammunition, food and fuel to Britain, rather than trying to sink warships. In the Pacific, on the other hand, both the Americans and the Japanese decided the most urgent priority was to use their boats against the enemy navy. In the case of the US Navy, the preferred strategy was to send their long-range submarines all the way to the major Japanese naval bases and there to set up an effective blockade to sink as many Japanese warships as possible.

Japanese theory was slightly different. In the sense that all navies tend to become the victims of their successes and failures in earlier conflicts, they were obsessed with their victory over the Russian fleet at Tsushima in 1905, which first proclaimed the professionalism of the Imperial Japanese Navy on the world stage. In that case, the enemy had made a marathon journey all the way from European waters right around the globe to meet the bitterness of defeat on Japan's doorstep. If the Russian fleet had thought it worthwhile to do that with small and slow warships, it seemed to Japanese commanders that the more powerful American fleet must have a similar objective once war began.

The Japanese planned to operate unrestricted submarine warfare from the first day of hostilities, but then ordered submarine commanders that merchant ships were the lowest priority as potential targets, worth a single torpedo at most. Instead, they proposed to threaten American bases in the Philippines to persuade the numerically stronger US Navy to send its battle fleet out across the Pacific to fight them.[1] Ranks of powerful battleships with a twenty-one-knot top speed would need to be attacked all the way across the ocean, so enough of their strength could be whittled away before the fleets met on a more equal basis, when Japanese ingenuity and fighting spirit could triumph against a weakened enemy.

It seemed logical enough, and Japanese submarines were designed with this exact role in mind. Apart from the smaller boats produced for coastal defence, the rest were intended for fleet operations. Consequently they carried heavy armament and several were equipped to carry seaplanes to help search for the approaching US fleet. Virtues like long-range, high surface speed and powerful torpedo armament were seen as essential for their role. The ability to survive attacks from enemy anti-submarine forces by making them manoeuvrable under water and able to dive to great depths to avoid destruction was seen as irrelevant in the kind of fast-moving fight they expected. Yet the experience of their German allies showed that virtues like these made all the difference between death and survival.

This kind of naval myth was proof even against logical thinking. The Japanese eagerly adopted naval aviation, with a powerful fleet of fast carriers, carrying modern aircraft and highly trained crews, but they still insisted that the battleship held pride of place in naval warfare. So when the dive bombers, torpedo bombers and escort fighters returned from Pearl Harbor to report the damage they had inflicted on the warships moored along Battleship Row, their jubilation was complete. The fact that the truly vital American carriers were at sea and missed the attack seemed to escape them, even though those carriers, every bit as formidable as their own strike force, would change the entire balance of the war in the Pacific in five minutes at the climax of the Battle of Midway the following summer.

Instead, this failure of the US fleet to behave as the Japanese predicted had left their submarine force without a primary role. Instead of ranks of ponderous battleships, heavily protected by cruisers and destroyers, Japanese submarines found they were up against much faster and more elusive carrier groups, and their few successes in the early phase of the war were too few to affect the outcome. It was only thanks to their speed, their long range and their deadly torpedoes – the submarine Mark 95 version of the Long Lance oxygen- and paraffin-powered weapons used by the Japanese surface ships to such deadly effect – that individual submarines were sometimes able to strike lucky. Simply by being in the right place at the right time, they often finished off a damaged warship lacking its normal defences of speed, manoeuvrability or heavy escorts.

For example, on 9 January 1942, just over a month after the attack on Pearl Harbor, *I18* reported seeing an American carrier with a cruiser and an escort of two destroyers to the west of Johnston Island, but had lost contact before she could deliver an attack. The Japanese formed a picket line of submarines southeast of Pearl Harbor, and for once the tactic worked as it was intended to. *I6*, the third boat from the northern end of the line, spotted their quarry two days later and succeeded in working into a favourable attack position

The pre-war American destroyer uss *MacDonough* escorted the carrier *Saratoga* in the Guadalcanal campaign and carried out ASW escort duties for US warships and supply vessels for most of the Pacific war.

(The Floating Drydock)

Quick reaction: US warships carry out an ASW hunt in Ulithi lagoon on 20 November 1944 following the sinking of an auxiliary by a Japanese submarine.
(US National Archives)

in spite of her low underwater speed. She was finally able to fire a spread of torpedoes at this prime target at an astonishing range of more than two miles. She then dived to avoid the inevitable depth-charge attack which, when it came, pounded the submarine mercilessly. Nonetheless, while sinking into the depths, the crew had heard two distinct explosions.

When finally the attack ended and they were able to surface, the crew of the *I6* found there was no sign of the ship they had attacked and they reported they had sunk an American carrier. In fact the ship they had torpedoed was the USS *Saratoga*, suffering a hit in one of her boiler rooms, but she had survived and managed to reach port for repairs. However, *I6*'s efforts had left the Americans with just three carriers operating in the Pacific, although there had been innumerable opportunities to catch one of the others on their way in or out of Pearl Harbor at the time.[2]

Nevertheless, there were several other occasions when Japanese submarines were able to do the job they were intended for, and sink major US warships. At the Battle of Midway, in June 1942, the carrier *Yorktown* had been virtually crippled by Japanese dive bombers, with engines put out of action and fires blazing below decks. Heroic efforts by her damage-control teams put out the fires and repaired the engines, so that she was able to steam at twenty knots and operate her fighters, until a second Japanese attack, this time by torpedo bombers, crippled her a second

time. Two torpedoes hit their target, the ship began to list and her crew was ordered to abandon her.

She was still afloat the following morning, and salvage teams went back on board to see if she could be brought back to Pearl Harbor for repairs to be carried out. Her luck finally ran out on the morning of 5 June when a floatplane from the Japanese heavy cruiser *Chikuma* spotted her and radioed the fleet. Orders were sent to the submarine *I168*, which had been carrying out a lone bombardment of Midway Island, to find and sink the carrier. Because of an incorrect position report (out by 9 degrees of latitude)[3] *I168* took a long time to track down her target, but on the morning of 6 June she found the carrier lying still in the water, with the destroyer USS *Hamann* alongside, providing power for the pumps keeping her afloat.

The submarine skipper, Lieutenant-Commander Yanachi Tanabe, took his time manoeuvring into a favourable firing position, and at 1.05pm – with the carrier beam on to his boat – fired a spread of four torpedoes. One of them ran shallower than the others and hit the *Hamann*, blowing her in half. The two halves sank quickly, setting off the depth charges on her stern, which killed many of the men in the water. The others hit the carrier, and she began to sink, so slowly that she only vanished beneath the surface at 6am the following morning.[4]

Worse was to come two months later. In August

Escort destroyers like the uss *Levy* had a vital role to play in the Pacific War too, though by the time she arrived in the operational area in August 1943, much of the Japanese submarine fleet was no longer a serious threat. She spent her time escorting transports and supply ships and bombarding Japanese held islands until at the very end of the war she accepted the Japanese surrender on Mili Atoll in the Marshall Islands, on 22 August 1945, and of Wake Island, one of the first US held bases to fall to the Japanese at the start of the Pacific War, on 3 September 1945, the day after the surrender ceremony in Tokyo Bay.

(US National Archives)

1942, at the start of the bitter fighting on Guadalcanal, seven large fleet submarines of the Imperial Navy's 1st Squadron of the 6th Submarine Fleet were ordered to form a picket line to the southeast of the island chain of the Solomons, across the route that US naval reinforcements and supply ships would have to take to reach the islands from their base at Espiritu Santo. Significantly, these boats had been recalled from a promising foray against Allied merchant ships in the Indian Ocean to carry out their primary responsibility, and they were reinforced by other large boats from the 3rd Submarine Squadron recalled from sinking merchant ships in the waters around Australia.

The numbers were sufficient to form two lines, one across the entrance to the island chain and another as an advance-warning picket 200 miles to the south of them. They patrolled up and down in their individual sectors at right angles to the predicted approach of the enemy, and at dawn those equipped with float-planes launched them to extend their range of vision. At last, on 31 August, *I26* sighted the recently repaired *Saratoga* at dawn, to the east of San Cristobal Island.

She managed to fire a full spread of six torpedoes, before an alert escort destroyer, the uss *MacDonough* spotted the torpedo tracks from just thirty yards away and, following them to their source, tried to ram her. The two were so close that the destroyer's hull actually scraped against that of the submarine as she plunged into the depths. So fierce were the destroyer's depth-charge attacks, lasting for four hours in all, that the submarine had no chance to verify whether or not the carrier had been sunk. In fact only one of

her torpedoes had hit the *Saratoga* at her after end. Once again she survived, but the US Navy was deprived of her value while she spent another three months in dry dock having repairs carried out.

On 15 September two US carrier groups, one based around the *Wasp*, the other around the *Hornet*, were escorting a convoy of troopships carrying the 7th Marine Regiment and its stores and supplies to Guadalcanal, when they too ran into the Japanese picket line. Commander Taikachi Kinashi of the *I19* spotted the *Wasp* in the early afternoon, when she and her escort group were eight miles away. Only when the American force made two alterations of course, designed to throw submarines off the scent, did he finally find himself within a thousand yards of his target, whereupon he fired a full spread of six torpedoes at her.

The *I19* had to dive deeply to avoid powerful anti-submarine attacks, but Kinashi thought he heard four explosions. In fact, three torpedoes hit the carrier, the uss *Wasp*, crippling her so severely that she later had to be torpedoed by US destroyers. The remaining torpedoes headed onwards, directly on course for another carrier group around her sister ship *Hornet* twelve miles away, and far beyond Kinashi's range of vision. Astonishingly, the Japanese type 95s continued running on course, and a lucky chance led to one impacting against the armoured hull of the new battleship uss *North Carolina*, putting her out of action for two months for repairs. Another lucky hit smashed into the destroyer *O'Brien*, causing massive damage. She was ordered to head back to the USA for heavy repairs but broke up and sank en route when her overstressed hull gave way on 19 October. Only the sixth torpedo ran its course without hitting anything. Kinashi himself knew nothing of this, and only a near neighbour from the picket line, the *I15*, was able to report that a badly damaged American aircraft carrier had sunk.[5]

Other Japanese submarine successes included the torpedoing of the heavy cruiser USS *Chester* by *I176*. The cruiser survived but had to return to the USA for repairs to be made. Less lucky was the USS *Juneau*, torpedoed by the *I26*, which hit her magazine, causing her to blow up and sink immediately, with heavy loss of life. Finally, in the closing weeks of the war, when the Japanese Navy was a truly spent force, the heavy cruiser USS *Indianapolis* was torpedoed midway between the Marianas and the Philippines. She was returning from a secret assignment delivering the components for the atomic bomb which would be dropped on Hiroshima to the air base on the island of Tinian.

Long before this, however, the advantage in the anti-submarine war had passed almost completely to the US Navy. Using the new purpose-built escort destroyers and powerful new weapons like Hedgehog, which in the clearer waters of the Pacific proved especially formidable, they hunted down Japanese submarines with chilling efficiency.

In early May 1944, the Imperial Navy set up a patrol line across the gap between the Admiralty Islands and the Carolines to watch for the approach of American warships. Because they picked up American signals reporting the presence of one of the patrol line, the rest were ordered to take up new positions and this signal was read in turn by the Americans, who sent a Solomons-based hunter-killer group of three escort destroyers to hunt them down.

On the afternoon of 19 May, USS *England* detected the echo of *I16* and made a series of Hedgehog attacks. The first salvo missed but the next two hit causing the submarine to explode violently, in the second successful Hedgehog attack in the Pacific. Three days later the group caught *RO106* on the surface charging batteries. She dived, they picked up her echo and *England* fired a Hedgehog salvo. The submarine exploded. Another RO class was spotted on the surface on the following day - USS *George* and USS *Raby* attacked without success, but the second Hedgehog salvo from the *England* sank her with all hands. A day later another surfaced Japanese submarine dived as the group approached, and USS *England*'s first attack sank her.

The group then returned to base to refuel and rearm, but en route they encountered the surfaced *RO108* at the southern tip of the patrol line. *Raby* attacked first and then *England* sank her with Hedgehog. When they returned to the fight on the 29 May they were ordered to join a nearby carrier group, whose escorts had flushed another submarine from the patrol line, the *RO105*. The submarine evaded a series of determined attacks, but on the following morning the *England* was called in and blew her to pieces with her first salvo, her sixth victim in less than two weeks.

This amazing achievement by a single ship, commanded by Lieutenant Commander W B Pendleton, showed the Japanese submarine arm was finally beaten. Yet it also made two crippling mistakes. From start to finish it failed to grasp the opportunity presented by the United States' complete dependence on shipping to transport its invasion forces from island to island, and to keep them supplied and reinforced during the long struggle across the ocean wastes of the Pacific, to the doorstep of Japan itself. Japanese submarines did sink merchant ships on occasion, but only as targets of opportunity when nothing more prestigious materialised, and in comparison with the sinkings of the U-boats, who were striving to win a real tonnage war, their successes were trivial. During the whole of 1942, when events were still largely moving in favour of Japan, and with the whole Pacific open before them, Japanese submarines sank little more than 100,000 tons of merchant shipping, less than a sixtieth of the tonnage sunk by the U-boats of Japan's allies in the same period.[6]

Much more surprising, in view of their involvement in the Atlantic battle, is the American failure to realise the equal vulnerability of their enemies. In one respect the USA moved quickly, declaring a policy of unrestricted submarine warfare throughout the Pacific within days of Pearl Harbor. Nevertheless so much time was wasted using the benefits of radio interception to try to track down and attack Japanese warships that in the first six months of the Pacific War, American submarines only sank thirty-five Japanese merchant vessels. German U-boats sank this number in weeks.

During the whole of 1942, the Americans sank some 700,000 tons of Japanese merchant ships, but the U-boats sank nearly ten times as much Allied shipping over the same period. More significantly for the Pacific campaign, Japan's own shipyards added another million tons to her merchant fleet, so that the net tonnage available to her actually increased by 300,000 tons. Even 1943 saw only a partial improvement in Allied results; US submarines were crippled for a long time by grossly unreliable torpedoes and over-cautious skippers – more than a third of them were eventually replaced by younger men. Following official reluctance to accept that anything was wrong with the torpedoes, the necessary modifications only brought about a real improvement by 1944. Even before this, Japanese merchant shipping tonnage sunk by US submarines doubled in 1943, though in tanker construction particularly, new construction outstripped losses.

CHAPTER 16

AMERICAN MAYHEM
1944–45

Just one of the vast number of Japanese merchant ships to fall victim to US submarines. The freighter *Sunko Maru* on her last plunge into the depths, seen through the periscope of uss *Skipjack*, the boat which sank her. (US National Archives)

AFTER neither side in the Pacific War had capitalised on the potential of their submarines to mount a trade war against their enemy, it was only in 1944 that the US submarine campaign really hit its stride, and when it did the Japanese had no effective reply. US boats had achieved some remarkable successes against major warships of the Imperial Navy. On 21 November 1944, for example, the uss *Sealion* torpedoed the battleship *Kongo* and one of her escorting destroyers off the northwestern coast of the island of Formosa. On 28 November, the uss *Archerfish* sank the huge Yamato-class battleship *Shinano*, undergoing her final sea trials after conversion to a much-needed major aircraft carrier. But during this same month, the Japanese submarines achieved little, except the loss of seven of their own dwindling numbers.[1]

In finally turning to attack the huge amount of supply traffic on which the Japanese island conquests were so dependent, the US Navy adopted wolf-pack tactics. Radio intelligence was used to find convoys, so that submarines could be sent where the traffic was at its densest; the greatest weakness that prevented the Imperial Navy countering this new American campaign was its own ignorance of modern ASW tactics.

Not so the US Navy. During the campaign to retake the Marianas campaign, American air and sea escorts destroyed no less than ten of the twenty-six submarines deployed by the Japanese in defence of their islands, and not one Allied ship was hit by a submarine's torpedo.[2] This was a remarkable tribute to the vigilance and efficiency of the escorts charged with the defence of the vast invasion fleet.

Compared with American efficiency in anti-submarine tactics, gained from experience against German U-boats, Japanese ASW proved largely a failure. Because their own submarines lacked the structural strength of German and American boats, they assumed that their own depth-charging of American targets was successful, with little or no supporting evidence. Sometimes, they did indeed sink enemy submarines, as US and British loss figures testify, but on other occasions the Japanese called off the hunt when more perseverance might have brought real success.

This was compounded by the mismanagement of the Japanese submarine force. At one time, they sent their best boats and most experienced skippers to carry out futile bombardments of the American, Canadian and Australian coasts, at great risk. They were forced to use submarines as gun platforms in the land campaign in operations like Guadalcanal, and then, as the tide of war began to run against Japan, they found they had to use the submarines to reinforce and resupply land garrisons. As it became more and more costly for surface ships to undertake these tasks, more and more work devolved on the submarines.

Only in mid-1942 was there a concerted Japanese

Searching for targets. A US Navy officer at the periscope of an American submarine in the Pacific.
(US National Archives)

Pacific sailed in escorted convoys from almost the very beginning, for the Japanese there was no priority, no pressure, no technological advances and no new ideas (apart from an effective MAD system that was outstandingly promising, in theory) for protecting their shipping. Initial assumptions about the merchant shipping losses to be expected from US submarine attacks were comfortingly low, and grossly under-estimated. In addition, the downgrading of the importance of protecting this shipping from attack meant that the officers responsible for planning it had little status within the rigid hierarchy of the Imperial Navy. Just as in Britain, and to a lesser extent in the USA, it was not a sound career move for Japanese officers to specialise in ASW.

The cumulative effect of these assumptions and attitudes was that, on the day after the Pearl Harbor attack, there was still no unit charged with the duty of protecting merchant shipping. Furthermore, the only convoys were those involving military shipping where the mounting of a particular operation depended on ships making a voyage in company. 'No convoy was organised in the case of non-military shipping. Civil-controlled ships were encouraged to sail independently in order to secure the highest possible shipping circulation.'³ At that time, Japan had 2,529 merchant ships totalling some 6,337,000 tons. Of this total, the Army controlled 519 ships of 2,160,500 tons, and the Navy another 482 ships of 1,740,200 tons. Civilian ships accounted for the remaining 1,528 vessels with a total tonnage of 2,436,300. Eight months later, in August 1942, following a sweeping tide of Japanese conquest right across the Pacific, the total tonnage had dwindled slightly to 6,266,800 tons and in January 1943 to a total of 6,066,700 tons, reflecting the slow US response to this tempting and vital target. Nevertheless, the most significant part of these statistics was that the civilian shipping tonnage, at 2,629,300 tons in January 1943, was appreciably lower than the limit of 3 million tons stated to be essential before the start of the war.

By this time, it was almost too late to do anything about it in terms of creating and equipping an effective anti-submarine force. As with all other navies, destroyers were at a premium, needed for every kind of operation from escorting major surface units to acting as high-speed troop transports and supply ships. Belatedly, the Navy had attempted to tackle the problem in the same way as had the British and US navies, by building larger numbers of specialised escort vessels. The programme had begun slowly, with four frigates authorised during 1941, but even these were not officially acknowledged as anti-submarine escorts and were officially classified as coastal defence ships (*kaibokan*) or even as fishery protection vessels. By June 1943, the anti-submarine warfare branch of the Navy, aware of what was likely to be heading their way, requested a total of 360 of

effort against Allied merchant shipping. The *I10* sank no less than eight merchant vessels east of Madagascar in June alone, totalling almost 39,000 tons, while others sank merchant ships off the coast of New South Wales. In all, Japanese submarines sank thirty cargo ships of a total tonnage of almost 150,000 for the loss of only one of their number (*I28*), which was torpedoed off Truk by an American submarine, USS *Tautog*, on a completely different errand from the anti-commerce campaign. However, this promising tactic could not last for the Japanese, as more and more Imperial Navy boats were being diverted back to their original primary purpose – defending the navy's surface ships from attack by US units – and in time they would even have to help the army, risking losses in carrying out supply and evacuation missions in the island campaign.

The most crippling effect of Japanese ignorance about ASW was shown in their own feeble efforts to defend their merchant shipping from US submarine attacks. Whereas American merchant ships in the these craft to be able to fulfil their trade protection commitments. They received just forty, while first priority went to the building of carriers, submarines and high-speed transports.

Not until 10 April 1942 did the Imperial Navy form its first two escort groups. The 1st Escort Group was made up of ten older destroyers, reinforced by two torpedo boats and five converted gunboats. This was given the huge task of protecting merchant vessels sailing between Singapore and Japan, a route fully 2,500 miles long. The 2nd Escort Group was smaller, made up of four elderly destroyers, two torpedo boats and a single gunboat, charged with protection of merchant ships sailing between Japan and the base of Truk in the Marshall Islands, a distance almost as great. The only bright spot from the Japanese point of view was that the total inadequacy of the forces they had committed to anti-submarine warfare was partly hidden by the continuing American problems

Lieutenant Commander Dudley 'Mush' Morton, one of the foremost American submarine aces in the Pacific War as the commander of the uss *Wahoo*, describes his successful third patrol at a Pearl Harbor debriefing.
(US National Archives)

with the reliability of the torpedoes issued to their submarines.

Only by August 1943 did the sudden increase in merchant ship sinkings reveal two changes in the anti-submarine war, neither working to the advantage of the Japanese. Not only was it increasingly apparent that American torpedoes were now working properly, but it was also obvious that their submarines were now definitely beginning to focus on according a new importance to merchant ships as potential targets. By this time, total Japanese merchant ship tonnage had dipped again, to 5,460,000 tons, not in itself a catastrophic loss but one which did not bode well for the future.

By now Japanese forces were being forced into retreat, to shorten lines of supply and communications and create a more defensible perimeter to their island conquests. Even this regrouping process called for huge quantities of shipping, as every kind of wartime requirement affected shipping in a country with such meagre natural resources. Increasing the output of the aircraft industry meant increasing imports of bauxite – the ore from which aluminium is smelted – and these and other priorities meant that the military would need to demand that a quarter of a million tons of shipping be requisitioned from civilian trade. This urgent need galvanised the naval high command into setting a limit for merchant ship losses for 1944 to a maximum of a million tons. It was also intended to make more efficient use of existing resources by boosting the strength of the escort forces to ensure that convoys were formed more quickly and sailed more frequently.

Losses continued to climb. In September 1943 they reached a new high of 172,000 tons. By November, the losses had climbed to 265,000 tons for the month and the official limit of a million tons in twelve months was already looking impossibly optimistic. The official response was to bring the two escort groups formed so far under a new command, the Grand Escort Command Headquarters (GEHQ), under a senior admiral with real authority. Unfortunately the one thing he and his GEHQ lacked was the ships they needed. All they had were fifteen twenty-year-old destroyers, some even older destroyers barely capable of ocean voyages, and four converted gunboats. Most other ships were smaller than eight hundred tons apiece, and not really up to the job. The only promising developments for the future were represented by four small escort carriers, roughly equivalent to the CVEs that were doing such damage to the U-boats in the Atlantic battle.

First these had to undergo repairs, and then the 901st Air Group, which was to provide the aircraft and crews, had to carry out a comprehensive training programme, a huge mountain to climb when there had been no real attempt to work out tactics and procedures for attacking submarines from the air. If this were not already bad enough, losses were still continuing to rise, and they would soon face pressure to transfer the carriers and their air groups to other objectives. Even on those occasions when the carriers operated with convoys, they proved fatally vulnerable to the US submarines they were supposed to be hunting – more like HMS *Courageous* than USS *Card*!

Communications proved to be another in a seemingly endless succession of weak points and limitations. Each convoy area used a different system, and there was no universally agreed tactical doctrine to enable different ships and commanders to work together as a team. Equipment was generally obsolete,

The uss *Archerfish*, which sank the huge Japanese carrier *Shinano*, converted from a *Yamato* class battleship, on her way for fitting out on 29 November 1944.

(The Floating Drydock)

and the escort fleet, for example, only received essential items like radar in late 1944, after all the major warships of the Combined Fleet. A working radio telephone system for escorts was partially introduced, though not extended to any of the merchant vessels in their charge.

But the greatest shortcoming was the belated introduction of the convoy system. By the time it was being seriously considered, pressure on merchant shipping was so heavy that convoying was seen as hopelessly cumbersome and time-consuming. One alternative that was seriously considered was to use mine barrages, shore-based radar and sonar and regular sea and air patrols to establish a defence line between the islands of the Ryukyus south of the Japanese mainland, Taiwan, the Philippines and Borneo, to create a Japanese lake in the Taiwan Strait and the South and East China Seas, the Yellow Sea and the Sea of Japan, where merchant ships could sail independently, free from the submarine threat. Like the Royal Navy's attempts to bar U-boats from the northern North Sea, it was doomed from the start. Mines were in short supply and minelayers even scarcer, and before other preparations could begin, the Americans were already approaching Okinawa as the final prelude to an invasion of Japan proper.

In the meantime, the rudimentary convoy system (such as it was) was proving hopelessly vulnerable. Two small oil tanker convoys were attacked in February 1944. One in the East China Sea consisted of two tankers escorted by a frigate, and both tankers were sunk by an American submarine. The other, in the South China Sea, included five tankers, also escorted by a frigate. All five tankers were sunk. With severely limited escorts,

the only way to boost the protection was to follow the lead of the Allies in the Atlantic and run larger convoys, though in this case the average size would be about fifteen ships, the maximum it was thought the escorts and merchant skippers could cope with.

By this time, the only fitful ray of hope for those charged with protecting Japanese convoys from American attack was the new frigates. They were being commissioned in larger, though still inadequate numbers, and their presence might enable some retaliation to be delivered against the all too effective American submarines. However, the sinking by those same submarines of four of the five promised escort carriers was a major blow.[4]

In the wider maritime world, defeat was succeeding defeat with the Japanese withdrawing from the Marshalls and other island bases under unremitting US pressure. At the same time when the need for merchant shipping was reaching its peak, losses of those merchant ships through submarine attacks increased still further. When the need for shipping reached its highest level yet, in January 1944, another 240,840 tons of merchant shipping were sunk, with an even larger total of 256,797 tons lost in February. In response to these losses, and the clear need to protect what was left as securely as possible, convoys were increased in size to some twenty ships apiece, but US submarines still presented an extremely potent threat. Through delivering a low-key version of what the U-boats had achieved during their most successful days the long-range US boats were proving far more aggressive and successful than their German opposite numbers had done. So bad had the situation become that even Japanese warships were not immune. A vital series of training missions for Japan's surviving carriers undertaken as part of their preparations before the Battle of the Philippine Sea had to be abandoned when four of the destroyers sent out to sweep the area clear of submarines as a precaution were torpedoed by American submarines in quick succession.

Even at this late and terminally discouraging moment, the Japanese were eager to find any grounds for hope. At first it seemed that the switch to larger convoys might have been successful since for two months losses actually declined. Unfortunately this proved to be a false dawn, as American submarines then returned in greater numbers with a switch to what the Japanese concluded were wolf-pack tactics, which were much more successful than those of Doenitz in their intention of overwhelming the enemy's escort forces. If this were not disappointment enough, the only trained ASW air unit, the 901st Air Group, had been thrown into the air battles off Taiwan against the US attack carrier task groups, and was virtually eliminated.

By autumn 1944, Japanese ASW was almost at its last gasp. Though the American submarines had suffered grievous losses in their far-reaching and hard-pressed campaign, their Japanese opposite numbers had suffered an attrition rate proportionally similar to that of the Germans. Of a total of 174 submarines – sixty of them built prior to Pearl Harbor and 114 more built during the war – no less than 130 were lost, a loss rate of almost 75 per cent.

Unlike the campaign against the U-boats, the greater part of this destruction was achieved by US Navy surface escorts, responsible for sinking seventy Japanese submarines on their own and another eight in conjunction with air attacks. A further fourteen Japanese submarines were destroyed by air attack alone and four were lost in US minefields, and no

fewer than nine were sunk by US submarines, with the remaining twenty-five being lost by accidents and unknown causes. But dwarfing these statistics was the appalling loss of Japan's merchant fleet. By August 1945, American submarines had sunk more than 1,300 ships, totalling 5.3 million tons, or almost 84 per cent of the Japanese merchant marine at the start of the Second World War.

Yet it could have been far less one-sided. At the eleventh hour of the anti-submarine war in the Pacific, Japanese tactics and weaponry belatedly improved.[5] In October and November 1944, two of the months during which American submarines seemed to be finally triumphing over their enemies, eight of them failed to return, many of them sunk by Japanese attacks. Two that narrowly survived had some lurid tales to tell. uss *Salmon* torpedoed an escorted 10,000-ton tanker on 30 October 1944, when she was attacked and heavily depth-charged by four escorts. There followed a heavy and accurate attack that all but blew the submarine to pieces. Hatches and vents started leaking, hydroplanes were jammed and the engine rooms were filling with water. After plunging twice to depths of 500 and 600 feet respectively, the crew managed to reach the surface and carry out emergency repairs before dodging the escorts chasing them by vanishing into a convenient rain squall. When she returned to base, parts of her pressure hull were found to have been forced inwards by up to two inches by the pressure of the explosions and the depth to which she had plummeted.

On 14 November, uss *Halibut* was subjected to an even more frightening experience, not least because of its unusual nature. Part of a wolf pack operating against Japanese convoys, the boat was at periscope depth when, just after launching torpedoes against a freighter, the crew heard a loud, high-pitched buzzing

The US submarine uss *Salmon* served in the Pacific where she carried out eleven successful patrols against Japanese shipping. On her last she was heavily attacked by Japanese ASW forces, but succeeded in surfacing and driving off her attackers using her deck guns.

(The Floating Drydock)

By the time the submarine uss *Tench* reached the Pacific in early 1945, other US submarines had almost swept the seas clear of Japanese merchant shipping. However, on her three war patrols she managed to sink most of the small ships she encountered, including two freighters and a small tanker.

(US Naval Institute Press)

noise circling around them four times before a heavy explosion close on their port side. There was none of the usual noises of depth charges dropping prior to the explosion, and the submarine dived to more than 400 feet, accompanied by the noise of more explosions and considerable internal damage. The skipper reported a strange and inexplicable greenish glow in the control room, which accorded with descriptions from other submarine commanders, but no one could account for what this might have been.

Finally, *Halibut* too was able to surface and make her way back to base, to find similar damage to the pressure hull, which led to this boat also being declared a total loss. Only when the skipper of one of the other boats in the pack made his report did it reveal what had attacked them. Large flying boats had been seen through the periscope circling backwards and forwards over *Halibut*'s position, and it was clear that they had been using *Jikitanchiki*, the Japanese MAD system that, in this case at least, made possible an accurate and crippling attack.

This was one of the few areas in which Japan had developed new technology well up to Allied standards. It was a semi-automated system in which the pilot of the patrolling aircraft was alerted by a lamp lighting up on the instrument panel, and a slick of aluminium powder was dropped into the sea as a preliminary marker. The pilot maintained his course until the aircraft passed out of the zone of magnetic disturbance, whereupon another slick was dropped automatically. He then had to turn and fly a course at right angles to the line joining the first two slicks

and crossing it halfway between them. Once again the apparatus would release markers automatically as the aircraft flew in and out of the zone of magnetic disturbance, and an attack could be delivered on the basis that the submarine was in the centre of the pattern formed by the first, second and fourth slicks, but aimed according to a table that took into account how long the dropping of the markers had taken. Then the aircraft could attack with its own bombs or depth charges, or direct surface escorts to the markers showing the target's position, as was believed to be the case with *Halibut*.

So sensitive was the equipment eventually made that boats could be located down to 400 feet below the surface and even, with a skilled pilot flying forty feet above the sea, down to a depth of 800 feet, well below the crush depth of US submarines. This formidable weapon might have achieved much more, but by the time of its introduction, aircraft and aircrew capable of operating it were in such short supply that it made little difference. The last US submarine to be lost in the Second World War, the *Bullhead*, was caught on the surface in the penultimate week of the conflict by an aircraft of the Japanese Army. The bomber crew flew overhead and dropped their bombs, claiming two direct hits. This time the submarine vanished, leaving an oil slick, and never returned to its base. This was on 6 August 1945, the very day the first atomic bomb was detonated over Hiroshima. It seemed as if Japanese ASW had matured at last, but too late to achieve the change of fortunes which might have prolonged the struggle.[6]

CHAPTER 17

THE NEW POST-WAR THREAT

1945–54

Following their realisation of the speeds of the final generation of U-boats, the Allied navies modified several of their wartime submarines for greater underwater speed: this is HMS *Satyr* of the Royal Navy after her streamlining treatment.

(www.navyphotos.co.uk)

THROUGHOUT the First and Second World Wars, anti-submarine forces had one huge advantage over their opponents. For all the menace presented by the U-boat and by Japanese, Italian, American and British underwater craft, not one was a true submarine, able to operate in its chosen medium without crippling restrictions. All were submersibles, boats able to slip beneath the surface for very limited periods for concealment or escape, at the cost of most of their performance. Even lying on the seabed to ride out depth charge attacks was no real answer – battery life and limited air supplies meant that an escort which could stay with its target for long enough would sooner or later force it to the surface. Equally, forcing a submarine to dive robbed it of speed and endurance so that it presented a much reduced threat until it was free to surface once again.

Only in the closing months of the Second World War did submarine design begin to close the gap with the defences against those submarines. Both the Japanese and the Germans built streamlined high-speed conventional submarines with greatly reduced drag and greatly enhanced battery power to enable them to outrun existing anti-submarine forces in a short, high-speed underwater dash before surfacing when safely clear of pursuit. In addition, Germany experimented with hydrogen-peroxide-powered boats as the first true submersibles. These proved promising in theory though so dangerous in practice that they would be unusable on operations. Instead, it was decided to embark on the construction of two new U-boats that would have greatly enhanced underwater speed and range, to make them much more formidable adversaries.

The more promising was the large type XXI. This was modified from the design for the type XVIII hydrogen-peroxide-powered submarine, but using the large and carefully streamlined pressure hull to house conventional diesel engines and electric motors but with treble the normal battery capacity and a number of new features, like a high-speed torpedo reloading system, two extra tubes and more reloads. It was similar in length to the type IX, with a greater displacement, but its maximum underwater speed was increased to sixteen knots and its maximum endurance at the economical five-knot cruise speed was increased from forty-five hours to seventy-two. In addition to all this, it was much quieter and tended to give a smaller sonar echo. Tests carried out by the US Navy after the war showed the type XXI was as quiet at fifteen knots submerged as the US Balao class running at eight knots.[1]

Performance on this scale might have given existing Allied escorts a very hard time, but this was to ignore wartime realities. The Germans were embarking on these radical new submarines against increasingly effective Allied bombing of the shipyards. To cope

A Terrier BW-1 guided missile leaving the after launcher of the USN guided missile destroyer uss *Bainbridge*, and just prior to boost phase blast, during an anti-submarine warfare/fire power demonstration on 15 August 1963, to make a direct hit on the drone target seconds later.
(US Naval Historical Center)

An ASROC missile leaves its launcher on uss *Bainbridge*, during an anti-submarine warfare/fire power demonstration, 15 August 1963.
(US Naval Historical Center)

with this disruption, it was decided to switch to modular construction. The pressure hull was divided into a series of eight sections, or modules, each one similar to a thick slice across the overall pressure-hull sausage, complete with all the inside fittings and pipework. These modules would be built by a wide range of specialist construction plants, and then transported to a berth in a conventional shipyard for final assembly.

It was a desperate expedient for a desperate situation, and a recipe for chaos. Designing and making such a radical new warship was a big enough challenge in any

case, but doing so with such an unconventional construction technique was bound to result in huge technical problems, especially when the time available to solve them was extremely limited. For example, once the process of welding the completed modules together was begun, it could not be interrupted even during air raids, and so a series of attacks destroyed the German submarine force's future on the slipways and in the dockyards rather than on the open sea.

As a result, relatively few of these new submarines were built, and only a handful sailed on patrol before the war ended, though their effectiveness against the convoy escorts gave a chilling demonstration of what might have happened in the Atlantic battle had they been introduced a year or two earlier. Fortunately, before they could be perfected, the final surrender saw the U-boat force broken up and scattered, with the more advanced boats distributed among the victorious Allied navies.

There still remain two sharply differing viewpoints on the threat presented by the type XXI. On the one hand, it could:

... cruise as far as the Pacific without refuelling and reach a spring speed when deeply submerged of 16 to 17 knots; as fast as most Allied convoy escort vessels ... during a pursuit at this speed the noise caused by water rushing and bubbling along the pursuer's own hull would deafen his sonars. When dived to maximum depth under attack the Type XXI could cruise for nearly 300 miles at 6 knots on her electric motors, as against barely 10 miles and 2 knots by the type VIIC U-boats ... the anti-submarine forces' existing operational arithmetic of search and kill would thus be rendered null and void; whereas the area unit in searching for a traditional U-boat had been 31,400 square miles, it would be 282,000 square miles for the Type XXI. In sum, the Allied navies had no ready technical or operational answers to the Type XXI.[2]

On the other hand, perhaps they would never have needed any, even if more type XXIs had been completed before the war's end. Clay Blair remained much more sceptical of the design and criticised what he described as its 'crippling faults'.[3] These included poor structural integrity, as the modules were crudely made and badly fitted together, giving the finished hull a shallow failure depth, underpowered diesels and an impractical hydraulic system with most of the pipes outside the protection of the pressure hull.

Yet the fact remains that the type XXI and the smaller type XXIII coastal electro-boats between them caused a severe fright among some Allied naval circles. These included officers of the calibre of Admiral

Sir Max Horton, commander-in-chief Western Approaches, and the First Sea Lord, Admiral Sir Andrew Cunningham. Neither was a man who shirked a challenge, but they warned of the possibility of increased merchant ship losses at the hands of a resurgent U-boat fleet made up of electro-boats.

The greatest significance of the type XXI design was how steeply it raised the bar for the kind of potential threat that post-war anti-submarine forces would have to deal with, rendering a whole generation of escort craft obsolete almost overnight. Once the wartime Allies realised what the Germans could have achieved given more time and resources, it became clear that other naval powers would do even better in the less chaotic peacetime world. As a result, it was decided that future anti-submarine craft would have to deal with submarines having underwater

speeds of fifteen knots, and diving depths – given a better and more carefully assembled hull than the type XXI, of up to a thousand feet.

This was to lead to huge developments in naval sensors and weaponry, to locate faster submarines at greater ranges and then sink them. Finding them still depended on sound location – the term 'sonar', already in common use in the US Navy, replaced 'Asdic' from the end of the war – but the capabilities of new versions were greatly extended. By the early 1950s, the Royal Navy was being equipped with the immediate successor to the late-war 144/147 combination, which gave the necessary depth read-out for arming the Squid mortar charges. This was a type 166 combination of two sonars, each with a slightly different objective: the early-warning type 174 sonar with a maximum range of 4,000 yards, backed up by the type 164, 1,500-yard range attack sonar, which was more reliable than its predecessors and fitted with a means of compensating for the movements of the attacking ship in recording the bearing of the target.

Even as these were being brought into service, the radically new type 170 attack sonar was about to be introduced. This had a transducer divided into a four-square arrangement, to enable a split beam pulse to reveal the target's depth as well as its range and bearing from the attacking ship, out to a limit of 2,000 yards. This was also fitted with automatic stabilisation to compensate for the pitching and rolling of the ship, and it was linked electrically to the heavier, and more accurate, Limbo ahead-throwing anti-submarine mortar with a 1,000-yard maximum range, which was beginning to replace the wartime Squid. So successful did the new sonar prove on trials that it was also fitted to smaller anti-submarine ships linked to the existing Squid system.

By now, the only surface ships with a realistic hope of coping with the suddenly even more urgent ASW requirement – given the huge resources the Russians were devoting to building up an even larger submarine force than Doenitz could have dreamt of – were those already capable of operating with the fleet, like the traditional destroyers. In terms of escort requirements, the wheel had come full circle and reverted to a situation like that of 1939, where destroyers would be scarce and over-committed elsewhere.

Once again, the solution would have to be a huge new programme for building fast frigates to undertake this role instead. Fortunately, since completely new construction was impossible on cost grounds together with building time, the opportunity already existed for a cheaper and more quickly available alternative. The Royal Navy and the US Navy had a surplus of wartime destroyers that had the necessary speed and carrying capacity. Converting the sensors and weaponry needed to fit them for their new role was much cheaper, simpler and more straightforward than designing and building new ships.

The American destroyer USS *Rich* underway in Chesapeake Bay on 17 April 1967 with a DASH drone anti-submarine helicopter seen on her deck.

(*US Naval Historical Center*)

The modern ASW patrol aircraft, like this S-3B Viking, deploys a formidable array of sensors and weapons to reveal today's more elusive submarine targets.

(US Naval Institute Press)

To produce escorts with the performance needed to catch the faster post-war submarines, most navies began by converting destroyers to the ASW frigate role. This is HMS *Terpsichore,* an intermediate destroyer conversion for the Royal Navy.

(www.navyphotos.co.uk)

The first of the Royal Navy's fast frigate transformations were built in two versions: the type 16 interim destroyer conversion, and the more radical and expensive but ultimately more successful type 15. Type 15 conversion involved removing the destroyer's main armament of guns and torpedo tubes, and replacing them with a twin 4-inch mounting of the type fitted to the wartime escort sloops and a twin Bofors mounting for token anti-aircraft capability. The new main armament was provided by a pair of Limbo mortars, and the traditional open bridge and Asdic hut of the wartime escorts gave way to an enclosed bridge on the US pattern with a fully protected operations room where submarines could be trailed, tracked down and attacked in much more comfortable, all-weather conditions. To maintain stability, the new superstructures used a high proportion of aluminium to reduce additional weight.

The conversions cost some £600,000 each, and took eighteen months to complete. However, with ever-greater pressure on the defence budgets, it was decided to pursue a simpler and lower cost alternative that could be completed for around half the cost, and could be completed inside six months. The type 16 conversion involved removing the main armament to reduce the top weight, but the anti-submarine mortars were Squids and the superstructure was not changed as part of the conversion. In all, twenty-two destroyers were given the full type 15 treatment, and another seven type 16s. All of them, thanks to their pedigree ancestry, had a top speed of thirty-six knots.

Their numbers were boosted by the newly built type 14 frigates which were slower (twenty-seven knots) smaller and much lighter (1,100 tons rather than 2,200–2,300 tons) having only three Bofors guns and a pair of triple-barrelled Limbos. This attempt to boost numbers by producing cheaper second-rank ships was limited to twelve ships before the type was discontinued. Nonetheless, the requirement remained, and was eventually filled by the Tribals, which were fitted with a single 4.5-inch gun mount front and rear, space for an anti-submarine helicopter and a Limbo mortar.

The US Navy also followed the destroyer conversion route to cash in on the huge wartime building programmes as a quick and simple means of providing fast anti-submarine ships, though they retained the destroyer designation. The first step was to complete four half-built Gearing class destroyer hulls as prototypes of two new classes of anti-submarine ships – DDK hunter-killers that could operate alone to find and sink modern fast submarines and DDEs, which would work in groups to achieve the same results.

New anti-submarine weapons included the American Weapon Alfa project, which operated like a Gatling gun with a rotating drum magazine, but firing 12.75-inch rocket-propelled depth charges in quick succession. When firing at full bore, it could launch a rocket every five seconds, and promised a powerful punch. In practice it was ahead of its time, as the mechanism proved to be over-complicated and called for lengthy and complex maintenance routines. As a stopgap the US Navy continued to use Hedgehog, which they rated marginally better than the Squid used by the Royal Navy and they developed a rapidly trainable version to cope with submarine targets located at fairly close ranges.[4]

The DDKs were fitted with 3-inch guns and different combinations of depth charges, Hedgehog and Weapon Alfa, while the DDEs had Weapon Alfa in B gun position, a trainable Hedgehog and fixed tubes for launching anti-submarine homing torpedoes.

Later in 1958, the Fleet Rehabilitation and Modernisation Program (FRAM) resolved the confusion with a more unified approach, involving converting more Gearing class destroyers by removing the torpedo tubes and one of the guns, and replacing them with an ASROC missile battery and facilities for handling a DASH ASW RPV drone.

This was experimental weapon that proved too far ahead of its time. The drone anti-submarine helicopter (DASH) was a remotely piloted drone that could be flown far enough from the ship operating it to launch homing torpedoes within their 200-yard range at a submerged submarine, up to five miles away. In theory this was a promising weapon, but in practice the drones proved difficult to control at sea, and more than half were lost. Once it was decided to provide the additional flight deck and hangar space aboard anti-submarine ships for operating conventional piloted helicopters, these soon replaced the drones as more reliable and more effective alternatives.

Other navies, including the Soviets, pursued similar objectives, either by conversions of existing ships or building new faster frigates, and equipping them with more powerful weapons with a longer reach. For the moment, changes in anti-submarine warfare were largely limited to increasing performance of ships and weapons to keep pace with submarine developments, while the tactics involved were still closely based on those developed so laboriously during the two World Wars. Searching by sonar for elusive sub-surface echoes, followed by launching weapons at the resulting echoes, would have seemed immediately understandable to escort commanders of the Second World War and to the U-boats that were trying to evade them.

It was the Royal Canadian Navy which, pursuing

HMS *Grenville*, a wartime destroyer given the longer and more expensive full ASW frigate conversion.

(www.navyphotos.co.uk)

their chosen post-war specialisation of ASW, began operating helicopters from escort vessels on a large scale. As far back as 1958 they were able to land and take off a Whirlwind helicopter from a tiny flight deck set up on a wartime River class frigate, and by the 1960s they were using the large Sea King on their larger destroyers. To make this possible on an all-weather basis, they invented the helicopter haul-down and rapid securing device (HHRSD) more commonly known as 'Bear Trap'. This consists of a retractable main probe and secondary probe mounted beneath the helicopter, which can be extended on landing to lock into a substantial grating assembly set into the flight deck and achieve a positive hold-down while the rotors are still delivering lift. The auxiliary probe, set further back, engages with a similar grid to prevent the helicopter from swinging around under torque reaction or strong crosswinds, and positions it for easy access to the hangar.

Helicopters soon became indispensable for a range of anti-submarine duties. Because they could fly out to considerable distances from the ship operating them, they could be used to drop sonobuoys or hover with dipping sonar equipment, to extend the reach of the ship's detection facilities. In addition, once lighter-weight versions of the ship-launched homing torpedoes were introduced, they could assume the hunting role as well. However, given the higher operating speeds of post-war submarines, it was essential to develop faster versions of the homing torpedoes used by both sides during the Second World War. For example, the US Navy's Mark 20 homing depth charge had a top speed of twelve knots, which was clearly inadequate, as was the fifteen-knot capability of the Mark 43 homing torpedo. Much more promising was the Mark 44, introduced in the mid-1950s, which had a top speed of thirty knots and at 450 pounds weight could be carried by the more powerful anti-submarine helicopters.

Another means of extending the range of anti-submarine weapons was the rocket, and the US Navy carried out a great deal of development work on ship-launched rockets that could be fired in the direction of a submarine contact, to drop a homing torpedo into the water in the vicinity of the target, whereupon the torpedo would acquire the target and home in on it. Early models proved unreliable in that they would not always prove sufficiently accurate to drop the torpedo close enough to the submarine for it to home in on it. But the later ASROC version used the Mark 44 torpedo, which proved a much more formidable weapon, though the launcher installation was too large to fit the smaller anti-submarine ships.

The Soviet Navy also made wide use of anti-submarine rocket launchers in addition to homing torpedoes on their anti-submarine surface ships. However, their problems included the relatively short

range of their surface ships' sonars, which meant that the long-range torpedo-launching rockets had to be guided en route to their targets by one or more helicopters using dipping sonar. Having to hover in the combat area to make an attack possible, these were especially vulnerable to being attacked in turn, not by the submarines they were hunting but by hostile fixed-wing aircraft in the combat area, and this constituted a major weak point in the anti-submarine system.

The final link in the ASW chain remained, as it had in both wars, the anti-submarine maritime patrol aircraft. With the advent of jet engines, post-war patrol planes had much greater speed, endurance and weapons-carrying capability, well able to keep pace with the transformation in submarine performance. The first genuine post-war design used on US Navy and Royal Canadian Navy carriers for anti-submarine patrols was the Grumman CS2F Tracker, which was

LEFT HMS *Andromeda,* one of the Royal Navy's successful Leander class of ASW frigates.

(www.navyphotos.co.uk)

BELOW USS *Knox* is a modern US Navy frigate with ASW capability.

(The Floating Drydock)

The Royal Navy's Type 22 frigates like HMS *Chatham* are general-purpose ships with ASW capability.

(www.navyphotos.co.uk)

The Royal Canadian Navy has built on its successful wartime ASW experience with a selection of modern ships, like the frigate HMCS *McKenzie*

(www.navyphotos.co.uk)

originally designed to fly from the wartime-built escort carriers, replacing the Grumman Avengers that had been so deadly against the U-boats.

These aircraft carried a progressively more complex and capable assembly of sensors and weapons. The MAD equipment of wartime operations was refined and improved to become able to detect schnorkelling submarines at longer distances, and deeper contacts were revealed by dropping patterns of sonobuoys — floating platforms which relayed information from their hydrophones back to the aircraft that had dropped them. The data was also fed into computer systems which could work out the whereabouts of submerged contacts and systems like the JULIE and Jezebel anti-submarine systems, which were computer-aided audio spectrum analysers capable of recording and maintaining a record of the acoustic signatures of surface and submarine target vessels. Individual vessel names could then be routinely identified and stored for later retrieval. Later carrier-borne anti-submarine aircraft and their land-based equivalents like the Lockheed Neptune and the RAF Shackleton (based on the Lancaster bomber airframe) and the Nimrod (based on the Comet civilian airliner) would extend the capability of these systems still further.

Until the 1950s and beyond, the technology of anti-submarine weapons had made them faster, cleverer at finding and hitting targets and capable of delivering a heavier punch at longer range, far beyond what had been possible in 1945. The tactics employed to use them, however, remained much the same as before, as had the submarines themselves. Though faster and more robust, they were still detected in the traditional way using active sonar to reveal bearing, range and depth, and they still had to surface from time to time to replenish air supplies and recharge batteries. Though this now needed to be done at much longer intervals than before, and could be postponed through careful use of the schnorkel, the submarines were still essentially submersibles, however much their qualities had improved. Yet on the last day of September 1954, the world of ASW would be changed forever. The coming of the true submarine would call for a revolution in tactics as well as in technology to try to contain the threat it represented.

CHAPTER 18

THE NUCLEAR REVOLUTION
1954–the present

Early post-war attempts to produce genuine submersibles tried to build on German experiments with hydrogen peroxide as an air-independent fuel, but foundered on the volatility of the substance which made it unsuitable for operational use – the RN's HMS *Explorer*, one of two hydrogen peroxide powered boats of the 1940s was known to her crew as HMS *Exploder* and finished her days as a high-speed target.

(www.navyphotos.co.uk)

THE preceding chapter showed the enormous implications of the capabilities of the German type XXI U-boat design on post-war anti-submarine ships, detection systems and weapons, in order to be able to combat vessels with these huge increases in performance. However, since the few completed type XXIs were available to be studied by the victorious Allies, they also had a radical effect on the design of new submarines as well. For example, it was clear that the key to the XXI's performance was an emphasis on much greater battery power and, to an even greater extent, a clean and carefully streamlined hull where underwater speed was seen as much more important than top speed on the surface.

Given the harsher conditions under which submarines of any country would now be expected to operate, this change in priorities was definitely to be encouraged, and hull streamlining for higher underwater speed became the new imperative. In the Royal Navy, the A class patrol submarines of the late 1940s succeeded the wartime T class and at first both classes adopted the usual submarine shape with a semi-enclosed deck gun and a casing honeycombed with drain holes which produced colossal drag when submerged. During the 1950s, they were progressively streamlined, replacing the old conning tower with a slab-sided sail that enclosed the periscope standards and schnorkel, and removing guns and external torpedo tubes. In the case of the T class, for example, lengthening the pressure hull to provide space for extra batteries helped double the electric power to 2,900 horsepower, and increased their underwater speed from nine knots to fifteen knots.

The US Navy went much further. In 1946, they embarked on the 'Guppy' programme for Greater Underwater Propulsive Power, which involved applying a similar prescription to that of the Royal Navy submarines to a range of fifty boats, with underwater speeds of up to eighteen knots. The Soviet Union also used type XXI technology and design features to produce the high performance Zulu and Whisky classes of the 1950s, featuring high underwater speed and increased battery power. By then, however, the US Navy had taken two huge steps further forward in submarine development.

The first was fairly straightforward, the fruit of a programme that had begun as far back as 1944 to determine the ideal hull shape for maximum underwater performance. This was effectively a clean sheet of paper approach rather than the popular post-war expedient of cleaning existing submarine hulls of their greatest sources of hydrodynamic drag. Over several years a long series of wind-tunnel tests determined that a tubby tear-drop shape similar to that of an airship produced the lowest drag for a given displacement, and in November 1950 a contract was issued for $20 million to develop the first full-size prototype, to be commissioned as USS *Albacore*.

She was built at the Portsmouth Navy Yard in New Hampshire and commissioned in December 1953. She was unarmed and her smoothly contoured hull was constructed from low-carbon steel with her sail positioned approximately one-third of the way along the hull from the rounded bow. With conventional propulsion, she exceeded her design performance by a huge margin. Instead of a predicted surface speed of fifteen knots, she managed twenty-six, and – more significantly – instead of twenty-five knots submerged, she managed thirty, and this was at the start of twenty years of development.[1] Her other great virtue was her underwater stability at speed, which absolved her crew from the problem of compensating for unwanted dives and climbs, and allowed them to exploit her excellent manoeuvrability to the full.

The second step forward emerged just a month after *Albacore*, but was an even more ambitious project, and one that would change the face of naval warfare forever. For years navies had been seeking the Holy Grail of underwater warfare, to develop a propulsion system that could run without air and create the true submarine for the first time. Wartime Germany had sought it in the designs of Professor Helmuth Walther, using the exotic and volatile hydrogen peroxide. In the Walther 'direct' system, the hydrogen peroxide was passed over a catalyst to break it down into steam and high-temperature oxygen. The mixture was fed into a combustion chamber where the oxygen supported the burning of fuel oil, raising the energy level of the mixture still further so that it could be used to drive a turbine to propel the boat.[2]

Several prototypes were built and showed truly astonishing underwater speeds by the standards of the time – twenty-five knots in 1944 – and after the end of the war *U1407*, a Walther type XVII boat was taken over by the Royal Navy and commissioned as HMS *Meteorite*. In terms of its volatility and difficulty of control, the name was ironically appropriate, but the Navy persevered with what they thought of as the propulsion of the future, even though it took five years to put it into commission. By the mid-1950s they had produced two unarmed prototypes of their own with a more modern and, it was hoped, a more practical version of the hydrogen-peroxide system named HMS *Explorer* and HMS *Excalibur*. The fact that the crew of the first referred to her as HMS *Exploder* gives a vivid impression of the problems encountered and the two boats were later downgraded for use as high-speed targets where they reached underwater speeds of twenty-seven knots,[3] though they had been revealed as a blind and dangerous alley in terms of submarine development.

The American approach was even more radical and infinitely more successful. At the time when others were hoping they could solve the problems of hydrogen peroxide as a much lower cost alternative, the USA decided to undertake the cost and complexity of fitting a working nuclear reactor into a submarine, and using the colossal heat energy it produced to raise steam and drive turbines. Because nuclear fuel needed no oxygen for it to generate heat and raise steam, and because modern technology made it possible to purify the air within the submarine over and over again without it having to surface, the result promised to be a genuine submarine at long last. The other huge advantage of nuclear propulsion was the minute amount of fuel needed for almost unlimited cruising.

The world's first nuclear submarine, USS *Nautilus* was commissioned in January 1954 and went underway under reactor power for the first time a year later. Because of the size of the reactor she had to be considerably larger than conventional diesel electric boats, with a submerged displacement of 4,000 tons, but her performance was astounding. She could dive to 600 feet, maintain twenty-two knots on the surface and twenty-five knots submerged, and continue at that speed right around the world. In ninety hours she sailed all the way to Puerto Rico in the West Indies, a distance of more than 1,300 miles, and she did it underwater throughout. A huge building programme during the rest of the decade resulted in the Skipjack and Thresher classes of nuclear patrol submarines, soon to be followed by Russian, British and French nuclear submarines. And as each successive boat was commissioned, the questions arose – what were the limitations to what these boats could be used for, and what kind of tactics and equipment could be used to neutralise enemy nuclear submarines?

Paradoxically, in view of their plans to build the largest submarine fleet ever seen, this was a question that the Soviet Union found particularly difficult to answer. With the disappearance of the U-boat threat in 1945, the Soviet Navy downgraded anti-submarine capability to a low priority. They remained much more concerned with the powerful US Navy carrier groups, which they realised could launch powerful air attacks on different parts of the Russian homeland if war should break out. To meet this threat, the Soviet Navy continued to evolve during the late 1940s and early 1950s, along Second World War lines, with large gun-armed cruisers escorted by conventional destroyers and designated as anti-carrier striking forces.

The American introduction of the nuclear-powered submarine created a revolution in Soviet naval planning, especially when the increasing numbers of nuclear patrol submarines were joined by the even larger and more powerful missile boats, armed with ranks of nuclear ballistic rockets to deliver the ultimate deterrent to a pre-emptive strike. They reasoned that the only secure defence against this threat was to have ships that could sink these submarines at much greater

The real answer to the true submarine requirement proved to be uss *Nautilus*, the world's first nuclear submarine.

(The Floating Drydock)

Another highly important American submarine design was the uss *Albacore* which explored the best hull shape for underwater performance and set the pattern for all of today's submarines.

(The Floating Drydock)

ranges. Not only did this mean locating them at greater distances, but also using weapons with a heavier punch and a longer reach.

A handicap that had to be faced from the start was that Soviet sonar capability was not as good as that of Western navies. Another difficulty was that the later ships – powered by gas turbine engines to give them the high speed and endurance needed to chase nuclear submarines – were inherently noisy. The problem was compounded by a tactic commonly used by gas-turbine powered Soviet warships, which was to shut down one engine and its accompanying propeller for long-range low-speed cruising where fuel economy was needed. Unfortunately, since the blades of Soviet marine propellers at the time could not be feathered like those of Western warships, this meant the anti-submarine ship generated enough noise and turbulence to deafen its own sonar.

In terms of anti-submarine weapons, the Russians relied heavily on rockets, like the 12-barrelled rocket launchers that had a range of some three miles. These would usually be fired as a broadside at any close-range submarine target, on a similar principle to the wartime Hedgehog. If any of the rockets hit the target at that close a range, it would almost certainly be crippled and possibly destroyed. Other weapons included six-barrelled launchers firing heavier rockets and 21-inch anti-submarine torpedoes, which could be launched from quintuple mountings on the larger anti-submarine ships.

The *Kresta* class of the late 1960s had a more seaworthy hull design than earlier Soviet anti-submarine ships, suggesting a capability for longer-range operation, but the weapons for use against submarines were as before. Even though the ships were equipped with onboard helicopters, these were not anti-submarine capable. Only the large *Moskva* class helicopter carriers of the late 1960s took ASW seriously, with helicopters that were fitted with dipping sonar, sonobuoys and MAD equipment. They could also carry different weapons, including nuclear-tipped or conventional depth charges, mines or anti-submarine homing torpedoes, and were capable of operating at distances of up to 160 miles from the ship.

On the ships themselves, the usual mix of rockets and torpedoes was reinforced with solid fuelled nuclear-tipped anti-submarine missiles with a range of up to sixteen miles, fired from launchers on deck.

These were thought to be intended for an all-out war situation, where the time needed for the missile to reach its target at extreme range would mean that the position of a nuclear submarine trying to evade attack would be so uncertain that only the lethal radius of a nuclear detonation would do the job reliably.

When the first Soviet nuclear submarines started to appear in the late 1950s, Western navies realised that their high performance (many featured twin reactors for maximum speed) would call for heavy weaponry to neutralise them effectively. A series of nuclear-tipped torpedoes and depth charges were developed to meet the threat. These included the 'Lulu' and 'Betty' nuclear depth charges weighing half a ton and one ton respectively, and the 500-pound air-dropped B57 combined bomb and depth charge. As with Soviet thinking, this requirement was not principally because the submarines were so strongly constructed that a nuclear blast was needed to destroy them. Instead, a charge was needed with a large enough lethal sphere to sink the submarine, even if it was moving so quickly that its exact location was uncertain following the deployment and dropping of the weapon.

These weapons were joined by different types of nuclear-tipped torpedoes, like the Mark 45 ASTOR wire-guided weapon with a command-detonated

Eventually the stealth, speed and range of nuclear submarines made them ideal vehicles to deliver the nuclear deterrent, like this American ballistic missile boat USS *Ohio*.

(The Floating Drydock)

The only nuclear submarine
to fire a torpedo in anger
was the Royal Navy's
hunter-killer boat
HMS *Conqueror* which sank
the Argentine cruiser
General Belgrano during the
1982 Falklands War.

(www.navyphotos.co.uk)

Both the US Navy and the Royal Navy joined, together with the Soviet Navy in realising the potential value of the submarine as an anti-submarine weapon, as they could operate at whatever depth gave the best conditions for sonar searching for their targets. This called for special submarine passive sonars, able to pick up non-nuclear submarines when most at risk, using schnorkels to evade air detection while recharging their batteries, at ranges of ten miles or more.

In the meantime, for surface anti-submarine ships, there were two ways of dealing with the problem of sonar and temperature layers. One was the so-called 'bottom-bounce' technique where the sonar beam would be directed downward towards the seabed at an angle too steep for it be reflected at the next temperature layer, so that it continued to the sea floor and was then reflected upwards. Not only did this allow the sonar beam to be propagated for longer distances below the thermal layer transition, but a submarine hiding below that transition would be struck by the beam and an echo would be returned in the normal way.

Another, more reliable method was to use variable-depth sonar, or VDS: a sonar transmitter–receiver mounted on the end of a long cable could be lowered from an escort vessel below the thermal layer transition, where it could clearly see concealed submarine targets as if the thermal layer problem did not exist. VDS was primarily developed by the Royal Canadian Navy after the war, in response to the extremely difficult sonar conditions between the cold deeper layers and the warmer surface layers of the Gulf of St Lawrence and the Canadian east coast.[4]

By 1958, their SQS-504 VDS was outranging the orthodox hull-mounted 144 sonar used by the Royal Navy by a factor of five, and by the early 1970s Canadian destroyers were achieving sonar ranges of fourteen miles. Several other navies became enthusiastic users of the equipment, and the Canadians adapted a version for use with their experimental high-speed ocean-going anti-submarine hydrofoil, designed with a view to having the necessary performance to cover distance quickly to a locality where submarines might be found and then the capability of loitering on station using the VDS to monitor movements below the deeper thermal layers.

Accurate detection was also made more difficult by the switch to lower-frequency sonars to increase detection ranges. The result of using lower frequencies in the sound beam is that the resulting echo from a hard metallic object, like a submerged submarine, is no longer the sharp ping produced by the higher frequency sonars of the past, but a flatter and less distinct sound that is harder to identify with any certainty as a submarine echo. Another aid that was commonly employed to confirm a submarine target

warhead, introduced in 1959, and its successor the SUBROC, introduced in 1966. In time, however, it became clear that these weapons were extremely dangerous to the users as well as the targets in anything short of a hot-war situation, since they might well ignite a global nuclear holocaust. Furthermore, even in limited-war situations, the deafening effect of nuclear detonations on anti-submarine sonars made it essential to develop better conventional weapons, like the wire-guided Mark 37 torpedo of the 1960s and the heavier and faster Mark 48 of the 1970s.

Another limitation of 1960s ASW technology in countering nuclear submarines, was the effect of having to use sonar at longer ranges to give adequate warning of a nuclear boat's presence. With ranges of up to ten or twelve miles for powerful active search sonars, there was a greater premium on operator skill, as the equipment itself became less discriminating. Difficulties with the amount of background noise from a wide range of sources made contacts less reliable. Given the enhanced deep diving abilities and the limitless underwater endurance of nuclear submarines, another area of concern was their ability to hide below deeper thermal layers where conventional sonar beams were likely to be reflected upwards by the transition between different thermal layers and the surface. Russian submarines had been able to exploit the interaction between the warmer Gulf Stream and the colder waters beyond to evade long-range sonar detection.

in the past was the presence of the 'Doppler effect', a perceptible change in pitch between the outgoing beam and the returning echo imposed by the relative movement between the submarine and the ship operating the sonar. This too was proving to be less distinct with lower-frequency sonars, and the stronger the efforts being made to extend sonar ranges through even lower frequencies meant that these problems tended to worsen.

A less obvious problem concerned the time taken for the beam to reach the target and the echo to return over such long ranges. Where the range reaches 10,000 yards this process takes some twelve seconds, a long time for the operator to retain and then compare the characteristics of the outgoing signal with the returning echo. Furthermore, over even longer ranges, additional errors would have crept in because the sound beam tends to follow a curved path. Simply translating the echo return time to estimate the target range, as was normally done in the shorter-range sonars of the past, could easily result in an appreciable error, which would have been compounded by the movement of the operating ship and its target during that time. Finally, longer search ranges meant there was almost no chance of determining the depth of the target submarine, which, given the increased depth limits of nuclear submarines, became an increasingly important factor. The basic trigonometry of the depth-finding sonar used in the later stages of the Second World War was simply not possible over these hugely expanded distances.

In addition to all these limitations of long-range active sonar, there was one overriding vulnerability that, given the more powerful weaponry and the longer reach of the elusive nuclear submarines, made it less attractive as an anti-submarine sensor. It gave any hostile submarine in the vicinity an absolute indication of the presence and position of the anti-submarine ship itself, and made it an inviting target. It was rather like an armed soldier looking in the dark for equally well-armed adversaries. By using a powerful torch, the hunter would betray his position and become one of the hunted. Instead, by remaining in the dark and watching for his opponents' movements, his chances of surviving to disable that opponent would be greatly increased.

By this time, the single real weakness of the early nuclear submarines had become apparent: it was noisy (as detailed further in the next chapter). A nuclear boat could be heard over passive sonar for surprisingly long distances, without the danger of the anti-submarine ships betraying their positions and intentions. Consequently, the advantages of passive sonar became more appreciated. Listening for the noises emitted by a hostile submarine without giving away one's own position made much more sense, particularly where local oceanographic conditions constrained the range of

movement of a nuclear submarine in a particular locality. There was only one real disadvantage to passive sonar: it could indicate the bearing of a sound source like a hostile submarine or surface ship, but like the hydrophones it gave no precise information on range. All that could be done was for a submarine to sprint to another position far enough away to provide a cross-bearing to the sound source to allow an estimate to be made of its position, but this risked emitting additional noise and was cancelled out if the potential target made a similar move.

Success in simply listening for the enemy rather than a positive active sonar search called for the quietest acoustic background possible against which the sounds of a hostile submarine could be heard. This importance of sound reduction for successful use of passive sonar over long ranges meant two major changes in ASW tactics.

The traditional world-war experience of operating close escorts to protect convoys from submarine attack gave way to a more distant defence, using escort vessels on the fringes of a wider sanitised area free of submarines, well away from the high noise levels produced by the merchant ships under their protection. This was the thinking behind the idea of the NATO anti-submarine Striking Force. This was a more powerful equivalent to the support groups of the Second World War – intended to strike against Soviet submarines in a doctrine called the Forward Maritime Concept – sited well ahead of the NATO Fleet using the ships' own towed array sonars and helicopters operating dipping sonars and sonobuoys, and making use of other resources like long-range maritime patrol aircraft.

These forces came into their own where long-range detection became increasingly vital. Because of their speed and range, they could extend any hunt for submarines over huge areas, yet when they deployed their MAD and sonobuoy sensors they suffered few of the accuracy or detection problems of long-range sonar.

However, this was only part of the solution, applicable where specific ships or other high-value targets had to be protected. In the wider oceans where single targets abounded, even maritime patrol aircraft found it difficult to cover enough area in a given patrol, and the clear answer was to prove both more logical and more radical. If nuclear submarines could operate in places so remote from surface anti-submarine vessels, where severe range limitations on sensors and weapons reduced their effectiveness as submarine hunters, the answer was to set a thief to catch a thief. The best way to exploit the undoubted qualities of the nuclear submarine as a potential target was to send another nuclear submarine after it, a nuclear submarine dedicated to a new role, an anti-submarine vessel in its own right: the ultimate stealth weapon in the form of the hunter-killer submarine.

CHAPTER 19

STEALTH AND SILENCE AND UNDERWATER HUNTING

1960–1992

The sleek and threatening shape of a Russian Alfa class hunter-killer submarine.

(US Naval Institute Press)

T HE introduction of the nuclear-powered submarine proved enormously successful. So successful, in fact, that the only anti-submarine vessel realistically capable of tracking it down and destroying it proved to be another nuclear submarine. The main reason for this was that only another nuclear submarine could match its speed, stealth and underwater performance, not to mention its huge sensor capacity resulting from the almost limitless power provided from its reactor. Consequently, the most effective tactics to use against nuclear submarines involved submarine-versus-submarine operations. Because of the power of modern sensors and weapons, the old realities of ASW had effectively been turned on their heads. The nuclear hunter-killer submarines (SSKNs) that would undertake this role were the modern, and much more effective, equivalent of the ineffective hunting groups of both world wars. In this case they were protecting carrier groups and convoys and other vulnerable surface targets by sailing on aggressive patrols against their adversaries instead of providing close escorts to those convoys and task groups and waiting for the enemy nuclear boats to come to them.

The result was a succession of encounters between the heavily armed and highly capable hunter-killer submarines and ballistic missile submarines of both sides in the Cold War. This was a highly dangerous game involving eavesdropping on one another's operational methods, their performance and their sound signatures in a campaign of underwater hide-and-seek. The price of this close watch had been more accidents, with eleven known collisions in the last thirty-five years, damaging several submarines and believed to have resulted in the sinking of at least one Soviet boat. The benefits include valuable additional intelligence on the way the Soviet submarines would be used in a major confrontation or in full-scale war, the kind of exercises in which they were involved, the tactics they used and how they co-operated with surface units or attacked potential targets, and the routes they used to reach their objectives and return to their bases afterwards.

To help British and American hunter-killer submarines find their elusive targets in the first place, a chain of passive sonar arrays was mounted on the seabed to keep constant watch for passing submarines. This trip-wire system was effectively a modern equivalent of the hydrophone arrays of the First World War intended to monitor the noises made by passing U-boats in restricted waters like the narrow sections of the English Channel. It originated as Project Caesar in the early 1950s, at about the time the first nuclear submarines appeared, and tests showed that submarine noise signatures could be picked up at ranges of up to six hundred miles in ideal conditions.

By 1960 Caesar barriers had been established off both

the western and eastern coasts of the United States. They were later succeeded by the Sound Surveillance System or SOSUS, which was deployed further out into international waters and natural choke points like the Greenland, Iceland–UK (GIUK) Gap, where submarine traffic was at its most dense and where particularly good passive sonar signals were picked up. By 1981 SOSUS chains also operated in UK waters, off Turkey and Japan and the Aleutian island chain, off Hawaii and Puerto Rico, off Bermuda and Barbados, Canada and Norway, Iceland and the Azores, Italy and Denmark, Gibraltar and Panama, the Philippines, Guam and Diego Garcia.[1]

SOSUS used low-frequency analysis and recording (Lofar) narrow-band techniques to identify specific sounds in the ocean associated with the submarines of actual or potential enemies. Since the 1970s the system has been developed to enable it to call anti-submarine resources such as patrol aircraft into an area sufficiently small for them to stand a good chance of picking up the echo of the particular submarine that triggered the original SOSUS alarm.

This was only possible because of the relatively high level of noise it created, which meant it could be heard and identified from a long way away. All these passive systems, and the techniques used by hunter-killer submarines to find their opposite numbers from the other side of the Cold War confrontation, either as objectives for peacetime intelligence gathering or as wartime targets, depended on this one serious limitation.

The noise was created from three main sources. The first was propeller cavitation, from the formation and collapse of voids or bubbles along the faces of the propeller blades, as they drove the boat along at high speed, though this was less important as the noise emission tended to reduce as the submarine dived to greater depths. The second source was low-frequency resonances from operating machinery, which were conducted through the hull and out into the sea beyond. The third source involved transients resulting from specific operations like the opening of the torpedo tube doors.

In addition, the nuclear reactor itself needed to be kept cool by motor-driven pumps that ran continuously. To compound the problem, the steam turbine drove the propeller shaft through a gear train, and these too were particularly common sources of noise on Soviet nuclear submarines. The first generation of Soviet nuclear reactors tended to suffer from reliability problems, so there was much system duplication in the designs of the early boats. All these factors made them larger, less manoeuvrable and more easily detected than their Western equivalents. Nevertheless, they were extremely robust, often using double hulls to increase their safe diving limits and enable them to minimise the damage that might result from being hit by an anti-submarine conventional warhead torpedo, and this was reinforced by large amounts of reserve buoyancy.

However, the Soviets eventually realised how vulnerable their noise emissions had made their nuclear boats from cipher data passed to them by the Walker spy ring over seventeen years of espionage, which enabled the KGB to read more than a million secret messages. Some of these referred to noise emissions from Soviet submarines, and they began to embark on a belated improvement programme, using all the noise-reduction techniques used by the British and American navies. These included natural circulation systems for the nuclear reactors to reduce the dependency on cooling pumps, and the fitting of quieter pumps where these were still needed. The main items of machinery were made quieter by mounting them on rafts supported by noise-insulating mountings within the pressure hull, and by using dead water or some form of sound insulation material in between the inner and outer layers of the pressure hulls. In the longer term, improved hull shapes caused less turbulence, and larger propellers turning more slowly could all help reduce the sound signature of a submarine.

From the 1960s onwards, it also became clear from new construction that the Soviets were giving increased priority to ASW, and were almost certainly intending to use nuclear submarines to escort their ballistic missile submarines to their wartime positions if war became likely. However, even the Victor class hunter-killer submarines of 1968 were too noisy to escape retaliation, and it was only with the Victor III class of 1978 that sound reduction had begun to prove successful. Nevertheless, by the late 1980s, the newer Soviet boats were almost as quiet as their Western adversaries, and it was thought likely that continuing espionage by the likes of the Walker spy ring had given them the data needed

The US hunter-killer submarine uss *Thresher*, lost with all hands off the east coast of America in April 1963 during deep diving trials following an earlier overhaul of her systems.

(The Floating Drydock)

The Arctic pack ice offers concealment to nuclear submarines searching for one another on the main undersea routes between Russia and the US, which has kept boats making regular exploratory visits to the area.
(US Naval Institute Press)

to achieve this. Three classes in particular, the latest 671s, the Sierra class and the *Akula* class, which used raft-mounted machinery, had been made quiet enough to put passive sonar target finding in doubt.

Until then, though, tracking Soviet boats was straightforward enough for well-handled SSKNs with experienced crews. Their high-quality passive sonar equipment could not only hear the noises emitted by a Russian nuclear submarine, but analyse the different components of the sound to identify the class and often the individual boat, using a library of sensor recordings made on earlier intelligence-gathering confrontations. Since all nuclear submarines would be aware of the danger of being trailed by the opposition in their turn, they would use different tactics to reveal whether or not they were being tracked.

For example, Soviet boats often manoeuvred sharply without warning, sometimes turning in a full circle, to expose whether or not a Western submarine was hiding in the blind spot dead astern. In other cases, their most valuable missile submarines would often be accompanied by a nuclear hunter-killer boat as escort, which could cover any blind spots without the need for distracting manoeuvres. The counter-tactic to this was for the shadowing NATO submarine to keep the less-wary missile boat between it and the more alert escort, trusting that its own quieter noise emissions would be covered by the noise output of

both Russian submarines, though this called for great care and rapid responses.

Choke points, where the huge ocean spaces were narrowed down because of land masses or underwater topography, posed particular problems to a shadowing boat, since it would be forced closer to the boat it was trailing. One tactic was to use the restricted space to advantage. Once it became clear the target was heading for a particular choke point, the shadower could sprint ahead to lie in wait on the other side of the restricted area, but this too called for great care, moving ahead slowly until the range increased, so that the inevitable increase in noise resulting from greater speed was not heard by the target.

Apart from lower noise emissions, until recently, Western submarines enjoyed another huge advantage over their adversaries, in the high quality of their sonar equipment. For example, the BQQ5D system used on the US Navy's Los Angeles class nuclear submarines – designed to support high-speed carrier battle groups as essentially underwater escort vessels – consisted of a fifteen-foot radius[2] spherical sonar array mounted in the bows of the submarine, with both active and passive options, and a low-frequency array mounted around the bow for longer-range passive searches. Higher-frequency sonars are also able to search for mines or obstacles under pack-ice. The main sonar system uses a technique called digital multi-beam steering to track a series of different contacts at the same time, In addition, the boats had an acoustic intercept receiver that acted as the underwater equivalent of the U-boats' Metox radar detector, giving warning of any other vessel's active sonar emissions, or signals from incoming weapons.[3]

Sonars like these consume huge amounts of power – seventy-five kilowatts for the BQQ5D and a staggering 570 kilowatts for the BSV-2 combat system installed in the later Seawolf class hunter-killer boats of the US Navy. British sonars too are extremely capable. The S and T classes of nuclear hunter-killer boats were fitted with 2001 and later the 2020 bow sonars as the heart of a computer-controlled tracking system. Even as long ago as 1973, the electronics aboard these boats made it possible to track up to twenty-four different contacts at the same time, compared with the limit of two or possibly three using the old manual methods;[4] sensor and computer capability have been greatly improved since then.

One way of evading the attentions of hostile submarines, or ASW forces in general, was to make use of geography in other respects. From the very beginning, nuclear submarines have operated below the polar ice-cap. There they can operate without fear of aircraft spotting them either directly on the surface, or by using dipping sonar or dropping sonobuoys. Another advantage of operating beneath the ice was that the lower surface of the pack ice is not smooth but studded with jagged downward-facing ridges called keels, caused by pressure and sometimes reaching to depths of 150 feet or more. These provided excellent cover and were opaque to sensors and even to weapons in most cases. Finally, the polar area is itself extremely noisy, with the continuous breaking up of the pack ice under different stresses, which provides excellent cover in an area where sonar conditions are already problematic because of layers of different density created by mixing currents of salt and fresh water.

Polar anti-submarine operations became increasingly important as the Soviets improved the range of their submarine-launched ballistic missiles. No longer would their SSBNs (nuclear-powered missile submarines) have to undertake the dangerous voyages to launching sites off the American coast if war threatened. Instead, they could stay back under heavy naval protection from submarines, aircraft and surface anti-submarine ships in what became known as 'bastions', located closer to their own coasts and potentially more difficult for NATO submarines to reach. These bastions included the Bering Sea, the Sea of Okhotsk and the polar regions where the Soviet colossal, new Typhoon boats in particular, assembled from two Delta type pressure hulls side-by-side within a huge streamlined outer casing, and displacing some 25,000

The latest British hunter-killers include HMS *Tireless*. (www.navyphotos.co.uk).

Royal Navy hunter-killer submarine HMS *Swiftsure* leaving harbour. (www.navyphotos.co.uk)

tons fully loaded, would lurk in a war situation.

Early in the 1980s, a joint US–UK operation was sent to the polar region to try to determine how it might be possible to locate and attack Soviet submarines using this area for protection. HMS *Valiant*, a British hunter-killer submarine and an American SSKN were able to use what amounted to a firing-range beneath the polar ice. This was created by sending a C130 military transport plane to land on the ice and organise the lowering of sonobuoys through holes specially drilled through the ice cap. The two submarines made mock attacks on one another, firing practice torpedoes that were then retrieved by burning holes through the ice, and as a result modifications to weapons and tactics to make the best of these unusual conditions were evolved.

At one time the West seemed to have a ten-year lead on the Soviets in terms of sonars, weapons and noise reduction. The first measure of how much that lead had been eroded was underlined by the introduction of the first of the *Akula* class in 1984. This hunter-killer boat carried sophisticated sonar, displaced some 10,000 tons and had an observed top speed of thirty-five knots, yet it was also extremely quiet. Normally the faster a boat travels, the noisier it is, and since it cannot travel at high speed and listen for other targets at the same time, surveillance tactics usually involve covering long distances in short sprints broken by periods of listening at slower speeds.

This put new pressure on Western navies to develop sonars that could still hear these quieter Russian submarines. One solution was to use existing towed array sonars originally developed in the 1970s, which consisted of a long array of hydrophones arranged on a cable up to half a mile long, which could be streamed astern of both submerged submarines and surface anti-submarine vessels alike. The principal advantage was that this allowed the sonar to trail so far behind the ship carrying it that it operated well clear of its wake and machinery noise, and was therefore well placed to hear the lower-level sounds emitted by the newer submarines. Where passive hull-mounted sonars could previously pick up Soviet submarines at ranges of between ten to twenty thousand yards, this effective range was greatly reduced as the Soviet vessels were made much quieter. Towed array sonar was effectively much more sensitive and the range was therefore extended again.

By the end of the 1970s, using advanced computer techniques to process the data from long towed array sonars had made them capable of detecting relatively quiet targets at ranges of a hundred miles and beyond. For best results, the sonar arrays needed to be streamed as far away from the towing ship as possible. This was more straightforward aboard a surface ship than it was aboard a submarine, where the cable often had to be attached at the start of a patrol and only stowed once it was over, and manoeuvrability was restricted by the need to let the towed array stream out astern after each turn. Furthermore, getting the most from towed array sonars needs high speed, as it can easily take a matter of hours to resolve the bearing and movement of a potential target, over which time the target could move between fifty and a hundred miles. To carry out a full target motion analysis (TMA) can take even longer, up to ten to fifteen hours or even more.

By the early 1980s the surface escort ship was becoming more important as a detector of hostile submarines once again. During the 1980s, passive sonar was the mainstay of anti-submarine operations in both the Royal and United States navies. The US Navy developed the powerful SQQ-89 sonar and control system for surface ships to integrate passive sonar with both towed array systems and the helicopter-deployed sonobuoys launched from US escorts. Later the emphasis switched from using helicopters simply as one part of the system dedicated to locating hostile submarines to actually carrying out their own search-and-attack procedures rather than simply dropping sonobuoys to feed data to the ship. In this respect longer-range aircraft like Sea Kings allowed them to extend operations out to the full range of the high-performance towed array systems, and maritime

The huge Russian Typhoon class of ballistic missile submarines displaces as much as an old-time battleship and may be able to survive one or more torpedo hits.

(www.navyphotos.co.uk)

patrol aircraft with more capable computer systems and homing torpedoes were able to mount independent searches of their own over much wider ocean areas.

Towed array sonars even had a part to play in the wider strategic ASW picture. Information from the towed array sonars of NATO submarines and surface anti-submarine vessels were used to create a net called

SURTASS–LFA (surveillance towed array sensor system–low frequency active), which uses active low-frequency sound to improve its detection capabilities, fed into the Acoustic Research Center in California and then into the US Navy's ASW Center Command and Control System to provide a worldwide picture of submarine movements and local tactical data under the Integrated Undersea Surveillance System (IUSS) scheme. Nevertheless, with the end of the Cold War, monitoring the movements of large numbers of Soviet nuclear submarines became relatively less important, and there has tended to be a shift back towards active sonars and the use of both surface anti-submarine ships and both fixed-wing aircraft and anti-submarine helicopters with MAD equipment, sono-buoys and dipping sonars.

As always with anti-submarine warfare, the ultimate purpose of spotting, identifying and tailing a hostile submarine is, in a wartime situation, to sink it, and in this respect anti-submarine weapons have developed far beyond those of even the early post-war era in terms of speed, destructive power and target-finding abilities. Though the Russians have done a great deal of catching up more recently, anti-submarine weapons, quality was another area in which they previously lagged well behind the West. Their lightweight anti-submarine torpedoes, for example, were invariably bigger and heavier than their Western counterparts.

Since the old type of homing torpedoes were effectively limited to targets with ranges of up to a mile or two because of gyro errors or the target taking evasive action, Western navies have turned to wire-guided torpedoes to hit targets at longer ranges. As the wire is paid out at a similar rate from the submarine at one end and the torpedo at the other, the wire remains almost stationary in the water. A Soviet submarine attacked by one of these weapons would be likely to fire less capable and much noisier homing torpedoes back down the bearing of the incoming weapons to try to persuade the launching submarine to part the cable as it takes evasive action. In addition, because the earlier Russian submarines were noisier than their Western counterparts, they were forced to develop a range of static and self-propelled decoys. If they heard incoming torpedoes they would try to evade by going into a full-speed dive, releasing decoys ready to use in stern tubes.

Because of the high speeds of which nuclear submarines are capable, current anti-submarine weapons have to be even faster, in many cases using gas-turbine propulsion, and the British and American navies have relied on advanced long-range high-speed torpedoes with heavy warheads. The Royal Navy Mark 24 Tigerfish battery-driven wire-guided torpedo was originally introduced in 1980, but persistent teething troubles with such a complex weapon meant it took almost the entire decade for it to reach its full potential. The US Navy's Mark 48 torpedo, which first appeared as long ago as 1971, has been upgraded into a faster 'advanced capability' or ADCAP version which is capable of sixty knots, fast enough to catch any Russian nuclear submarine trying to run for safety.

This torpedo was fitted with a larger fuel tank to increase its range to twenty-five nautical miles. With a total of twenty miles of guidance wire, the submarine using it has the chance to clear away from the launch position and still continue guiding the torpedo towards its target. If the launching submarine has to cut the wire, the torpedo has its own homing head, which uses electronically steered sonar beams, to find its target for itself over a 180-degree hemisphere and then steer it to the point where its 650-pound warhead can do the most damage. In addition to all this, it has sophisticated anti-jamming facilities to prevent itself being seduced by the target firing off decoys, and it can also send information from its seeker head back to the parent submarine.[5]

Standard tactics with an ADCAP torpedo involved trying to hit the hostile submarine at the stern, where at the very least it would destroy the target's propulsion system even if it failed to sink it. Furthermore, the shock of the detonation might well have burst the weak points around the seals for the propeller shaft, flooding the engine room and probably sending it to the bottom. These torpedoes can be launched – effectively floated out of the launch tubes – in quiet

The American nuclear submarine uss *Seawolf,* first of the latest class of fast attack submarines.
(US Naval Institute Press)

wire-guided mode, and if different temperature layers are present, the torpedoes can be steered under a transition zone to hide the noise they make from the intended target. If the enemy submarine does hear the incoming torpedoes, the standard counter-tactic would be to launch torpedoes of its own on a reciprocal bearing. In that event, the US submarine would almost certainly cut the wire-guidance link and leave the torpedoes to use their own homing systems to lead them to the target, while itself turning and running at full speed to evade the Russian weapons, firing decoys to distract them if they should succeed in closing the range. In a contest like this, if the Russian submarine should survive the attack with heavy damage, the final result would merely be postponed. Any physical impact would almost certainly increase the noise the submarine transmits because of extra turbulence around damaged parts of the hull, and make it that much more vulnerable to a second attack.[6]

Ironically, just as the submarine Cold War reached this final peak of sophistication, and the closest balance of capabilities yet between the submarines of either side, the situation was transformed by the break-up of the former Soviet Union and the sharp decline in the number and operational readiness of the Russian submarine force. Though a core of the best nuclear submarines still remains at Russian bases – both hunter-killer and ballistic missile boats – financial restrictions have inflicted severe cuts on the number at sea at any one time. For example, only two of the massive Typhoons are believed to be operational, backed up by half a dozen Delta IVs and several Delta IIIs. The new Borey class was supposed to number six, but so far one boat is almost three-quarters complete, another half complete and a third was laid down in the spring of 2006. So far as boats on patrol are concerned, there were three SSBNs at sea during 2005, two each in the two preceding years and none at all in 2002.[7]

Instead, the nature of the threat facing anti-submarine forces has shifted, almost heading back to complete the full circle towards the diesel-electric submersible of U-boat days. More and more countries unable to afford the vast cost of nuclear boats have chosen the cheaper option, and recent developments have ensured that this type of submarine is taking over as the main potential adversary for current anti-submarine warfare operations. Though these boats lack the astonishing performance of the nuclear-powered submarine, the huge developments that have taken place since 1945 make them much more formidable propositions, and ASW tactics and technology have had to evolve to deal with the threat they present. This latest development in the long story of the submarine and how to contain and defeat it will be covered in the final chapter of this book.

CHAPTER 20

THE 21ST-CENTURY SUBMARINE THREAT

1991–the present

The Lockheed Neptune ASW patrol plane was also supplied to the RAF as the Mercator during the 1950s. The sting tail contains the much more capable MAD equipment developed from that used during the war.

(US Naval Institute Press)

*U*31 was a type VII German submarine, commissioned on 28 December 1936. She was sunk for the first time, with all her crew, on 11 March 1940 in the Heligoland Bight by a Blenheim of Bomber Command (see Chapter 8). Lying in relatively shallow water, she was raised and repaired and recommissioned. She was then sunk for a second and final time almost eight months later northwest of Ireland by the British destroyer HMS *Antelope*, this time with only two casualties. Now another *U*31 has joined the German Navy, this time a type 212A; in some ways she resembles her unfortunate predecessor, but in others she is much much more formidable, and an ideal example of the latest challenge to face anti-submarine forces in the twenty-first century.

Like her forebear, the new *U*31 is equipped with diesel power, electric motors and lead-acid batteries. However, her other equipment, and the overall performance it provides, is something that those who crewed her predecessor could only dream about. Unlike earlier types of air-independent propulsion (AIP) systems like Stirling engines, which have had to contend with different limitations, she is the first of four new-generation U-boats for the German Navy, and the first submarine in the world to have a fuel-cell converter linked directly to her propulsion system. Her electric motor is powered either by nine silent-operation Siemens polymer electrolytic membrane fuel cells that can allow her to stay fully submerged for up to a month, or by high-performance lead-acid batteries that can either increase that overall endurance, or be used to allow her to sprint up to a maximum underwater speed of seventeen knots. Not only is the chemical reaction in the fuel cells completely silent, but the only by-product of the reaction is distilled water, so pure it can augment the crew's washing and drinking allowance. To keep noise levels as low as possible, she has a single seven-bladed 'skew-back' propeller which produces almost no cavitation and her control room and engine room are both mounted on rubber buffers inside the pressure hull to stop sound emissions reaching the outside.

If fuel cells and batteries become exhausted, she can deploy a schnorkel to use her single diesel engine for recharging. Her sonar equipment includes a towed array, a mine-detection sonar and a system that can monitor the submarine's own noise emissions to be aware of what an enemy vessel might be able to hear. Her search periscope is fitted with the usual optical range-finder but also with a thermal imager and a GPS receiver. She also carries a torpedo counter-measures system consisting of four containers each with up to ten discharge tubes for releasing effectors, small underwater vehicles similar in shape to torpedoes, but emitting signals that enable them to decoy incoming torpedoes and which are based on a system already used for Germany's latest frigates.

Her main armament consists of six torpedo tubes, each one capable of launching a 21-inch DM2A4 heavyweight torpedo using a water ramjet expulsion system. The torpedoes are guided not by wires but through optical fibres that give extended range and faster data transmission, and she carries a full set of reloads. She is one of four 212As built for the German Navy with another two for the Italian Navy. Her export equivalent, the type 214, is already winning overseas customers, with four ordered by Greece and three by Korea so far. While the maximum diving depth of the type 212A remains classified, the type 214 can go deeper than 1,300 feet, and can launch missiles as well as torpedoes. Fifty examples of her predecessor, the type 209, have been sold to a dozen different countries, and other modern diesel-electric boats have been produced for worldwide sales by Sweden, France and Russia.

Originally, the type 212 was designed to operate in shallow waters like the Baltic during the Cold War to

The capable and sophisticated Lockheed Orion, from its introduction in 1959 through to the present day, provides an essential part of the kind of multi-platform weapons systems needed to find and attack modern submarines.

(US Naval Institute Press)

attack Soviet transports and supply ships in an invasion of the West, or to seal off the choke point of the Skagerrak and Kattegat to deny the Soviet Baltic Fleet access to the North Sea and the Atlantic. Now she and her sisters are more likely to be used to enforce UN or NATO weapons embargoes or to operate against pirates or terrorist groups seeking to hijack merchant vessels.

Above all, this state-of-the-art design is the shape of the submarine for the twenty-first century. Though the world total of operational submarines had fallen to 390 by the end of 2003, roughly half those operational a decade before, there has been a shift in emphasis. Operators of nuclear submarines like the Russians, the Americans and the British have sharply reduced their nuclear submarine forces with the end of the Cold War. On the other hand, the number of

these new semi-submersibles has increased, and is likely to go on increasing, among countries without the means or the know-how to commission their own nuclear boats.

As a potential target for anti-submarine warfare, these boats present a formidable challenge. Though they lack the speed, endurance and firepower of the big nuclear submarines, they pack a heavy punch and promise to be exceedingly difficult to detect. As such, they have triggered a sharp difference of opinion among commanders of the navies that might have to deal with them in earnest – how should ASW develop to meet this resurgent problem from its own history?

This leaves ASW development in a state of some confusion: some feel only the nuclear hunter-killer submarine can neutralise these new submarines. Others insist that the way forward is a multi-faceted anti-submarine team of surface escorts, fixed-wing maritime patrol aircraft, helicopters, dipping and towed array sonars, homing torpedoes, SOSUS hydrophones, IUSS data, sonobuoys and cruise missiles. The truth of the argument can only be proved in action, but would surface anti-submarine ships be too vulnerable if they have to use active sonar to find their elusive targets, and risk betraying their position in doing so? Or would a varied anti-submarine team present even the most elusive submarine with far too many adversaries?

To some extent, ASW since 8 May 1945 has been a combination of technology and prediction. In the century since the submarine was developed into a deadly naval weapon, the only time when ASW technology was put to the test of combat operations was in the Second World War. The six decades since Doenitz's surviving submarines surrendered to their Allied adversaries has meant that ASW tactics and technology have remained as unproven as ICBMs and anti-missile defence systems. Furthermore, while the highly sophisticated equipment now available to both sides is a matter of fact, some insist that ASW has been rendered obsolete by the end of the Cold War, and the money being spent on new technology would be better spent on other naval ships and weapons, an echo of the ideas fashionable between the wars. However, the same paradox still applies: no one can prove who would triumph in actual combat between one side and the other if snoop became shoot.

What has been shown by the most detailed and realistic ASW exercises has been highly disconcerting. Diesel-electric submarines have penetrated US Navy defences and survived to make simulated attacks on the highest-value targets like carriers and logistics ships. In 1982, the diesel-electric Argentine submarine *San Luis* effectively eluded the ships from the Royal Navy that were searching for her during the Falklands War.[1] In 1996, US Navy units could not find Chilean diesel submarines in a joint exercise, and a year later

An Orion patrol aircraft flies over an American warship intercepting a Soviet freighter during the blockade of Cuba following the 1962 Missile Crisis.

(US Naval Institute Press)

a Russian Oscar was able to tail the command ship USS *Coronado* for a matter of days without being detected, and in joint Pacific exercises in 2000, several Royal Australian Navy submarines succeeded in evading US Navy anti-submarine defences.[2]

All of this has created a new emphasis on the need for effective ASW, particularly for the US Navy to operate safely in the coastal areas needed for effective power-projection operations. These sites certainly favour the newer, smaller submarines, with different density layers resulting from the combination of salt water with fresh water from river estuaries creating difficult sonar conditions, and being a much noisier environment than the open ocean. Consequently a battery of new technology under the overall umbrella of Command, Control, Communication, Computers, Intelligence, Surveillance and Reconnaissance (C⁴ISR)

is being developed to meet this threat, with more sophisticated anti-submarine aircraft, and littoral combat ships (LCS) carrying their own ASW-capable helicopters to attack the submarines as well as a wider range of systems to find them.

These new location technologies include distributed sensor networks seeded across wide areas of water, and non-acoustic methods like bioluminescence, electro-optical, electric field and electro-magnetic methods and infra-red and chemical wake analysis. Future ASW tactics may also involve sabotage methods in the enemy's own harbours and bases by special forces teams, including ways of hampering submarines' performance or tagging them to make them easier to find and destroy when they emerge on operational patrols.

At the same time, the quietness of the latest submarines has added a new importance to the use of

HMS *Upholder* was one of four British diesel electric submarines built during the 1980s to explore this technology, but since sold to the Canadians.

(www.navyphotos.co.uk)

More and more navies are tending to rely on carriers, equipped with ASW helicopters, to combat the threat presented by modern submarines. This is the Spanish ASW carrier *Principe de Asturias*.

(www.navyphotos.co.uk)

A *Krivak* class ASW cruiser of the Soviet Navy, one of a series of heavily armed vessels built to combat Western submarines.

(www.navyphotos.co.uk)

active sonar, on both surface ships and helicopters. Dipping sonar lowered from helicopters hovering over the sea has come back into popularity, this time involving low-frequency, long-range active sonars. For the Royal Navy, where operations in the shallower waters of the continental shelf are extremely important, the newer frigates are likely to use active sonars like the 2050, which has software that prevents it being confused by false echoes off the seabed, and which can operate in shallow water conditions at ranges of several miles. Towed array sonars for future ASW operations are likely to be combined with active transmitters.

The danger is that unless a boat moves a considerable distance between one active transmission and the next, it will be attacked by anti-submarine forces that have picked up on its transmissions and know its position. If, however, a SSKN nuclear-powered attack submarine has picked up its target by information from allied ASW units – like surface escorts or helicopters using sonobuoys or dipping sonar – or by its own passive sonar, then it may only need two sonar pulses to give the range and position information it needs for fire control, enabling it to be faster to the draw and launch torpedoes before its adversary does so. Another option for the longer term is to fit wide-aperture array sonar at the bow and stern of the larger nuclear boats, to provide the equivalent of the old optical range-finders, so as to allow the range and position of a target to be fixed accurately without the need to send out an active pulse of acoustic energy.

Of course, even these new and more efficient submarines have their weak points, as does every submarine ever made. If operational demands call for increased speed from time to time (and today's merchant ships and their warship escorts are appreciably faster than their wartime predecessors), then their endurance is greatly reduced, and they would have to resort to schnorkelling to recharge the batteries so that they can continue to operate underwater. This imposes severe penalties on a submarine trying to remain concealed. Although design improvements mean that using a schnorkel is quieter than it was in the Second World War, it still degrades the boat's ability to listen for potential threats, while the latest hunter-killer nuclear submarines can hear a schnorkelling submarine at ranges of ten miles or more.

Likewise, the commander of one of these hybrid-drive submarines has a series of difficult decisions to take over the balance between range and performance. For designs like the latest German boats, the economical cruising speed is eight knots, for a maximum submerged endurance of some eight thousand miles. However, if operational requirements mean the boat has to increase to maximum speed to reach a favourable firing position, then her power reserves can be depleted at more than sixty times the cruising rate. Furthermore, while AIP systems are able to offer even higher combinations of range and performance for the future – one Italian design claims a speed of up to thirty knots for up to three thousand miles – the fact remains that none of them are as efficient or as independent of the outside world as the

A new generation of U-boats is represented by the *S171*. Like her sister ships and their successors, they are known by two numbers – the traditional German 'U' designation and their standard NATO 'S' number.

(www.navyphotos.co.uk)

Canada has built up formidable expertise in deploying capable helicopters on small escort vessels: HMCS *Frazier* carries a Sea King as a vital part of her weapons system.

(www.navyphotos.co.uk)

nuclear reactor. In addition, these smaller diesel-electric submarines are far too small to survive a direct hit by missile or torpedo, unlike some of the largest multi-hull Russian nuclear boats.

Two other, less quantifiable factors concern cost and expertise. These sophisticated smaller submarines are anything but cheap, and three of the German boats offered for sale to Portugal were priced at around $2 billion in total. The other limitation concerns the infrastructure and experience needed to keep these submarines in the peak of mechanical condition once they have been paid for, with well-trained crews and powerful weapons ready whenever they may be needed. This may well prove to be impossible on a longer-term basis for countries who simply buy submarines as a relatively cheap and simple way of increasing the threat they present to their perceived enemies. Where the opportunity to enhance their performance does arise, such as through the addition of a low-cost, low-power nuclear source for increased underwater endurance and to therefore reserve battery power for high-speed emergencies, these promise to be too costly and complex for many

operators of these submarines.

At the same time, a whole range of promising tactics and technologies may also provide anti-submarine forces of the future with the means of redressing the balance against larger numbers of these stealthy submersibles. In theory, some of the performance improvement possibilities now being pursued for nuclear hunter-killer boats might also be available for the smaller boats they would be hunting, but the reality is that the technologies and the resources to exploit them will belong primarily to those countries already operating nuclear submarines. They include more efficient hull shapes and surface coatings for higher speed, possibly with the ejection of gases or liquid additives to the boundary layer surrounding the hull to reduce friction with the water. Other advances in propulsion systems, such as the use of new technologies like magneto-hydrodynamic drive or electromagnetic ramjet propulsion may not only improve performance but also make it possible for nuclear boats to move faster without any increase in sound emissions. Finally, larger hulls and stronger materials may well make the larger submarines more difficult for their smaller adversaries to destroy.

Even the active sonar conundrum may be soluble using ingenious technology. Research is continuing into the feasibility of camouflaging active sonar transmissions as random ocean noise, or by concealing them in different parts of a wider range of frequencies. Other possibilities include the potential to disguise an active pulse by making it seem like a gradual increase in the types of sounds emitted by whale or dolphin conversations or shrimps chirruping. Even now, one of the tests of a top-quality sonar operator is to distinguish whether the increase in shrimp noise in reaction to the passing of a submarine is caused by his own boat, or another undetected one far too close for comfort.

Other possibilities include the opportunity to solve the active sonar problem by avoiding it, and developing another means of detection altogether. The existing undersea arrays like SOSUS could be made accessible to friendly submarines within range, so that they could interrogate the arrays' sensors – active or passive – and receive three-dimensional information on the positions and movements of potential targets in the vicinity. Other search criteria for future systems could include extreme low-frequency (ELF) electric fields, magnetic anomalies and thermal scarring resulting from a submarine's passing through a particular area beneath the surface. Sophisticated sensors could monitor the temperature changes resulting from the discharge of coolant from a hostile submarine's propulsion system.

Even the turbulence of the wake or the almost imperceptible surface bulge caused by the water displacement of a passing submarine could be measured

The ultimate ASW asset –
and most vital submarine
target – the US Navy's
nuclear attack carrier USS
Eisenhower is the centre of
a complex array of ships,
aircraft sensors and
weapons to combat even
the stealthiest and most
powerful underwater craft.
(The Floating Drydock)

by the right kind of sensors. For example, one report claimed that among the information passed to the Chinese by spies in the US was satellite radar that could detect nuclear boats well below the surface and even identify individual submarines by their propeller characteristics.

The report explained that the satellites used low-angle 'polarimetric and interferometric radars to see through clouds and pick up very small changes in the ocean caused by a submarine' and that

> the relatively low angle of the satellite in the sky enables it to detect the subtlest of changes in sea level. Advanced computer signal processing is then used to analyse the radar images. This eliminates any movements in the ocean due to the motion of waves and takes account of diffraction effects (when different parts of the submarine's wake interfere with one another) to determine the speed of the submarine and the direction in which it is travelling.[3]

If this technology exists now, or in the future, the data could all be passed on by airborne or satellite sensors to an ASW submarine.

Another possibility is the submarine equivalent of the Patriot anti-missile missile, or the anti-torpedo torpedo. Researchers at Pennsylvania State University

have produced a model of a weapon looking like a scaled-down pump-jet Mark 48, reduced to a diameter of 6.25 inches in order to fit existing decoy tubes, so that it could be launched from either ASW submarines or surface ships, using a short towed array for its information. The Russians also claim to have developed both an anti-torpedo torpedo and a rocket that fires to impact when an incoming torpedo crosses a preset line.[4]

Finally, perhaps the greatest savings to be made in ASW operation might be made by the use of unmanned underwater vehicles (UUVs), using a combination of remote-control and highly automated systems. Essentially, this would involve modifying existing technology used to develop the highly sophisticated and successful unmanned aerial vehicles (UAVs) that are capable of loitering unobtrusively over heavily defended areas, sending back information to their bases and even launching attacks with their own weapons when directed. Because of their smaller size and reduced power requirements, these UUVs could be made even more undetectable than the quietest submarines. Against a future as promising but as unpredictable as this, only one fact is certain. So long as the submarine remains a viable weapons system, then the technology and tactics of anti-submarine warfare needed to defeat it will remain an essential part of naval operations.

BIBLIOGRAPHY AND SOURCES

ARCHIBALD, E H H, The Fighting Ship in the Royal Navy, 897-1984, Poole 1984.

ARTHUR, MAX, Lost Voices of the Royal Navy, London 2005.

BAILEY, JIM, The Sky Suspended: a Fighter Pilot's Story, new paperback edition, London, 2005.

BAKER, RICHARD, The Terror of Tobermory: An Informal Biography of Vice-Admiral Sir Gilbert Stephenson, KBE, CB, CMG, London 1972.

BARNETT, CORELLI, Engage the Enemy More Closely: the Royal Navy in the Second World War, London 1991.

BAUER, VICE-ADMIRAL HERMANN, Als Fuhrer der U-boote im Weltkrieg 1914-18, Leipzig, 1943.

BAXTER, JAMES PHINNEY III, Scientists against Time, New York 1947

BEAVER, PAUL, The British Aircraft Carrier, Sparkford 1987.

BEAVER, PAUL, U-Boats in the Atlantic, Sparkford 1979.

BEESLY, PATRICK, Very Special Intelligence, The Story of the Admiralty's Operational Intelligence Centre in World War II, London 1978.

BLACKETT, PROFESSOR P M S, Studies of War: Nuclear and Conventional, London 1962.

BLAIR, CLAY JR, Silent Victory, the US Submarine War against Japan, New York 1975.

BLAIR, CLAY, Hitler's U-Boat War, (2 volumes), London 1997-99.

BOWMAN, MARTIN, Mosquito Bomber/Fighter-Bomber Units 1942-45, London 1997.

BOWYER, CHAZ, Men of Coastal Command, London 1985.

BOYD, CARL and YOSHITA, AKIHITO, The Japanese Submarine Force and World War II, Annapolis 2002.

BRENNECKE, JOCHEN, The Hunters and the Hunted, German U-boats 1939-45, Annapolis 2003.

BRIDGLAND, TONY, Sea Killers in Disguise: Q Ships & Decoy Raiders, London 1999.

BROWN, CAPTAIN ERIC, Wings of the Luftwaffe, Shrewsbury 1987.

BROWN, CAPTAIN ERIC, Wings of the Navy, Shrewsbury 1987.

BUCHHEIM, LOTHAR-GUNTHER, U-Boat War, London 1978.

BUELL, THOMAS B, Master of Sea Power: A Biography of Fleet Admiral Ernest J King, New York 1980.

BURN, ALAN, The Fighting Captain, Barnsley 1993.

CHALMERS, REAR ADMIRAL W S, Max Horton and the Western Approaches, London 1954.

CHESNEAU, ROGER, Aircraft Carriers of the World, 1914 to the Present, London, 1992.

CHURCHILL, WINSTON S, The History of the Second World War, Vol I, the Gathering Storm. London 1948.

CLANCY, TOM, Submarine: A guided tour aboard a nuclear submarine, London 1993.

CLARK, RONALD, The Rise of the Boffins, London, 1962.

COLES, ALAN, Three before Breakfast, Havant 1979.

COMPTON-HALL, COMMANDER RICHARD, Submarine versus Submarine: the tactics and technology of underwater confrontation, Newton Abbott 1988.

CORRIGAN, GORDON, Mud, Blood and Poppycock: Britain and the First World War, London 2003.

COSTELLO, JOHN, The Pacific War 1941-45, New York 1981.

CRAVEN, W F and CATE, J L, The Army Air Forces in World War II, Chicago 1949.

CREMER, PETER and BRUSTAT-NAVAL, FRITZ, U333: The Story of a U-boat Ace, London 1984.

CROSLEY, R 'MIKE', They Gave Me a Seafire, Shrewsbury (UK) 1986.

DONITZ, KARL, Memoirs – Ten Years and Twenty Days, London 1959.

DORLING, CAPTAIN TAPRELL, Endless Story, an Account of the Work of the Destroyers, Flotilla-Leaders, Torpedo-Boats and Patrol Boats in the Great War, London 1932.

EDWARDS, BERNARD, Dönitz and the Wolfpacks: the U-Boats at War, London 1996.

FRANKS, NORMAN, Conflict over the Bay, Momentous Battles fought by RAF and American aircraft against the U-Boats, Bay of Biscay, May-August 1943, London 1999.

FRANKS, NORMAN, Dark Sky, Deep Water, First-Hand Reflections on the Anti-U-boat war in WWII, London 1997.

FRANKS, NORMAN, Search, Find and Kill: Coastal Command's U-Boat Successes, London, 1990.

FRIEDMAN, DR NORMAN, British Carrier Aviation, London 1988.

FRIEDMAN, DR NORMAN, British Destroyers & Frigates: the Second World War and After, London 2006.

GANNON, MICHAEL, Black May: the epic story of the Allies' defeat of the German U-boats in May 1943, London 1998.

GANNON, MICHAEL, Operation Drumbeat, London 1990.

GARDINER, ROBERT (editor) Navies in the Nuclear Age, London 1993.

GIESE, OTTO and WISE, JAMES E JR, Shooting the War, the Memoir and Photographs of a U-Boat Officer in World War II, Annapolis 2003.

GOLDRICK, JAMES, The King's Ships were at Sea: the war in the North Sea, August 1914 – February 1915, Annapolis 1984.

GRETTON, VICE-ADMIRAL SIR PETER Crisis Convoy: the Story of HX231, London 1974.

GRETTON, VICE-ADMIRAL SIR PETER, Convoy Escort Commander, London 1964.

GUNTON, MICHAEL, Dive ! Dive ! Dive ! – Submarines at War, London 2003.

HACKMANN, WILLEM, Seek and Strike: Sonar, Anti-Submarine Warfare and the Royal Navy 1914-54, London 1984.

HAGUE, ARNOLD, The Allied Convoy System, Its Organisation, Defence and Operation, London 2000.

HALPERN, PAUL, A Naval History of World War I, London 1994.

HASHIMOTO, M, Sunk: the Story of the Japanese Submarine Fleet, London 1954.

HEALY, MARK, Midway 1942: Turning Point in the Pacific, London 1993.

HESSLER, GUNTHER, The U-Boat War in the Atlantic: 1939-45, revised and reissued London 1989.

HINSLEY, F H et al, British Intelligence in the Second World War, (3 volumes) Cambridge 1981-84.

HIRSCHFELD, WOLFGANG, Hirschfeld: the secret diary of a U-boat, reissued London 1998.

HMSO, British Vessels Lost at Sea, 1914-18 and 1939-45, Sparkford 1988

HMSO, The Battle of the Atlantic, London 1946.

HOLT, THADDEUS, The Deceivers: Allied Military Deception in the Second World War, London 2004.

HOPE, STANTON, Ocean Odyssey, A Record of the Fighting Merchant Navy, London 1944.

HOUGH, RICHARD, The Great War at Sea, 1914-1918, Oxford 1983.

HOUGH, RICHARD, The Longest Battle, The War at Sea 1939-45, London 1986.

HOWARD BAILEY, CHRIS, The Battle of the Atlantic, The Corvettes and their Crews: an Oral History, Sparkford 1994.

HOWARTH, STEPHEN and LAW, DEREK, (joint editors) The Battle of the Atlantic 1939-45: the Fiftieth Anniversary International Naval Conference, London 1994.

HOWSE, DEREK, Radar at Sea: the Royal Navy in World War 2, Annapolis 1993.

HOYT, EDWIN P, The U-Boat Wars, London 1985.

HUTCHINSON, ROBERT, Submarines: War Beneath the Waves, from 1776 to the Present Day, London 2001.

IENAGA S, The Pacific War: World War II and the Japanese, 1931-1945, New York 1978.

IRELAND, BERNARD, Battle of the Atlantic, Barnsley 2003.

Jane's All the World's Aeroplanes, Jane's Publishing Company, 1946 – revised and republished 2001 by Random House as Jane's Fighting Aircraft of World War Two.

Jane's Fighting Aircraft of World War One, Jane's Publishing Company 1919 (revised 2001) published by Random House.

JONES, GEOFFREY, Defeat of the Wolfpacks, London 1986.

JONES, PROFESSOR R V, Most Secret War: British Scientific Intelligence 1939-45, London 1979.

JORDAN, DAVID, Wolfpack, The U-Boat War and the Allied Counter-Attack 1939-45, Staplehurst, Kent, 2002.

JORDAN, JOHN, Soviet Warships, The Soviet Surface Fleet 1960 to the Present, London 1983.

KAHN, DAVID, Seizing the Enigma, London 1991.

KAHN, DAVID, The Codebreakers, London 1966.

KAPLAN, PHILIP and CURRIE, JACK, Convoy, London 1998.

KAPLAN, PHILIP, and CURRIE, JACK, Wolfpack, London 1997.

KAPLAN, PHILIP, Run Silent, London 2002.

KEMP, PAUL, Convoy Protection: the Defence of Seaborne Trade, London 1993.

KEMP, PAUL, U-Boats Destroyed: German Submarine Losses in the World Wars, London 1997.

KILDUFF, PETER, US Carriers at war, revised London 1997.

KUENNE, ROBERT E, The Attack Submarine: A Study in Strategy, Yale 1964.

LATIMER, JON, Deception in War, London 2001.

LAVERY, BRIAN, Churchill's Navy: The Ships, Men and Organisation 1939-45, London 2006.

LONGMATE, NORMAN, The Bombers, The RAF Offensive against Germany, 1939-1945, London 1983.

MACINTYRE, CAPTAIN DONALD, The Battle of the Atlantic, London 1961.

MACINTYRE, CAPTAIN DONALD, U-Boat Killer, London 1956.

MARDER, PROFESSOR ARTHUR J, From the Dreadnought to Scapa Flow, Oxford 1961-70.

MARRIOTT, LEO, Modern Combat Ships 3: Type 42, Leo Marriott, London 1985.

MARRIOTT, LEO, Modern Combat Ships 4: Type 22, London 1986.

MARRIOTT, LEO, Royal Navy Destroyers since 1945, London 1989.

MARS, ALASTAIR, Submarines at War, 1939-1945, London 1974.

MARTIENSSEN, ANTONY, Hitler and his Admirals, London 1948.

MASON, DAVID, U-Boat – the Secret Menace, London 1968.

MESSIMER, DWIGHT R, Find and Destroy: Anti-submarine warfare in World War 1, Annapolis 2001.

MIDDLEBROOK, MARTIN, Convoy, London 1978.

MIDDLEBROOK, MARTIN, Task Force: The Falklands War, 1982, London 1987.

MILLER, DAVID, U-Boats, the Illustrated History of the Raiders of the Deep, Limpsfield, (Surrey) 1999.

MILNER, MARC, North Atlantic Run, Toronto 1985.

MONSARRAT, NICHOLAS, Three Corvettes, reissued London 2001.

MOORE, CAPTAIN J E and COMPTON-HALL, COMMANDER R, Submarine Warfare: Today and Tomorrow, London 1986.

MORISON, PROFESSOR SAMUEL ELIOT, History of United States Naval Operations in World War II, Oxford 1948-56.
Volume I, The Hunters 1939-42,
Volume II, The Hunted, 1942-45.
Volume 1, The Battle of the Atlantic 1939-1943,
Volume 3, The Rising Sun in the Pacific,
Volume 4, Coral Sea, Midway and Submarine Actions,
Volume 10, The Atlantic Battle Won.

NESBIT, ROY CONYERS, The Strike Wings, Special Anti-Shipping Squadrons 1942-45, London 1984.

NESBIT, ROY CONYERS. An Illustrated History of the RAF, London 1990.

NIMITZ, ADMIRAL CHESTER W, ADAMS, HENRY H and POTTER, E B (joint editors), Triumph in the Atlantic – The Naval Struggle against the Axis, London 1960.

OI, ATSUSHI, Why Japan's antisubmarine warfare failed, in 'The Japanese Navy in World War II, in the words of former Japanese Naval Officers' (second edition), Annapolis 1986.

OWEN, DAVID, Battle of Wits: A History of Psychology and Deception in Modern Warfare, London 1978.

PADFIELD, PETER, Donitz – the last Fuhrer, London 1984.

PADFIELD, PETER, War Beneath the Sea, Submarine Conflict 1939-1945, new paperback edition London 1997.

PAWLE, GERALD, The Secret War 1939-1945, Re-issued London 1972.

PEARCE, FRANK, Running the Gauntlet, The Battle for the Barents Sea, London 1989.

POOLMAN, KENNETH, Periscope Depth, London 1981.

PRICE, DR ALFRED Aircraft versus Submarine in Two World Wars, Barnsley, Yorkshire, 2004.

PRICE, DR ALFRED, Aircraft versus Submarine, London 1973.

PRICE, DR ALFRED, Skies of Fire: Dramatic Air Combat, London 2002.

RAYNER, COMMANDER D A , Escort: The Battle of the Atlantic, London 1955.

RING, JIM, We Come Unseen, The Untold Story of Britain's Cold War Submarines, Jim Ring, London 2003.

ROBERTSON, TERENCE, The Golden Horseshoe, London 1955.

ROBERTSON, TERENCE, Walker RN, London 1966.

ROHWER, PROFESSOR JURGEN, Axis Submarine Successes of World War II, Annapolis 1999.

ROHWER, PROFESSOR JURGEN, The Critical Convoy Battles of March 1943: the Battle for HX229/SC122, London 1977.

ROSCOE, THEODORE, United States Submarine Operations in World War II, Annapolis 1949.

ROSKILL, CAPTAIN S W, The War at Sea, London 1954-61.

ROSKILL, CAPTAIN S W, Naval Policy Between the Wars, London 1954-61.

SCHULL, JOSEPH, The Far Distant Ships, Ottawa 1961.

SEBAG-MONTEFIORE, HUGH, Enigma – the Battle for the Code, London 2000.

SETH, RONALD, The Fiercest Battle: the story of North Atlantic Convoy ONS5, 22nd April-7th May 1943, New York 1961.

SHOWELL, JAK MALLMANN, The U-Boat Century: German Submarine Warfare 1906-2006, London 2007.

SHOWELL, JAK MALLMANN, U-Boats under the Swastika, London 1973.

SLESSOR, MARSHAL OF THE ROYAL AIR FORCE SIR JOHN, The Central Blue: the Autobiography, New York 1957.

SONTAG, SHERRY and DREW, CHRISTOPHER, Blind Man's Buff, the Untold Story of Cold War Submarine Espionage, London 2000.

STAFFORD, EDWARD P, Subchaser, Annapolis 2003.

STERN, ROBERT C, Battle beneath the Waves, London 1999.

TARRANT, V E, The Last Year of the Kriegsmarine: May 1944-May 1945, London 1994.

TARRANT, V E, The U-Boat Offensive, 1914-45, London 1989.

TERRAINE, JOHN, Business in Great Waters, the U-Boat Wars 1916-1945, London 1989.

TERRAINE, JOHN, The Right of the Line: The Royal Air Force in the European War 1939-1945, reissued London 1998.

THOMAS, DAVID A, The Atlantic Star 1939-45, London 1990.

THOMPSON, JULIAN, The War at Sea, London 1996.

VAN DER VAT, DAN, The Atlantic Campaign, London 1988.

VAUSE, J, U-Boat Ace, the Story of Wolfgang Luth, Shrewsbury 1992.

WADDINGTON, C H, O. R. in World War Two: Operational Research Against the U-boat, London 1973.

WERNER, HERBERT A, Iron Coffins, A Personal Account of the German U-Boat battles of World War II, London 1972.

WHINNEY, CAPTAIN REGINALD, The U-Boat Peril, An Anti-Submarine Commander's War, London 1989.

WILLIAMS, MARK, Captain Gilbert Roberts R.N and the Anti-U-Boat School, London 1979.

WILSON, KEVIN, Bomber Boys: the Ruhr, the Dambusters and Bloody Berlin, London 2005.

WINTERBOTHAM, GROUP CAPTAIN F W, The Ultra Secret, London 1974.

Y'BLOOD, WILLIAM T, Hunter-Killer, US Escort Carriers in the Battle of the Atlantic, Annapolis 1983.

INTERVIEWS:
Commander R 'Mike' Crosley, DSC, RN, 1990
Captain Eric 'Winkle' Brown DSC, RN, 1990.
The late Major Oliver Patch, Royal Marines, 1990.
The late Professor R V Jones, November 1992.

NOTES

CHAPTER 1

1 Hutchinson, *Submarines: War Beneath the Waves, from 1776 to the Present Day*, p 9, says 'the armament consisted of a 150 lb gunpowder mine, intended to be screwed into the wooden hull of the target warship by using an augur or gimlet attached to the vertical propeller of the submersible', though presumably attached to the propeller *shaft* would be a better description.

2 Captain Peter Hore, RN Retd, 'A Secret Journey to Halifax', *Naval History*, (US Naval Institute) June 2002.

3 Hutchinson, *Submarines*, p 16, said that the trials in Liverpool Bay were 'encouraging enough to interest a still sceptical Admiralty, which asked Garrett to mount a demonstration at Portsmouth'.

4 Ibid, pp 38–9.

CHAPTER 2

1 Goldrick, *The King's Ships*, p 129.

2 Coles, *Three Before Breakfast*, p 14.

3 Coles, ibid, p. 67, says the ship sank quickly because the torpedo explosions set off the magazine holding ammunition for the 9.2-inch main armament, but Goldrick, *The King's Ships*, pp 129–31, makes no mention of the magazine explosion, and suggests that most watertight doors had been left open allowing the hull to flood quickly from the water pouring into the engine room.

4 Coles, *Three Before Breakfast*, p 76, claims the second torpedo passed astern of the target because she had gone to full ahead when lookouts spotted the approaching torpedoes, and her movement was enough to carry her clear.

5 Halpern, *A Naval History of World War I*, p 33.

6 Tarrant, *The U-Boat Offensive*, p 17.

7 Ibid, p 21.

8 Ibid, p 24.

9 Ibid, p 25.

10 Messimer, *Find and Destroy:*, p 70.

11 Tarrant, *The U-Boat Offensive*, p 22.

12 Ibid, p 36.

13 Bridgland, *Sea Killers in Disguise*, p 59.

14 Terraine, *Business in Great Waters*, p 27.

15 Bridgland, *Sea Killers in Disguise*, pp 70–1.

16 Ibid, pp 71–5.

17 Tarrant, *The U-Boat Offensive*, pp 32–3.

18 Terraine, *Business in Great Waters*, p 34.

19 Messimer, *Find and Destroy*, pp 145–6.

20 Terraine, *Business in Great Waters*, p 29.

21 Tarrant, *The U-Boat Offensive*, p 37.

22 Hough, *The Great War at Sea*, pp 306–7.

23 Terraine, *Business in Great Waters*, pp 49–50.

24 Hough, *The Great War at Sea*, pp 307–8.

25 John Terraine, in *Business in Great Waters*, says on p 59:

> Those who believe the Admiralty should have acted earlier are unlikely to change their minds. [Sir Maurice] Hankey, a warm advocate of convoy since February [1917] was one of them, and his biographer may be given the last word on the subject:
>
>> In sum, although no one can reasonably criticise the Admiralty for their slowness and reluctance to introduce the traditional strategy, it is also reasonable to ask why Lloyd George should escape all the blame for the delay in starting convoy and be accorded so much merit for the change, when Hankey's original memorandum on the subject had been in his hands since 1st February. If the Admiralty was slow to accept convoy, the Prime Minister and his colleagues in the War Cabinet showed no very marked alacrity in picking up the ball which Hankey had placed at their feet …

In the other sources used the initiative is credited to the Admiralty (Dwight Messimer in *Find and Destroy* (p 148) says the delay was because only when the threat appeared serious enough did it seem worthwhile to undertake the colossal organisational task involved in setting up a watertight convoy system).

26 Marder, *From the Dreadnought to Scapa Flow*, Vol IV, p 187.

CHAPTER 3

1 Terraine, *Business in Great Waters*, p 60, and Halpern, *A Naval History of World War I*, p 360.

2 Admiralty MS, 'Convoy: The Core of Maritime Strategy', p 9, quoted in Tarrant, *The U-Boat Offensive*, p 56.

3 Terraine, *Business in Great Waters*, p 92.

4 Hackmann, *Seek and Strike*, p 9.

5 Messimer, *Find and Destroy*, pp 222–4.

6 Tarrant, *The U-Boat Offensive*, p 59.

7 Messimer, *Find and Destroy*, pp 226–7.

8 Ibid, pp 245–7.

9 Hackmann, *Seek and Strike*, p 40.

10 Kahn, *The Codebreakers*, p 133.

11 Ibid, pp 68–9.

12 Price, *Aircraft versus Submarine*, pp 18–19.

13 Tarrant, *The U-Boat Offensive*, p 68.

14 Rohwer, *The Critical Convoy Battles of March 1943*, p 11.

CHAPTER 4

1 Blair, *Hitler's U-Boat War*, Vol I, 'Prologue', which provided much of the background for this section.

2 The 'Z' stood for 'Ziel-Target' or 'Ultimate Target'.

3 Macintyre, *U-Boat Killer*, p 3.

4 Hackmann, *Seek and Strike*, pp 130–1.

5 Ibid, p 188, footnote 72.

6 Blair, *Hitler's U-Boat War*, Vol I, p 49.

7 Blair, *Hitler's U-Boat War*, Vol I, p 37. Other information from this chapter from Tarrant, *The U-Boat Offensive*, pp 77–80 and Mason, *U-Boat – The Secret Menace*, pp 16–51.

8 In the case of attacking warships, detonating the torpedo beneath the hull would avoid the armour protection along the target's sides, while in the case of merchant ships it was hoped they would break the target's back rather than blow a possibly survivable hole in its side plating.

9 Most submarine powers were more inclined to see their submarines as weapons for use against warships – unsurprisingly, given their experience in the previous war – the Germans knew Britain's chief weakness was her dependence on supply by merchant ships, and this remained their first and clearest priority. Moreover, attacking an opponent's warships was always dependent on potential targets emerging from their bases, while merchant ships would always be at sea if Britain were to be kept in the war.

10 Terraine, *Business in Great Waters*, p 253.

CHAPTER 5

1 Roskill, *Naval Policy Between the Wars*, p 228, quoted in Terraine, *Business in Great Waters*, p 176.

2 Ibid, p 177.

3 Hessler, *The U-Boat War in the Atlantic*, ch I, p 11.

4 Ibid, p 12.

5 Quoted in Hessler, *The U-Boat War in the Atlantic*, ch I, p 16.

6 Barnett, *Engage the Enemy More Closely*, p 67.

CHAPTER 6

1 Sinkings and timings from Rohwer, *Axis Submarine Successes of World War II*, p 45. However, Terraine, *Business in Great Waters*, p 314, and Macintyre, *The Battle of the Atlantic*, p 76, both say *UA* was so badly damaged by depth charges that she left the attack on 7 March and headed back to base.

2 Description from Macintyre, *U-Boat Killer*, pp 32–3. Blair, *Hitler's U-Boat War*, Vol I, describes an earlier attack by *Wolverine* being the one that sent *UA* heading back to base, but claims the one that produced the underwater glow was inconclusive. Kretschmer maintained for the rest of his life his conviction that Prien's boat had been lost by a rogue torpedo that had malfunctioned and turned back to hit the boat which had launched it.

3 Blair, *Hitler's U-Boat War*, Vol I, p 255, claims the escorts depth charged *U110* after this first attack, but Macintyre himself, in *U-Boat Killer*, pp 33–4 says they found no trace that they were able to attack at this stage.

4 Blair states that *Erdona*, torpedoed earlier, was severely damaged but towed safely to Iceland, and Rohwer, *Axis Submarine Successes of World War II*, p 46, records her as having

been damaged by Lemp's original attack. Macintyre says (pp 33–4) she was lost and that the corvette *Bluebell* was sent to pick up survivors, without success. To compound the confusion, Hague, *The Allied Convoy System*, p 131, does not list her among the losses from HX112.

5 Descriptions of the battle of HX112 taken from Blair, *Hitler's U-Boat War*, , Vol I, pp 255–8, from Macintyre, *U-Boat Killer*, pp 34–42, and Robertson, *The Golden Horseshoe*, pp 139–51.

6 Tarrant, *The U-Boat Offensive*, p 90.

7 Gannon, *Black May*, p 48.

CHAPTER 7

1 Blair, *Hitler's U-Boat War*, Vol I, pp 449–50.

2 Gannon, *Black May*, p 100.

3 Williams, *Captain Gilbert Roberts RN and the Anti-U-Boat School*, p 87.

4 Ibid, p 90. Coincidentally, this was Sir Max Horton, soon to take over at Western Approaches. The lack of prior discussion between escort commanders and submariners was remarkable, given that this tactic of launching attacks from within a convoy had apparently already been practised by Royal Navy submarine crews.

5 See later in this chapter for an explanation of HFDF (high-frequency direction-finding).

6 This is described more fully in Chapter 13, together with the 'Foxer' sound decoy device.

7 Price, *Aircraft versus Submarine in Two World Wars*, pp 104–5, states that 'The shore Huff-Duff stations could not give accurate bearings on transmissions coming from more than three hundred miles away'. Tarrant, *The U-Boat Offensive*, p 101, says that 'Huff Duff' gave 'errors in direction of up to 30 percent'.

CHAPTER 8

1 Blair, *Hitler's U-Boat War*, Vol I, pp 90–1.

2 Mason, *U-Boat – the Secret Menace*, p 26.

3 *Jane's Fighting Aircraft of World War Two*, pp 97–8.

4 Terraine, *Business in Great Waters*, p 246.

5 Terraine, *The Right of the Line*, p 232.

6 Ibid, p 43.

7 Churchill to the (like-minded) First Sea Lord, Admiral of the Fleet Sir Dudley Pound RN, 20 November 1939, quoted in *The History of the Second World War*, Vol I, p 669.

8 Terraine, *Business in Great Waters*, p 247.

9 Brown, *Wings of the Navy*, p 29.

10 Blair, *Hitler's U-Boat War*, Vol I, p 88.

11 Beaver, *The British Aircraft Carrier*, p 55.

12 Blair, *Hitler's U-Boat War*, Vol I, p 86.

13 Quote from Terraine, *Business in Great Waters*, p 246.

14 Gannon, *Black May*, p 73.

15 Hough, *The Longest Battle*, p 48 and Bowyer, *Men of Coastal Command*, pp 58–63 – this incredible battle is described more fully in Chapter 13.

16 Kemp, *U-Boats Destroyed*, p 64.

17 Price, *Aircraft versus Submarine in Two World Wars*, p 47. U31 was raised from the bottom eight days later and put back into service at the end of July 1940, only to be sunk on 2 November 1940 by HMS *Antelope* northwest of Ireland.

18 Notes from the author's interview with the late Major Patch, January 1990.

19 *Jane's Fighting Aircraft of World War Two*, p 166.

20 Brown, *Wings of the Luftwaffe*, p.8

21 Monsarrat, *Three Corvettes*, pp 64–5.

22 Figures from Hague, *The Allied Convoy System*, pp 176–7, though Blair, *Hitler's U-Boat War*, Vol I, pp 338–9 says 'eight small vessels for about 14,000 tons'. In fact even the smaller total represents a loss of one-third of the convoy.

23 *Jane's Fighting Aircraft of World War Two*, p 103.

24 Churchill, *The History of the Second World War*, Vol II, p 537.

25 Quoted in Terraine, *Business in Great Waters*, p 366.

26 The U-boat men referred to the Air Gap as the 'Black Pit' using the English words rather than the German, Hessler, *The U-Boat War in the Atlantic*, p 86 and footnote.

27 Price, *Aircraft versus Submarine in Two World Wars*, pp 52–3.

28 Barnett, *Engage the Enemy More Closely*, p 258.

29 Price, *Aircraft versus Submarine in Two World Wars*, p 58.

30 Quoted in Terraine, *Business in Great Waters*, p 369.

31 *Jane's Fighting Aircraft of World War Two*, pp 110–11.

32 Hough, *The Longest Battle*, p 44.

33 Beaver, *The British Aircraft Carrier*, p 97.

34 Hough, *The Longest Battle*, pp 44–5.

35 Friedman, *British Carrier Aviation*, p 180.

36 Monsarrat, *Three Corvettes*, p 284.

37 Friedman, *British Carrier Aviation*, p 182.

38 Brown, *Wings of the Luftwaffe*, p. 14.

CHAPTER 9

1 Franks, *Dark Sky, Deep Water*, pp 5–7.

2 Price, *Aircraft versus Submarine*, p 62.

3 Bailey, *The Sky Suspended*, p 69.

4 Franks, *Dark Sky, Deep Water*, p 5.

5 Gannon, *Black May*, p 87.

6 Ibid, p 88.

7 Ibid, p 89.

8 Waddington, *O.R. in World War Two*, p 175.

9 More information on these intriguing aspects of wartime Operational Research can be found in Waddington, *O.R. in World War Two*, p 176 onwards, in Price, *Aircraft versus Submarine*, pp 68–70, and in Gannon, *Black May*, pp 88–92.

10 *Jane's Fighting Aircraft of World War II* quotes the range of the B17 as 1,100 miles and that of the B24 as 1,540 miles (bomber versions with normal tanks in each case). It gives the maximum range of the Lancaster and the Halifax as 'approximately 3,000 miles' for the standard-tankage bomber versions.

11 Longmate, *The Bombers*, p 299.

12 Blair, *Hitler's U-Boat War*, Vol I, p 340–7; Padfield, *War Beneath the Sea*, p 162; Terraine, *Business in Great Waters*, pp 364–5.

13 Price, *Aircraft versus Submarine in Two World Wars*, pp 79–80.

14 Blair, *Hitler's U-Boat War*, refers (in a footnote on Vol I, p 569) to the *Torelli* being hounded 'into Santander, Spain, where she was "interned". A month later she "escaped" and limped into Bordeaux.' The implication is that internment and escape were staged as a matter of collusion between two Fascist countries, but Price and Franks both describe strenuous diplomatic efforts being made to avoid internment, and official (and presumably genuine) Spanish anger at the successful escape attempt.

15 Barnett, *Engage the Enemy More Closely*, p 592.

16 ADM 234/578.

17 Price, *Aircraft versus Submarine in Two World Wars*, pp 94–5.

18 PRO, AIR 41/47, Peyton-Ward, *RAF in Maritime War*, Vol III, pp 495–7 (quoted in Gannon, *Black May*, p 100).

19 Waddington, *O.R. in World War Two*, pp 220–5.

20 Van der Vat, *The Atlantic Campaign*, p 458, and Gannon, *Black May*, p 75.

21 Blair, *Hitler's U-Boat War*, Vol I, p 612.

22 Price, *Aircraft versus Submarine in Two World Wars*, p 146.

23 Terraine, *The Right of the Line*, p 278.

24 PRO, CAB 86/3, A.U.(43)40, 'Progress of Analysis of the Value of Escort Vessels and Aircraft in the Anti U-Boat Campaign'.

CHAPTER 10

1 Crosley, *They Gave Me a Seafire*, Appendix 4, pp 214–15, and interview with author, RNAS Yeovilton, 1990.

2 Ibid, p 91.

3 Blair, *Hitler's U-Boat War*, Vol II, p 112.

4 Rohwer, *Axis Submarine Successes of World War II*, p 136.

5 Chesneau, *Aircraft Carriers of the World*, p 110.

6 Y'Blood, *Hunter Killer*, p 4.

7 Ibid, pp 105–6.

8 Werner, *Iron Coffins*, pp 171–2. Though the author mentions helium as the gas used to fill the balloon, both Price, *Aircraft versus Submarine in Two World Wars*, p 190 and Miller, *U-Boats*, p 112, specifically refer to hydrogen. This seems the most likely as the USA was the source of most of the world's production of helium and it was the withholding of this as a strategically valuable material from Nazi Germany before the war that led to the huge transoceanic airships *Graf Zeppelin* and *Hindenburg* having to use the more buoyant but highly inflammable hydrogen instead. This was a major factor in the *Hindenburg* disaster of 6 May 1937, when the

huge airship was destroyed after fire broke out while she was preparing to pick up her mooring at Lakehurst NAS, New Jersey following a flight from Europe.

9 Price, *Aircraft versus Submarine in Two World Wars*, p 118.
10 Wilson, *Bomber Boys*, p 86.
11 Hessler, *The U-Boat War in the Atlantic*, ch VI, p 86.
12 Ibid, ch VII, p 4.
13 Jones, *Most Secret War*, pp 410–11, and interview with the author, Aberdeen, 1992.
14 Hessler, *The U-Boat War in the Atlantic*, ch VII, p 21.
15 BdU War Diary, 31 July 1943.
16 BdU War Diary, 14 August 1943.
17 Price, *Aircraft versus Submarine in Two World Wars*, pp 162–3.
18 Author's interview with the late Professor Jones, Aberdeen, 1992.
19 Hessler, *The U-Boat War in the Atlantic*, ch VIII, p 35.
20 Ibid, ch VII, p 4.
21 Price, *Aircraft versus Submarine in Two World Wars*, p 121.
22 Ibid, p 155.
23 Blair, *Hitler's U-Boat War*, Vol II, p 359, describes the Whitley as having to ditch in the sea, whereupon her crew was rescued by a French trawler with the unusual name *Jazz Band*, which landed them in France en route to a POW camp. Price, *Aircraft versus Submarine in Two World Wars*, p 157, on the other hand, describes the Whitley as limping off and heading back to base, only to report being attacked by German fighters before disappearing without trace. Franks, *Dark Sky, Deep Water*, p 87, says that Benson radioed base to report damage to the aircraft's hydraulics from German gunfire, and some two hours later an engine failed on the return journey forcing the crew to ditch in the sea. After two days in a dinghy they were then picked up by a French fishing boat, and that Benson himself was informed of his promotion to Warrant Officer and the award of the DFM (Distinguished Flying Medal) while still in his POW camp.
24 Miller, *U-Boats*, pp 100–1.
25 Hessler, *The U-Boat War in the Atlantic*, ch VII, p 11 – also says *U441* carried two single 20-mm cannon, not identified by other sources.
26 These are recorded in Miller, *U-Boats*, p 34, which contains a detailed history of different types and sub-types of German submarines, their equipment and eventual fate. Blair, on the other hand, *Hitler's U-Boat War*, Vol II, p 316, has *U650* in addition to the others.
27 Blair, *Hitler's U-Boat War*, Vol II, p 389.
28 Price, *Aircraft versus Submarine in Two World Wars*, pp 151–2 and Blair, *Hitler's U-Boat War*, Vol II, pp 363–4.
29 Hessler, *The U-Boat War in the Atlantic*, ch VII, p 13 said it was a Mosquito. Both types were twin-engined, though only the Wellington carried depth charges.
30 War Diary of *U106*. However, sources differ on the final fate of the rescued crew. Damerow (who ought to know at first hand) clearly implies the submariners were picked up by the three 600-ton fast but lightly armed torpedo boats sent to escort them home, and Blair *Hitler's U-Boat War*, Vol II, p 393, says that 'the [German] torpedo boats rescued Damerow, his log book, and thirty-five other Germans'. On the other hand, Franks, in *Search, Find and Kill*, p 98, states clearly that 'The 40th [Royal Navy] Escort Group later picked up 37 men, including Damerow', and again in *Conflict over the Bay*, p 158, rather more confusingly after having explained that the Royal Navy had sent out two additional destroyers to reinforce the [Escort] Groups in the bay that

The 502 Squadron Halifax finally made a bombing attack on the torpedo boats before he had to leave, but his three A/S bombs missed by 100 yards. Shortly afterwards the *ships* found the survivors of *U106*, rescuing 36 men, including the submarine commander. Having lost the torpedo boats, the *ships* turned for home. Another 502 Squadron Halifax found the three *boats* later but when night came they finally got away [emphasis added].

As a further pointer, Blair (above) refers to Damerow not surviving the war, a fate statistically much more likely if he had succeeded in reaching home and continued to serve in the U-boat arm rather than sitting out the war in the relative safety of a POW camp.

31 Price, *Aircraft versus Submarine in Two World Wars*, p 160.
32 Hessler, *The U-Boat War in the Atlantic*, ch VII, p 14.

CHAPTER 11
1 Figures taken from Rohwer, *Axis Submarine Successes of World War Two*.
2 The Allies were able to read Enigma signals referring to Axis convoys, but the fact that the U-boats in the Mediterranean used a different Enigma cipher from those used in the Atlantic gave them a valuable extra measure of protection.

CHAPTER 12
1 The HX convoys switched their assembly port from Halifax, Nova Scotia to New York from HX208 onwards in September 1942. The SC convoys switched backwards and forwards between Sydney, Nova Scotia and Halifax until September 1942 and convoy SC102, when they too were transferred to New York until 31 March 1943 and SC125, whereupon they were transferred back to Halifax for the remainder of the war. Hague, *The Allied Convoy System*, pp 134–5.
2 Quoted in Middlebrook, *Convoy*, p 153.
3 Ibid, p 309.
4 Ibid, pp 316–17.
5 Blackett, *Studies of War*, p 232, quoted in Gannon, *Black May*, p 111. Blackett calculated that sending 180 merchant ships as two 90-ship convoys instead of three 60-ship convoys would cut losses in half.
6 PRO/CAB 86.2, quoted in Gannon, *Black May*, p 112.
7 Hague, *The Allied Convoy System*, p 132.
8 Blair, *Hitler's U-Boat War*, Vol II, pp 277–8.
9 Hessler, *The U-Boat War in the Atlantic*, ch II, p 96.
10 PRO, CAB 86/3, A.U.(43)40, 'Progress of Analysis of the Value of Escort Vessels and Aircraft in the Anti U-Boat Campaign, Report by Professor Blackett', ff 241–3, quoted in Gannon, *Black May*, pp 112–13.
11 Williams, *Captain Gilbert Roberts RN and the Anti-U-Boat School*, p 115.
12 In peacetime, a Great Circle course would be the normal procedure, but in wartime, the selection of the course was a balancing act between fuel economy and the need to evade U-boat concentrations, which would tend to be most common along the Great Circle courses between the main convoy ports. In this case, fuel shortage was such a limiting factor that it was thought best to accept the additional danger of taking the most direct route.
13 Gretton, *Convoy Escort Commander*, p 135.
14 Hessler, *The U-Boat War in the Atlantic*, p 105.
15 Turbulent conditions made it more difficult to pick up the return echo which warned of the submarine's position.
16 Hessler, *The U-Boat War in the Atlantic*.

CHAPTER 13
1 Burn, *The Fighting Captain*, p 69. Alan Burn was Walker's gunnery officer on HMS *Starling* and as such had an unrivalled first-hand view of the actions of the 2nd Support Group.
2 Robertson, *Walker RN*, p 95.
3 Ibid, pp 96–7.
4 Hackmann, *Seek and Strike*, p 304.
5 Miller, *U-Boats*, p 111.
6 Burn, *The Fighting Captain*, p 78.
7 Gerald Pawle, *The Secret War 1939–1945*, gives a detailed account of the achievements of DWMD, and the combination of inspiration and inter-departmental rivalry that resulted in the development of these weapons.
8 Naval shore station.
9 J M Kirkby MA, PSO, Admiralty Mining Department in an address to the Institution of Mechanical Engineers, 6 February 1948.
10 Pawle, *The Secret War 1939–45*, p 139.
11 Whinney, *The U-Boat Peril*, p 116.
12 Ibid, pp 118–19.
13 Ireland, *Battle of the Atlantic*, p 94.
14 Williams, *Captain Gilbert Roberts RN and the Anti-U-Boat School*, p 128, describes *Lagan* being towed back to base by *Escapade* with the destroyer going astern to protect her shattered

bows from the sea. Blair, *Hitler's U-Boat War*, Vol II, p 422, says the frigate was towed by the deep-sea salvage tug *Destiny* under the escort of the anti-submarine trawler *Lancer* while the less crippled destroyer made port under her own steam – a much more likely procedure, confirmed by Ireland, *Battle of the Atlantic*, p 157.

15 Ireland, *Battle of the Atlantic*, p 132.

16 Miller, *U-Boats*, p 88.

17 This reference to Hagenuk in the original is almost certainly directed at the Wanze receiver which was made by the Hagenuk company.

18 BdU War Diary, 23 August 1943.

19 'Considerations Regarding the Convoy Operation with the Available Weapons', document contained in the BdU War Diary, 21 August 1943 and quoted in Hessler, *The U-Boat War in the Atlantic*, ch VIII, p 24.

20 Blair, *Hitler's U-Boat War*, Vol II, pp 422–3.

21 Hackmann, *Seek and Strike*, pp 280 onwards, covers the technical background to these sonar developments in considerable detail.

22 Extract quoted in Burn, *The Fighting Captain*, pp 187–8.

23 Ibid, p 131.

24 Robertson, *Walker* RN, p 168.

25 The details were chiefly taken from Burn, *The Fighting Captain*, pp 124–43. Burn, who was actually on the spot as *Starling*'s gunnery officer received a letter from the Historical Branch of the UK Ministry of Defence after the war confirming the numbers of the three U-boats sunk by the 2nd Support Group that night but stating it was impossible to say with certainty which was which. Since then, Clay Blair, *Hitler's U-Boat War*, Vol II, p 498, has confirmed their identities as given here.

26 Blair, *Hitler's U-Boat War*, Vol II, p 498, identified the culprit as the former flak-boat *U256*, which launched an acoustic torpedo at *Woodpecker* and blew her stern to pieces.

27 Cremer, *U333: The Story of a U-Boat Ace*, p 188.

28 Tarrant, *The Last Year of the Kriegsmarine*, pp 150–4.

29 Hessler, *The U-Boat War in the Atlantic*, ch IX, p 58.

30 Werner, *Iron Coffins*, pp 299–300.

31 Hirschfeld, *The Secret Diary of a U-Boat*, pp. 196–7.

CHAPTER 14

1 Hackmann, *Seek and Strike*, pp 313–17.

2 BdU War Diary for 12 May 1943, quoted in Price, *Aircraft versus Submarine in Two World Wars*, p 130. The reference also quotes the use by Doenitz of the term *Fliebotreffer*, an abbreviation of *Fliegerbombentreffer*, or 'hit from an aerial bomb'.

3 Some confusion still exists over credit for sinking the submarine. Miller, *U-Boats*, p 186, credits the kill to 86 Squadron, but gives the date as 13 May 1943. Blair, *Hitler's U-Boat War*, Vol II, p 328, says the submarine was sunk by the large and modern destroyer HMS *Opportune*, while Franks, *Search, Find and Kill*, p 23, names the RCN corvette HMCS *Drumheller* and the RN frigate HMS *Lagan* as the ships responsible.

4 Hessler, *The U-Boat War in the Atlantic*, ch VI, p 106.

5 The story of these carrier operations against the U-boats is graphically told in Y'blood, *Hunter Killer*, pp 82–7.

6 CTG 21.14 Action Report pp 5 and 6, quoted in Y'Blood, *Hunter Killer*, p 91.

7 Later the title was amended to Magnetic Anomaly Detector, but the acronym remained the same.

8 Price, *Aircraft versus Submarine in Two World Wars*, p 189.

9 Ibid, p 192. Blair, *Hitler's U-Boat War*, Vol II, p 494, describes events slightly differently, claiming it was gunfire from the destroyers which finally persuaded the Germans to abandon ship, and saying that forty-nine of the crew were rescued, including the skipper, Horst Geider, with eight killed in the sinking, including the chief engineer, and another dying later in a Gibraltar hospital. David Miller, *U-Boats*, appendix, pp 194–5, agrees with Blair's casualty and survivor figures.

10 Price says this happened on 5 May, Blair, *Hitler's U-Boat War*, Vol II, that the U-boat was lost on 15 May, and Miller agrees with Blair.

11 Terraine, *The Right of the Line*, p 282.

12 Bowman, *Mosquito Bomber/Fighter Bomber Units 1942–45*.

13 Ibid, p 69.

14 Hessler, *The U-Boat War in the Atlantic*, ch X, p 70.

15 Price, *Aircraft versus Submarine in Two World Wars*, p 198.

16 War diary of U-Boat Headquarters, 15 September 1944, quoted in Hessler, *The U-Boat War in the Atlantic*, ch X, p 79.

CHAPTER 15

1 Costello, *The Pacific War*, p 82.

2 Boyd and Yoshida, *The Japanese Submarine Force and World War II*, p 64.

3 Ibid, pp 84–6.

4 Healy, *Midway 1942*, pp 77–84.

5 Boyd and Yoshida, *The Japanese Submarine Force and World War II*, pp 98–9 and Padfield, *War Beneath the Sea*, p 251. Costello, *The Pacific War*, p 347, says the *I15* sank the *Wasp* while the *I19* saw the *Hornet* and deliberately aimed at her, but this is not supported by other sources.

6 Blair, *Hitler's U-Boat War*, Vol II, appendix 18, and Vol II, appendix 20, give a total of 6,149,473 tons.

CHAPTER 16

1 Roskill, *The War at Sea*, p 228.

2 Ibid, pp 197–8.

3 Atsushi Oi, *The Japanese Navy in World War II, in the Words of Former Japanese Naval Officers*, USNI Press, 1986, provided much of the information for this section on the failure of Japanese ASW.

4 Roskill, *The War at Sea*, p 229.

5 Ibid, pp 230–1.

6 Padfield, *War Beneath the Sea*, pp 445–8, and Price, *Aircraft versus Submarine in Two World Wars*, pp 227–9.

CHAPTER 17

1 MILLER, U-BOATS, P 61.

2 Barnett, *Engage the Enemy More Closely*, p 854.

3 Blair, *Hitler's U-Boat War*, Vol II, pp 709–10.

4 Gardiner, *Navies in the Nuclear Age*, p 143 says the US Navy rated the Hedgehog 28 per cent effective compared with Squid at 26 per cent effective, but that the Royal Navy thought Squid was twice as effective as Hedgehog in the more demanding conditions under which they operated.

CHAPTER 18

1 Hutchinson, *Submarines: War Beneath the Waves*, pp 116–17.

2 Miller, *U-Boats*, pp 73–6.

3 Archibald, *The Fighting Ship in the Royal Navy*, pp 281–8.

4 Gardiner, *Navies in the Nuclear Age*, p 151.

CHAPTER 19

1 Ring, *We Come Unseen*, p 165.

2 Clancy, *Submarine*, in a detailed treatment of the Los Angeles class sensors, says the spherical sonar array is 15 feet in diameter!

3 Clancy, *Submarine*, pp 78–80.

4 Gardiner, *Navies in the Nuclear Age*, pp 150–1.

5 Clancy, *Submarine*, pp 117–21.

6 Ibid, pp 201–2.

7 US Naval Institute, *Proceedings*, June 2005, pp 86–7.

CHAPTER 20

1 Martin Middlebrook, in *Task Force*, p 130, says that the *San Luis* was chased by HMS *Brilliant* and HMS *Yarmouth* and a pair of Sea King helicopters in an area twenty miles north of Port Stanley and that the Argentine submarine 'reported making a torpedo attack on a British ship ... but there is some doubt about this', and that 'she was not resolutely handled during the war and may have been keeping well out of the way of trouble'.

2 US Naval Institute, *Proceedings*, December 2003, p 43.

3 *Daily Telegraph* (London), 15 May 1999.

4 US Naval Institute, *Proceedings*, July 2003, p 6.